VERNON E. ANDERSON, Ph.D. University of Colorado, is Dean of the College of Education and Professor at the University of Maryland. He has held positions as Director of Curriculum for the State Office of Superintendent of Public Instruction, State of Washington; Director of Curriculum for the Portland (Oregon) Public Schools; and Professor and Director of the Curriculum Center at the University of Connecticut. Dean Anderson is a contributor to Douglass: *The High School Curriculum*, Third Edition, and is co-author of Anderson-Gruhn: *Principles and Practices of Secondary Education*, Second Edition, both published by The Ronald Press Company.

PRINCIPLES AND PROCEDURES OF

CURRICULUM

IMPROVEMENT

VERNON E. ANDERSON

University of Maryland

Second Edition

THE RONALD PRESS COMPANY • NEW YORK

2 M

Library of Congress Catalog Card Number: 65-12741

PRINTED IN THE UNITED STATES OF AMERICA

To my wife
ALICE P. ANDERSON
and my daughter
MARY A. STONE

PREFACE

New influences and new forces in society have caused educators and scholars to examine both the process and content of the curriculum in order to bring them up to date with developments in the behavioral sciences and in the disciplines. The ferment in curriculum change is undoubtedly one of the more significant trends in education today as well as in the foreseeable future. For schools cannot stand still while the world moves ahead. The book takes full cognizance of these changes and what they may mean for the curriculum.

In this Second Edition, seven of the chapters are entirely new and approximately 60 per cent of the total content is new since all of the remaining ten chapters have been revised or rewritten. The basic theme of the book is maintained: human relationships are the key to the curriculum improvement process since curriculum change is dependent upon changes in people, and the focus on quality of experiences is the essence of curriculum improvement in the classroom. Recent curriculum developments which are discussed in the new chapters include the national curriculum projects in the disciplines; the new "curriculum makers"; the change of scope and direction of content; the pressures on children; the consequences of technological change; the structure of the disciplines; the interest in curriculum research; the experimentation with team teaching, television, data processing and computer science, programmed instruction, and independent study; the study of more difficult concepts at an earlier age level; the continuity and open-endedness of learning; programs for the culturally disadvantaged and children with other handicaps; programs for the talented, the gifted, and the creative; and other developments in elementary and secondary schools that tend to advance or obscure attention to individual differences.

This is intended to be a comprehensive book on curriculum improvement, written for teachers, administrators, other curriculum leaders in schools, and college professors and students who are mutually engaged in that task. The book is designed for courses in curriculum, for workshops, for local programs of curriculum im-

provement, and for independent study. Principles based on knowledge about human development and learning, about the culture, and
about democratic ideals and values are illustrated with descriptions
of school practices.

Part I is devoted to dynamics and processes of curriculum change;
Part II, to the sources from which the curriculum and curriculum decisions are derived; Part III, to the means of planning curriculum
improvement in the schools; Part IV, to trends in the elementary and
secondary school curriculum; and Part V, to cooperative teacher–
pupil planning of the curriculum.

The book stresses a search for answers rather than final answers.
Although it takes a position in favor of an experience-centered,
problem-solving approach, it also recognizes that the heart of that
approach is an open mind and experimental and research-mindedness.
Curriculum improvement is regarded as resulting from people's study
of their own problems and evaluation of the changes made. Beginning with Chapter 2, the end of each chapter presents different points
of view of educators on the various problems and issues as they now
appear.

The author wishes to express appreciation to Bernard J. Lonsdale,
former Supervisor of Elementary Education, State of California, for
writing Chapter 10 and to Gilbert Schiffman, Supervisor of Corrective-
Remedial Reading, Baltimore County Public Schools, Maryland, for
writing Chapter 11, the two chapters which focus particularly on
curriculum developments in elementary schools; to school leaders
who furnished information for the examples; to Harl R. Douglass,
for his guidance and helpful criticisms; to others who furnished suggestions; and to Alice P. Anderson, who typed, edited, and corrected
the entire manuscript. Appreciation is extended to the publishers
of copyrighted materials who have given permission to quote from
their publications.

The illustrations in this book are used by courtesy of the following public schools: Alameda County, California, Public Schools;
Covina Valley Unified School District, Covina, California; East Baton
Rouge Parish, Baton Rouge, Louisiana, Public Schools; Glencoe, Illinois, Public Schools; Milwaukee, Wisconsin, Public Schools; Mont-
gomery County, Maryland, Public Schools; Portland, Oregon, Public
Schools.

VERNON E. ANDERSON

College Park, Maryland
January, 1965

CONTENTS

cies: State Legal Requirements. State Agencies. Accrediting
Agencies. Colleges and Universities. *National Curriculum Programs
and Influences:* Federal Government Participation.
Professional Organizations. Academic Organizations and Programs.
Publishers, Producers, and Authors. Foundations. *Issues
and Points of View. Selected References.*

II. SOURCES OF CURRICULUM DECISIONS

III. PLANNING AND ORGANIZING FOR CURRICULUM STUDY

IV. CURRICULUM DEVELOPMENT IN ELEMENTARY AND SECONDARY SCHOOLS

Foreign Language. The Evolving Area of Communications. Emphasizing Experimentation and Discovery. New Directions in Elementary School Science. Modern Mathematics. *Innovations in Staff Utilization and Organization for Instruction:* Use of Television. Team Teaching. Programmed Instruction. Changes in Elementary School Organization. Other Organizations and Groupings. *Issues and Points of View.*

I
DYNAMICS OF
CURRICULUM
IMPROVEMENT

1

THE MEANING OF
CURRICULUM CHANGE

Curriculum improvement is sought by teachers, administrators, scholars, parents, and the general public. All of these groups have a common goal: a better school experience for children. While they may not agree on what is "better," they are aware that the increase of knowledge alone requires changes in the school curriculum. To those who thoughtfully ponder the question, improvement means change: updating content, rewriting textbooks, doing research on learning and child growth, using the findings of the behavioral sciences, re-educating teachers. Change may mean many things, for example, a reorientation of thinking, an upsetting emotional experience, a discovery of new meanings, a use of paperbacks, an insight into human nature, more drill, a new device for scheduling, or a new method of cleaning chalkboards. It may be monumental, trivial, forward-looking, or regressive.

A promising sign is that more people are asking frank, searching questions. Is the change an improvement for our schools? Does it mean our children will have higher quality of experiences? Why is this change being made? Are we riding someone's private bandwagon? What difference does curriculum study make to those who teach? What evidence can we find that another way is better? Who says that a change is "good"?

The ideas and suggestions in this book do not propose the answers. They point out guiding principles that may govern behavior. These ideas will assist in finding answers, but more often than not they may raise additional questions lest the reader take the easy way. The examples indicate what schools seriously working at curriculum improvement are doing, but these are presented only as possible means. The suggestions and examples are tentative, not prescriptive, and are subject to further exploration and research.

In this chapter, the meaning of curriculum and the purposes of curriculum study are clarified. These statements represent a point of view, which the reader is not called upon to accept. It is hoped that he will develop his own.

POINTS OF VIEW ABOUT CURRICULUM

It is impossible to attempt to define *curriculum* without exhibiting a point of view. However, one's concepts about it will determine the way he goes about developing or revising it. The values that are inherent in the definition will in a measure control actions in curriculum study. Any teacher may, of course, choose his own definition. But he should be fairly sure of the consequences of the choice he is making. Several concepts of the curriculum are presented in this section.

Curriculum as the Course of Study

In the early history of curriculum development, the course of study was often interpreted to mean the curriculum. For the most part, the curriculum was regarded as a written course, and revision of the curriculum consequently meant revising the course outline. The curriculum was first produced by a committee, then installed in the schools, next tested in practice, and finally revised again. This curriculum was considered something that could be brought in from the outside and transplanted into school life. Adoption of a single text to serve as a guide to the content manifests the same belief, since the textbook becomes the course of study.

In the modern concept, the *course of study* is a written resource guide to the curriculum, incorporating suggestions to teachers as to objectives, study of pupils, learning experiences, content, materials, and means of evaluation.

Curriculum as Courses Offered

An implied definition of the curriculum on most college campuses is the list of courses offered by the various schools and colleges, combined into sequences for students with a specific educational objective. Generally, each department or college has an official "curricula and courses committee" whose sole function is to make proposals for adding or dropping courses from the program and for revising the requirements for graduation. Few are the committees that suggest any changes in either the content or the experiences provided in any professor's course. The underlying assumption is that the curriculum will be similar for each student if the description appears stated in a certain way under a specific title in the catalog. To a degree, however, the realization that the course title or description means very little to students or instructors is leading to action in a number of institutions. College departments are cooperatively studying the nature of the courses in the department and determining the objectives of these courses.

The term with the most precise meaning for the list of courses offered and for the grouping of required and elective courses to attain some educational objective is *the program of studies.*

Curriculum as Subject Matter Content

One of the most commonly accepted definitions of the curriculum is that it consists of the subject matter taught to the students. Curriculum study focuses on revising the content, adding new subject matter brought about by scientific discoveries, social change, or more recent literature. Method serves the purpose of presenting more interesting ways by which the pupil will learn the subject matter.

As a result of this point of view, some subjects, such as physical education, art, and music, have not been readily accepted on a par with other subjects. Secondary schools and colleges often have not considered them "solid" subjects, a rather subtle and invidious distinction between traditional and newer subjects. The content of the arts and physical education has been difficult to assess because it is not typically found in the usual books read and studied. Consequently, these subjects have often been relegated to the "extracurricular" (a term which implies lower status) or to the non-credit or orientation classification.

Subject matter is evaluated largely on the basis of its cultural values, timeliness, or usefulness as preparation for the adult world: the facts, habits, and skills which have been found useful in the past and which are most useful to successful adults living today.

Curriculum as Planned Experiences

The definition of the curriculum in terms of pupil experiences under the guidance of the school is a point of view which has generally been accepted in the professional literature on curriculum since Caswell and

Campbell's significant work in 1935.[1] Subsequent writers have re-fined and extended the definition to include purpose and to emphasize the school's relation to its surrounding culture, undoubtedly implied in the former definition.

In this book, the curriculum is defined in terms of the quality of pupil experiences in the school environment. Douglass' definition makes a useful distinction between the school's point of view as the learning environment provided and the pupil's point of view as the experience he perceives that he has in that environment.[2] Experience is, of course, interaction; but judgments concerning the quality of a person's experiences must consider the type of environment and the conditions that are provided for learning. The pupils' experiences are planned, organized, and guided by the school as a social system to serve the purpose of the society in which it exists. The *kind and quality* of experience provided and planned in the school culture are pre-eminent. To guide these experiences, the school must furnish a fertile learning environment. The teachers, the pupils, other adults in the school, the physical plant, the equipment, the learning materials, the course content, and the procedures used are all important factors interacting in the total environment. Changing the curriculum involves changing these interacting forces. Understood in this way, the curriculum is the means by which pupils' behavior is changed.

When the curriculum is conceived of as experiences which the pupils undergo within the culture of the school, content and method can no longer be regarded as separate entities. The selection and organization of experiences that will help children grow in socially desirable ways is a process that encompasses both content and method. The pupil and the teacher share in that process as part of the school society.

The curriculum includes not only classroom experiences but also the extraclass activities: the planned school services such as the library and health services, the field trips into the community, the school assemblies, and the entire school community as used for learning experiences (such as the buying and selling of goods, and traffic regulation). All of these are deliberately planned by the school to serve social purposes.

[1] Hollis L. Caswell and Doak S. Campbell, *Curriculum Development*, New York: American Book Co., 1935, chap. iv.

[2] Harl R. Douglass, "The Function and Nature of the Curriculum," in Harl R. Douglass (ed.), *The High School Curriculum*, 3rd ed., New York: The Ronald Press Co., 1964, chap. 2.

This definition is one that makes sense to parents, whose chief concern is what happens to their children as a result of schooling. Two rather extreme examples are used in order to illustrate the point.

Let us for a moment place ourselves in the position of a parent who has a choice of two teachers for his child. One teacher is a domineering, aggressive, and sarcastic person. He secretly considers children obnoxious and apparently rejects them in many ways. He blames his unhappiness in life on circumstances and on others. He is narrow in both vision and learning. Few are his genuine friends. He considers his job a bore, hurries out the front door ahead of the children after school, and thinks any suggestion for improvement of his work is an insult to his competence.

The other teacher is a witty, alert, cheerful, well-read person, one who makes parents feel at ease. He has had some tragic experiences in life but has adjusted to them well and does not blame the world for them. It is evident that he likes children; he can usually be found surrounded by a group of them at noon or after school, on the playground or in his room. His fellow teachers respect him. In his professional responsibilities, he strives constantly to improve himself. He likes teaching and shows it.

Let us further assume that both of these teachers follow the same course of study, use the same textbooks and other materials, teach the same content. Their procedures would, apparently, differ. We may suspect, too, that the clarity and understanding of their own goals would not be the same. If we had to choose between these two as a teacher for our child, our choice would not be based exclusively on content taught. Personality, competence, effect upon the child, and other factors would be considered.

What happens to the course of study in the hands of these two teachers? The experiences of the children in their classrooms would be radically different. The chances are good that at least some of the children working for a year with the frustrated and aggressive teacher would tend to become somewhat frustrated themselves.

Differences in any other significant aspect of the total environment can be analyzed in the same way. The curriculum is determined by an interaction of many complex factors: the room environment; the fellow classmates; the attitudes, competency, and personality of the teacher; the course of study; the content; the materials available; the other members of the staff. A modification of any one of these factors can change the environment and the experiences pupils have in that environment.

THE PURPOSE OF CURRICULUM STUDY

One of the basic issues that teachers must face in entering upon curriculum study relates to acceptance of new ideas. Are we willing to modify our ways? Will we look for the facts and arrive at conclusions after thoughtful study, or will we set out to prove that we are right? Will we seek information for the solution of our problems in any areas that give data on human behavior? Will we take whatever action we may conclude desirable based upon objective data? Unless we can frankly answer "yes" to these questions, curriculum tinkering will be the result, with a dab of the new here and a deletion of an inconsequential bit of the old there. It is extremely doubtful if the energy and time expended on curriculum study are worth the effort if we are not honest and sincere about our desire to change the curriculum.

This principle applies with special force to those in leadership positions. Administrators should not ask teachers to enter into curriculum study unless they are willing to accept the conclusions reached as to changes that need to be made.

Meeting Cultural Demands

The rapidity of social change is a pertinent reason for curriculum study. Changes in society seem to be rushing with the speed of a jet plane, while curriculum changes seem to crawl like a tortoise. The scientific advancement in nuclear energy alone, with its world-shaking consequences, spells a need for change in the curriculum. The ferment and demand for independence among the people of Asia, Africa, and Latin America, accompanied by the cancerous growth of communism and totalitarianism, make essential a new perspective on these areas of the world. Books giving romanticized versions of these people are no longer sufficient. Understanding of others' ways of looking at life becomes a more important objective. Peace has become a vital necessity for the survival of civilization, not a luxury that can be dispensed with to further the individual goals of nations.

Teachers and children are subject to various kinds of pressures from professional and community groups who want more of this or less of that. Safety organizations ask that safety be taught, to halt the slaughter on highways. Some people want more geography taught. There is increasing demand for citizenship education, for better teaching of the skills, for attention to moral and spiritual values. Some groups want aviation education; others, intercultural education; others, the sciences; still others, more of the humanities. These pressures for curriculum change are manifestations of social change. They represent a need for curriculum study.

Solving Instructional Problems

When educational groups meet, formally or informally, knotty problems usually come to the fore: How can we best help the slow learner? What can we do for pupils no longer interested in learning or in school? What can we do for the culturally deprived youngsters? How can we obtain continuity in the social studies throughout grades 1 to 12? What can we do to improve our reading program? There are no simple answers to questions that involve inquiry into complex skills and human relations, insight into children's maladjustments, and understanding of the cultural influences on children. Such questions require study, to which some people are devoting a lifetime of research.

However, these are the kinds of problems that confront the schools and demand solution. In this book the hypothesis is presented that study of one's own problems will lead to significant curriculum changes. Curriculum study ought to deal with these problems; many seemingly insurmountable ones can be solved by getting people together in face-to-face situations in a favorable environment where they can explore and test out ideas, and arrive at tentative conclusions. Others need to be scrutinized by research over a longer period of time.

Changing People's Ways of Behaving

There are undoubtedly teachers who go through the motions of curriculum study to obtain the required number of in-service credits. There are graduate students who study curriculum as an academic exercise, reading required books, preparing required papers, and taking final examinations. That they will change their mode of behavior by so doing is questionable.

On the other hand, there are many principals, teachers, and graduate students who are concerned that they become better teachers or administrators through in-service study. No curriculum study of any kind, in a school or in a college classroom, is fruitful unless it results in change of the behavior of those who participate. Out of such study should come changed values and ideas, new concepts and information, new perceptions of one's own and others' role in the school, improved selection of content, better ways of working with children, deeper insights into one's own and the pupils' behavior.

Curriculum change, from this point of view, is not a matter of going through musty printed pages to alter the words. It is not making an administrative decree that certain new curriculum practices shall be adopted. It is a change in behavior on the part of the teacher, the administrator, the pupil—all who are involved in the process of curriculum development.

As adults with the chief responsibility for selection and organization of curriculum experiences of children, we probably do not go into curriculum study with the conscious purpose of changing ourselves. We want to try out new ideas, to discuss ideas with others, to learn more about our subject and human nature, to find out how we can give children a more worthwhile experience. In the process we develop different attitudes, change our point of view, or become more skillful in teaching. These understandings, skills, and attitudes are the controls of our behavior; consequently, we are changing.

Changing Perceptions

People, however, do not change in a vacuum. Any change a teacher makes in his way of operating or thinking is related to the total social structure of the school of which he is a part and the community in which the school exists.

The school in a sense is a social system, including a network of rules, regulations, rituals, and traditions within which people work together. There is a pattern of relationships in a school building, an established way of living in which each one plays a certain "role" or behaves in an expected way. One teacher may be the person who always finds time to see that the coffee is ready at the meetings; another, the one to whom beginning teachers turn for help; another, the one who has his hand on the pulse of public opinion, to whom the principal turns for advice; another, an "old nester"; another, a constant complainer. The principal may see himself as a person who is supposed to make decisions, or as someone who facilitates arriving at decisions cooperatively. Social psychologists have pointed out that we retain these roles because they give us satisfaction. The "old nester" finds it most comfortable to sit and do nothing different. The complainer finds satisfaction in airing his criticisms because he may have no other means of communication with fellow teachers.

As these perceptions of one's own role in a school are changed for the better, the climate for curriculum change becomes more favorable.

Improving Pupils' Experiences

Change of teacher behavior is not an end in itself. Curriculum study is not therapy. To change the ways and ideas of teachers, administrators, and supervisors is a means toward an improved learning climate for pupils. If teachers and their supervisors see themselves differently, develop new insights into working with each other, clarify their concept of the purpose and use of subject matter, and examine their values, children will have a different kind of experience. If through the very experiences of curriculum study, teachers become more alert, sensitive, and well-informed, they cannot fail to provide a different atmosphere for children. The community can justifiably demand that any curriculum improvement program should result in an enriched school life for its children.

HUMAN RELATIONS AND CURRICULUM CHANGE

"It was the first time that my ideas counted for anything." This statement was made by a teacher who had been a member of a workshop in which human relations had been considered a significant factor. The value that teachers place on getting to know each other as individuals, learning to work together, understanding each other, and being understood is evident in evaluations of group experiences in curriculum study. Nor are such statements mere manifestations of sentiment. The evidence from research in group dynamics shows that improved human relations are not to be written off as inconsequential results.

It would appear from studies of human behavior in groups that curriculum improvement finds nourishment in an atmosphere of friendliness, the spirit of give and take, and genuine attempts to understand one's associates' ideas and points of view. On the other hand, sarcasm, ridicule, humor at someone else's expense, and ostentatious parading of knowledge seem to hinder real progress. Where the human relations factor is ignored, there is little inclination to use others' ideas or to look at one's values. The best idea will not work unless there is a will to make it work.

Human Relations Structure

Curriculum improvement is a social change that involves a change in the human relations structure among individuals within the school society. It is a process of changing the interrelationships among school faculty, the perceptions of teachers' and administrators' roles in relation to each other, the way in which teachers view their actions in the school system in which they work. Teachers behave in what they feel are accepted ways. Much of their behavior tends to be shaped by those with whom they associate. Thus, mathematics teachers may associate only with mathematics teachers in a large school system or a college, and their actions will be influenced by what their associates feel is acceptable.

The findings of research in group dynamics in such centers as the Research Center for Group Dynamics at the University of Michigan bear directly on how a group of people in a school system go about changing the curriculum (viewed as a social process) and what tends to block curriculum change. The following are illustrative of the findings:

1. The group determines much of the individual's attitudes toward himself and others.
2. Groups develop pressures toward group uniformity and solidarity among their members. The persistent deviate tends to be rejected by the group.
3. Groups establish standards for the performance of their members.
4. Individuals select information received in terms of group beliefs, sanctions, and stated positions. They sort out what already conforms to the group beliefs.
5. People tend to avoid communication with those who threaten, make them feel anxious, or give them other types of unrewarding experiences (those with ideas, ways of doing, education, background distinctly different from their own).
6. People find frustration or happiness in their organizational roles, which either suppress their talents or give them a chance to express those talents.
7. Whether group members work for group goals rather than individual goals depends upon the extent to which the members understand the group goals.
8. Productivity increases with more helpful interdependence among group members, with increased awareness among group members of the mutual need for each other's work, and with increased trust in one another.
9. Groups in which members see themselves as interdependent will have greater cohesiveness, greater interest in the group task,

and greater interest in completing the task than groups in which perception of interdependence is absent.[3]

Business organizations, government organizations, the military, labor unions, and voluntary associations have been among the groups studied. These studies suggest that if curriculum improvement is to occur, teachers need to find new satisfactions within the group in which they work. Supervisors who concentrate on giving information and at the same time create fear and distrust through rating of teachers, or simply through bad human relations, are likely to fail in any effort at change. The remoteness of administrators or supervisors from teachers is based upon a concept of maintaining authority. When human relations are sound, such a concept is not necessary, and changes are more likely to be brought about and genuinely accepted.

The approved patterns of behavior evident in any school building may be the more obvious routines that make teachers accepted and respected: firm discipline, children marching to and from the class-room in drill fashion, and order and neatness in the classroom. The more subtle unwritten rules are those dealing with the acceptance of new ideas concerning instruction. In some schools it is comfortable for the principal to leave teachers alone, and the teachers have found it comfortable also. Teachers are not asked for their opinions in regard to policy, and they have learned that they can get home earlier by not becoming so involved.

In the social structure within a school, there is a hierarchy of status, highly developed in formal situations and negligible where the faculty works cooperatively as a total group. In large school systems there tends to be more of a definite "peck order" where superintendents are above supervisors, supervisors above principals, and principals above teachers. The line-and-staff type of organization tends to perpetuate the hierarchy, which may even manifest itself in social groupings, where elementary principals associate only with elementary principals and elementary school teachers only with elementary school teachers. In other words, a person's role stems from the status relationships, and where a premium is placed upon status differences, interaction and change are likely to suffer.

This concept of curriculum improvement as changing the human relations structure places emphasis on group processes and group

[3] *Institute for Social Research*, 1946–1961, Ann Arbor: University of Michigan, 1962, 40 pp. A detailed summary of research in this field can be found in Dorwin Cartwright and Alvin Zander (eds.), *Group Dynamics: Research and Theory*, 2nd ed., New York: Harper & Row, Publishers, 1960, 826 pp.

work, through which changes in the group structure can be effected. It throws considerable doubt on the value of any curriculum study that does not involve the teachers concerned. It also centers the attention on the way faculties work together, know each other, understand each other, and see themselves and others.

The Teacher's Personality

Within this social structure the teacher acts as he does because of the various kinds of experiences he has had. The roles that he plays and his personality make-up are a result of the influence of his environment. Sharp's thesis is that the curriculum develops basically as the result of the development of teachers' personalities.[4]

An analysis of what happens when an attempt is made to change the values of a teacher who has become set in his ways is invaluable for understanding the uncertainty and hostility that a person experiences in the process of changing as an individual. For example, a teacher who changes from teaching with a single textbook in an authoritarian manner to cooperative problem-solving through the use of many sources of information actually changes his whole frame of reference. He changes in his concept of growth, in his philosophy, in his concept of learning, and in his values and beliefs—to say nothing of his changed skills in working with pupils.

The process of re-education is a difficult one. The individual teacher must work through it with the help of the principal, superintendent, supervisor, or other leader. The leader plays a crucial role in helping the teacher to grow, since he establishes to a large extent the kinds of relationships that exist among the members of the group. He needs to create an atmosphere in which the teacher will be free to express his own problems, no matter how trivial they may seem, and to help the teacher solve his problems through gaining greater insight into them.

Morale of Faculty

Anyone acquainted with schools and school faculties does not have to be in a building very long before he can sense the morale of the faculty. There is a certain good feeling, a sense of joy in their work, a unity of purpose, and a liking and respect for each other that constitute what is known as high morale.

The morale of a group influences its productivity—in the case of

---

[4] George Sharp, *Curriculum Development as Re-Education of the Teacher*, New York: Bureau of Publications, Teachers College, Columbia University, 1951, p. v.

teachers, the degree to which they can create a good environment for learning. Working conditions, such as wages, safety, and promotional policy, affect the morale of the group. However, research in industry has discovered that once good relations between supervisor and worker are established, special benefits such as rest periods or free morning lunches can be taken away without decreasing the output. When workers have a part in policy-making, when there are good relations between employer and employees so that the latter understand and approve of technical changes to increase efficiency, increased production occurs. Forward-looking practices, such as the profit-sharing plan in some companies, illustrate this point.

The uncertainty, anxiety, and hostility felt by teachers in a school where they are subject to changes by decree, or are kept in the dark about reasons for the administration's policies, are signs of low morale. Morale drops where uncertainty exists, where there are conflicts and tensions, and where the teachers' expectations are not realized.

Where teachers have a sense of belonging, have confidence in the administrator, and are given an opportunity to be creative individuals, curriculum improvements occur more readily.

Group Decisions

Experiments in work production, food habits, prejudice, leadership training, and other areas have shown that a group decision to change makes it easier for an individual to change. Alcoholics Anonymous is an example of a well-known organization that illustrates the point. In an experiment in industry, a group of workers had a low production rate when they were simply notified of changes. These workers raised their rate considerably when they had an opportunity to participate in decisions.[5] Lewin's experiment in getting housewives to use inferior cuts of meat during the war is an illustration of how behavior is best changed when the group norms first change in the desired direction.[6] When a group as a whole decides on a certain course of action, more individuals within the group are likely to go along with the decision.

This is an important principle for curriculum improvement, one that experience in curriculum study in schools has substantiated. The focus of curriculum study, therefore, should be on the group, not on the

[5] Lester Coch and John R. P. French, Jr., "Overcoming Resistance to Change," in Cartwright and Zander, op. cit., chap. 18.

[6] Kurt Lewin, "Group Decisions and Social Change," in Theodore M. Newcomb and Eugene L. Hartley (eds.), Readings in Social Psychology, New York: Holt, Rinehart and Winston, Inc., 1947, pp. 334-37.

individual. For example, when a school makes some major change such as instituting the ungraded classroom in an elementary school, encouraging the few teachers who are willing and ready to experiment to do so is probably better than attempting an over-all change. But, at the same time, the decision to experiment should be that of the entire faculty. It should be a group experiment decided upon and evaluated by the whole faculty. The abrupt dislocation of the social framework in which teachers have become accustomed to work builds up hostility and resistance to the change if it does not come about as a result of group study and cooperation. How often have the home-room, the new marking system, or other innovations become the scape-goat of many of the teaching staff! These observations suggest a re-examination of the whole concept of supervision that is based on classroom visitation and individual contacts with teachers.

Quality of Leadership

The kind of role that the leader takes in relation to the members of the group is one important factor in determining the productiveness of the group. Studies of leadership in both adults' and children's groups give evidence that highest productivity occurs in groups under democratic leadership.

In this section the findings from research in group leadership [7] are translated into a school situation where curriculum study is going on. The four situations described below are only some of many possibilities. They describe different kinds of climates in which these events *may* well occur. They indicate how a principal or leader may behave in these situations.

In the school atmosphere of the *authoritarian or autocratic* type, there is no "nonsense about soft democracy." As far as the principal is concerned, the teachers know where he stands, for he does not hesitate to tell them. He visits teachers' classrooms to see what they are doing, insists on quiet hallways and clockwork scheduling, and boasts that he has a well run school. At the beginning of the year, he has some meetings to interpret the course of study to the teachers. From then on meetings are routine, held because the school district requires them once a month, not because there is any particular need for them. The principal wants a "smooth school," builds his success in life upon his managerial ability, and bases his skill in managing

[7] Ralph White and Ronald Lippitt, "Leader Behavior and Member Reactions in Three 'Social Climates'," in Cartwright and Zander, *op. cit.*, chap. 28.

people on fear rather than on confidence. However, people working under him can develop definite opposition to him. Unified through fear, teachers can support each other and develop ways of outwitting the principal. Since he is really not a member of the group, this principal knows little about what is actually going on. Teachers have developed some group rules of their own for behavior in teachers' meetings and in other contacts with the principal, passing the word along when he is visiting classes. Few are inclined to take responsibility for tasks other than those which the principal asks them to perform. For the failure of their pupils, teachers tend to pass the buck to the policy of the central office, the lack of equipment, the neighborhood, or the parents. Little effort for improvement of instruction is evident—all on an individual basis. Changes the principal suggests are carried out halfheartedly.

An atmosphere of *benevolent despotism* is more difficult to identify. The principal believes himself to be democratic in his paternal attitude toward his teachers. He may be a jovial kind of person, easy to get along with, and may have considerable influence in the community. Teachers like him, for he is friendly and encourages them in the work they are doing. To outsiders he talks about "his school and his wonderful teachers." Actually, he secures dependence on himself because decisions are always made between the individual teacher and the principal. It is a one-to-one relationship rather than a total group interaction. When teachers have a problem, they are encouraged to come to him and are well received. The danger is that each teacher may feel happy and secure in this submissive role. Only the more astute see the situation as it is: If they want to try to bring about a major change in the curriculum, there is only the single-lane avenue. The suggestion may be pigeonholed by the principal. Changes in instructional policy come about through individual conferences with teachers, the final decision being made by the principal. Unified opposition is difficult. Since few perceive the reality of the situation, the minority group can do little. Whatever they may attempt is considered unethical. Most teachers do their work well. All experimentation is done by individual teachers, but initiative to experiment is generally lacking.

In the *laissez faire* atmosphere, the principal is often described by his teachers as one who "is afraid of his own shadow." He takes refuge in the office, doing routine work that any clerk could do as well or better. When his teachers come to him for decisions on what to do about something that clearly involves school policy, he shifts the responsibility back to them. He allows each teacher to decide for himself what changes, major or minor, are to be made in the curriculum and expends no energy to see that there is any effort on the part of the faculty to improve instruction. Actually, few do anything about curriculum change, for there are no channels and little encouragement for group improvement. Teachers do not work together, since they have no leadership for group study. They cannot go to the principal with suggestions, for he would make no effort to carry them out. There is the least freedom of action in this type of atmosphere. The teachers are insecure in their work, for they do not know what is expected of them nor to whom to turn for leadership. In such a school situation, no improvements in the curriculum are likely to occur.

In a *democratic* atmosphere the principal is a member of a team. Some people misinterpret democratic leadership as the laissez faire type. The principal does not abdicate leadership but gives responsibility to those who can and are willing to take it. He makes it possible for the staff to plan together and to cooperate in developing policy. Then he carries out that policy to the best of his ability. Where there is sharing in decision-making, teachers understand why certain practices and policies exist. Since they participate in deciding what the school is to be like, they feel it is their school and take responsibility for the success of its program. In this kind of an atmosphere, although they may not always be happy, teachers tend to enjoy their work. Even though they work a good deal harder, holding more meetings and serving on more committees, they are also more relaxed, because the tensions of unpleasant interpersonal relations are absent. The group feels that the responsibility rests with them for making their own plans work. They know that they have the power to change plans, since they helped to formulate them.

Obviously, in these four hypothetical cases the lines are drawn too rigidly to apply to all situations. Many principals are more—or less—benevolent, autocratic, or democratic than each illustration implies. Then, too, the community conditions affect the atmosphere in a school. Just as it is more difficult for a teacher to be democratic in an autocratic school, so it is harder for a school to develop a democratic atmosphere in a community that tends to be authoritarian in its relationships.

A faculty working in a democratic situation can be expected to accomplish the most; a faculty working in a laissez faire situation, the least. Both quality and quantity of production are highest in the democratic group. There is a self-propulsion and initiative when the leader is absent, as well as in his presence.

PACING CURRICULUM CHANGE

If the concept of curriculum change as involving a change in people and their relations to each other is accepted, it is reasonable to conclude that changes should be made only as fast as people are able and willing to change. There are those who want to "change the curriculum by Christmas." Their notion is that committees appointed to work on curriculum revision can turn out a product within a few months' time, even if it involves the revision of the whole elementary school curriculum! Human relationships do not change in such short order. The task of improving the curriculum through modifying the teachers' behavior toward each other and toward their pupils, the administration's behavior toward the teacher, the teacher's concept of his own behavior, and the interpersonal relations of faculty and lay public is a far more complicated task than making a change in the course of study.

Difficulty in Making Changes

Changing our ways of working or living is hard for us all. We are reluctant to change because we have a certain vested interest in keeping things as they are. The attitudes we have built up, our comfortable habits, our skills, the tools we use, and the routine to which we are accustomed may all be disrupted or outmoded by taking on new ways and customs.

It is doubtful if the seriousness of the upheaval that occurs in making major changes in professional habits and procedures has been fully realized by those who inaugurate the changes. It means more work and new materials. Even for the teaching of a new unit, there are hours of planning to be done, illustrations to be gathered, and books to be selected. A change which involves teaching controversial issues in the classroom or making field trips for the first time means bringing the public into the planning. It is far easier to use the same units, the same lecture notes, the same questions or problems, or the same materials that we used last year.

Lack of Security in the New

How much more difficult it is for anyone to change to a new approach, such as the experience-centered curriculum, which even requires a recasting of the ways of thinking! The venture may result

in a return to the safety and success of the old ways if something does
not work out as well as expected. Because teachers do not know
how to plan with pupils, many will be afraid to try, a perfectly normal
reaction. Most important is the need to experiment to gain the necessary confidence in their own abilities.

Workshops for in-service education are a good illustration of the
need for gaining security in a new process. Students tend to be more
secure in an atmosphere of lectures, single textbooks, term papers, and
examinations. They know what is expected of them, what they will
be required to do. When they are first introduced to planning the
course with the instructor, some will object that it is a waste of time.
Some will remark: "Why doesn't he tell us what to do?" Others will
say: "I came here to learn something from the instructor." At this
point, it would be much easier for the leader to revert to procedures to
which the group is accustomed. He may have some anxious and uncomfortable moments, but, as he helps the group members to see the
powers and resources that they have within themselves, the group
gains confidence in the process. Education, by definition, is a leading-
out, not a pouring-in process.

There is a lack of security for some in the very idea of change
itself. Values are thought of by an individual as his own personal
values unless he has learned to look at them more objectively. Teachers may feel that a status leader's belief that a change is needed implies something wrong with their ability.

Importance of Correct Pacing

How fast, then, can we expect curriculum changes to take place?
The answer is inherent in the situation, depending upon the previous
experiences of the group in decision-making and group study, the
skill of the leader, the genuineness of the problems studied, the human
relations pattern already built up within the group, and the resources
available.

Some are impatient with the process of change in human beings.
They try to attack the problem head-on with inspirational speakers,
meetings to stimulate interest, over-all programs, a publicity campaign.
and decrees to "speed up things." Or they may demand "tougher
courses." They do not take into consideration that they cannot change
people; they can only provide situations favorable to change and help
make it possible and easier for people to change.

These high-pressure methods have little lasting influence. Pushing
too fast results in frustration, antagonism, and insecurity. The time

when the superintendent, principal, or dean will move on to some other position is talked about. The aggression which results from a frustrating condition may actually take such forms as collusion between a group of teachers and dissatisfied community people to get rid of the school leader.

When school systems have reverted to previous practices, one can be fairly certain that neither teachers nor citizens actually had changed in their values or their perceptions. Learning and change involve conflict, frustration, and ambivalence; it takes time, leadership, and a desire to change in order to resolve problems and conflict. Some give up too easily, before the modifications have ever had a chance to prove their value.

Modification of Forces Affecting Change

Lewin's concept of the state of equilibrium in social change is a useful one in understanding the speed with which curriculum changes can be expected to occur. Lewin states that there are social forces operating in the total situation, some for change and some against it. When these two types of forces are equal, a state of equilibrium or one of no change is present. In order to effect change, either the opposing forces must be reduced or the driving forces strengthened. Reduction of the opposing forces and a gradual increase in the driving forces results in less tension than would come from increasing the strength of the driving forces alone. In order for the change to be permanent, the new conditions must then be stabilized.[8]

A curriculum committee chairman may decide that he wants more involvement in group discussion. He proposes that the committee pay attention to improvement of discussion skills. The group may be accustomed to listening to the leader talk. The forces *against* making this change may be: (1) the threat to the security of listening to the leader and not getting "involved" in more work, (2) the natural reluctance to change, (3) the belief that the more vocal will dominate the faculty, (4) the belief that group discussion is a waste of time, (5) the aggression caused by use of unfamiliar terms of group dynamics (which is a real danger in cases where people want to show off new knowledge). Forces operating *for* change may be: (1) the boredom with meetings where the major portion of time is spent in listening, (2) the desire of some staff members to develop more democratic procedures, (3) the experience of a few in curriculum conferences or workshops using good group techniques, (4) the desire to have a part

[8] Lewin, *op. cit.*, p. 344.

in policy-making, (5) dissatisfaction with the present state of some practices.

The leader's chief problem would be to change the attitudes against group discussion by making it fruitful; by eliminating fear of unfamiliar terms through not using them; by guiding the discussion so that everyone has a chance to say what he wants; and by seeing that some decisions are arrived at and action taken as a result of those decisions. Moreover, the stabilizing of the new way of conducting meetings would come about through further experience in group decision-making and continuous attention to improvement of group discussion.

Change in Beliefs

The values and standards held by an individual or a group are powerful determiners of behavior. In their desire to bring about change in people, some schools have begun curriculum study with the formulation of a philosophy. The theory is that the establishment of a philosophy at the beginning will prepare the way for change and point out the gaps between philosophy and practice. It is extremely doubtful that a study of philosophy apart from practice has resulted in any significant curriculum change.

A new set of values or beliefs for the individual grows out of his experience and the cultural values of the social group of which he is a member. He tends to accept new ideas as group values change or as he finds belongingness in a new group. A practical idea may seem to teachers impractical and foolish because it does not fit into the framework of the thinking and ways of acting of the group with which they identify themselves. For example, a high school teacher may regard a policy of social promotions as ridiculous because it does not fit within the frame of his experience, whereas an elementary teacher may have a different point of view since he is a member of a faculty that has long accepted the practice.

The study of philosophy is not something to precede curriculum study; it grows out of a group's attack on solving problems, finding its own facts, and applying the facts to its situation. One of the main reasons secondary and elementary school teachers are at variance in their thinking is that they lack opportunities to work and think together. Each group sees the problem from a different angle. As their values change and they change their frame of reference through analyzing others' viewpoints, they will adopt new practices that are in conformity with newer values. This is one of the reasons why curriculum improvement is a slow process. Curriculum change can occur no faster than change in beliefs of those concerned.

CONDITIONS FOR CURRICULUM IMPROVEMENT

The preceding analysis has been concerned with what happens to individuals and to groups in the process of curriculum change. The analysis suggests that focus in curriculum study should be on the group. However, some teachers are undoubtedly happy in a school where they are not called upon for many meetings or committee work. Others would not even consider accepting a position where teamwork was not evident. How have the experiences of the latter been different? What have they been like?

There are some essential elements of a group situation in which people will grow individually and professionally. They constitute basic principles for curriculum improvement.

1. *Leadership that knows how to work with people democratically.*

Leadership of this type permits maximum participation in determining policies. It creates opportunities for teachers to work together. It realizes the creative potentiality of individual teachers and even capitalizes on idiosyncrasies. It develops leadership through delegating responsibility to members of the staff.

2. *Acceptance of people and respect for their contributions.*

In a school where differences are considered an asset rather than a liability, a teacher is accepted as a human being with likes and dislikes, joys and sorrows. His associates make him feel that his contributions are of value. They have the belief that it is a good thing for people to differ. The practice of labeling people as "traditional," "old fogies," "older teachers," or "progressive," has hurt many teachers deeply. It has served to alienate them from those who do not agree with them.

3. *Faith in group judgment.*

Whenever confidence is bestowed upon groups, they come out with sensible and reasonable decisions. Their decisions are better than those any one individual can make because they represent the collective thinking of many minds. As groups make judgments, they also grow in their ability to judge. Progress in curriculum improvement can be made if the school staff has a right to make decisions based on the best available evidence.

4. *Opportunity to know individuals as persons.*

It is no accident that faculties arrange for coffee hours before meetings in the afternoon or that conferences or workshops are held at a camp by a lake or in the mountains where people may be informal and enjoy recreation together. These experiences make it possible for people to get acquainted with each other. There is a leveling of status where the principal or teacher becomes known as a person, not a position.

5. *Freedom for schools and teachers to experiment.*

In an atmosphere conducive to curriculum improvement, the group standard is experimentation. Teachers make changes because they are encouraged to try out new ideas, perhaps new only in the sense of being unfamiliar. They feel secure that the mistakes that inevitably occur in exploring will not be held against them. They find encouragement and assistance in experimentation and evaluation of results. Within the school building, there is freedom to develop as a school unit which serves its own community and has an individuality of its own.

6. *Study of the problems of the people concerned.*

When faculties begin curriculum study as a group, they may propose problems that seem minor. The study of poor attendance or pupil conduct may lead into various ramifications of child development, home background, the child's life outside of school, good learning situations, or development of attitudes. These are curriculum problems in the sense that their study can lead to changes in experiences provided for pupils. Only as people in curriculum study seek a solution to problems that are real to them will any appreciable action take place as a result of study.

7. *Assumption of the mutual growth of all concerned.*

Teacher, superintendent, principal, and parent are all involved in the process of curriculum change. Sometimes the leader urges his teachers to take courses and arranges for in-service education for his school, but he stays on the sidelines. Somehow the queer notion has developed that teachers are supposed to grow but that the leader has reached his maximum growth. Yet, cooperative study for curriculum improvement must assume such mutuality if the leader is to be an accepted member of the group, one who can give the most effective kind of democratic leadership. Curriculum improvement is a dynamic process involving teacher, parents, pupils, supervisors, and administrators.

8. *Formation of a real group structure.*

To a sociologist or social psychologist, the definition of a "group" includes more than an aggregate of individuals. A group consists of more than a sum of its parts. (For example, the tourists who visit Mt. Rainier National Park in one day do not constitute a group.) It has characteristics of its own. The persons who constitute the group share norms and ideals and have a certain dependence on each other. It takes time for a collection of individuals to become a group. The particular class using this book, for example, may or may not become a group before the course is over. These tests are suggested as a checklist to determine whether there is a cohesive group structure and solidarity that will be productive for curriculum improvement:

Members identify themselves with the group and take pride in it, referring to "our group" or "our school."

There is an interdependence among members; they freely give and receive help.

They enjoy being together.

They resist leaving the group when requested to change to some other group.

There is adequate communication among members.

The ending time of group meetings comes too quickly.

There is freedom for different members to express their beliefs.

They can reach a consensus through study and discussion.

They are clear as to what the group is trying to do.

There is a free work atmosphere.

Members know how to handle conflict without acrimony.

The group analyzes its ways of working and reaching decisions.

Value is placed on individual contributions.

These are optimum conditions for curriculum study that seeks to improve pupils' experiences, that is based on the concept of change in people, that is cognizant of difficulties people have in making changes, and that places high value on good human relations in a school faculty.

2

PROCESS OF GROUP STUDY

Group study is an essential ingredient of optimum curriculum improvement. In this study, teachers, administrators, supervisors, community members, and sometimes pupils participate. The teacher is the medium through which the improvement is translated into action in the classroom. His is a most vital part in this process.

If this principle is accepted, the teacher's responsibility for knowing how to work with fellow teachers, how to give leadership to curriculum study, and how to prevent ceaseless hours of inept committee deliberations becomes unmistakably clear. The supervisor and the teacher share this responsibility.

The dynamics of school leaders and teachers working together as a group is examined in this chapter. Practical suggestions are derived from the research in group process.

PURPOSES OF STUDYING GROUP PROCESS

Any faculty group can afford to take time to improve its skills of working together. Many are woefully inept in these skills. It is foolhardy to expect such groups to perform well or to arrive at decisions quickly without an understanding of, and skill in, group processes. The "stars" and individualists do not become good team members in a day, nor do those who by bitter experience have learned that it is wiser to listen than to talk.

Getting a Job Done

Some will say when they are first introduced to group process: "Why should we waste our time discussing process when we have a job to be done? Let's get it done as quickly and as well as we can." The question is asked sincerely; it indicates a worthy purpose. The leader's task is to show how attention to group process can help get that job done more effectively.

When any teacher accepts an appointment as a member or chairman of a curriculum committee, he is anxious to see that it accomplishes something. Yet he may be somewhat apprehensive. Perhaps he has been on committees that did not get anywhere; the members just talked and seemed unable to arrive at any decisions. There was always someone who enjoyed probing philosophical questions or someone who was a stickler for defining terms. Perhaps it was a group in which the chairman dominated the discussion and the decisions. Or perhaps the committee had two factions that were unable to arrive at agreements. He justly wonders if the new committee too will flounder.

Why is it that some groups are so much more productive than others? Why does it take so long for some committees to clarify their problems and begin their work? Why are some faculties seemingly incapable of defining their problems? As soon as we begin to ask questions of this nature, we are concerned with the dynamics of groups, their structure, and the processes which make them successful.

The study of group processes is not an end in itself except for those concerned with research in group dynamics. When groups become so absorbed in the process, terminology, and rituals that the real goal is obscured, the criticism that time is wasted is valid. The study is not intended to be an academic exercise but a tool for the improvement of problem-solving by a group. As such it has value in curriculum improvement, where there is no dearth of problems.

Improving Skills in Group Work

Any group that does not intend to remain a collection of individuals needs to clarify its purposes, consider how it will accomplish those purposes, arrive at some conclusions upon which the group agrees, and take action upon these decisions. At the outset each of these steps in group work seems a formidable task. The history of curriculum study is marked by the skeletons of curriculum committees that have expired because they could not cope with one or another of these steps.

The leader is responsible for assisting the group in evaluating its procedures. He cannot do it merely by lecturing about group dynamics. No amount of study *about* process will by itself make members of a group more skillful in solving their problems. They will learn the skills by practicing these skills, by being helped to analyze why they have or have not been successful in moving ahead.

PRODUCTIVITY OF A GROUP

Although practice in group work is the medium whereby skills are learned, mere repetition of poor or mediocre practices without critical appraisal will be sterile and unfruitful. Only the self-critical and those with an objective attitude toward their way of working can be expected to improve. The self-satisfied may find analysis too disturbing and disrupting. There are certain skills to be learned in becoming a capable group member. Many of these skills deal with human relationships and the ability to communicate sympathy and understanding of feelings; a number have to do with the communication of ideas; only a few depend upon the ability to talk fluently.

Groups in Action

The procedures described below exhibit varying degrees of effectiveness in the use of group processes. The six types in the order listed represent only roughly group productiveness from a low to a high level.

1. *The group that is used to serve someone else's purposes.* This type of group meets because some status person or agency has certain aims to be accomplished—perhaps to sell an idea, to indoctrinate, or to create a semblance of democratic procedure. Members have little or no chance to express their desires. Sometimes they do not realize that they are being used to rubber-stamp policy that has already been determined. Actually, this is not an organic group with cooperative interaction and unity, for it has no dynamic quality or wholeness. A student or faculty council that merely carries out the principal's wishes is an example.

2. *The group that presents a series of individual reports.* It is quite a common practice for committees to divide their topic or problem into subproblems, assigning them to different individuals or subcom-

mittees. This is an accepted way for committees to function. However, the whole committee may not get a chance to consider the findings of each subgroup. In reality, none of the reports represents total committee thinking or committee action. The subcommittee report may be the product of group deliberation; however, in no other sense can the report be termed a "committee" or group report.

3. *The group that settles its differences by bargaining and compromise.* A characteristic procedure in arbitration of labor–management disputes is to try to arrive at some compromise proposal that will be accepted by both factions. The final decision, although accepted, may not be genuinely satisfactory to either party. Differences of opinion are still likely to be sharp and feelings bitter. Some faculties in schools and colleges are composed of several factions that bargain for advantage but rarely reach any conclusion that represents the cumulative thinking of the group.

4. *The group that follows the principles of majority rule through parliamentary procedure.* This is one of the most typical practices in committee or group action in schools or in government. Majority rule is an important concept in a republican form of government. Children in school are given practice in parliamentary procedure so that they may know how to participate in organizations and meetings. However, there may be no organic or cohesive group formed, since one faction may go home disgruntled and belligerent over the majority decision. The New England town meeting is a good example. Where there has been a spirited fight over the location of school buildings, the disruption of community harmony is quite evident in the town meeting and its aftermath.

5. *The group that arrives at conclusions based upon free discussion.* Some groups freely give and take ideas in the discussion of common problems. This kind of group is found in the modern educational conference. In these discussion groups, the members usually reach conclusions upon which they agree and often develop some kind of report that represents group thinking. No action necessarily results from the discussion. Such groups have been especially effective where attention has been paid to the group process skills.

6. *The group that takes action based upon a consensus.* This kind of group, and the above-mentioned one, reach a consensus. The final conclusions represent the cooperative thinking of the group. It is interesting to note that the derivation of the word "consensus" is "thinking with." Consensus is different from compromise in that no original proposal is necessarily adopted in total or in part. The final

conclusions may be far different from any that the individual members started with; consequently, they are superior for that particular group concerned. Attempts to reach consensus represent a higher quality of democratic action than parliamentary procedure. This group goes further than arriving at a decision; it also takes action based upon that decision. It is a type of action group found in committees and faculties that have a substantial part in making policy for their school.

These six types represent some of the characteristics of groups who work together. Teachers can undoubtedly name others from their experiences. The degree of cohesiveness obviously differs. Some are more suitable than others for a specific purpose or for a meeting of a certain size. The last two mentioned, however, best meet the criteria for group structure. These are the two with which this chapter will be concerned. Such groups hold the most promise for curriculum improvement, particularly if their deliberations lead to action. Obviously, in large faculties, there needs to be a combination of procedures used in the fourth, fifth, and sixth groups described.

Stages in Group Growth

Out of the research at the National Training Laboratory on Group Development, Thelen and Dickerman have identified four stages in the growth of a group, marked by certain characteristics, which are the labels they use to designate the phases: (1) individually centered; (2) frustration and conflict among stereotypes; (3) attempted consolidation of group harmony; (4) individual self-assessment, flexibility of group process, and emphasis upon productivity in problem-solving.[1] Data were gathered from sound recordings of discussion groups and written records of group observers. These stages are used as a basis of the discussion below. The following observations are also taken from similar, more recent data. The interpretation of these four stages depicting types of group behavior is placed within a curriculum study group framework.

1. *The individually centered stage.* At the beginning of the work of the group, members tend to act like individualists. Each has certain proposals that he believes ought to be accepted. He wants the chance to talk to bolster his own ego, or he has a problem of his own that he wants the group to solve. Generally, members feel that every-

[1] Herbert Thelen and Watson Dickerman, "Stereotypes and the Growth of Groups," *Educational Leadership*, 6:309–16, February, 1949.

one must talk. They are sizing up the leader and showing dependence upon him. Quite characteristic is the impatience and compulsion to "get on with it." The group must be "learning something" or doing something, such as passing resolutions, making lists or outlines on the board. Silence is considered a sign of weakness.

2. *The frustration and conflict stage.* In this phase there tends to be conflict in ideas about what the leader's role should be. To what extent should he exert a strong influence on the direction in which the group is moving, and how much initiative should be taken over by members? Considerable conflict arises about how much attention should be paid to group process. Members tend to take comments personally. Curriculum study groups are often frustrated because of the length of time consumed in setting up and achieving goals. The frustration is generally expressed toward the leader, who is held responsible for the progress of the group. Members of a group, after working together for some time, say that they were dissatisfied at first because the leader had not told them definitely what to do, or because they did not seem to be getting anywhere. Critical comments of this nature at this point are a good sign, since members express their feelings in the group rather than outside.

At this point the leader needs to be thick-skinned. Considerable courage is required to go through this phase with a group that has had no experience in group process. It would be much easier to revert to lectures or directive procedures. Undoubtedly, this is the "dropout" stage for some groups that had started out with a sincere desire to use democratic procedures. Actually, the leader ought to be concerned if groups *do not* go through this phase. If everything runs smoothly, in all probability he is giving too much direction.

3. *The attempted group harmony stage.* In the next phase in the growth toward becoming a cohesive group, the members seem to be bending over backward to avoid conflict, which may have been uncomfortable for them. Their major concern seems to be the achievement of harmony. Everyone must be made "happy"; disagreements are frowned upon. Differences of opinion are likely to be avoided because they are disturbing to "harmony." This is the "sewing society" stage, where groups try to develop a more pleasant atmosphere than existed before. The group may try to help an individual solve his problem rather than get on with its problems.

This stage represents a step forward in consciousness of responsibility for the group, in the attempt to get a feeling of oneness, and in the development of skills for successful group work.

4. *The productivity in problem-solving stage.* When groups become more aware of their responsibility and power as a group and gain greater maturity through experience, they find it easier to concentrate on what they are trying to accomplish. At this stage, members are more objective about ideas and arguments. Consequently, they can arrive at decisions representing consensus. The members recognize that the differences that exist among themselves are of value and that everyone has something worthwhile to contribute. The permissive atmosphere encourages members to express their feelings without defensiveness or hostility. The members understand that their power as a group depends upon utilizing the resources within the group. At this point in a curriculum study, behavior that exhibits an unwillingness to listen to the ideas of others is less likely to occur.

Undoubtedly, these four phases in the growth of a group are not mutually exclusive nor do they fall into a rigid time sequence. The group will not be "individually centered" for three meetings, "frustrated" for two meetings, and so on. The assumption can be made that factors which will cause variations in the growth of a group include the previous experience of members in group process and the homogeneity of the group. The purposes for which people come together will make a difference in the time that it takes them to become a cohesive, productive group.[2]

Principles of Productive Group Thinking

While the following principles apply to group work in general, they are specifically pointed toward group thinking and discussion. They are intended to be of help to in-service curriculum study groups, faculty meetings, and curriculum classes which employ discussion as a technique for getting their tasks accomplished.

The four aspects of productive discussion outlined here furnish criteria for the evaluation of group discussion.

1. *Clarity of goals.* Many groups accomplish little because their goals are not clearly defined. Stating what a committee hopes to do should be a simple task. Evidently it is not. Some committees begin by recommending the changes they would like made in the curriculum. Often such recommendations express desires of various individuals; usually they involve change on the part of someone else.

---

[2] "Group Cohesiveness: Introduction," in Dorwin Cartwright and Alvin Zander (eds.), *Group Dynamics: Research and Theory,* 2nd ed., New York: Harper & Row, Publishers, 1960, chap. 3, summarizes research on how to achieve cohesiveness in a group.

A statement of goals should be made in terms of the problems that the group wants to tackle. A committee may, for example, decide to find out how many children drop out of school, why they drop out, and what the school can do about it. These are problems that need to be explored and answered. There can be no valid predetermined answers based on judgment unsubstantiated by data. One of the essentials for effective curriculum committee work is to approach the task with an open mind.

The group should list its goals, breaking them into subpoints if necessary, and later refer to these goals occasionally during the discussion. A blackboard recorder is helpful during the time that a group is exploring its goals.

If the leader finds that when the goals are relisted on the blackboard the members begin arguing about them, he can be sure that the group is uncertain of what it is trying to accomplish. The failure of the group to know its purpose and direction is evidenced when goals set down in the recorder's notes do not really represent the thinking of all the members. They are not group goals. It may be that the leader or a powerful clique has decided what the group is to do.

A member of a group who is clear about the group's goals is more likely to feel that he is a group member, to be more interested in his task, and to work toward the group's goals rather than his personal goals.

A group should attempt to establish realistic goals, but it should by all means be willing to change them. A danger is that a group will set its aspirations too high, beyond possibility of attainment within the time available for group work. The leader who doggedly insists that the group stick to its original goals shows signs of insecurity. He fails to recognize that a group working at its own purposes also has the power to change those purposes. New insights acquired during the discussion may call for a re-evaluation of the original goals, a more intelligent action than persisting in the original purpose if the new data clearly indicate a change of direction is needed.

2. *Quantity and quality of participation.* The two aspects to be considered with regard to participation of members in the discussion are the quantity and the quality of their contributions.

The number of members that participate, the number of times a person talks, and how long he talks are of importance in a discussion. Obviously, good interaction cannot be achieved if a few members monopolize the time. Long speeches by people who feel they need to be heard are detrimental to the progress of group discussion. However, the *quantity* of participation has been far overstressed in the evaluation of group process. Considered alone, it is a poor measure to indicate the fruitfulness of a discussion.

Some of the more quiet members may find it difficult to phrase what they want to say, or it may have already been said by someone else. They show a clearer perspective than the chatterbox who talks incessantly without saying anything. Many group members feel their difficulty is that they are not "quick enough on the trigger"; someone else always speaks first. Yet a formal, orderly procedure that permits each one to speak an equal number of times would be the very antithesis of democratic group processes.

Nevertheless, if some members remain silent during several discussion periods there is a real danger that they may not feel free to talk. It would be unwise to pass over non-participation lightly, for it may indicate the group has not achieved a free atmosphere.

More significant is the *quality* of participation: how the members participate in the discussion, the value of what they say, and their concern for each other as human beings. It should be obvious that what a person says is of great importance. In evaluating quality we should look for evidence of thoughtful ideas and also of a sensitivity to the feelings of others. Those who make cutting, sarcastic remarks about others are no better group members than they are teachers.

It is quite evident when people in a group are sensitive to others. They recognize that some may be easily offended; they try to call attention to a person's interests or accomplishments to help bring him into the discussion; they show interest in the ideas of other members. Utilization of the contribution of all members and respect for what they have to say, even though there are differences in opinion, are earmarks of good group membership.

There are other indications of high quality of participation in a discussion:

> The group explores a worthwhile point brought up by a member instead of jumping rabbit-fashion from point to point without continuity.
>
> The discussion does not wander far from the main topic unless the group has consented.
>
> Discussion is directed toward the group as a whole rather than to a certain individual.
>
> The flow of the discussion is from member to member rather than through the leader.
>
> The group gathers information for its discussion to help clarify points; members volunteer to get the data needed.
>
> The members show a willingness to change any plans or procedures as necessity arises.

3. *The type of atmosphere.* One of the most useful concepts in the study of group dynamics is that of building a permissive atmosphere: a group situation in which people feel at home, free to say what they think, uninhibited by status and by individuals who "know so much more than I do." It does not mean a lack of respect; indeed, a permissive atmosphere is one in which there is the greatest respect for people's personalities and feelings. The person who warrants the respect of others is the one who earns it.

We have all experienced situations in which no one has any problems to suggest at the beginning of a discussion. Later on, as the group becomes acquainted and learns to work together, many problems are raised. Permissiveness cannot be expected of a group of people who come together for the first time. Since the members will probably spar around and may be wary of the leader, friendliness and informality must first be established.

If this situation continues, the group leader can justifiably be suspicious when many people hesitate to speak. Do they really feel free to express their ideas? Or are they thinking that others will dismiss their ideas as of little value? Actually, when persons in the group feel free enough to express their complaints, even toward leaders, considerable progress has been made. An unhealthy group is one in which people either stifle their dissatisfaction until they leave the meeting or shut off ideas that others bring up.

As the anxiety level is raised in a group, all kinds of peculiar behavior come out. If the level goes too high, people cannot function effectively. The hidden agenda may be an obstacle to group functioning. The leader needs to see that these agenda "items" are laid on the table and discussed frankly and freely. When members bring out of hiding their concerns, they are well on their way to becoming a mature group.

A leader can help to create a permissive atmosphere by his own actions toward others and his receptiveness to what they have to say. Ideas can be listed on the board as expressed, without being changed to more flowery phrases or dismissed as not worthy of consideration.

In a friendly atmosphere, members of the group do not resent criticism of their suggestions, because they have learned that once an idea is expressed it belongs to the group. They are not personally offended by disapproval of their ideas. This principle is one of the most significant for fruitful group discussion and argument that does not leave scars of rancor.

In addition, a friendly group is not afraid of silence. When the atmosphere is tense, leaders feel that someone must be talking all of the time. They are not secure enough to tolerate a period of silence, a time when much fruitful thinking may be going on. One of the difficult things for group members to learn is to be comfortable during such a time. They are like the hostess who keeps up a conversation with the newly arrived guests at all costs although the guests would like nothing better than to relax after a tiring journey!

4. *Function of leadership roles.* Leadership of the democratic type discussed in Chapter 1 is a function of the group. In committees or discussion groups, the status leader's responsibility is to see that leadership is diffused among members of the group. At times someone who makes a pertinent suggestion takes over as leader while the group explores the proposal. Another group member leads the discussion when the resources available to the group are explored. Another helps the group to evaluate itself. The leadership shifts from one individual to another, often without anyone's awareness of the shift.

There are four more common status leadership roles: leader, recorder, resource person, and observer. Some of these may be omitted, but they all serve useful functions. Whether or not an observer needs to be selected will depend on the members' experience in group processes. It should be noted that the terms "leader" and "recorder" are used instead of "chairman" and "secretary." The former terms are useful since they designate somewhat different types of roles from those ordinarily taken by a chairman and secretary of a meeting. Each of the four roles is discussed more fully.

The *leader* sets the tone for the group by his relations with other members. It is his responsibility to get the group started, to lead the original planning of a working schedule, to keep the discussion focused on the problems selected, to summarize as needed, to see that various members have an opportunity to contribute, and to move on to conclusions and actions.

Some leaders are tempted to do a good deal of the talking and to come with a well prepared outline of what the group ought to do. Too many groups allow the leader to do the work for them. Actually, he must exercise care that his opinions are not given more weight than those of other group members. Good group leaders have to learn to listen well.

It is important to realize that leadership duties are really responsibilities of the group as a whole. The effective democratic leader will delegate others in the group to carry on leadership functions. The experienced group member does not wait for the leader to summarize. Instead, the member summarizes at an opportune time. He also feels a responsibility for pulling the discussion back from byways. He helps to make others feel that their contributions are accepted. Such is the acid test of shared leadership.

The *recorder* leads the group by keeping a record of what it has said. He deals with the content, not the process. A recorder differs from a secretary in that his function is to select important points and trends in the discussion rather than to keep only a record of official actions. He can also help the group members become acquainted by providing mimeographed sheets with names and information about the members. A good recorder is not necessarily someone who can take short-hand notes, but rather someone who is able to use judgment in selecting problems, issues, ideas, facts, and decisions to record.

He makes available to the group, when it wants such information, specific items that have been previously discussed or decided upon, such as the original goals or decisions about procedure. In addition, he summarizes as he sees a need for it. When resolutions or final reports are expected, he works with the group in the preparation of these statements. At such times he is, of course, serving as a leader of the group. He also makes necessary contacts with other groups. In an effective group, many of these functions are shared by other members.

A blackboard recorder is usually someone other than the designated recorder. However, groups need to be careful in listing the high points of the discussion on the blackboard. This technique is useful to focus a group's attention on certain points, such as the goals; but if a report is to be given, a group can easily start bickering about wording and phrasing. When that happens, ideas are often lost sight of. Editing is likely to receive the most attention.

The *resource person*, or consultant, is someone who has been invited to become a member of the group, perhaps for a certain session, to contribute specific kinds of information. In a good group discussion, the consultant is accepted by others as a member of the group. To reveal who are the resource persons may be unwise in a conference, for the tendency will be to ask them for the answers. This precaution is not necessary in a mature group that has learned to work together and to realize that every member is a resource person whose potentialities should be utilized.

The *observer* is a type of leadership role that may be strange to many groups. His responsibility is to observe the process and to assist the group in the improvement of process skills. When a person is appointed as observer for the first time, he is likely to focus on what is said, the content or ideas of the discussion. Ordinarily, there is someone in a group with some experience in group process who can take his turn first in serving as observer.

The observer watches the aspects of the process discussed in this section of the chapter. The observer's job is to help the group answer the questions: "Why didn't we get further along on our problem?" "What hindered us?" or "What helped us to move toward our goal?" The best kind of observation is that which diffuses this type of leadership among the group. There is a temptation for the observer to show off his skills or to show up weaknesses of the group. Instead, he ought to help the group analyze its own weaknesses. He should be given some time at the end of each session for this purpose. However, he and other members of the group should feel free at any time to stop the discussion for a brief analysis of what is wrong or to move the discussion ahead if it is lagging. A high quality group is one in which everyone accepts his responsibility, without any special designation of an observer.

The form and the checklist on pages 43–44 will be useful to an observer. He can help the group in its self-evaluation by keeping such data as a flow chart of the discussion, showing by lines how the discussion proceeded from member to member, or showing the amount and distribution of participation by checking the number of times each one participates. However, he needs to focus largely on the quality of the discussion. The observer should be regarded as an assistant leader helping the group raise its sights for accomplishments.

ESSENTIAL GROUP SKILLS FOR CURRICULUM STUDY

Teachers and administrators engaged in curriculum study want specifics on how to apply to their own situation what has been found valuable in group dynamics. The principles presented in the preceding section are practical suggestions to assist faculties or committees in their work together. As a further help, certain steps to take in group work are outlined here. Obviously the steps from "getting started" to "evaluating results" may overlap considerably. For example, evaluation should occur throughout the entire study if it is to be of maximum value. These "steps" are best learned through practice.

Getting Started

Groups have found that taking some time at the first session to identify group members and their duties is worthwhile. Usually members will have good suggestions for the procedure. Some groups have each person introduce his neighbor; some use informal "buzz" sessions for small groups to get together; others have each member introduce himself. If the latter method is used, the leader ought to set the pace by introducing himself first or asking someone who has experience in group work to introduce himself. The object is to get individuals to talk about themselves, their jobs, their hobbies, or special experiences or skills that will help the group utilize all of its resources. If the first person mumbles his name in a timid manner, others will also be likely to give only their name. Such introductions are not particularly helpful.

During the early stages of group work, the leader can be on the lookout for opportunities for a social get-together in order to develop good interpersonal communications. A dinner or luncheon is usually a possibility. Members should be encouraged to suggest ideas. In curriculum study carried on after school, the coffee cup is the best possible socializing agent. Some schools would not think of having an after-school staff meeting without serving coffee.

Introducing Group Procedures

A second step for the leader might be to suggest to the group possible ways for keeping a high level of efficiency in its work. In a conference, the orientation session can be an effective means for introducing people to the idea of evaluating process. A demonstration on the stage has been used successfully for this purpose.

In small groups, a demonstration can involve the entire group, with a few members previously selected to play typical roles of group members. In addition to the leadership roles, such designated roles as the blocker, the person who tries to harmonize differences, and one who always wants to talk, can help to create some fun in the consideration of process. The "devil's advocate" should, of course, be identified as such after the demonstration.

In a school or class situation, the leader can begin by taking time at the end of the meeting for an analysis. Some may prefer to leave the consideration of group process until the group gets into its problem, using some form of end-of-the-meeting evaluation slip.

Selecting Leadership Roles

In many instances the leader is a status person selected by virtue of his position. In committee work the leader should be selected by the group itself whenever possible. The group at the beginning chooses its recorder and its observer. The leader and the recorder usually function over a period of time to give continuity to the work. If a true democratic leadership exists in the group, everyone shares in these activities. It is preferable to have several people act as observers, rather than have one person function for all the meetings. This is a role that people may be reluctant to accept. Rotating this role assures that several have an opportunity to practice leadership for self-evaluation. Consultants, or resource people, are selected as the needs arise.

Taking a Problem Census and Setting Up Goals

If curriculum study is not to be based on the problems of the chairman or the supervisor, time must be spent with the faculty or committee to develop the goals of the group. There is a distinct possibility that the easy way will be to choose a respectable "problem," such as improvement of the social studies program, or revision of the course of study, which may not be a problem at all. In fact, time spent in preliminary discussion of some of the originally stated problems will bring out others beneath the surface. Care must always be exercised so that people do not suggest only superficial problems.

In a small staff, the group can work as a whole in these preliminary goal-setting stages. In staffs of thirty members or more, the group can be broken into sections of about ten people each to develop the items that need to be studied by the staff. One school system had the members of the total staff list their "gripes," which were then tabulated by a committee. These lists were used as work sheets in a two-day conference of the entire faculty, when small groups selected those points that they felt needed to be studied. In these instances, it will be noted that everyone had a chance to have his say. Only then can curriculum problems be considered problems of the teachers.

The best place to begin curriculum study is with the concerns of the teachers. Teachers in their planning as a group show genuine concern for factors that have bearing on improving the child's experiences. In high schools or departmentalized situations in elementary schools, one of the valuable experiences for the teachers is to work together on all-school problems that need attention. This fact should be considered in the selection of problems by an entire faculty or by a workshop.

In groups planning together as a whole, such as workshops or elementary school units, one or two meetings should be devoted to the problem census. The leader will find that it pays to discuss briefly and clarify each suggested problem before moving on to another. He should *not* reword, omit, or express any judgment on the suggestions made. When all are satisfied that the problems listed include points they would like to see the group study, some reclassification and consolidation can be done by a small committee or by one individual who will be careful to avoid losing the original meaning of the suggestions.

The group then needs to plan the sequence of the problems that will be discussed or to select those that should have priority. Since all problems selected are those of the entire group, time should be provided for the committee or faculty to discuss thoroughly what is to be done about each one. Consequently, it would not be wise to choose too many problems. The next step is to divide into subgroups if needed.

Gathering Information

Teachers are aware of the need for pupils to get some facts as a basis for their discussion of any question. The need is as evident in group study by adults. As a group clarifies what it wants to accomplish, it will pose questions that need to be answered if the problem is to be solved. For example, the problem may be pupils' lack of interest in the school. As the group considers the problem, it raises questions such as: What do pupils do that shows a lack of interest? Who are the pupils that lack interest? What is their attitude toward school? Are they "repeaters" or "failures"? Do they come from certain types of homes? What does the family attitude have to do with it?

These questions lead to the gathering of information. One source of information for many problems is the material in professional books, pamphlets, and periodicals which include empirical evidence and recommendations of practitioners and scholars. However, this is only *one* source. Surely, in the problem posed above, the pupils, their families, and the faculty would be the best sources. Yet these are often neglected. Consultants from universities, colleges, state departments of education, and community agencies can be invited to furnish additional information.

Many groups have to be helped to see the importance of gathering data to solve problems. They, like pupils, sometimes tend to discuss and to try to arrive at solutions to these problems without the necessary information.

Arriving at Conclusions

Considerable discussion is necessary in order to analyze data, hear different points of view, and finally arrive at a consensus regarding what should be done. If the group has planned its goals and decided upon the kinds of data needed and the procedural steps to take, it has had practice in making decisions and will find it easier to arrive at agreements. Although consensus will not always be possible, it is the goal to strive for. If the principles of group discussion described earlier in this chapter are applied, agreement is a possibility.

Decision should not be delayed too long. The group may find that it can arrive at some conclusions early to present as preliminary recommendations for the consideration of the total faculty.

Taking Action

Action should follow careful study. Too much curriculum study has ended with drawing conclusions and making recommendations. In the files of some superintendents, deans, and principals repose committee and staff reports that represent many hours of extra work for teachers. The sad part is that the committee members have never heard what happened to their report or why it was not accepted. An administrator has an obligation to his staff to explain to them why recommendations cannot be adopted or to report what happens to committee recommendations. Otherwise good staff morale cannot be maintained. If the administrator works constantly *with* the committee, he can discuss what can and cannot be done within the financial structure and board regulations, and these problems can be ironed out as the work progresses.

In some instances committees may be overanxious to institute changes before those concerned—including the community—are ready for such changes. It is the duty of the leader to see that those concerned study the possible obstacles involved, and develop sound pacing and timing for introducing the desired change and plans for evaluating the change.

Evaluating Results

As in all evaluation of learning, the process is a continuous one. The heart of the study of group process is self-evaluation, looking for those factors that make a group productive. The basic question is:

"How much progress did we make?" Groups that stop at that point, however, have not laid a foundation for further improvement. The objective analysis that follows, which can occur at any point in a meeting, and ought to occur throughout group work, is the sign of a mature group.

It is helpful to give the group some material that suggests ideas about what to look for.[3] A checklist such as the following is often used.

How Does the Meeting Look?

1. *Goals*

   What is the group trying to accomplish?

   How clear do you think this is to the members?

   Who decides what the group does?

   To what extent do we understand how we are going to reach our goals?

   What did I do to help clarify goals?

2. *Leadership*

   Does the leader encourage others to talk?

   How much interest does he show in what the members think and want?

   How much weight is given to the leader's opinion?

   How effectively does he summarize and help make the discussion clear?

   How sensitive is he to the feelings of individual members?

   Does he use fully what the members know and can contribute to the group?

   How does he help to keep the group on the topic under discussion?

   Is leadership assumed by various members?

   What did I do to help in the leadership?

3. *Participation*

   Did contributions indicate that those who made them were listening to what others said?

   Does the discussion seem to bring out what the various members may be able to contribute?

   Does overparticipation by some keep others from participating?

   How much of the talking is done by the leader? By various members?

   To whom are questions or remarks usually addressed?

[3] See Alex F. Perrodin, "Participation Adds a Third Dimension to Teachers' Meetings," *NEA Journal,* 43:490–91, November, 1954, for a good checklist for self-evaluation purposes.

Is the discussion usually directed to the group as a whole, or to individual members?

How well does discussion stay on the point?

To what extent are we blocked by lack of information?

Are members willing to revise their thinking in light of the situation?

What did I do to help in the participation?

4. *Atmosphere of the meeting*

How well is the group working as a team?

Do members feel free to express their ideas even if they do not agree with the majority?

Do members encourage others to express their feelings?

Is everyone's point of view considered?

How open-minded does the group seem?

Was the atmosphere of the group friendly? Informal? Co-operative?

To what extent does the group feel united by a common purpose?

To what extent were we able to subordinate individual interests to the common goal?

What did I do to help create a desirable atmosphere?

5. *Results*

How much progress was made at the meeting?

Did we come to any conclusions and plans for action?

Do members seem satisfied with results?

How well do you think we will follow through on our decisions?

Another device is an evaluation sheet passed out to members of the group to fill in at the end of the meeting. An observer could use such information for a report to the group at the beginning of the next meeting as a stimulus for improvement of weaknesses. A suggested form in general use follows:

END-OF-MEETING SUGGESTION SLIP

What did you think of this meeting? Please be frank. Your comments can contribute a great deal to the success of our meetings.

1. How did you feel about this meeting? (Check)
   ( ) No good   ( ) Mediocre   ( ) All right
   ( ) Good   ( ) Excellent
2. What were the weaknesses?
3. What were the strong points?
4. What improvements would you suggest? [4]

[4] Ronald Lippitt, "Group Self-Analysis of Productivity in the Work Conference," *Adult Education Bulletin*, 12:377–78, February, 1948.

Determining Size, Setting, and Time

Questions often arise regarding the optimum size of the group, the physical setting, and the most desirable length of time for a group to work together. The answers will depend upon the purpose of the work group and the conditions that exist. Some helpful suggestions from experience can be made.

The size of discussion groups varies with the nature of the group. Discussion and work groups must be small enough to permit all members to participate and yet large enough to have a variety of skills and backgrounds represented. In an experiment with discussion groups in a Boy Scouts' summer camp, the findings indicated that as the size of the group increased from five to twelve members, consensus decreased when the time for discussion was limited.[5] From five to fifteen people is a desirable range for the size of committees. For conference discussion purposes, a group of five is rather small; groups up to twenty-five or thirty have functioned successfully. In school faculties of seventy-five to a hundred people, some breakdown into groups for discussion or committee purposes is necessary. In curriculum courses in which consideration is given to obtaining experience in group work, the size of the subgroup depends upon the size of the class. In any curriculum study, the question of how many problems can be effectively handled by the total faculty through subcommittees or subgroups must be considered.

The physical setting has a direct bearing upon communication and, consequently, the achievement of a group. Rooms with screwed-down seats are intended for the "telling" type of meeting where one or more persons stand in front of the rest. The leader should be able to sit with the group in a circle, square, or rectangle. Cafeterias and libraries usually make good meeting rooms in schools since they have tables that can be arranged in various ways. Rooms with tab-arm chairs are also adaptable to group discussion. Rooms with easy chairs are excellent when they can be found. An important factor is the informality of the setting. Cafeterias or lounges where coffee can be served and where members may have smoking privileges make for an informal, relaxed atmosphere.

Cohesive groups are not formed in one short meeting. In conferences, discussion groups may find that they do not get "warmed up" until the second or third meeting. When they are ready to go home,

---

[5] A. Paul Hare, "A Study of Interaction and Consensus in Different Sized Groups," *American Sociological Review*, 17:261–67, June, 1952.

they feel they have just begun to accomplish something. Two- to five-day conferences are replacing the old one-day gathering. Generally about two hours are provided for a group meeting, although groups may forget to pay attention to the clock when they become absorbed in their own purposes.

SOME MISCONCEPTIONS ABOUT GROUP PROCESS

That misunderstandings are likely to arise concerning group processes is understandable. More research on group work within classes is needed. Mistakes will be made in using this relatively new procedure. Moreover, those who have adopted group dynamics as a cult have not helped the situation. Some common misconceptions that may arise when people are first introduced to group process are these:

1. *Group cohesiveness refers only to a group that is meeting together.* Some of the best groups are those that work side by side as a faculty. The members know each other, know each other's potentialities, and have learned how to live together with respect for each other. Not all faculties meet the criteria for a group—not by any means—but there is opportunity to form a cohesive group in a faculty of a school building. Working together in staff and committee meetings is an important phase of forming the group.

2. *Group action is incompatible with efficiency.* Some teachers believe that spending time in group deliberation to determine curriculum policy is an inefficient use of time. They fail to realize that in no other way will they get as efficient adoption of the best policy for the group, through acceptance and real change. In the same vein, others are reluctant to devote part of an hour's time of meetings to consideration of group process. They are amazed at groups that no longer find an hour a week sufficient for curriculum study! This misconception is actually an evidence of lack of faith in democratic principles.

3. *Everybody in a group must talk.* One could also add "and talk an equal amount." Nothing is more ridiculous if one admits that people are different. Only if the atmosphere is such that people fear to talk frankly on the one hand, or tend to overindulge in conversation on the other, is there cause for concern.

4. *Exchange of experiences has no place in group discussion.* The observation is sometimes made in conferences using small group discussion that the exchange of experiences in groups signifies a low

level of group process. Such comments do not take into consideration the purposes that a group may have. It is certainly legitimate for a group to exchange experiences as well as ideas if the relating of those experiences helps to clarify the problem. Often, discussion of specific cases is the best means for forming a common ground for analyzing certain principles or proposals. Exchange of experiences without direction or purpose, however, may be merely a "gabfest."

5. *High-level group process does not permit clash of opinion.* In other words, everybody must be kept happy; therefore, we do not want to hurt anyone's feelings. A rational look at this concept reveals its absurdity. Argument and clash of opinion are essential elements in any society where people are allowed to differ. The important factor in group discussion is that people learn to be objective about such differences.

6. *Group discussion about a problem sets up the same dynamic situation as group attack upon solving a common problem.* This misconception is also evident in conferences. When a group of people get together for two to four days' discussion, the situation is quite different from committee work in a school. Consequently, all principles of group process cannot be expected to apply equally to these two types of groups. In a conference, people want to clarify ideas, get new insights, and find general professional stimulation. In a school curriculum committee, there is a specific job to be done. The fact that the committee can arrive at a conclusion and carry it into action makes the situation radically different from that of a discussion group. There is a difference between discussion and action-centered discussion.

ISSUES AND POINTS OF VIEW

Few issues dealing with procedures for curriculum study have been discussed with as much fervor and emotion as group dynamics. It would often appear as if there were no middle ground between the extreme protagonists and antagonists.

1. *Is group dynamics a worthwhile field of scholarship, research, and study in the basic social sciences, with useful theoretical developments growing out of these studies, or is it a pseudo-scientific approach, a cult, or a squandering of precious time that should be devoted to more practical questions?*

No doubt much of the antagonism toward group dynamics has resulted from the extravagant claims, the near-cultish behavior, and the specialized vocabulary of the extreme proponents of the idea. In certain cases, such as the earlier conferences into which group dynamics with the use of an observer was introduced, many teachers and supervisors who found both the language and the behavior strange felt like the great unwashed who had not yet received the word. As toward any excesses in education, the hard-headed research-minded reacted as they would toward anything they felt was pseudo-scientific, or what they thought was mere sham.

This was a new idea, something exciting to grab hold of, that offered possibilities for improving curriculum study by the many committees and groups. Some were carried away with it. Others became more skeptical. As is usually the case, the excesses led to a reaction that made it unpopular to focus conscious attention on group process either in a conference or in a curriculum study.

When teachers—and even more so, professors and supervisors—have to look critically and analytically at their own behavior, they may feel uncomfortable and quickly shift to some other topic. Note how difficult it becomes for some to analyze their *own* teaching procedures. With supervisors or college professors, the topic is most likely to turn to discussion of teacher behavior in general. Consequently, it is small wonder that the idea of evaluating one's own behavior in a group is not a popular one.

Yet, group dynamics is a respectable area of research by psychologists, sociologists, and other specialists in the behavioral sciences. Groups such as the Research Center for Group Dynamics and the Institute for Social Research at the University of Michigan have made valuable research contributions to the field. Education, public health, social work, business, industry, and other fields have profited by their research.

2. *Is evaluation of what the group is doing useful for any curriculum study group or class?*

This is usually the question argued. The issue is not that simple, however. The research shows that any group that studies its own procedures in an objective manner, and is able to move from emotion and airing of prejudices toward becoming more objective both toward itself and toward data, will improve in its functioning. The extent to which a curriculum study group needs to use observation techniques, the observer, and self-analysis sessions depends upon its ability to work together and its maturity in understanding group process.

The answer for any study group depends also upon its interest in improving itself. For a class, the purposes that it has are important.

A human relations workshop or a curriculum class that has as one of its objectives to improve curriculum study, has valid reasons for evaluating itself. A faculty that seeks to improve its meetings has good reasons for using evaluation instruments.

As in any subject, the teacher or leader must understand group process and the skills essential to productivity in a group if he is to use it successfully.

3. *Is there a danger that group work submerges the individual's goals in those of the group and will lead to loss in individual, creative contributions by teachers in the school?*

In other words, this question asks: Should all curriculum study be group study? Although the teacher never ceases to be a member of a group (committee, faculty, group of third-grade teachers), he does not make all of his contributions to curriculum improvement in a group curriculum study situation. Much of it may grow out of such a situation where people have ideas and are willing to discuss them, but his own creativity is evidenced largely by how he works with children in a class. Here much of the curriculum development occurs.

This question genuinely troubles many thoughtful people. Some argue that a research worker cannot be creative anywhere except in his laboratory, working alone. The same may be true for the teacher in his "laboratory." Perhaps it is the "groupy," those who would herd people into groups at the smallest provocation, who do the most toward submerging creative ideas. Yet, group sessions have proved fruitful for new ideas for a group that works together.

Some people are individualists who are not happy working in a group. They are not good team members, but nevertheless their contribution may be outstanding.

People try to avoid groups that have failed in their tasks. Such groups frustrate them and create emotional tension for them. Yet, it is from group life that the individual usually draws some of his greatest satisfactions as well as his keenest conflicts.

4. *Should leaders promote their own ideas and plans in a group, or should they always wait for plans to evolve from the group?*

Many sincere leaders in schools feel that all proposals should stem from the group. Appraised in its true sense, as these leaders see it, this concept means that the group must make all the decisions.

On the other hand, some leaders hold it a weakness to expect such evolvement. This notion borders dangerously on the autocratic concept of leadership, if one can think objectively of this emotionally charged concept.

Perhaps a better way of stating the issue is whether group leadership is a matter of exerting influence on the group or serving the group. Leadership studies, and the modern situational theory of leadership, indicate that it is some of both. The strong leader is not strong in the sense that he always vigorously promotes his ideas, but he stands for what he believes, promotes his ideas when he senses they are of value for the group, but also accepts change of his proposals as well as defeat of them. He is also a servant of the group who sees that conditions are established which will make it possible for people to be creative and to enjoy their work because it offers opportunity to do something that the individual feels is a worthwhile contribution of his talents.

Research has shown that a person faced with a large majority of his group making deliberately wrong responses will be more likely to make errors of judgment. Teachers may follow such a behavior pattern to avoid ridicule or censure from principals, supervisors, or parents. In curriculum study, the expected "correct" response may be given. If the power of supervisor or principal over teacher is great, the teacher will be more likely to conform and less likely to broach his own ideas. Thus, with status-quo-minded supervisors, the tendency for creativity to arise from the teacher is small indeed.

5. *How can a group keep the aggressive individual from monopolizing time or determining conclusions?*

One of the most difficult problems a group faces is helping the domineering individual to see his influence on the group in its true perspective. He may be someone who just likes to talk. He may be a compulsive individual who feels he has to make a speech to the group. Or he may be so intense in arguing for his position that he forgets that there are other members of the group who should express their opinions. Sometimes, this type of person does not care to hear others' views or deliberately filibusters to shut off other arguments. In the latter case, he should be dealt with directly by the leader, who has a responsibility for giving all who wish the opportunity to have their say.

In most cases, the person who monopolizes discussion has no ulterior motive for doing so. What does the group do then to assist him? For that is the key to the problem. He needs help, not censure. Every member of the group has a responsibility to try. Group pressure is a powerful incentive to change. Kindly but firm pressure usually works the best. Group participants can indicate they would like to hear a specific member's opinion. They can raise questions directed at someone else. The observer, or others, can indicate that the discussion should be diffused more throughout the group.

However, the chief responsibility that a group member has is to speak out on issues under discussion. Otherwise, he allows this situation to continue by default. What occurs then is that decisions of the group are largely determined by a few persons' opinions, the vocal ones. Democratic participation in policy-making is as much a responsibility to speak out as a right to be heard.

3

THE CURRICULUM MAKERS

The first two chapters have dealt with principles of the curriculum improvement process, focusing on the change in people and in the relationships among people. These principles, derived largely from studies in human relations and group dynamics, were presented as ideals which would result in the greatest amount of growth of all those involved in the process—teacher, pupil, parent, citizen, supervisor, administrator, consultant.

However, the realities of the situation are not the ideal. The power politics, the orders and directives, the pressures and capitulation to pressures, and the practical decision-making that go on day by day are also very much a part of the dynamics of curriculum-making. Whether or not they result in any long-range or permanent improvement is a question for exploration.

Curriculum change as a political process, a "study of influence and the influential," has been examined by Mackenzie, applying to the curriculum process the type of analysis made by political scientists. He points out that curriculum change can be achieved through direct action of administrative authority and "through the political processes of using resources, symbols, and coalitions among influential groups" as well as by changing the teacher or by in-service education.[1] This chapter focuses on the roles of individuals and organizations in the total curriculum-making process: the part of the teacher, the local community, the state, regional agencies, the federal government, and national organizations. The part played by the pupil is discussed in Chapter 17.

[1] Gordon N. Mackenzie, "The School Context of Curriculum Change," *Theory into Practice*, 1:189, October, 1962.

WHO ARE THE DECISION MAKERS?

Does the teacher actually have anything to say about the curriculum in his classroom? Are all of the decisions made by administrators and outsiders? What responsibility has the teacher for curriculum-making? What are the responsibilities of the local board and of the state in curriculum planning? How are the two related? What is the federal government's responsibility? Is it desirable to have a national curriculum? What influences do the extralegal organizations have on the curriculum? Questions of this nature are of concern to the teacher, for all of these individuals and groups impinge upon what he does in the classroom.

Shifts in Influence

Rather drastic shifts in the influential groups in curriculum-making have occurred in recent years. New groups have gained power. The public listens to a new class of experts. No longer do the taxpayers' groups, Chambers of Commerce, professional organizations, labor organizations, or parent–teacher associations hold the most dominant positions. Accelerated by cultural and technological changes, this shift has almost seemed imperceptible. Professional organizations and individual teachers and administrators have sometimes acted as though no change had taken place. Some curriculum leaders have proceeded with the usual curriculum improvement activities as though they were entirely unaware of these new influences.

What has bothered educators most, however, is that much of this shift has been toward indirect action groups that have no legal authority to make curriculum changes. The philanthropic foundations, the learned societies, the academic scholars, the scholarship testing programs, and the Rickovers and Conants have exercised an authoritative voice in curriculum affairs. One of the characteristic responses has been for the school authorities to step up their power-decisions. As a consequence, more decisions tend to be made on the basis of authority held by the person than on authority of knowledge gained from research.

Another shift has been in the direction of centralization of control. With the advent of the National Defense Education Act in 1958 and the National Science Foundation in 1959, the federal government moved out from its traditional area of vocational education into the business of curriculum-making in academic fields, and on a scale never attempted before. The federal decision-making activities made their influence felt in the fields of science, mathematics, foreign language, guidance, audio-visual aids, and higher education programs and research, and more recently have expanded into the fields of English and social studies. Funds were provided for selected kinds of activities and programs. Another branch of the federal government, the courts, moved into direct action affecting the curriculum through its decisions on segregation and religious activities in the schools.

Innovators and the Adoption of New Ideas

The influential groups and individuals discussed in this chapter are all curriculum makers, whether or not they make the final decisions. In many cases they do, for the failure of the status leaders to act in the midst of a social revolution is an abdication of authority. The ideas, pronouncements, and recommendations of outsiders fill in the vacuum. These organizations and individuals then become the innovators. They have prestige, funds, and access to publicity with which to influence public opinion.

The question of how much of an innovator in curriculum-making the school administrator or curriculum director can be depends upon both the human relations and the political process of the situation. He is looked to for leadership and, in many cases, shares it with teachers. Where the principal is not hamstrung by stringent administrative rules for approval of experimentation, nor by curriculum committees that see their function as approval of innovations, he may well be the chief innovator in the school system. The competent principal who wants to make improvement but finds himself enmeshed in hierarchical chains of command wisely encourages the individual teacher to move ahead.

The research done by rural sociologists on the adoption of new ideas and practices in farming has pertinence for the curriculum-making process, especially in gaining insight into who is responsible for the innovations and for using the influential sources. Some of these selected findings are as follows:

1. In adoption of new ideas and practices, information sources vary in their functions.
2. In the adoption process, people go through a continuous series of stages of awareness, interest, evolution, trial, and adoption.
3. Individuals are important sources of information.
4. The person sought for advice is usually more competent.

5. Persons sought for advice are usually more exposed to direct information sources.

6. In communities where a premium is placed upon quick, successful adoption of new practices, the key communicators and influentials are likely to be much more receptive to new ideas and more prone to change.

7. Influentials and innovators are not always the same persons.

8. Persons sought for advice frequently have higher status than the seekers.

9. Skeptics may play a useful role in adoption.

10. The easily demonstrable practice may be more quickly adopted.

11. The prestige of groups concerned influences adoption.

12. People are influenced by groups of which they are not members.

13. Value-changes result from widened horizons.

14. Those quickest to adopt new practices are inclined to use objective facts in their decisions and to rely on institutionalized sources of information.

15. Formal education is associated with adoption of new ideas and practices.[2]

According to the New York State study that analyzed how instructional changes were made in over 100 schools, and who brought about the changes, large-scale instructional innovations are chiefly initiated by the principal, teacher planning is utilized in the most successful changes, visits to observe successful programs are persuasive incentives to change, and commercial publishers and other organizations are powerful initiators or inhibitors of change.[3]

Kinds of Decisions

The answer to the question of who makes the decisions also depends upon the type of judgment needed. The broad policy-making decisions seem appropriately made at the higher levels, with participation of all ranks of educators. The more practical decisions are then made at the local level. It should be remembered that school systems vary greatly in size, and "local" may mean either the school district in relation to the state educational agency or the school building in relation to the central administrative staff.

[2] Adapted from Herbert F. Lionberger, *Adoption of New Ideas and Practices*, Ames: Iowa State University Press, 1960, pp. 3–17.

[3] Henry M. Brickell, *Organizing New York State for Educational Change*, Albany, N. Y.: State Department of Education, 1961, pp. 19–62.

The point has been aptly made by many professional organizations that the school system should have a policy and a systematic procedure for studying and utilizing the recommendations that come from influential groups and individuals. The school should also have a policy for utilizing outside funds and for including evaluative studies in its own instructional budget. Each administrative unit within the school organization needs some safeguards that will insure flexibility and a chance for creativity to operate.

Policy-making that is looked upon as gate-keeping of the rules rarely gives the teacher any opportunity for significant decisions. The gate is likely to be closed to many innovations that might originate at home instead of from outsiders.

The administrative structure of the school may be geared to the echelon concept with only minor decisions made by the lowest echelon, the teachers. The man in the middle, the principal, finds himself busily implementing decisions filtering down from the top. The appellate type of decision, which comes from the bottom up, is better suited to curriculum decisions, if people are going to have a part in deciding what affects them. However, it too may get caught in the gears of the chain-of-command machinery and never emerge.

The major problem seems to be to free the principal and the teacher for the creative type of decision, where a novel situation is visualized and carried out. These solutions occur only in a few instances and only where people value individuality rather than organization. In these creative kinds of decisions, the teacher is more highly valued as the curriculum maker.

THE TEACHER

The teacher is the most important of the curriculum makers. He is the expert working in a classroom with a group of children, putting into practice what many others have had a part in deciding. He determines, in the final analysis, what he shall do with the course of study, what content shall be utilized in the immediate situation, whether or not pupils will have a part in determining their activities, and what activities will be used.

Decisions that others make either expand or restrict the boundaries of these activities carried on by the teacher. The kind of role that other individuals and agencies play in the process affects the teacher deeply and helps to make him as effective as he is. State legislation, state examinations, community attitudes, pressure groups, the board of education's and the administration's policies, accrediting agencies, professional and academic organizations—all affect his capability as a curriculum maker.

Responsibilities

The teacher's primary role in the curriculum development process is teaching in the classroom. The day-by-day decisions that he makes reflect his knowledge of pupils as individuals, his knowledge of the subject taught, his understanding of the learning process, his understanding of the society in which he lives, the clarity of his objectives, and the recognition of his responsibilities to the school system.

The decisions about classroom teaching should be the responsibility of the teacher within the limits set by the cooperative planning done with his colleagues and by the school's regulations. In some schools, the teacher is given a great deal of freedom as a curriculum maker. He is considered as a mature person who can be trusted with an important charge. All types of assistance are given him to do his job well, such as supervisory help, instructional materials centers, testing service, counseling assistance, and in-service education.

In other schools, the restrictions that prevent him from having any great latitude in moving toward curriculum improvement are legion. Hedged in by rules made by pedestrian gatekeepers, by outdated textbooks, by skimpy materials with which to work, by community pressures, and by pressures from teachers who have succumbed to the environment in which they find themselves, the teacher soon loses his enthusiasm. He becomes a different kind of curriculum maker, but nevertheless his decision to give in to the system just as surely helps to determine the curriculum for his pupils as if he had pursued a different course.

In any kind of school environment, however, the teacher's first responsibility is to his pupils. He is responsible for giving them the best kind of educational environment possible in spite of any handicaps under which he may work. He cannot excuse his own lack of knowledge about new developments, or treatment of children with little respect, or indifference to what each one's potential might be.

The teacher is responsible for collecting data about his pupils, information upon which to base intelligent curriculum decisions. He is responsible for selecting materials for use in his teaching, whether they be sparse or abundant. He is responsible to the school district for carrying out its policies regarding the curriculum.

In almost all school systems today, teachers have some opportunity to take part in developing courses of study, in selecting texts and other materials, and in determining curriculum policies. Those who take advantage of the opportunities have a greater part in decision-making.

However, there has been a growing tendency to object to committee participation, curriculum study, and extra responsibilities. This is due, in part, to the greater number of married women teachers who have children to whom they feel a responsibility after school hours. In part, it is also due to the reaction against the many kinds of monitoring, clerical, and maintenance-type duties asked of teachers by boards of education that are not able to see the advantage of employing non-teaching personnel for such duties.

But the responsibility for participation in curriculum improvement activities and in-service education cannot be shrugged off. Every teacher has an obligation to engage in some type of self-improvement as well as in cooperative curriculum activities.

Approach

The way the teacher sees his role is determined to a large extent by his approach to curriculum development. How a teacher uses subject matter, sets up goals, develops experiences, measures progress, and guides and controls the learning situation, constitute this approach. Based on his understanding of the psychological and social foundations of education, it is a system of values, a framework within which curriculum decisions are made. The attitudes which he has formed regarding the teaching process—what a teacher does to or for pupils, how he helps them learn, and how he decides what children should learn— form a pattern of behavior that can be described objectively.

Every teacher believes that he is interested in improving the experiences that his pupils have. But "better" experiences may have entirely different meanings for teachers. The value judgments as to what is better will depend upon how the teacher looks at the means and ends of the teaching process.

Elsewhere the author has used the concept of the experience-centered and the subject-centered approaches to describe the behavior of teachers in the classroom.[4] The two basic approaches are described by a number of statements as to what is the position of the teacher who takes either approach. Few teachers follow either the extreme subject-centered approach or the extreme experience-centered approach.

[4] See Vernon E. Anderson and William T. Gruhn, *Principles and Practices of Secondary Education*, 2nd ed., New York: The Ronald Press Co., 1962, pp. 109–17.

Yet, the teacher is usually so involved emotionally with how he behaves as a teacher that it is difficult, perhaps impossible, for him to look at his own behavior objectively. The fact that someone attaches a label to describe a pattern of behavior makes him even more upset, especially if somehow the label conveys inferiority. "Subject-centered" and "experience-centered" are perfectly neutral words. But they are not neutral in teachers' minds. The connotation of "experience-centered" may bring to his mind aimlessness, frittering away time, and letting pupils "run the show." Or he may conceive of "subject-centered" as traditional, backward, and refusing to accept modern procedures.

Even though the concepts are useful for analysis of the way a teacher functions in curriculum development in the classroom, they are ineffectual for the person who refuses to look at his own behavior objectively, at whatever level he teaches.

For the teacher who wishes to examine his approach to curriculum development as exemplified in behavior, the characteristics of each of the two approaches are briefly listed here.

The subject-centered approach:
Subject matter in distinct compartments represents what is to be learned.
The subject matter to be covered and the kinds of experiences pupils will have are determined before the course begins.
Minimum standards and a predetermined pattern govern what is to be learned.
Skills are taught as separate entities.
The teacher acts as the external authority who exercises control over the learning situation.

The experience-centered approach:
Subject matter is used as a means to an end, to lead to desirable outcomes in behavior changes.
The development of the child or adolescent, his mind, body, emotions, and social nature, all are considered important.
The content is a series of planned experiences growing out of the pupils' background, needs, interests, and daily living, and out of the social and physical environment.
The teaching of the fundamental skills is done in relation to their use.
The experiences are selected cooperatively by teachers and pupils, based on a study and knowledge of those pupils and their previous experience.
The teacher is concerned with the growth and development of each individual pupil rather than with preconceived ideas of what the mythical "average pupil" should know at a certain grade level.

The Competency and Role of the Teacher

Much research has been done on predicting teaching success but no reliable predictors have been found. Relatively little progress has been made in defining quality teaching or in specifying distinguishing characteristics of competent teachers. Yet, these are factors that relate quite definitely to how the teacher conceives of and puts into action curriculum principles and programs.

The problem lies in the fact that characteristics of a good teacher are likely to vary with the situation, the particular culture in which the teacher functions, and the goals and purposes of that culture for education. It is one thing to train people to carry on technical skills with a high degree of perfection; but quite another, to educate highly creative research specialists or statesmen highly skilled in human relations and knowledgeable in world affairs. The characteristics of a good teacher most likely vary also with different grade levels and different subjects taught and with the intellectual and other characteristics of the pupils taught.

The definition of teaching competence is a rather slippery problem to grab hold of because the role of the teacher has not been sufficiently clarified. Sociologists who have studied the question indicate that the role a teacher plays depends upon the way the community conceives of the teacher. Is he a model for the young, an idealist, a person of culture, a participant in community affairs or a stranger in the community, a person who knows, a judge of achievement, one who keeps discipline, one who gives guidance and advice, a substitute for parents—what does the community demand of him?

In his role as teacher, a person may be expected to function effectively as a director of learning, a guidance worker, a member of the profession, a member of a school, a member of the community and the nation. It is extremely doubtful that agreement could be obtained about which roles are most important. Then, too, is it not possible that the teacher's role is changing in our society? For example, what will ever increasing perfection and utilization of educational media such as television and programmed learning do to the role that the teacher performs? It is not news to us that teachers are very much concerned about what these modern devices will do to them.

The different concepts of the teacher's role at times cause considerable conflict. Perhaps one of the reasons is that we have failed to distinguish clearly what is required for competent teaching at the college, high school, and elementary school level, or within the various subjects taught. Some talk as though what is good preparation for a secondary school teacher is also good for a teacher of young children, and are entirely oblivious to the differences in children's maturity.

Probably the breakthrough will not come until we can change some of our hoary concepts that good teachers must all fit into one mold without regard for the circumstances, without regard for what they teach and whom they teach, without regard for the fact that teachers differ in their qualities and strengths.

THE COMMUNITY AND LOCAL POLICY

Every administrator and teacher knows that certain things can or cannot be done in his community. Some know what persons wield the major influence in the community and who must be seen in order "to get things done." The kind of community, its traditions, its mores, its attitudes, its prejudices, and its pressure groups are of great importance to the curriculum of its schools.

Sociologists define the community as an area or neighborhood that has common elements, such as manners, traditions, modes of speech, and interests. The days in which people in a community depended upon each other for virtually everything, in the intimate face-to-face association of the primary group, have disappeared. Today it is difficult to know what "community" one is talking about: the school district; the parents of the youngsters in a particular school; or the town, city, or rural area which the school serves. This discussion refers to the immediate community which has an interest and a stake in a particular school system through paying taxes or through having its children attend the schools within that system.

Community Patterns

The community of even a few decades ago has been changed radically by war, mobility of population, facility of transportation, and new media of communication. Industrial development has concentrated large masses of people around urban centers. People continue to move out of cities to settle in nearby communities. Over half of the young people who live on farms will some day move to urban areas. Agriculture with its mechanized farming and absentee ownership has become more like a business. In some sections of the country, a declining industry such as coal is causing unemployment, extreme poverty, and disillusionment. The small town in farming areas struggles for existence. Burgeoning suburban or "bedroom" communities with their huge shopping centers and impersonal supermarkets offer diversion but not community spirit nor cohesiveness. Large cities have their sections of differing socio-economic levels: nob hill, the ghetto, the middle-class family, and the slum.

The big-city area, which has come in for special study in recent years, is characterized by early dropouts, unemployed youth, juvenile delinquency, and children on welfare rolls. Children may grow up not knowing their parents, with the derelicts, "pushers," drunks, and prostitutes as their models. The streets are their playground and the gangs their only friends.

The community—whether it be a slum or a wealthy suburb—is, in a sense, the most powerful of curriculum makers. Its hopes, despairs, attitudes, and values, and the disruptions caused by change, affect what the school can do or what the community allows it to do. By no means is a well-fed, self-satisfied suburban community the place where the most dynamic curriculum can always be found. Where ingenious leadership exists, curriculum forefronts may instead be found in a community struggling to overcome adverse conditions.

The type of community, its organizational patterns, modes of living, and traditions have an important bearing upon planning experiences for school children. The slum child may face a make-believe world in a school that does not take cognizance of the conditions under which he lives. The rural child has no basis for understanding stories depicting city life. Crowded conditions place on schools additional responsibilities for recreation and physical education. Changing community patterns and their effects on people need to be understood. A vital study of community life goes beyond visits to the dairy, to industries, or to museums.

Criticisms and Pressures

The public school is subject to a variety of criticisms and pressures from organized groups and individuals within the community. Almost anyone can get a hearing about a school issue, whether it be in the living room of a friend, at a school meeting, or in the press. Magazines and newspapers feed on controversy, something that makes news and will be read: "How Can We Catch Up?" "Are the Public Schools Doing Their Job?" "Who's Trying to Ruin Our Schools?"—these titles shout at the reader to gain his attention.

The curriculum is often the point in focus, although anyone who wishes to attack the school can find his favorite whipping post in almost any issue that deals with expenditures, morals, discipline, standards, fundamentals, politics, religion, or radical change.

In recent years, organizations critical of the schools have demanded more stress on the fundamentals, or "returning" to "basic" education; firming up the control of pupils; cutting the frills; raising standards; eliminating religious holiday programs; teaching more phonics; eliminating content dealing with evolution, the United Nations, communism, or any topic that deals with controversial issues. They have accused public schools of teaching socialism, being godless and anti-intellectual, undermining American institutions, misspending time, lacking a rigorous enough program, teaching useless life adjustment, or invading through tests the private concerns of the family and the child.

In the face of this situation, many school administrators and teachers shudder at the thought of pressure groups. They have come to regard these groups in a community as undesirable. Pressure groups can have an influence upon public opinion quite out of proportion to their size through skillful use of the press, the radio, television, and other communications media. However, the pressure group in itself is an expression of the democratic principle that any group has the right to be heard and to try to bring about changes.

Some of the concerns of pressure groups are valid; some are smokescreens for concealed purposes. Some represent the sincere convictions of a group of thoughtful people; others are matchsticks for rabble-rousers and fuel for the maladjusted and malcontent. The task of sifting out purposes is far from an easy one.

Yet, pressure groups and critics are political realities of the life of the public school teacher. Some kind of classification should be helpful in the sifting process that is a part of intelligent action. Pressure groups may be classified according to the type of interest they have in the public schools.

The first type is made up of organizations primarily concerned with school policy, such as parent–teacher associations, school–community councils, citizens' advisory groups, and citizen groups that have been formed outside of the school largely to influence school policy. A number of these, such as the P.T.A., have as their purpose the improvement of understanding between school and community. Some other organizations are frankly critical of the schools and are concerned largely with changing certain school practices. All of them, however, are supporters of the public schools.

A second type includes organizations which, as a secondary purpose, seek to influence public elementary and secondary school education while their main purpose lies in some other area. They are also supporters of public education. Typical of such groups are the National Association of Manufacturers, the American Association of Railroads, other organizations representing industry and business, and labor unions. Most of their influence is exercised through publications, films, speakers, and cooperation with the school as illustrated by the typical "industry–school day." A newer type of group of this nature is the learned society composed largely of college professors, discussed later in this chapter.

A third type of organization interested in school policy is one that deliberately attacks the schools. These organizations have often been labeled as "fronts" for other interests. Thirteen characteristics listed in the Association for Supervision and Curriculum Development's 1953 Yearbook help to identify an organization with such purposes. These activities, as true today, are as follows:

1. Meets initially under authorized group, perhaps; may then begin holding secret or off-record sessions.
2. Tends to work under cover and to use devious means of evading school officials and faculty.
3. Attracts emotionally unstable people to it and often these are given command of the group.
4. May break away from an honest, firmly established group and set up its own splinter organization with high-sounding title, indicating patriotic motives or unselfish concern for public education.
5. Uses smear literature, poison pamphlets, usually imported from the outside, or lifts phrases, slogans, and titles from them.
6. Introduces extraneous issues, rather than concentrating on the agreed-upon area of discussion.
7. Accepts rabble-rousing techniques, "dust-throwing," "name-calling."
8. Permits only one side of the issue to be presented fully.
9. Frequently passes resolutions without thoughtful deliberation and regardless of all the evidence. Persons making such resolutions are frequently fanatically critical of the schools.
10. Attacks personalities—the superintendent or principal becomes the "whipping boy."
11. Makes a pretense of getting the facts, then issues ultimatums to be answered in a limited amount of time. Sometimes these attacks take the form of a list of questions to the school officials or to the board, often given to the press simultaneously.
12. Frequently uses press in the campaign.
13. Secures funds through collections and through gifts solicited, not through regular constituted membership.[5]

[5] Association for Supervision and Curriculum Development, *Forces Affecting American Education*, 1953 Yearbook, Washington, D. C.: National Education Association, 1953, pp. 47–48.

A more recent phenomenon in American society is the super-patriotic organization that represents extreme conservatism in the broad area of political action, which often includes the schools. The John Birch Society, America for Americans, and the Christian Crusade typify these groups. Many of them have access to large financial resources, are successful in collecting money, and often include influential citizens in their membership. They tend to be well organized, with a program that calls for action of some type. The action may be seeing the board of education, writing to Congress, censoring textbooks, "booknapping," conducting anti-communism "schools," impeaching a prominent public figure, getting elected to school committees, or "straightening out" P.T.A.'s. They have discovered that political action takes more than passing resolutions at conventions. Infiltration tactics are commonly used.

The Commission on Professional Rights and Responsibilities of the National Education Association estimated in 1962 that there were over 250 such organizations, varying, of course, in their specific objectives and methods.

Their demands or criticisms tend to fall in the areas of anti-communism, censorship of texts, teaching the free enterprise system, "Americanism," and teacher participation in politics. Generally, they are characterized by an overriding concern for the internal threat of communism; a scorn for democracy; opposition to civil rights laws, the U. N., economic planning, the income tax, and foreign aid; and a suspicion that both Democrats and Republicans are socialists.

The radical right, whose methods often resemble those of the radical left, may represent one of the most serious threats to American democracy and the teaching of its principles in the public schools. They are often the groups that feed on hate and help create an atmosphere of the kind that led a disturbed malcontent in Dallas to kill President Kennedy.

They have every right to be heard and to promote their own point of view. This basic tenet of democracy is the very one that they threaten to stifle, for freedom to read about and discuss controversial issues is what they oppose.

In this day and age of attempted thought control throughout the world, Harold Benjamin rightly said: "Free men cannot be taught properly by slaves. Courageous citizens cannot be well educated by scared hired men." Forces that would limit the freedom to teach all ideas would have schools teach a certain dogma, a certain philosophy, or point of view. Some would like to use the school for political ends.

Limiting the schools merely to teaching the facts of geography, history, science, and other subjects, without giving the pupils the equipment with which to analyze social issues and problems, should be seen in its rightful sense as an anti-intellectual force which would preserve the status quo. Groups are trying to place a millstone around the necks of teachers when they do not want pupils to be given all the facts and to be allowed to make decisions for themselves. Actually, this is the most insidious kind of thought control; it bores from within and in many instances operates under the guise of Americanism.

Irresponsible attacks that use innuendo and misrepresentation have a debilitating effect on the school curriculum. Destructive criticism distorts facts, attacks personalities, and uses sensationalism rather than reason. All of these methods of criticism erode curriculum improvement. They are destructive of good education and effective in suppressing ideas and in wasting creative human resources.

Responsible criticism, on the other hand, should be welcomed by the school. The public should always have an opportunity to voice its opinions about the schools.

Freedom to Teach and Learn

The teacher's freedom to teach objectively and the student's freedom to read liberal as well as conservative thinkers, to learn, and to know can be seriously impaired by radicals on the right or on the left. Loyalty oaths, censorship of reading, investigations of textbooks, the use of self-selected investigating committees are deliberate means to bring about conformity.

Censorship of instructional materials is another of the most insidious forms of thought control. A number of organizations have taken up this cause. Book-burning comes in many forms. It is but a stone's throw away from the witchcraft trials of old Salem in the Massachusetts Bay Colony. The witchhunts that engulfed that village still go on, but in a different guise. The teacher who needs to refresh his memory about the hysteria of that day and to compare it with modern witchhunters should read Marion L. Starkey's *The Devil in Massachusetts; A Modern Inquiry into the Salem Witch Trials,*[6] a colorfully written account of the horrible emotional orgies of a community led by terror rather than by reason.

Book censors have been active in many communities, especially in Florida, Texas, and California. They have been successful in removing books from sale, purging libraries, causing withdrawal from use of standardized tests, distributing lists of objectionable books and

6 New York: Alfred A. Knopf, Inc., 1950.

authors, labeling books that they find objectionable, and influencing boards of education to change book adoptions or even to change certain passages in books. Such respectable publications as *The Christian Science Monitor, The New York Times,* and *The Nation* have all come under their censorship stamp. Fortunately, well established publications with good reputations can withstand the onslaughts of petty censors, but such is not always true with school boards, administrators, and teachers.

These techniques of the book burners are clearly a violation of the principle of free inquiry. In an atmosphere in which liberal ideas and liberal thinkers are often classified as subversive or communistic by those who disagree with them, this kind of a pressure group has caused considerable damage to the school curriculum. For example, attacks upon the United Nations and upon UNESCO as subversive and un-American organizations have caused teachers in some communities to shy away from teaching about these organizations. More serious, however, is the general effect on the attitudes of teachers toward teaching controversial issues.

Under such influences, some teachers have tended to return to the three R's, with little else to enrich the curriculum. Numerous schools have been hesitant to introduce changes that might become convenient points of attack. Teachers have reverted to older and more traditional methods of teaching which were used in schools that the children's parents attended.

The requirement that teachers sign loyalty oaths, singling them out as a special group; the investigation of textbooks; the proposals that the Congressional committees should investigate the schools, on the suspicion that they are teaching communism; the various attempts at censorship—all are symptoms of a social illness which suspicion and fear of a social evil, communism, have brought about. All tend to bring about an atmosphere of conformity and to push people to the far right. Authors and publishers become more cautious. Textbooks become more bland. The safer course may be taken in curriculum innovations.

Organizations such as the National Council of Teachers of English, American Book Publishers Council, The National Council of Social Studies, and the American Library Association have taken a courageous stand against book censorship. One example of an organization's policy is the Library Bill of Rights of the American Library Association:

The Council of the American Library Association reaffirms its belief in the following basic policies which should govern the service of all libraries:
1. As a responsibility of library service, books and other reading matter

selected should be chosen for values of interest, information and enlighten-
ment of all the people of the community. In no case should any book be
excluded because of the race or nationality or the political or religious
views of the writer.

2. There should be the fullest practicable provision of materials presenting all points of view concerning the problems and issues of our times, international, national, and local; and books or other reading matter of sound
factual authority should not be proscribed or removed from library shelves
because of partisan or doctrinal disapproval.

3. Censorship of books, urged or practiced by volunteer arbiters of
morals or political opinion or by organizations that would establish a co-
ercive concept of Americanism, must be challenged by libraries in maintenance of their responsibility to provide public information and enlighten-
ment through the printed word.

4. Libraries should enlist the cooperation of allied groups in the fields
of science, of education, and of book publishing in resisting all abridgment
of the free access to ideas and full freedom of expression that are the tradition and heritage of Americans.

5. The rights of an individual to the use of a library should not be de-
nied or abridged because of his race, religion, national origins or political
views.

6. As an institution of education for democratic living, the library should
welcome the use of its meeting rooms for socially useful and cultural activities and discussion of current public questions. Such meeting places
should be available on equal terms to all groups in the community regardless of the beliefs and affiliations of their members.[7]

School Policy-Making

The policies of the board of education and the administration are
indicative of community attitudes. If the community feels that teachers ought to live in the town in which they teach, there may be a
written or unwritten rule to that effect. Boards may feel constrained
to place restrictions on teaching about a particular subject. These
actions may be taken as a result of some community pressures and
may not be the result of considered judgment and study involving
many elements of the community. That this sets a dangerous precedent
is obvious.

The board of education has an obligation to enact policies that will
protect the teachers' freedom to teach fearlessly and objectively about
any issues of importance to the life of the people whom it represents.
In this manner, it exercises its powers constructively as a curriculum
maker. For example, a board of education in a large county school
system adopted a policy statement "to strengthen the commitment to

[7] Adopted in 1948 and amended in 1961, Chicago: American Library Association.

our American values and the teaching about communism." Another adopted a set of basic principles for the selection of materials for school libraries.

One of the important policies of a school system deals with the use of the course of study. The school administration may believe in working with the community to analyze what is at stake educationally, what uniformity is desirable, and what serves best to bring about agreement on objectives, or it may solve the problem by requiring teachers to follow rigidly courses of study. Inflexibility of the curriculum can be imposed either by state legislation, board of education regulation, or administrative operational policy.

Other types of policies may limit the curriculum. Some schools have restrictive policies concerning field trips, which limit the kinds of experiences that a teacher can give pupils in the school community. High school graduation requirements may limit what can be done to change the curriculum. In many instances, these regulations and requirements have never been questioned by the teachers and the easy "calf-path" of traditional practice has been followed. In other schools, teachers and administrators work together with community people to help set up such policy, and the entire faculty is constantly reviewing requirements and participating in a democratic way in developing school policies.

STATE AND REGIONAL POLICIES

The state agencies that have the legal responsibility for the schools of the state have, in some form or other, exercised control over the school curriculum. The state is the legal curriculum maker. Regional agencies, such as accrediting associations, work closely with state agencies in regulating practices so that adequate standards are maintained.

State Legal Requirements

Traditionally, states have legislated curriculum for the public schools. In the period prior to the late 1920's, the state legislatures were active in enacting curriculum prescriptions, largely from the belief of the public that certain requirements were essential in order to develop good citizens. Uniformity was demanded. In the period from the late 1920's to 1950, these requirements were relaxed in some legislatures. Again, in the 1950's a new wave of legislation began.

The earlier legislation centered around teaching American history and the Constitution, citizenship and civics, conservation, health and physical education, standard areas of the elementary school curriculum such as language arts and arithmetic, and the effects of alcohol. Some required celebration of certain days, such as Bird Day or Arbor Day. Others forbade certain content, such as the teaching about evolution. Later came demands for teaching about state history and government.

More recently, laws were enacted to require driver training and education. As usual, state legislatures turned to the schools to correct a social condition that the people seemed to have no desire to control. In a sense, the schools become the escape valve for a bad conscience that states have about a social evil. In another sense, the action represents an inherent faith in the schools.

Included in the newer wave of legislation that affects the school curriculum has been mandatory state-wide testing programs. In 1961, the California state legislature enacted a law requiring each school district to administer an achievement test related to the course of study approved by the State Board of Education.

The Project on Instruction of the National Education Association, in an important deliberative report, has recommended that state legislatures "should not prescribe curriculum content or legislate specific courses" but should, instead, "set forth general goals for the schools, provide adequate financial support, and delegate broad powers of implementation to the state and local educational authorities." [8]

State Agencies

In the same report, the function of the state educational agency was recommended as to "establish standards for public school instruction, provide adequate resources for their achievement, and give dynamic leadership to curriculum development, experimentation, and innovation in local schools." [9]

State departments of education and state boards of education have the responsibility for maintaining public school programs. They specify the areas of the elementary school program if not mandated by law. At the secondary school level, the state department sets graduation requirements. State boards of vocational education designate in some detail the curriculum for vocational courses that come under the federal acts for special funds.

[8] National Education Association, *Schools for the Sixties,* New York: McGraw-Hill Book Co., 1963, p. 124.
[9] *Ibid.,* p. 124.

The modern role of the state department of education tends to be a facilitating one. Although state departments have responsibility for enforcing state laws on education, they plan programs and work with public schools for curriculum improvement in a cooperative way. They sponsor workshops and committees to develop units, curriculum guides, and state projects. They initiate state curriculum studies and programs, sponsor state conferences, serve in a consultant capacity to local schools, furnish supervisory assistance, and collect and disseminate information concerning good teaching practices.

In the field of instructional materials, state departments produce suggested curriculum guides rather than prescriptive courses of study. State curriculum centers make available to schools curriculum bulletins and other types of bulletins and, on a loan basis, books and audio-visual materials.

A newer service has been research departments that collect and disseminate data, conduct state-wide research projects, and consult with schools concerning local research projects.

State testing programs, in the few instances where they have been developed, have not been particularly auspicious in improving schools. A study of instructional change made for the New York State Education Department declared flatly: "The Regents Examinations, beyond any question whatsoever, inhibit educational change in the State of New York." [10] The investigators found that copies of previous examinations constituted at least 10 per cent of the curriculum in the typical high school academic course. The same condition existed in Minnesota when state examinations were abolished in the 1930's. Nevertheless, state examinations of any type are determiners of the curriculum, since teachers tend to teach for the tests.

Accrediting Agencies

Regional accrediting agencies, such as the Middle States Association of Colleges and Secondary Schools, have been developed by member organizations to accredit secondary schools and colleges. State departments of education also accredit secondary schools and colleges.

Influence on the curriculum has been exerted by the regional accrediting agencies through regulations for secondary schools and through certification that graduates of accredited schools are eligible for admission to colleges. Mainly the externals have been specified, in the form of course requirements or the number of credits or units required for graduation. Equipment, facilities, staff, and instructional

[10] Brickell, *op. cit.*, p. 40.

materials have generally been evaluated through report forms and visitation by accrediting committees at intervals, or upon application for accreditation. These agencies too are changing their approach to emphasize experimentation and local evaluation in terms of the philosophy and objectives of the school. An example is the *Evaluative Criteria* of the National Study of Secondary School Evaluation, used as a basis for school evaluation by local staffs and teams of school people from outside the school.

In his influential book, *The Education of American Teachers*, James B. Conant has recommended that regional associations become merely advisory bodies to local school boards.[11] Such a move would lessen their influence on the curriculum of secondary schools.

Colleges and Universities

No doubt colleges and universities have had an influence on the American public school curriculum, not only through teacher education, but also through research, curriculum centers and laboratories, consultation by faculty, conferences, and publications. Especially public state universities and a few large private ones have worked closely with schools on research and field studies through bureaus of research and field services. Their influence through experimentation and demonstration in laboratory schools on campuses has been less noticeable. Many such schools have been used for teacher education rather than for these purposes; others have not been outstanding schools.

Another kind of indirect influence on the high school curriculum has been exerted through college entrance requirements. Many colleges and universities require completion of specified subjects in high school as a basis for admission. These requirements have had a marked influence on what is required for completion of a high school program.

NATIONAL CURRICULUM PROGRAMS AND INFLUENCES

Traditionally, the United States has had a decentralized system of education. Curriculum development has been the function of local and state school systems. The federal government's role has been that of gathering and disseminating information concerning programs and practices. In recent years, not only has the federal government

11 New York: McGraw-Hill Book Co., 1963, p. 217.

been changing its role in the influencing of curriculum improvement but extralegal agencies at the national level have come directly into the picture. Proposals, moreover, have been made for a national curriculum.

An examination of what is happening on the national scene is necessary to appraise the scope and influence of curriculum-making at this level.

Federal Government Participation

When the federal government entered the field of curriculum-making in vocational education in 1917, its influence became more direct than mere suggestion-making. The Smith–Hughes Act of that year, and subsequent acts, provided for federal aid and cooperation in vocational education in agriculture, trades and industries, home economics, and distributive education at the secondary school level. This has been strengthened by the Vocational Education Act of 1963, which provides for additional funds for vocational training for youth in and out of school, with a shift of emphasis to the industrial occupations. In approving of state plans for vocational education in order for states to receive federal funds, the U. S. Office of Education has exercised a great deal of control over these programs. The very fact that funds were provided for some types of courses and not for others influenced the direction of the curriculum.

This influence was considerably increased when the federal government also entered curriculum-making in the fields of science, mathematics, English, social studies, and languages. Funds were provided for secondary schools for equipment in these fields, for colleges and universities, and for in-service education of teachers, but largely on the terms specified by the special branches set up in the U. S. Office of Education to administer the programs. No doubt these specialized aid programs have greatly strengthened certain fields. But there is no question that the national government is involved in curriculum development, even though the desirability of its involvement is a question for debate.

Other examples of federal involvement in providing or encouraging programs for youth and adults have included physical fitness programs, the Civilian Conservation Corps and the National Youth Administration in the depression years of the 1930's, and the Peace Corps.

One of the newer developments, which is designed to aid universities, colleges, and public state and local school systems to find better answers to curriculum problems, is the Cooperative Research Program, discussed in Chapter 9. Even this program has encouraged studies of curriculum improvement in certain areas, such as special education and English.

Professional Organizations

The extent to which professional organizations have influenced curriculum improvement in the schools will perhaps never be known since the results of their activities are so diffuse and difficult to measure. Yet, the work of groups such as the National Council of Teachers of Mathematics, National Council of Teachers of English, American Vocational Association, National Science Teachers Association, National Council for the Social Studies, and Association for Supervision and Curriculum Development must have influenced their members through the years. These and similar professional organizations have conducted conferences; published yearbooks, periodicals, and bulletins; and appointed committees and commissions to carry on studies over a long period of years. Undoubtedly, the interchange of ideas through conferences and publications has influenced practice.

More influence has been exerted when funds have been available to organizations as in the case of the Eight-Year Study of the Progressive Education Association, the Experimental Study of the Utilization of Staff of the National Association of Secondary-School Principals, and the Project on Instruction of the National Education Association, all of which are discussed in this book.

There are some who believe that professional associations have little influence on practice. Lieberman thinks that the teachers' organizations have been unable to carry out programs for change in education.[12] Brickell is skeptical of the influence of professional associations because of their failure to understand the dynamics of instructional change.[13]

Yet, historically, the National Education Association through its Committee of Ten on Secondary School Studies (1892), Commission on the Reorganization of the High School (Cardinal Principles of Secondary Education) (1918), and Educational Policies Commission statements, and other influential reports, has undoubtedly had considerable influence especially on the secondary school curriculum.

---

[12] Myron Lieberman, "The Influence of Teachers' Organizations upon American Education," in *Social Forces Influencing American Education*, Sixtieth Yearbook, Part II, National Society for the Study of Education, Chicago: University of Chicago Press, 1961, chap. 8.

[13] Brickell, *op. cit.*, p. 56.

Academic Organizations and Programs

One of the most significant transformations in curriculum-making is the active participation of academic scholars and learned societies in curriculum studies. Up to the 1950's, few academic organizations had been interested in the public school curriculum. The absence of the interest of scholars in academic fields in curriculum studies at the local, state, and national levels had caused a lag in the introduction of recent findings and developments in content.

The events of the 1950's made professors in academic disciplines and the discerning public alike aware of the need for updating subject content in the schools. The secondary school curriculum quite naturally came in for first consideration, especially in the fields of mathematics and science. Some twelve to thirteen studies each in the fields of mathematics and science, under way by 1962, have been listed in two publications that describe the different programs.[14]

It was not long until scholars began to turn their attention to the curriculum of the elementary school. Modern foreign languages in the elementary school were the first areas given attention, although studies in mathematics and science soon followed. Studies in English and social studies followed about the same progression of development.[15]

It is not the purpose here to discuss the content of these studies. Instead, it is of importance to realize that educators have been joined by extremely powerful forces for the purpose of promoting curriculum improvement. The power rests in the knowledge possessed by scholars and in the respect they rightly command from the public. Their organizations have been able to secure large grants for the purpose of making studies. In many cases, the scholars in the subject fields, professors of education, and public school teachers and supervisors have joined in sponsoring and conducting studies, such as in the University of Maryland Mathematics Project. This is no transitory change but a permanent one that will make a difference in keeping content abreast of current developments and in the in-service education of teachers.

[14] Association for Supervision and Curriculum Development, *Using Current Curriculum Developments*, Washington, D. C.: National Education Association, 1963, 118 pp.

Dorothy M. Fraser, *Current Studies in Academic Subjects*, Washington, D. C.: National Education Association, 1962, 102 pp.

[15] In Chapters 10 and 12 on trends in the elementary and secondary school curriculum, further information regarding these studies is presented.

Publishers, Producers, and Authors

In the same sense that state courses of study influence the nature of the curriculum on a state-wide basis, textbooks, testing programs, and the authors of these publications affect the curriculum on a nation-wide basis. For the textbook is often the only curriculum guide that the teacher follows, or chooses to follow. Therefore, it is, in most cases, his course of study.

Texts and tests used in schools are selected by local administrators, supervisors, teachers, or committees, or by state authorities, but the fact that some textbooks are quite commonly used by schools in Massachusetts, Iowa, or Washington makes their influence national in scope. For example, whether mathematics textbooks in wide use for the upper and junior high school grades follow the modern mathematics approach or stress social arithmetic determines to a large extent what the curriculum will be like in those grades. Schools that choose to give college entrance examinations certainly do so in hopes that a good proportion of college-bound students will pass these tests. The structure of the program invariably feels this pressure.

The same can be said of producers of instructional materials, equipment, and programs on any media such as films or computers. The successful use of films, slides, or programmed instruction depends upon the quality of materials available. Television is a prime example of a medium whose shoddy programs have reduced to negative value its influence on adults' education. Moreover, once a product is on the market, a repeated sale or a change in the product may be related more to sales volume than to serving educational purposes.

The New York State study of educational change concluded that "commercial organizations tend to be a unifying influence over curriculum content and instructional methods, not only statewide but nationwide, probably holding the better schools and the better teachers short of the point they could reach while taking poorer school systems and less capable teachers further than they would otherwise go." [16]

Foundations

Whether one likes it or not, the private philanthropic foundations are becoming curriculum makers to be reckoned with. Beginning in the 1950's, the foundations began to exert a substantive influence on

[16] Brickell, *op. cit.*, p. 62.

the American college and public elementary and secondary school curriculum. More than 500 large foundations emerged in a twenty-year period from 1935 to 1954. There were in 1963 more than 15,000 private philanthropic foundations with assets of about $12 billion.[17] The Fund for Advancement of Education of the Ford Foundation, and the Carnegie Foundation have been especially interested in education.

There has been a growing awareness by school people that foundation funds can be used to shape school policy. If funds are available for only certain kinds of programs, those are the ones that will be stimulated. The developments are spurred by the money available for experimentation, equipment, personnel, and other costs. For example, Ford Foundation funds have been available for television, team teaching, flexible scheduling, and staff utilization studies. The funds have had a tremendous impact on the school program in these areas.

What disturbs some school people is the fact that other programs perhaps needed developing as well, but funds were not readily available for demonstration and experimentation purposes. Also disturbing to the research-minded is that these programs have largely been demonstrations without enough objective evaluation of results.

Perhaps this was the jolt needed to get schools out of established ruts, to push educational change. At any rate, this new, powerful phenomenon in American life has left its mark.

ISSUES AND POINTS OF VIEW

The issues in the question of who should be curriculum makers for the public schools are some of the most troublesome and disconcerting ones in the field of curriculum improvement. They shake the very foundations of our established traditions in education. They are often emotional issues, in a sense, since they involve change in ways of thinking and doing, and threats to one's vested domains, always extremely disturbing to people. The first and foremost of the twelve crucial decisions identified by the National Education Association's Project on Instruction was: Who should make what decisions about education?

Some issues have already been identified. Only a few of the major ones are discussed here.

[17] American Association of School Administrators, *Private Philanthropy and Public Purposes*, Washington, D. C.: National Education Association, 1963, 43 pp.

1. *Will a nationally developed course of study or curriculum program result in conformity and lack of flexibility for local communities, or will it be used as an aid to local schools?*

The question of federal aid is mixed up in this issue. Some people are scared stiff by the mention of federal aid since they believe it will lead to control of the schools. Yet, we have federal aid, with all the strings attached, supporting certain kinds of programs.

One side of the issue is that any kind of course of study, textbook, or program developed by a national agency, public or private—especially if there is money to support it—will result in an undesirable, inflexible kind of uniformity that may become fixed. The current groups writing textbooks are regarded with some skepticism because they operate on a national scope. Also, those who hold this point of view wonder whether it is not inherently dangerous to give any group of scholars the task of abstracting important concepts or values to be learned, in that someone's idea might be promoted at the expense of ideas of others.

Those who think otherwise see these efforts on a national scale as securing the best talents available to write materials for instruction—academic scholars, psychologists, educators. They argue that the American tradition will not easily accept one point of view, that local schools are free to use the materials or not. There is such a rapid development of knowledge and increased specialization in every field that specialists need constantly to examine content for the schools. After all, is not the question one of how the material is used? Can one hold the position that the teacher is the chief curriculum builder day by day in the classroom and expect that teacher not to be able to make decisions as to what materials to use? They point out that there is a great amount of free enterprise in the new science or mathematics programs, for example, with competing groups that do not always agree with each other.

2. *Should control over curriculum improvement be in the hands of educators, or should it be a shared responsibility with academic scholars and other experts in different fields?*

Note that this issue does not refer to control over the curriculum, as such, which is the legal responsibility of lay boards of education and the educators whom they employ to administer the schools and to teach the children. Instead, it refers to the question of who is the real curriculum maker behind the scenes. Whoever controls the funds for experimentation, studies, teacher in-service education, and research will also be a powerful force behind curriculum improvements.

Conant [18] has challenged the sole authority of "the establishment," organized professional education groups and executives of state agencies, in the field of certification and teacher education. This book is a manifestation of a direction that is evident in many aspects of educational life.

The issue seems to be a real one for many school people and academic scholars who have not yet learned to respect each other's competencies.

We, as educators, are probably a decade too late in taking the lead in this movement. The leadership was assumed by others when academic groups began the work of revising obsolete curriculum content and testing out the use of approaches and new content in the schools. Thus, the issue is in a sense an academic one.

The absence of sharing of responsibility for curriculum improvement was not wholly the educator's fault, for many professors of academic disciplines had been far from interested in helping in this process.

No longer can schools afford to be without expertness wherever it can be found. Sociologists, psychologists, anthropologists, and other behavioral scientists are also needed on the team to examine school programs and study the means and possibilities for their improvement. What is it that causes community, "establishment," or institutional resistance to change? What facilitates the adoption of new ideas? How can experts in many fields cooperate to accelerate curriculum improvement?

3. *Is a national curriculum commission necessary for a nation in a period of constantly accelerating change, or should the states and local school systems, with the cooperation of independent learned and professional associations, keep the curriculum up to date?*

A national curriculum commission or academy for curriculum design and research has been proposed for serious deliberation by scholars in the field of education, notably Paul R. Hanna of Stanford University.[19] Such a commission would formulate objectives, keep up to date on changes in knowledge, suggest curriculum models, and research and abstract the most important values and generalizations needed for the nation. It would coordinate efforts of national groups. The argument is made that scholars of the kind necessary to do these tasks either are

---

[18] *The Education of American Teachers, op. cit.*
[19] Paul R. Hanna, "A National Curriculum Commission?" *NEA Journal,* 49:25–27, January, 1960, and "Structure of Knowledge: The Interrelationship of Ideas," in *The Nature of Knowledge,* Milwaukee: School of Education, University of Wisconsin-Milwaukee, 1961, pp. 68–82.

not found on local and state staffs or do not have the time nor resources with which to do the job. The proponents of such a commission feel that the lag between the findings of research and its impact on the school curriculum could be greatly reduced. They question whether state and local units can be self-sufficient in this time of greatly expanded knowledge. They also advocate a minimum set of values, skills, and knowledge.

Others feel that such a commission is a dangerous venture which might well lead to uniformity and lack of experimentation. They will have nothing to do with a national curriculum. It is interesting to note, in this regard, that Hanna does not propose a national curriculum in the sense that the courses are mandatory for the schools, but instead would leave the final choice to the community. This would be a non-governmental agency without power to enforce its recommendations. Those who argue against the proposal also point out that packaged plans available in department-store fashion would not be feasible. Moreover, they feel that a commission which could spell out minimum standards would strengthen forces in American life that tend toward uniformity. They would prefer the diversity that exists in each state and local school system, as well as in private, independent groups, in conducting the experimentation and in making the studies.

4. *Should the schools utilize external state-wide and nation-wide testing programs for evaluative and selective purposes, or should tests be internal, selected, used, and controlled by the school system?*

External tests are of various types, selected, sponsored, and controlled by agencies outside the local school system for the purposes of the agencies. They are external to evaluating the schools' own purposes. One type, already discussed, is the state examination, such as the Regents Examinations in New York State. Other external testing programs are used to select students for scholarships or for college admission, such as the National Merit Scholarship tests and the College Entrance Examination Board tests. External testing conducted by a state for whatever purpose has long been criticized for its adverse effect on the curriculum. It has tended to make the test the determiner of the objectives, and to cause undesirable comparisons of schools and teachers.

The form of external test to select students of special aptitude for college scholarships is of more recent origin. These tests have multiplied since 1950 to the extent where there are more than twenty national testing programs being administered to sort out pupils.

Some professional organizations have called attention to the dangers and abuses of these testing programs.[20] The problems, they say, lie in the use of the tests and in the coordination of the testing programs. One problem is the willingness of the public to place a blind faith in the infallibility of the tests. Schools report that the testing programs exert undue pressure on principals, especially by the public, to participate. The multiplicity of the tests takes more time and money than warranted, since it would be possible for organizations to agree on one set of standardized tests for this purpose. The results of these tests and the number of scholarships achieved by a school have also been used as a means of evaluating the school without reference to the type of community in which the school is located.

The proponents of these tests, and the sponsoring agencies, feel that the tests have helped in evaluating the college potential of students, in encouraging scholarships in secondary schools, in encouraging industries to give additional scholarships, and in discovering talented youth some of whom would otherwise have no means of getting a higher education. External testing programs can be used as a basis for immediate decisions that need to be made. It is understandable that if they affect the lives of people, they should create anxiety and draw some criticism. The results are also used for valuable research purposes.

[20] American Association of School Administrators, Council of Chief State School Officers, and National Association of Secondary-School Principals, *Testing, Testing, Testing,* Washington, D. C.: National Education Association, 1962, 32 pp.

SELECTED REFERENCES

Alcorn, Marvin D., and James M. Linley (eds.). *Issues in Curriculum Development.* New York: Harcourt, Brace & World, Inc., 1959, chaps. 1–3.
The critics of education and the forces affecting the curriculum. Selections from the literature.

American Association of School Administrators. *Private Philanthropy and Public Purposes.* Washington, D. C.: National Education Association, 1963, 43 pp.
The influence of foundations upon education and the issues involved.

American Association of School Administrators, Council of Chief State School Officers, National Association of Secondary-School Principals. *Testing, Testing, Testing.* Washington, D. C.: National Education Association, 1962, 32 pp.
Points up the problems and pressures of national testing programs on the schools and the curriculum.

American Association of School Administrators, Department of Classroom Teachers, National School Boards Association. *Who's A Good Teacher?* Washington, D. C.: National Education Association, 1961, 54 pp.
An analysis of what research says about teacher effectiveness and its evaluation.

Association for Supervision and Curriculum Development. *Leadership for Improving Instruction.* 1960 Yearbook. Washington, D. C.: National Education Association, 1960, chaps. 2 and 3.
A significant statement of the modern concept of leadership, leadership roles, and how teacher leadership is utilized in curriculum study.

Association for Supervision and Curriculum Development. *Using Current Curriculum Developments.* Washington, D. C.: National Education Association, 1963, 118 pp.
A pamphlet describing national and regional curriculum projects in the subject fields.

Association for Supervision and Curriculum Development. "Who Should Plan the Curriculum?" *Educational Leadership,* 19:4–44, October, 1961.
The part played by the teacher, the pupil, the school board, the state agencies, and citizens in curriculum planning. Reprints published by National School Public Relations Association, Washington, D. C.

Bellack, Arno A. (ed.). *Theory and Research in Teaching.* New York: Bureau of Publications, Teachers College, Columbia University, 1963, 122 pp.
Studies of teacher and pupil behavior as observed in the classroom. Has implications for the role of the teacher and for curriculum development in the classroom.

Benne, Kenneth D., and Bozidar Muntyan (eds.). *Human Relations in Curriculum Change.* New York: Holt, Rinehart and Winston, Inc., 1951, Part III, Sec. A, and selected chapters.
Principles for group discussion, growth of a group, and analysis of human relations structure. Compilation of articles on earlier research in the field.

Bennis, Warren G., Kenneth D. Benne, and Robert Chin. *The Planning of*

Change: Readings in the Applied Behavioral Sciences. New York: Holt, Rinehart and Winston, Inc., 1961, chaps. 6, 10, 12.

An enlarged and more recent compilation of readings on group dynamics and related areas, a successor to Benne and Muntyan's *Human Relations in Curriculum Change.* Information on group process and planned change.

Bradford, Leland P., and Dorothy Mial. "When Is a Group?" *Educational Leadership,* 21:147–51, December, 1963.

Suggestions for effective conditions in developing a group and its effectiveness.

Cartwright, Dorwin, and Alvin Zander (eds.). *Group Dynamics: Research and Theory.* 2nd ed. New York: Harper & Row, Publishers, 1960, chaps. 1, 3, 9, 19, 25, 34.

Research on group dynamics, including stages in development in a group, the relation of leadership practices to productivity and morale, group cohesiveness, group standards and goals, and leadership.

Cox, Roy L. "Establishing Curriculum Requirements." *Educational Leadership,* 21:171–72, 183, December, 1963.

How state legislatures, state departments of education, and other state authorities exercise control of the curriculum.

Culbertson, Jack, *et al.* "Changing the School." *Theory into Practice,* 2:249–300, December, 1963.

An examination of innovators of change and barriers to change.

Cummings, Howard H., and Helen K. Mackintosh. *Curriculum Responsibilities of State Departments of Education.* U. S. Department of Health, Education, and Welfare, Office of Education, Misc. No. 30. Washington, D. C.: Government Printing Office, 1958, 76 pp.

A survey of legal and other responsibilities that relate to the curriculum and ways state departments of education work on curriculum improvement.

Douglass, Harl R. (ed.). *The High School Curriculum.* 3rd ed. New York: The Ronald Press Co., 1964, chap. 7.

This chapter deals with participants in curriculum determination.

Ehlers, Henry, and Gordon C. Lee (eds.). *Crucial Issues in Education.* 3rd ed. New York: Holt, Rinehart and Winston, Inc., 1964, Part I.

Deals with freedom and censorship in relation to education. Presents differing viewpoints of authors on these issues.

Fraser, Dorothy M. *Current Curriculum Studies in Academic Subjects.* Washington, D. C.: National Education Association, 1962, 102 pp.

Nationally oriented curriculum projects in five academic disciplines, and principles for use of these studies.

Gorman, Alfred H. *The Leader in The Group.* New York: Bureau of Publications, Teachers College, Columbia University, 1963, 82 pp.

Discusses in behavioral terms the main elements of group process involved in curriculum development: the group, the group members, and the status leader.

Guba, Egon C., and Shirley Lipson (eds.). "Changing The School." *Theory into Practice,* 2:249–94, December, 1963.

A special issue devoted to changes in education related to the teacher and the innovators' role in change, drawn from research in the behavioral sciences. Contains rather complete reviews of more recent publications on the topic.

Hall, Darl M. *Dynamics of Group Action.* 2nd ed. Danville, Ill.: Interstate Printers and Publishers, Inc., 1960, chaps. 1, 10–12.

Written for agricultural extension agents, this book contains many practical suggestions for group process, as a type of handbook for leadership teams.

Klohr, Paul R. (ed.). "Curriculum Planning and Development." *Theory into Practice,* 1:177–236, October, 1962.

Various authors discuss newer trends and issues in national curriculum programs, the politics of curriculum change, and conditions for curriculum change.

Leese, Joseph, Kenneth Frasure, and Mauritz Johnson, Jr. *The Teacher in Curriculum Making.* New York: Harper & Row, Publishers, 1961, chaps. 1, 3, 4.

This first complete book on the teacher's role in curriculum-making furnishes a valuable reference for the student who wishes to go deeper into the subject. These chapters deal especially with the teacher as a factor in curriculum change.

Miles, Mathew B. (ed.). *Innovations in Education.* New York: Bureau of Publications, Teachers College, Columbia University, 1964, chaps. 1, 9, 12, 17, and Part III.

A collection of studies of the nature of innovation and the change process in education. Research, theory, and case studies are included.

National Society for the Study of Education. *The Dynamics of Instructional Groups.* Fifty-ninth Yearbook, Part II. Chicago: University of Chicago Press, 1960, Section II.

Specialists in group dynamics discuss the socio-psychological characteristics of classroom groups.

Passow, A. Harry (ed.). *Curriculum Crossroads.* New York: Bureau of Publications, Teachers College, Columbia University, 1962, chaps. 2 and 4.

Two authors each discuss trends and issues regarding (1) the role of the teacher in decision-making and (2) the dynamics and politics of curriculum change.

Pritzkau, P. T. *Dynamics of Curriculum Improvement.* Englewood Cliffs, N. J.: Prentice-Hall, Inc., 1959, chaps. 1 and 2.

In these chapters, and throughout the book, the student can find challenging ideas regarding the teacher's responsibilities in curriculum development in the classroom.

Smith, B. Othanel, William O. Stanley, and J. Harlan Shores. *Fundamentals of Curriculum Development.* Rev. ed. New York: Harcourt, Brace & World, Inc., 1957, chaps. 17, 20.

The process of changing the curriculum as a form of educational engineering.

Strang, Ruth M. *Group Work in Education.* New York: Harper & Row, Publishers, 1958, chaps. 1, 14.

The dynamics of groups and the evaluation of group work. Written for the classroom teacher.

Taba, Hilda. *Curriculum Development: Theory and Practice.* New York: Harcourt, Brace & World, Inc., 1962, chaps. 23 and 24.

Deals with the strategy for curriculum change and group process in curriculum study.

Zacharias, Jerrold R., Chairman, Panel on Educational Research and Development, President's Science Advisory Committee. *Innovation and Experiment in Education.* Washington, D. C.: Government Printing Office, 1964, 79 pp.

An illustration of the influence of scholars in academic fields and of deliberative committee reports on the curriculum of the schools. Discusses developments and research needed in the subject areas, teacher education, learning, and the deprived child.

II

SOURCES OF CURRICULUM DECISIONS

4

CULTURAL VALUES
AND GOALS

Study and analysis of our society and its culture furnish guides to the school's objectives, content, and learning experiences. These are primary sources of information for making decisions as to what goes into a curriculum. The society that makes intelligent decisions about the curriculum of its schools and colleges first asks: What is our culture like? What are our primary values? To what principles do we hold? For their guidelines, our decision makers must look to cultural anthropology, social psychology, and sociology, and to statesmen who have formulated expressions of the principles that govern a democratic society.

THE RELATION OF THE CULTURE TO THE CURRICULUM

The Culture as a Socializing Agent

A culture is a common pattern of values and loyalties; ways of habitual acting, feeling, and thinking; and a common set of expectations. Each society has certain beliefs and customs concerning language, religion, song, dress, ideals, folkways, mores, art, and other characteristics that make up its ways of living. A society is made up of many subcultures, for example, those found in different sections of the United States or Africa, in different parts of a city, or in rural, urban, or suburban areas. Some nations, depending on many factors, have a common culture; others, a more diverse one.

These habitual ways of acting and expecting form the basis for values and, consequently, for choices concerning what is good. In the education of its young the society uses the culture in which children grow up as a socializing agent in order that they will learn to live in that society. The culture defines the problems with which the child must deal and how he shall deal with them. In this social environment, the child learns to accept certain values which are part of his heritage. If a child is reared in a rural Midwestern community, his beliefs concerning entertainment, other religions, foreign peoples, ways of meeting conflicts, and moral principles may be quite different from those of a child who has grown up in a slum district of a large city.

The society establishes schools for this socializing purpose, but if its schools are out of tune with the changes that take place in the culture, they serve less of a useful purpose as socializing agents. If the school environment is so strange that the child cannot cope with it, or if it deals with few of the problems defined by his culture, he is influenced almost wholly by his immediate neighborhood and by his peers rather than by what the school attempts to do. One of the problems that faces a rapidly changing society is keeping what is taught in the schools up to date, in order that the school may serve as an effective agent for teaching the young how to live in that society. For primitive societies, relatively unchanging as they are, the job is easy, with little need felt for their schools to perpetuate their traditions.

Cultural Values and the School's Objectives

Thus cultural values, heritage, and mores are the bases for what the school attempts to do. The curriculum varies according to the society and its principles and objectives. The school's objectives have a social orientation. Social and moral values are exhibited through a particular kind of conduct. These socially desirable ways of behaving form the objectives of the school.

Disagreement over these objectives arises in a complex society made up of many subcultures, since all do not hold the same values or agree on the part the school should play in perpetuating the ways of the culture. Moreover, there is often dispute—or more frequently, lack of understanding—of what the ideals and principles of that society mean.

Socialization into one culture makes it more difficult to grasp what it means to be a member of another strange and different culture.

This is as true for subcultures within our own country as it is for foreign cultures. We respond to other cultures in terms of our own values: what is "right" for us, we assume, should also be good for others. If a child has learned from his culture an entirely different sense of what is right or wrong, he finds it difficult to adjust to a school that teaches ways that are alien to his life. Stress on courtesy, reading, art, and deeds of kindness to one's neighbor means little to a child from a slum who has known only belt-lashes, deprivation, filth, and curses from his fellow humans.

In the process of growing up, any child will encounter conflicts between his own provincial beliefs and those of other communities, between the teachings of his religion and the values exhibited in daily life, between the teachings of his family and the activities and mores of his peers, between the values acquired in his larger social group and those held by his own economic and social class. In order to avoid these conflicts, his parents may place him in a private school catering to special group values, usually social or religious.

The public school, however, is one of the most unique institutions established to serve all of the people. It is an institution created to perpetuate the ideals of a larger society—the moral, social, economic, and political values that are held in common by that society. As an instrument of society, the school's functions are to study the heritage of that society, develop the skills and behavior necessary to live and succeed in it, clarify the significance of social values, and improve upon the ways of putting social ideals and values into practice. As we shall see, these tasks are becoming far more difficult to perform because we no longer live on a cultural island. Some of the school's objectives have changed because a technological revolution has made many values and ways of acting outmoded. It is far from simple in such a period of dislocation as we are living today—and will be living in the forseeable future—to stabilize values and agree upon the ones for the school to teach.

Directions for Curriculum Change

In this chameleonic age, when nothing in the future is certain except change itself, the question, "Where do we go from here?" is surely a sensible one to ask in the field of curriculum. Technological and social changes and scientific discoveries create new knowledge that must be utilized to prepare for living and working in a world inconceivable to those who formed a part of the childhood culture of

many who are living today. The significant changes which have made
our world so different from that of our forefathers have made curriculum revision imperative.

Immediately, bothersome questions arise. Should we give children
the freedom to think about serious issues of modern life, or should we
establish safeguards against dangerous and disturbing questions?
What part should children play in decisions affecting them? What is
necessary to teach, beyond the basic skills? Should we teach ninth-
grade pupils about ancient history or about their environment?

These questions, or any others that emerge, need to be seen in the
perspective of the cultural and social values which undergird the objectives of the school. Other sources of the curriculum, discussed in
this Part, obviously also help to derive sounder answers than do tradition, the universals of yesteryear, or the practices of a neighboring
school system. The cultural values and mores furnish directions for
change.

The fact that these directions are not as clear as they would be in a
less complex society or in a less complex age will be pointed out in
further discussion of changing social patterns and values. Yet, the
principles or ideals which form the goals of a society are the chief
guidelines that we have.

CURRICULUM CHANGE IN AN AGE OF UNCERTAINTY

Consequences of Technological Speed-up of Change

The fact that the automobile, the airplane, radio, television, anti-
biotics, sound movies, the space satellite, the high-speed computer,
and automation of various kinds have all come into use within the
life span of a single generation makes a resounding impact. But even
harder to comprehend are some other statistics and comparisons: the
majority of the scientists that the world has ever produced are living
today; scientific data are now being stock-piled in some 50,000 scientific journals; by comparison, the world has changed more in this
century than in the entire history of man.

These changes we accept as a matter of course and adjust to them
remarkably well, considering that they represent a technological
revolution as significant as the Industrial Revolution. But adjustment
to their social consequences is difficult. Although today the resulting
dislocations and upheavals are more in the realm of cultural values
than in economics, we can take little comfort in that observation. It
is probably just as distressing and painful to see the social and moral

values that seemed enduring and unchangeable crumbling as it is to face poverty and hunger. Fears, tensions, insecurities, emotional blows cannot be confronted as realistically as physical deprivations.

The effect of radio and television, the ease of communication, the telescoping of travel distances were predictable to a certain extent, even though predictions were not always made intelligently. Society and the schools could foretell with some probability better than chance what these developments might do to mobility, transmission of information, and human relations.

The adaptations that must currently be made to a suburban and urban culture and to living with peoples of other races and countries are likewise predictable. The demands of the technological advances for new technical skills, for literacy, and for changes in social institutions and arrangements are predictable up to a point. Communication with new "next-door neighbors" of India, Europe, and Japan demands new language skills, as does computer science, with a language of its own. An economy of abundance and of overproduction must be wrestled with; specialists at least have known facts to help them make some intelligent predictions of what these phenomena mean for the future. The greater need for stress on specialization, the fantastic increase in printed materials, the explosion of knowledge, the development of Telstar—all have meaning for education. The technological advancement that goes on with jet speed today and will go on with rocket speed tomorrow is fact, not fantasy. The facts of the social sciences at least give us a better insight into what might happen in the future. It is in the area of what these technological changes do to our values, our personal beliefs, that they become more bothersome, more difficult to cope with, since they seem to challenge everything we know and stand for.

One new fact resulting from technological progress has made the social institution of war outmoded and untenable; man is now able to destroy himself. This makes the future unpredictable. It is hazardous to predict what human conditions will be in the next ten to twenty years. It is difficult to realize the full meaning of this change, or even the fact that this is a permanent change, not one that will go away.

People tend either to shut out these facts as though they did not exist or to revert to irrational, primitive behavior of other kinds. One of the disturbing behaviors is what Kluckholm has called "the retreat to the orthodox." [1] When the rug of comforting ways is pulled out from under them, people have to find something to which to cling. So

[1] Clyde Kluckholm, "Foreword," in Theodore Brameld, *Cultural Foundations of Education*, New York: Harper & Row, Publishers, 1957, pp. xii–xiii.

we witness the ultraconservative, rightist type of movement, "un-American" labelers, the "Christian" front organizations, the groups that attract those who find security in values that are obsolete, bizarre, or irrational. In a period when one can be certain only of uncertainty as to the future, it is little wonder that people seek comfort in hideaways of their own making.

The proposed solutions of "back to" the fundamentals—McGuffey readers, progressive education, harsh discipline, or the one-room school—represent a desire for an age that no longer exists. Solutions viewed out of the context of technological and cultural changes are misguided ones. For there is no turning back. In spite of the uncertainties of the future, we must move toward them.

Not all social change can be regarded as good and wholesome progress, for certainly scientific change has not meant control of our total environment, nor has it been an unmitigated blessing. Even the progress in medicine, which has diminished the waste of human life, is helping to create a most critical social problem: overpopulation. Another result of technological progress is conformity to the ways of others, especially the tendency to conformity of thought that social analysts such as Riesman have pointed out.[2] For an individual who becomes more and more a place in the assembly line, the important things in life and conversation become the monotony of his job, petty gripes, routine and sameness. He becomes less important even in his own eyes and loses his perspective and sense of purpose in life.

Preparation To Cope with Change

What then are the qualities, the attitudes, the information, and the skills needed for tomorrow that the schools should teach, if we are not sure what future changes will bring? Those who have the one and only solution for education to save the world, a solution that has definitive answers, can command a good audience, for many people long for a comforting solution of such assurance. Others prefer a more reasonable course.

If the predictors of the future are less reliable, the young person's future world becomes an unknown to be explored. However, he is faced not only with doubts because of the vanishing of age-old cultural values but with the stark reality that he may not have a future.

Another dimension needs to be considered. What are the qualities, attitudes, and skills needed for survival in case of a nuclear war, if

[2] David Riesman, et al., The Lonely Crowd, Garden City, N. Y.: Doubleday & Co., Inc., 1953, 359 pp.

there are any survivors? This is a far different problem from survival in a technological, automated age. The survivor may find himself in the most primitive of conditions, with only the knowledge stored up in his mind to guide him. The most awful part of these situations, as pictured by novelists, would not be the complete isolation of the surviving communities or the utter uselessness of many things they valued, including money in any form, but the bands of unscrupulous marauders and the screaming, insane mobs who would stampede like herds of animals through the countryside. How does one prepare youth to cope with this eventuality? What deeper meanings of survival should the schools foster? These questions may be answered by the crusader on a white charger, who will solve it for us; by the retreat to the bomb shelter of our minds; or by holding on to past practices because those are the ones we know and in which we feel secure.

Changes in technology will undoubtedly mean a need for different knowledge, skills, and insights. These will include higher level specialized skills, new skills such as those related to computer science, new knowledge in almost any field, understanding of other cultures and other peoples, proficiency in human relations, and cultural and avocational interests. But first and foremost, in preparing for an age of change, young people need to be prepared to cope with change and eventualities.

Ancestor worship, even though modern in its forms, will not do the job. One step is to rid ourselves of the idea that the old, once useful and valuable, is the best for tomorrow's conditions. Outdated concepts or restricted forms of thinking are formidable barriers. If the advancement of knowledge in any field is to be achieved, steps must be taken to find, organize, and test out new knowledge. This is a basic attitude for men and women who will teach those who will be adults of the future.

Another step is to provide young people with a means of study, analysis, and thinking. Actually this process is an intellectual discipline that can deal with varied conditions, social conflicts, tensions. The unknown then can become an adventure, an exploration that is exciting rather than frightening. There is security in one's confidence in his ability to use the process of intelligence in human, social, and scientific problems. A curriculum directed toward these goals includes a process for interpreting, questioning, preparing for, and evaluating change.

The process of interpreting, questioning, and evaluating change can help cope with the constantly shifting problems of a rapidly changing culture. This process demands objective discussion of issues, looking at ways of propagandizing, studying the methods of thought control and the techniques of argument used by demagogues, self-aggrandizers, and anyone who wants to appeal to ignorance, prejudices, gullibility, or the mob spirit rather than to the intelligent approach to solutions. Independent thinking is of premium value in a culture that values differences, but of low or negative value in a society that attempts to bend people's thinking to its own dogma. The teacher who wishes to promote independent thinking needs to have tolerance for differences in views and for idiosyncracies. In a time when it is more difficult for a person to retain than to lose his individuality, divergence from the norm needs to be encouraged.

Along with independent thought, inquiry, reinterpretation of observations, and the study of issues, one of the leads to what prepares for change is the cultivation of creativity, uniqueness, and non-conformity of thought. A non-conformist has a sort of built-in revulsion for the orthodox. Many people are somewhat afraid of the creative individual, for to be creative he must think differently, and may disturb their patterns of thinking, or upset their neat arrangements of ways of doing things. Not only teacher behavior but curriculum organization also may tend to foster conformity. Are our convictions strong enough and do we have courage enough to value creativity in its fullest sense? It means, of course, tolerating and even welcoming pupils and colleagues who differ from us and irritate us at times, but who have managed to maintain an individuality in some relations with life and with others. Our goal here is to discover methods of learning that will foster a creative and inventive mind.

THE IDEALS AND PRINCIPLES OF DEMOCRACY

The most enduring aspect of our social world is the very heart of our democratic tradition, those values that have been commonly agreed upon as principles of a democratic way of life. For purposes of this discussion, these principles are considered under four main categories: individual liberties, group welfare, source of control, and the method of solving problems. They are discussed from the standpoint of what they mean for experiences provided by the schools.

These principles are moral values, for they express a deep concern for one's fellow man and the improvement of the welfare of all. They are grounded in religious beliefs. In a real sense, these principles are guides to the school's job of character-building.

What kind of learning environment should a society that believes in democratic principles provide? What meanings do democratic principles have for school practices? How do they serve as guides to curriculum objectives and experiences? In this day of individuals placing political expediency above public welfare, of attempts to narrow the limits of freedom in order to preserve freedom, and of pressures toward "safe thinking," it becomes all the more important for teachers, school faculties, and parents to analyze the meaning of democracy for their own and their children's behavior. Each principle will be examined as a basis for evaluating practices.

Respect for the Individual and His Liberties

In a democracy the individual is of prime importance. He is not merely a robot that serves the welfare of the state. Instead, the state, as the agent of society, makes laws to protect his rights. *Each person is regarded as important, with a contribution to make to society, and worthy of having his potentialities developed to the fullest extent.* The public school in this country is tangible evidence of faith in this principle, giving every boy and girl an opportunity for an education at public expense.

Great progress has also been made in teacher–pupil relations. No longer are harsh physical disciplinary methods countenanced, except perhaps by a few parents who expect the school to make up for their own failings. The modern school is concerned with each child as an individual. Such practices as studying children's growth and adapting discipline and classroom activities to individual needs testify to teachers' belief in this principle.

There still exist, however, coercion, whiplashings more severe than the physical kind, and lack of respect for children's individualities. For example, in one classroom a teacher asked the children to tell why they did not like a particular boy in the room. In another, a teacher asked a child suffering from cleft palate if he had mush in his mouth. These are school experiences that make the deepest kind of impression upon a child's personality. Each teacher should ask himself: Do I regard every child as equally important? What do ridicule and sarcasm indicate as to my respect for children?

One way by which teachers show respect for the individual personality is through a genuine interest in the child. The teacher attempts to find out as much as possible about the child's background, home, interests, peer relations, emotional problems, and abilities. Pupils tend to respond to teachers who have regard for them as human beings, in college classes as well as in the primary grades. Only in the proper emotional atmosphere can maximum learning take place.

The principle indicates that each person is respected for what he is. Many teachers make it a point to strive for objectives that concentrate on creating respect for others. People of other countries are studied as individuals with similar feelings, likes, and hopes, not as people who are "different." The aim is to understand the other person's culture, ideals, and ways of living. Insular, provincial attitudes have no place in a twentieth-century school. Intergroup or intercultural education extends beyond the bounds of the community or nation in which the child happens to live.

Do practices that support division of pupils according to social class backgrounds show respect for the worth of each individual? Inflexible ability grouping still abounds in a great many schools. The studies of social class structure indicate that enrollment in high school "courses" or curricula, such as commercial, general, or college preparatory, is significantly related to social class position.[3] Are they in essence any different from those divisions which separate other cultural groups?

Other practices, too, need to be examined critically. How much regard for individual abilities and interests is exhibited in blanket assignments and single textbooks suited in difficulty to some but not to all pupils? Do we give each pupil an equal opportunity for success? Do we consider each child's contribution as an important one for the school society? Do we give him a chance to make such a contribution? Are children of all races accorded equal esteem?

This principle is also concerned with differences among people, in a positive sense. *In a democracy differences among people are valued.* The problem of allowing for individual differences in the curriculum has long bedeviled teachers. One of the results has been that some teachers take the attitude: "Oh, if I could only have a group of all bright youngsters." Yet, if diversity is valued, teachers have an obligation to see that differences are considered and made use of in the school curriculum.

Are differences valued when pupils are labeled or segregated according to social or racial backgrounds or according to abilities in any way that may be embarrassing to the individual? Do teachers make it known and felt that it is important that one child has abilities of one kind and another child abilities of a different sort?

While conformity to social standards and moral principles is neces-

[3] See, for example, A. B. Hollingshead, *Elmtown's Youth*, New York: John Wiley & Sons, Inc., 1949, chap. 8.

sary to group living and the development of a healthy philosophy of life, conformity in all ideas is another matter. In a democracy people welcome differences of opinion and creative thought. The astounding progress in medicine, nuclear physics, and technology, as well as in the development of our own democratic form of government, has resulted from the inventiveness of individuals who were able to depart from accepted ways of thinking. What kind of an environment is provided for such creative thought to flourish in the classroom? It is a sobering thought, but what progress would be made in education, or in any other field, if all teachers thought alike?

Valuing differences means also that children are given experiences that will increase their respect for people of other religious, national, and racial backgrounds: the laborer as well as the executive, the African as well as the European, the man who speaks a foreign language as well as the one who speaks English. Snobbishness needs no reinforcement by the public school.

In the same vein *freedom of thought and expression are guaranteed by society* in a democracy. Thought control is a characteristic of a dictatorship. Some would extend thought control into the school. Fortunately, communities have prized their heritage of freedom to think, read, speak, challenge, and differ. It takes eternal vigilance to uphold freedom and liberty. There should be sufficient opportunity to discuss current issues—local as well as national or international—so that young people can find out for themselves the issues and facts involved.

In recent years some unfortunate attempts have been made to censor collegiate newspapers staffed by young people preparing in many cases to carry on in their life work the tradition of freedom of the press. As elementary, high school, or college teachers, we should think seriously about the amount of guidance pupils need in accordance with their level of maturity. To what extent do our own fears curb pupils' opportunities to express themselves about any school policies? These are realistic problems for class study and discussion.

We can have liberty only through social arrangements. Teachers who are alert to the forces that undermine liberties, and the factors in social organization that make freedom possible, give consideration to these matters in their classes.

Responsibility for Group Welfare

A necessary corollary to rights and freedom in a democratic society is the individual's responsibility to the group. *People show concern*

for the welfare of others and for the social consequences of their acts.
Freedom becomes license unless seen in this framework. Moreover,
there is an ever widening sphere of concern for others as people grow
in their ability to understand and apply democratic principles.

Teachers are discouraged to find that some pupils, when questioned
about the meaning of democracy, are more concerned with their rights
than with their corresponding responsibilities or the rights of others.
Pupils evidence lack of concern for others by rushing through halls,
pushing and shoving in lines, and grabbing the best seats in the audi-
torium.

Yet, are there not more significant actions that show a truly profound
feeling for fellow pupils than these behaviors, which may be manifestations of adolescent exuberance and thoughtlessness? Who looks after
the new pupil even at considerable inconvenience to himself? Who
is sympathetic with the unfortunate child who may be physically ugly
and mentally dull? Who helps other pupils by giving up something
important to himself?

Teachers with understanding look for the deeper meanings behind
actions. They help pupils to evaluate the consequences of actions by
utilizing mistakes as teaching opportunities. Under the teacher's
guidance, pupils discuss their mistakes; there is a conscious attempt
to think about how their actions affect others. They talk together
about how they can help the newcomer feel welcome. They plan for
ways of serving the school. In some instances classes have adopted a
school in a foreign country or in an underprivileged community in
order to help children in that school.

Student councils are a means of service to the school. Students take
charge of hall traffic, perform lunchroom duties, escort visitors in the
school, assist in the principal's office, and undertake many tasks that
are not necessarily pleasant but are essential for the good of the
school. Service clubs in schools and colleges perform similar functions.

Perhaps some of the time-honored ideas regarding how much responsibility children can take should be examined, such as demands
that pupils always study individually or the belief that one pupil's
helping another is cheating. Which kinds of practices develop re-
ponsible, law-abiding citizens who are concerned with helping others?
Do older pupils have an opportunity to examine social issues in terms
of human welfare? Do teachers help pupils evaluate the idea that
everyone needs to look out for himself? Do they constantly attempt
to extend the sphere of concern for people outside the immediate
group to a world-wide basis? The real point is what *kinds of expe-*

riences, what kind of social setting, are provided that will accomplish the democratic goal stated in this principle.

Control from Within the Group

One of the basic tenets for which our forefathers struggled is the guarantee to all members of a society of the right to share in determining the policies and laws under which they live. In recent history, the United States has been involved in similar endeavors in various parts of the world to prevent this right from being infringed upon by countries that would exploit people. The world is again threatened by autocratic beliefs and forces that would place decisions in the hands of the few.

Most citizens in democratic communities would agree upon the goal that *persons who carry out decisions should have a part in making them.* They understand that freedom is possible only under law, but that in a democracy people affected by laws have a part in making them. Not all agree upon the means of attaining this goal through education. Some do not believe that it applies to children. They feel that, if children are required to obey their superiors, under fear and threat if necessary, they will learn to respect law and order. Consequently, the teacher should see that order is maintained at all times. Others believe that children should be taught to discipline themselves, the teacher becoming less and less the decision maker as children learn to make and carry out decisions. They are all working toward the same goal: well ordered conduct. None of them believes in disorder, confusion, disrespect of authority, or misconduct, although each would vary the degree of freedom given youngsters.

The basic issues are: How does one learn the skills of self-control and self-government? When does a person attain the maturity to participate as a responsible citizen? If the community and the school can agree through careful study on some answers to these questions or at least spend time studying them, they will probably find that their views are not too far apart after all. Even the understanding that their goals are the same would be an accomplishment in some communities where the school is accused of letting children run wild, and the school people, in turn, make no attempt to meet with parents. All would undoubtedly agree that external control is necessary to maintain law and order; they have to reach some conclusions about how they can best help children and youth learn to practice self-discipline, participate in making laws, and respect law and order.

There are many primary-grade classrooms where children help

make their own regulations, abide by them, and conduct themselves in an orderly manner because this behavior is something they have learned and want to practice. Pupils in elementary schools as well as in secondary schools have successful student government that is given responsibility for conduct of activities in halls, study halls, and the lunchroom.

Let us examine two types of school environments in the classroom. In one, the pupils sit quietly at their desks in neat rows. When a child is asked to empty the pencil sharpener, pick up waste paper, or get the dictionaries at the proper time, he responds obediently. At recess and dismissal time, the pupils stand as a group and march out in rows when they are dismissed by the teacher. A visitor's attention is called to the quiet and order in the room. The teacher obviously makes the decisions and enforces them strictly.

In another school a visitor entering the room is greeted by a pupil, shown to a seat, and told what the class is doing. At the moment he does not notice the teacher who is sitting down, working with one of the five groups meeting in different parts of the room. There is a low hum of voices in the room as the children work together, but they are orderly in their conduct, and as they move about to get materials, there is no scuffling or horseplay. Rules of conduct and rules for use of room library books, drawn up by the committees, are posted on the bulletin board. Names of the clean-up committee for the week are also listed. As the teacher finishes his particular task, he comes to the visitor and suggests that they sit down and talk. The children keep on working in groups, and when the bell rings they straighten out the chairs, pick up the paper, and walk out in an orderly manner. A great deal more freedom is, of course, evident in this room.

These are actual descriptions of classroom situations which can be found in many schools from lower grades through high school. In which of the two are the pupils learning the skills of self-government? Which children are getting practice in the kind of behavior it is hoped they will exhibit as adults? More to the point, which kind of behavior do we want children to learn? There are, of course, situations in which there is overpermissiveness, where children have too little control. Freedom does not imply lack of discipline but it is predicated upon self-discipline.

One of the ingredients necessary to apply successfully this general principle is *faith in the ability of people to make wise decisions co-operatively*. In our own society there are those who believe the more "enlightened" should make the decisions for the rest, not as responsible elected individuals but as a self-chosen elite. In cases where administrators and teachers have placed faith in pupils to run their school government affairs through the student council, their trust has been justified. Policy-making authority has been delegated to the student body. Similarly, teachers who help pupils to make increasingly mature judgments have faith in pupils' ability to improve.

Use of Intelligence for Solving Problems

It is assumed in a democracy that man has the capability of becoming educated to the point where he can govern himself. Public education has been a concern of eminent leaders throughout the history of this republic. They have recognized that an illiterate mass of people who can be easily swayed in any direction cannot successfully cope with the responsibilities placed upon them in self-government.

In other words, *a democracy utilizes facts to arrive at intelligent solutions to problems.* Ignorance is a handy tool of would-be dictators. The level of operation of a government is a fair reflection of the ability of a people to study and decide problems with understanding. Another term used to describe the procedure is the scientific method.

To what extent are pupils helped to grow in the ability to use this method? The experiences of pupils can be evaluated by examining how the method operates. In simplified form, it involves recognizing the difficulty, considering possible solutions, gathering information about various points of view and data about the problem, testing tentative solutions and evaluating results, and taking action on the best possible solution. This is a learned kind of behavior which begins in its earliest stages when the child starts to reason things out for himself.

How do class procedures meet these rather rigorous criteria? Increasing evidence shows that teachers at all levels are becoming concerned about what has been termed the problem-solving method, in which students attack a problem of importance and carry it through to a reasoned solution. The curious inconsistency of some graduate school education, where good minds should certainly be able to use reasoned procedures, is that students are expected to be thoroughly scientific in their research studies but may get no such practice whatsoever in their class experiences.

CHANGE AND DIVERSITY OF VALUES

The core values in a democratic society are expressed in the principles of democracy, all of which center on the importance of the individual. These principles are guides to the way children are considered by teachers and to the kinds of experiences planned for them. The difficulty arises from the fact that the democratic creed is not universally accepted, at least not in practice. This section deals with some of these differences, how they arise, how they relate to technological changes, and what change and diversity of values mean for the curriculum.

Changing Value Systems

Values express a person's beliefs, his ideas about what ought to be, the rules by which he lives. These values are interwoven into a network of beliefs related to feelings and experiences. When the rules of the game are stable, or simple, and easily interpreted because everyone agrees upon them, the individual feels secure in these rules. He knows what is expected of him. This condition is true of a primitive society.

On the other hand, when these rules become complex, when people no longer agree on what is good and right, the individual finds himself faced with conflicts that are difficult to resolve. It is in such a situation that teachers find themselves today. In a changing society, there are fewer common values that are agreed upon. With little agreement upon what is universal and good, it is small wonder that the teacher faces a tug-of-war in the field of education. Some people want more mathematics and science, others, a greater stress on the humanities and social sciences; some, more consideration for religious instruction, others, no mention of religion or spiritual matters; some, a return to flogging, others, more consideration for mental health.

Related to these conflicts is the changing nature of the culture, the rapid transformation in ways of living brought about by invention and scientific discovery. What are the "good old days" of hard work, frugality, and close family ties to a father may be the "old fogy days" to his son, who lives in a time of abundance, few family responsibilities, and a rush of activities and organizations competing for his time. The automobile, television, and automation of home and farm have made some of the old values no longer acceptable to youth. Working hard for what one earns has become "get it while you can" and knowing the right people. Instead of conservation and concern for resources and property, bulldozers rip down groves of trees on the countryside, and refuse accumulates along the roads. Moral commitments change to moral relativity, the tendency to get by, or the respectability of cheating the government on the income tax. These are examples of the directions of changing values, not all traceable to technical advances, but affected by the change in transportation, mobility, and concentration of population, by the impersonal mode of living, and by other significant changes in the ways of living in an automated society.

The most serious change in modern-day values is the loss of individuality, for example, in the suburban complex of supermarkets, huge discount stores, and equally impersonal "personal" services, where the person is more likely to be a number in a line waiting to be served than a well-known and valued customer. Fromm stresses this anonymity and the influence of technology toward conformity in ways of living and working.[4] It becomes difficult to retain one's individuality in a setting of mass production, mass distribution, and a stress on owning material things, where contacts with others are few. Riesman emphasizes the tendency toward conformity in suburban living, so that a person becomes "outer-directed" rather than "inner-directed."[5]

In this cultural setting, the child finds it difficult to reconcile the values held by the school or the church with those of his peers, or the values exhibited in the actions of adults as contrasted with those taught by his parents. The old values that gave his parents security no longer hold in the society in which he lives, and he must grope for the stabilizing influences. The pressures for conformity are just as severe on him, if not more so in his adolescent stage of life, as on adults. To strike out for himself and be different is risky, even if "beatnik" dress and behavior are the accepted pattern of his in-group. The behavior in itself expresses a revolt against being one of the crowd. Studies showing that no significant difference in values exists between freshmen and seniors, or that inferior students tend to hold less traditional values than superior ones, are of special concern to the teacher who wants to assist pupils in the problems arising from transition and conflict of values.

Values and Social Class

American society's pluralism of values relates not only to the social changes occurring but also to the particular social class from which the individual comes. The studies of sociologists, such as Warner, Hollingshead, Havighurst, and others, have indicated that the kind

[4] Erich Fromm, The Sane Society, New York: Holt, Rinehart and Winston, Inc., 1955, p. 15.
[5] Riesman, et al., op. cit., pp. 24–48.

of education, the length of schooling, and the kind of job that a child gets depend to a large extent on the social class of his family.[6] These authors have described typical American communities and what it means to grow up in the particular subcultures of New England, the Midwest, the deep South, or other sections of the country.

While there are some common aspects of the culture in all social classes, the lower-class, middle-class, and upper-class subcultures vary a great deal in their beliefs about manners, morality, sex, education, and other facets of life. The middle class is the dominant group that sets the pattern of values for the society, usually accepted by the upper class. Schools and the mass media perpetuate middle-class values and attitudes.

The automation of industrial and business processes, and the requirements for a higher level of skill and education in greater numbers of occupations, have had an influence on the upward mobility of lower classes and the increasing proportion of the children of lower-class families who finish school and go on to college.

There are, however, definite relationships between social-class status and education that are of concern to the teacher. The lower class does not place as great a value on education as does the middle class. Neither the motivation nor the economic means to get more than minimum education is likely to be present for a child from a lower-class home. There is a greater likelihood that the child, once he has reached the end of the compulsory school age, will get a job if he can. Or he may just quit school.

Although there is no evidence that children who are deprived of cultural opportunities are genetically less capable than other children, the children from the lower classes do not succeed as well in school and do not participate frequently in extraclass activities.[7] The curriculum is geared to the middle-class child. Top honors, prizes, school leadership positions, and out-of-class help by the teacher are more frequently given to middle-class pupils. The lower-class pupil is more likely to be in difficulty with the school because of his behavior and is less likely to be regular in attendance. Disciplinary action for

[6] W. Lloyd Warner, et al., Social Class in America, New York: Harper & Row, Publishers, 1960, 274 pp.

Robert J. Havighurst, et al., Growing Up In River City, New York: John Wiley & Sons, Inc., 1962, 189 pp.

A. B. Hollingshead, Elmtown's Youth, New York: John Wiley & Sons, Inc., 1949, 453 pp.

[7] Vernon E. Anderson and William T. Gruhn, Principles and Practices of Secondary Education, 2nd ed., New York: The Ronald Press Co., 1962, pp. 85–92.

infringement of the rules tends to be more frequently enforced against lower-class pupils, according to the findings of class-status studies.

Much of what goes on in school has little relation to the life outside of school of the youngster who roams the streets, may go hungry, may not know his father or mother, and may have no one who particularly cares what happens to him. It is not only the primary-grade readers, with their emphasis on the home that has everything, including love and affection, that have little reality for this child. The values that are taught are foreign to him.

Understanding and Examination of Values

The values held by children from lower-class homes are of great significance to the teacher who wants to get next to these children and help them to succeed. The teacher does not need to approve their behavior but he should accept children for what they are. Attempts to improve behavior of any kind will probably fail unless the barriers that already exist between teachers from a middle-class culture and children from a lower-class one are broken down through understanding of the child as a human being who needs someone's affection and assistance.

The teacher may not like aggressive behavior. But this behavior is part of the cultural expectations of the home in which the children of lower classes grow up. In lower-class homes, children are encouraged to fight for their "rights"; a "sissy" is not tolerated by the father. Cursing and rough language may be everyday conversation. The attitude of "getting by" with something is prevalent. Such practices as skipping school frequently go unpunished.

The teacher needs to reflect on what happens to the child who finds himself caught between differing values at home and at school. Certainly, no conscientious teacher sanctions such behavior. But does he understand the home backgrounds of such children and through respect for their personality help them toward more acceptable behavior? In choices expressed by pupils for sociograms, children of working-class parents are frequently named as those with whom others do not care to associate.[8] In an exposé of the lurid and horror types of comic books many children were reading in a large city, the most revealing fact was that so few community leaders knew the situation

[8] Deborah Elkins, "Some Factors Related to the Choice-Status of Ninety Eighth-Grade Children in a School Society," unpublished Ph.D. dissertation, University of Connecticut, 1955, p. 196.

existed. Most teachers come from middle-class homes and have only a vague notion of how the lower classes live.

Understanding must precede guidance toward improved ways of living. A teacher deplores the fact that some children do not seem to care whether or not they receive high marks in school or fail to do their homework. Yet the values that teachers hold concerning marks and homework are middle-class values not always recognized as important in some homes. Some studies show that there is a high degree of relationship between a teacher's liking for pupils and the pupils' intellectual achievement. Teachers also tend to like pupils whose social beliefs are similar to theirs.[9] Some of the middle-class standards are that children should be quiet, pay attention to the approval of others, and obey without question. In furthering such values, to what extent do we also encourage docile behavior? Will the submissive, compliant types of behavior that teachers like furnish the creative minds and spirit-of-the-frontier courage necessary in solving the problems which face the world today?

The whole realm of values tends to be encrusted with rigid, fixed sanctions. Granted that young people need stability of values. But values have a blockade around them, especially those which deal with prejudices, parochialism, and local issues. The trouble is that these blockades to the school's discussion of sacrosanct values does not keep them out of young people's minds. They keep popping in and disturbing those who are sincere in their ideals and moral values.

A curriculum that prepares youth to deal with change recognizes that cultural values also are in the process of change and that the resulting conflicts make examination of values a necessity. Those who would control freedom of thought make this more difficult but more necessary. To look objectively at one's own values is not easy; to avoid looking at them is.

Where values of today are not permitted to be examined freely, would it not be possible to focus on those needed for the world of tomorrow? We need to look at what an unforeseen world may demand if certain alternatives occur. The attitude some people have expressed, that they would shoot a neighbor attempting to get into their bomb shelter in the event of an attack, is shocking enough to require examination of what is happening to values in our culture and why.

The principle that values be admitted to the classroom is an important one for the teacher who believes in an open, mobile society.

9 Robert Nelson Bush, *The Teacher–Pupil Relationship*, Englewood Cliffs, N.J.: Prentice-Hall, Inc., 1954, pp. 73–74, 79.

Values cannot be treated only with sentiment. If the teacher understands how frustrating value conflicts can be for children and how many contradictions and inconsistencies there are in a changing culture, he will make it a point to see that children can express their values, examine them, and make evaluations on the basis of intelligence rather than emotion alone. This applies to values expressing prejudice, bias, and hate, as well as those which deal with conflicts pupils face.

Unless values are examined and discussed in terms of meanings, the school will leave a vacuum that for some children will go unfilled by any other social agency in their entire lives.

The school's function with regard to understanding cultural values of others, especially the culture of other societies with a different history and language, is clear. This is a priority objective in an interdependent world. The tendency is for persons in one culture to think of others as strange. The process of developing cultural sensitivity needs a deeper examination of cultural values than the surface manifestations. The day of study of wooden shoes, igloos, and nose-rings as characteristics that identify people should now be past.

GOALS FOR AMERICAN SOCIETY

The goals of our society are best identified through statements of democratic principles. These are also basic goals for many people throughout the world. Schools of the society need to interpret, analyze, and examine these ideals for their meaning in everyday life, in politics, in social policy. The school has the functions both of perpetuating the culture and of improving it. Many specific statements have been made of these ideals.

The report of the President's Commission on National Goals, which was drawn up by a distinguished group of citizens in 1960, is based on the paramount goal of the United States, set long ago, to "guard the rights of the individual, to ensure his development, and to enlarge his opportunity." [10] The statement of fifteen goals spells out for the school its task in a world of changing ways of living. Some of these are cited here in part:

All our institutions—political, social, and economic—must further enhance the dignity of the citizen, promote the maximum development of his capabilities, stimulate their responsible exercise, and widen the range and effectiveness of opportunities for individual choice. . . .

[10] President's Commission on National Goals, *Goals for Americans*, Englewood Cliffs, N. J.: Prentice-Hall, Inc., 1960, p. 1.

Vestiges of religious prejudice, handicaps to women, and, most important, discrimination on the basis of race must be recognized as morally wrong, economically wasteful, and in many respects dangerous. . . .

The degree of effective liberty available to its people should be the ultimate test for any nation. Democracy is the only means so far devised by which a nation can meet this test. To preserve and perfect the democratic process in the United States is therefore a primary goal in this as in every decade. . . .

The development of the individual and the nation demand that education at every level and in every discipline be strengthened and its effectiveness enhanced. New teaching techniques must continue to be developed. The increase in population and the growing complexity of the world add urgency.

Greater resources—private, corporate, municipal, state, and federal—must be mobilized. A higher proportion of the gross national product must be devoted to educational purposes. This is at once an investment in the individual, in the democratic process, in the growth of the economy, and in the stature of the United States. . . .

Knowledge and innovation must be advanced on every front. . . .

The economic system must be compatible with the political system. The centers of economic power should be as diffused and as balanced as possible. Too great concentrations of economic power in corporations, unions, or other organizations can lead to abuses and loss of the productive results of fair competition. Individuals should have maximum freedom in their choice of jobs, goods, and services. . . .

Technological change should be promoted and encouraged as a powerful force for advancing our economy. It should be planned for and introduced with sensitive regard for any adverse impact upon individuals. . . .

We must remedy slum conditions, reverse the process of decay in the larger cities, and relieve the necessity for low-income and minority groups to concentrate there. . . .

An important welfare objective is to learn more about the causes and methods of prevention of juvenile delinquency and family breakdown. . . .

The basic foreign policy of the United States should be the preservation of its own independence and free institutions. Our position before the world should be neither defensive nor belligerent. We should cooperate with nations whose ideals and interests are in harmony with ours. We should seek to mitigate tensions, and search for acceptable areas of accommodation with opponents. The safeguarded reduction of armaments is an essential goal. . . .

The healthiest world economy is attained when trade is at its freest. This should be our goal. . . .

We should never lose sight of our ultimate goal: to extend the opportunities for free choice and self-determination throughout the world. . . .

Since a major nuclear war would be a world catastrophe, the limitation and control of nuclear armament is imperative. Disarmament should be our ultimate goal.[11]

11 *Ibid.,* selected statements from pp. 3–19.

ISSUES AND POINTS OF VIEW

The area of cultural values and goals is one in which innumerable issues can be identified. In fact, the process of identification and clarification of issues is itself a fundamental goal of education in a democratic society. Those outlined briefly here are representative of issues that might be discussed.

1. *Will the study of the past—its traditions, values, and developments—equip a person to deal with the technological and social developments of the future, or will he need new kinds of insights and vision for which the past can no longer be a sufficient guide?*

Some question the extent to which background knowledge is useful for coping with today's or tomorrow's problems. They hold that, since the world of tomorrow is a vast unknown, since the second Industrial Revolution is creating new conditions at such a rapid pace, there is little to be gained from looking at previous solutions. The past is no longer prologue. History is an intriguing subject of value for the knowledge of man's past but not for the future.

Others claim that the careful study of the history of man's ways of dealing with change, the obstacles he has faced, and the difficulties change has created are the best guides to the future even though it cannot be predicted. Man's actions can be predicted to a certain extent. The evolutionary and historical process is not without its lessons. There will still be basic ways in which people will react to situations, even though these become more complex, more frightening.

Much of this chapter has discussed aspects of this basic issue. It is doubtful that either extreme position will hold the clue to the best answer.

2. *Should moral commitments be taught through memorizing great religious documents or stating them without comment, or will they be taught best through conditions in which behavior toward others is examined and in situations that stir feelings and loyalties?*

Whatever the Supreme Court rulings concerning aspects of the use of religious exercises or any other matters pertaining to religion and the public schools, the issue will continue to be a live one. It is equally important for parochial or private schools. There is no evidence from psychological studies that commitments, or even understanding, comes from memorizing or stating something. Children can easily verbalize the Pledge of Allegiance or the preamble to the

Constitution without seeing its significance or giving any commitment whatsoever to its principles.

A question that ought to be of greater import to teachers is whether their religious experiences in their family and place of worship have any meaning for the lives of children, for the way they act in relationships with other children in school. The emphasis becomes quite a different one if the focus is upon behavior that exhibits an acceptance of the tenets of the great religions.

3. *Should the schools be laboratories to learn values and cultural orientation, or should these be learned entirely in the home and through contacts with other institutions and children outside the school?*

This is one of the big questions regarding what the scope of the curriculum should be. Those who would limit the scope to academic learning have little regard for anything that is not purely intellectual as the domain of the school. Yet the knotty question still arises as to what agency of society then does the job for the child who at best is initiated into the folkways of society through gangs on the streets or through actions of parents who neither care for society's rules nor for their children.

The other side of the coin is the fact that the school is a laboratory—whether we like it or not—just as is the home, for learning ways of acting and thinking. The other children with whom a child associates are his "teachers" in the incidental type of learning. For the teacher, the crucial question then becomes how these improved relationships within a school classroom can be brought under focus for instructional purposes.

The problem of whether one should teach middle-class values or also look at the values held by other classes is a related one. The different dimensions of class, such as occupations, customs, possessions, relationships within a family, and their effect on beliefs, may be intellectually examined.

4. *Shall sensitivity for other cultural mores and values be inculcated by studying about these cultures, or should the process be furthered by personal contacts dealing with feelings and values?*

While this is an issue, there is a good deal of evidence to show that feelings toward others whose ways are different do not change by studying about them. They tend to be curiosities that make fascinating reading. The student exchange programs, projects which bring high-school-age youth from foreign countries to live in homes in the United States and attend school here, seem to have greater promise. A person's attitudes toward another racial, religious, or ethnic group tend to change once he has a chance to know individuals as coworkers or friends.

This is also a question of whether schools should continue to foster ethnocentric values, as in the past, or work toward universal worldwide values. The perimeter of the cultural mores needs to be determined.

5. *Should the teacher encourage divergent thinking, or is it necessary to control the thinking of the immature?*

While it would seem that there should be only one possible answer to this question, there is certainly little agreement among societies of the world or even among groups within our own society. There are fundamentalist religious sects that strictly control the thinking of the young. There are parents who send their children to certain schools so that they will only associate with "their kind," a form of thought control.

The question is not simply one of whether parents or societies should inculcate in the young the values that they hold. For a democratic society, it is much more than that. As space travel opens up new fields of exploration, and computers, new vistas for the mind, the question actually becomes one of a preservation of the open-endedness, the experimental-mindedness of democracy itself.

Unless the issue is faced squarely by the teacher in his thinking and in his classroom actions, he is likely to fall into the trap of regarding the innovator as a beatnik, especially if he deals with social systems. Then the revolutionary, the rebel in ideas, becomes someone to be feared, except as the stalwarts of the Revolutionary War period are studied in retrospect.

6. *Should the school serve the children of all the people?*

A nation that has as its objective the education of all its young people to become intelligent, participating citizens in a democratic community, of necessity looks at its goals for general education differently from one that has no such convictions. This is the all-pervading question that relates to the kind of general education needed.

What goals are we willing to accept for American education? Do we want to support the elite concept of education, where the children of the upper classes are favored, or do we believe in universal secondary education? As contrasted with 500,000 students in public secondary schools (grades 9–12) at the beginning of the century, this country in 1964–1965 had about fifteen million students in public secondary schools (grades 7–12). We are approaching the ideal of universal secondary education, with approximately 90 per cent of the youth of secondary school age now in high school. This represents a steady progression every decade, underscoring the belief of the American public in universal, free, public education.

No more challenging task has ever been faced than to attempt to put into practice the democratic principle that everyone is worthy of the optimum development of his potentialities. The noble experiment of a democratic form of government, which is predicated on the assumption that the common man can be educated to govern himself and to make decisions for himself and for the good of others, is constantly being challenged. Those who question whether the mass of people should be given an education through secondary school in order to develop their capabilities, question one of the basic principles of a democratic form of government.

5

THE LEARNER AND THE
PROCESS OF GROWING UP

One of the most fundamental tasks of curriculum development is to bring into being situations in which it is possible for a child at a particular stage of growth to learn well what he should learn. The teacher is concerned with both the process and the product of learning. In his search for curriculum improvement, he uses knowledge about learning and about the growth process. He is interested in learning theories but he is not a theorist. He must apply to the school situation, with its complexities, distractions, and problems of human relations, what the psychologist has discovered in the laboratory—if he can. He must sift out from theory and research what is good and useful for his situation.

For the most part, teachers and curriculum leaders have to depend upon general principles and empirical data from observation rather than upon precise laws of learning or upon research that relates human development in any exact manner to curriculum development. Thus, the principles discussed in this chapter are of this nature, not laws but guidelines that can give some direction to the planning of curriculum experiences.

Learning and growth principles applied to the social setting of the classroom can be utilized in curriculum improvement programs. To that end, it is more appropriate to ask pertinent questions than to arrive at definitive answers. Knowledge about children's learning processes and capacities, about their nature and development in a particular kind of culture, is open-ended. The reader can find many references in addition to the few cited for this part of the book to satisfy his curiosity.

The questions of how the pupil learns and how he grows and develops are closely allied. In fact, growth other than physical development and maturation is often used synonymously with learning. The total growth process of the individual involves developing new behavior, insights, capabilities, integrations, generalizations, and differentiations. Those phases of growth which are attributed to experience are called learning.

THE PROCESS OF LEARNING

Learning Theories

What happens when a human being learns? None of the theories that have been developed explains satisfactorily all types of learning. Faculty psychology or mental discipline is no longer an acceptable theory to psychologists but its adherents live on in the classroom. Behavioristic theories, connectionism, conditioning, reinforcement, all of which stress accretion and discrete observable elements, have recently gained in popularity through research with programmed learning. Yet, they give no satisfactory explanation for insight, organization of thought, discovery, generalization, and purposiveness. Person-centered, motive-centered theories, those that stress the process of selecting and organizing and a learning situation with forces operating in it, include Gestalt, organismic, or field theories, phenomenological theory, and psychodynamics. The discreteness of the behavioristic theory appeals to the researcher because he can study only behavior that is observable. The wholeness of the Gestalt, which takes into its field the total situation, and phenomenological theory, which seeks to understand the person from his own perceptions, are often more appealing to the practitioner who has to deal with children as total individuals with certain backgrounds and perceptions of their world.

Learning as Acquiring Facts

Learning has frequently been thought of in terms of the facts, information, and intellectual and motor skills acquired by the learner. The idea that the curriculum consists of a certain body of materials to be learned fits in with this concept. The teacher does something to the pupil. He presents material to the pupil in order to get him to learn it. Many teachers who were trained under the more mechanical explanations of the learning process, such as the stimulus–response theory of learning, and who do not understand recent developments and research in this field, still hold this concept. The assign-recite-review-test and the lecture-study-test procedures are the outgrowth of a mechanistic view of learning which emphasizes a connection between a specific stimulus and response.

However, this concept falls short of explaining the complexity of the learning process. It does not adequately account for meanings, interrelationships, attitudes, or the influence of the total learning environment and the individual's reaction to that environment—aspects of learning stressed in theories of learning such as field theory or Gestalt.

Learning as Interaction and Change of Behavior

Learning is a dynamic, creative, active process. It is an interaction between the individual and his environment, between personal and cultural forces. It is the means by which man adjusts to his environment through modification of his behavior. Thus, the process is experiencing, undergoing, or doing, and the products of learning are behavior changes. These changes are modifications in attitudes, skills, understandings, and appreciations. For example, through undergoing successful experiences in school, a child can modify an attitude of dislike for school to one of liking school. Consequently, he will behave differently in his relationships to the school. Much of school learning, however, is by indirect rather than direct experiencing; some of the experiences necessarily have to be "synthetic" in nature.

Knowledge and information are, of course, an intrinsic part of these products of learning. Facts are of little value in themselves. The intelligent person knows how to use facts as a basis for thinking in order to arrive at solutions to questions or problems. There is a great difference between being able to recite rather isolated bits of information and having the ability to use facts to reason and think independently.

Learning as Goal-Directed Activity

Psychologists describe the elements of the learning process in terms of goal-directed activity. The process involves dissatisfaction or motivation; a perception of a goal which if achieved will satisfy the individual's desires; an obstacle or problem that prevents him from achieving the goal or temporarily blocks him; a choice of alternatives and an attempt to reach the goal; and an attainment of the goal through certain types of behavior that are successful in overcoming the obstacle and reaching the goal. The successful behaviors are what is learned.

Thus, the learning process is essentially one of problem-solving. To illustrate the process we can use the example of a teacher trying to solve a problem of pupils' behavior. A teacher is motivated to help children overcome their extreme passivity in the classroom. He faces a complex problem situation in which he does not know just what to do, especially because of the school's stress on obedience and quiet. He tries a variety of solutions, many of which fail to produce desired results. Finally, he finds that giving the pupils a greater opportunity to help plan goals and to evaluate and question findings tends to make the children less passive and submissive in their behavior. This, as the successful way to solve the problem, is what he learns to do.

Pupils are seeking such goals as approval by classmates, parents, or teachers; security; or self-enhancement. These psychological goals of the pupil are not the same as the ones that teachers write into their teaching plan or unit. When a pupil is blocked by an obstacle with which he cannot cope, he learns ways to "get around" that obstacle. He also learns "unfavorable" attitudes toward it. Thus, some children learn such attitudes toward reading when they are forced to read before they are prepared through previous experiences and maturation, or when they are given books too difficult in vocabulary and concepts.

Probably most important of all is the fact that whether or not a teacher is present the child learns. The teacher's responsibility is to see that his learning is channeled in the directions consistent with the goals of the school. These directions constitute the teacher's objectives, in the form of desired behavior changes compatible with the culture in which the child lives.

The elements in the learning situation are then (1) motivation toward a goal, (2) the problem situation, (3) varied activity to solve the problem, and (4) finding a successful way to attain the goal and satisfaction of the motive. Learning involves both a process and a product.

PRINCIPLES OF LEARNING

Although research in learning has not provided precise answers as to how learning takes place in the classroom, much has been discovered that is helpful to the teacher. These principles are presented as guides for the teacher in his decision-making. Curriculum improvement programs need to raise questions as to current practices, evaluating them against a set of criteria in which are included principles of learning. The principles are applied to a particular kind of social situation in a certain culture that has its own aims for its schools.

Purposes and Motivation

In an effective learning environment, pupils are working at purposes that are real to them. Real purposes are perhaps the most important factor in a good learning situation. Motivation is a condition that comes from within the individual, stimulating him to action. If he is prompted by purpose rather than by fear of failure and disapproval, his learning will be more effective in terms of changed behavior. A sense of satisfaction in achieving purposes that one has set for himself stimulates learning.

In the classroom this principle means that pupils have a part in setting up their goals and working with the teacher in developing the purposes for learning. They are also aware of progress made toward their goals since they have had a part in determining them.

All school learning is influenced by the child's cultural motivation. *Achievement is affected by the level of aspiration set by the learner.* Are the goals realistic for the pupil? How can a teacher know in a class of 30 to 100? Realistic goal-setting is a learned behavior with which children need help.

Learning is most effective when the child is motivated by goals which are intrinsic to the learning activity. In a type of activity such as helping in a community project, there are regulations to be studied, people to be interviewed, letters to be written, and reports to be given. Pupils have decided that they want to assist the community through performing a service. They see themselves as participating responsibly in the community's civic affairs. Such an activity may initiate in a service club, in a social studies class, or in a self-contained classroom. In the process pupils come in contact with town officials and learn about community organizations. The writing, speaking, interviewing, and reading activities involved are intrinsic in the learning activity itself.

Caring for pets in the elementary school classroom, as an inherent part of the activity, involves learning about the feeding and care of animals. Children find many opportunities to write, talk, and do further reading about what they are doing.

Developing, planning, and wanting to do something give an intrinsic type of motivation to the task. External incentives, such as marks and prizes, focus on those rewards as the goal. They, in turn, become the pupils' goals. Does a challenging learning activity need any incentives planned by the teacher?

The learner overcomes frustrations, obstacles, and difficulties when he sees the goal as worthwhile. The range of difficulty of a task needs to be within the child's probability of success, not too easy nor too hard. Is this principle an argument for marks and credits upon which society has placed a great deal of value? How does one evaluate long, difficult homework assignments in terms of this principle?

The learner who recognizes the need for acquiring new ways of behaving is conditioned for learning. If pupils see no purpose in learning more or acquiring new behavior, such as improved speech, they may be satisfied to "get by" with whatever the school requires. Why should a pupil learn new ways of gaining knowledge if he has always done well with rote memorization? Who taught him, in the first place, to memorize? If he is judged as to what he knows by a test for which he can memorize, why should he do otherwise? Is the place in the curriculum where the greatest number of awards are given, the least significant to children?

Meaning and Relationships

Learning is most effective when the situation has meaning for the learner. The relationship between purpose and activity is clear to the pupil. He understands why he is doing what he is doing. He also understands the meaning of words and concepts in the materials used.

Several studies have shown that pupils in social studies classes are proficient in giving factual information but lacking in reasoning and the ability to understand relationships. Obviously, children cannot learn something effectively if they cannot understand it. Pupils can repeat by rote many things that are isolated and meaningless. For example, children reciting the imports and exports of Brazil may fail to see their implications for that country's economy. They do not understand the relation of imports to exports, nor their effect upon the life of the people. But they can repeat the items on a test. This is evidence of a low-grade form of learning.

Meanings derived from experiences by the learner depend upon the meaning he brings to the situation. The learner sees meanings in terms of the relationship of new facts to what he has already learned.

This is the heart of meaning, to relate facts and ideas to each other so that new concepts can be derived. Reflective thinking involves organizing and relating experiences. One of the major characteristics of the newer content and approach in mathematics and science is to build meanings. Sometimes the pupil must unlearn what he has already learned because new meanings concerning the universe have been discovered.

Participation and Exploration

The learner should be given an opportunity to participate actively in the learning situation. The average layman understands this principle rather well. People often say, "Experience is the best teacher." It is the only "teacher." This is just another way of saying that we learn what we think, feel, or do, a principle that is most evident in relation to the learning of skills. Studies have clearly indicated that, if we wish to change attitudes, merely telling a person to change his ways is wholly ineffective. Giving pupils an opportunity to work in new kinds of situations, associating with different kinds of persons, on the other hand, is effective in changing one's attitude toward people.

What is active participation? The child's participation does not need to be physical or overt; he can participate mentally and emotionally as well as physically.

If there is freedom to make mistakes, the child sees the classroom as a safe place to explore or test his hunches. Some teachers feel that they must give children all types of aids or "crutches" to reduce initial errors, when in fact the child will profit more from learning through his own explorations. Some refuse to let pupils arrange for community speakers for the class because they think youngsters cannot do the job well. The teacher who bustles around giving minute directions to children when they present an assembly program is depriving them of a valuable learning experience.

The discovery approach to learning can never be put effectively into practice unless freedom from threat exists in the classroom. Any threatening atmosphere is hostile to experimentation. Errors are an important part of the learning process. Children who are permitted to make mistakes and then encouraged to discuss them in class will learn to do the job better the next time. This exploratory process is a crucial element of participation. It is basic to the discovery of new knowledge. Is it not possible that this is one of the most fundamental principles of learning?

Children are more likely to enter into a project if they have helped to choose and plan it. On the other hand, they are likely to react to continual teacher direction with apathy, conformity, or more or less subtle forms of resentment. If bedlam reigns when the teacher leaves the room, one can be sure that there has been little participation by pupils in planning what and how the work is to be done. How many rooms in the school building can carry on self-propelled when the teacher leaves the room? What have pupils learned who are able to do so?

Uniqueness and Creativity

Each child is unique in his ability to learn and in his rate of learning. There is a marked difference among children in rate of learning and in retention of what is learned. In a sixth grade, for example, children may vary in achievement levels from second grade to tenth grade. Is it realistic to expect all children in the sixth grade to learn equally well from the same sixth-grade textbook? Does the idea that all pupils should be at a similar point in achievement when they enter the seventh grade accord with reality?

If the full significance of this principle were grasped, much misunderstanding concerning homogeneous groups would be cleared up. In any group, no matter how selected, there will be pupils with varying abilities and interests. Some children of high mental ability will have difficulty in making social adjustments. Pupils grouped by ability on one type of test will vary over a wide range in other abilities.

Pacing instruction according to an individual's peculiar power to learn has rarely received much attention since it has seemed impossible in a class of thirty or more. Individualized procedures make pacing a possibility. Slow pupils who can pace their learning will have an advantage over those in a large group, who fall hopelessly behind.

If carefully thought through, this principle has a great deal of meaning for developing continuity in the curriculum.

Children have unique ways of learning. Recent learning studies point out that there are sex differences in the way children learn. Also, the mentally retarded child not only differs in rate and capacity of learning but in the way he learns. The person's mode of learning differs with the way he perceives himself as a learner. Research on creativity would indicate that some persons labeled as creative have different modes of learning, seeing meanings and possibilities not readily apparent to others.

One definition of creativity is "a new way of looking at problems as contrasted with doing what is expected." From studies of creativity, the creative person has come to be characterized as one who has originality, adaptability, flexibility, non-conformity; is imaginative, inventive, more playful; has the ability to synthesize and analyze, a desire to explore the unknown, talent to produce new ideas, to do divergent thinking. Such a person undoubtedly learns differently. Rote memorization and repetition bore him and he rebels against any learning activities that have as their goal conformity to the status quo. If a creative person, as Barron believes, thrives on disorder and responds to it by constructing for himself a new arrangement out of the mess with which he is confronted, he is tackling his learning from a different perspective and in a different way.[1]

If children have their own best way of learning, do schools need to organize the day differently for different pupils? Do some need abundant time for thinking, exploring, and developing ideas?

Human potentialities for learning are limitless provided the environment for learning does not set limits. There are indications from a number of behavioral sciences that the individual's capacity for learning may go far beyond any known estimates. The "ceiling" judged for him may be only the baseboard. Even the seemingly slow, such as the spastics sometimes given up as hopeless, may be misjudged in their limits.

The feedback type of learning, well adapted to evaluating what is learned and to mass teaching, sets definite limits on the child's possibilities for exploring new vistas. So do established thought forms and uniform expectancies. Moreover, anxieties, fears, failure, and other factors discussed in these principles, help to circumscribe potentialities. The best guarantee that a child will be able to deal with difficult problems is that he has been successful in previously dealing with them. Both the teacher who controls learning too rigidly and the one who believes children "cannot learn" are also potent factors in holding back learning.

This principle would suggest that independent study, experimentation, discovery of answers for oneself, opportunity to create new forms, opportunity for self-fulfillment, are means to open up vast new expanses in learning and to extend the "frontiers." Perhaps we have not discovered enough about what leads to an inquiring mind, to curiosity. What makes some children less curious about their world as they

[1] Frank Barron, "Creative Vision and Expression," in *New Insights and the Curriculum,* 1963 Yearbook, Washington, D. C.: Association for Supervision and Curriculum Development, 1963, chap. 13.

proceed through the grades? What has happened to dull their desire to poke around in unknown places? What types of learning are designed for conformity? For flexibility? How permissive with regard to learning activities should a teacher be?

Readiness and Continuity

A child learns best when the learning tasks are adjusted to his level of maturity and his readiness to learn. Not all children are ready to read at the same age, and forcing a child to read too soon may cause severe reading handicaps that may be difficult to overcome later. Nor does it make any more psychological sense to delay a child's reading just because his age-mate is a different human being who cannot learn to read early.

Readiness for new learning of any type is a complex product of many factors—among them, psychological and physical maturity, past experiences, home background, previous mastery or experience with success.

The idea that a child in the early grades can learn more abstract concepts if presented in simple form has been demonstrated in experiments with science and mathematics principles. Readiness is a relative thing.

The idea of being mature enough to undertake new tasks is not confined to the kindergarten and the primary grades. A high school student, or even a college student, must learn responsibility if he has never been given the opportunity previously. The ability to plan and evaluate, to organize one's work, and to do independent thinking are learned types of behavior. These are the kinds of objectives that must be worked at throughout all grade levels, adjusted according to the maturity of the child. Older groups not deprived of human relationships, because of their maturity may learn new skills more rapidly.

Learning is most effective when learning materials and activities are adjusted to the maturity and background of the individual.

The learning situation should provide for continuity of experience. Only if the child is provided with previous experience that makes him ready to learn the next step can there be any real continuity for him. The studies in programmed learning show that if such continuity is furnished, and the child can pace his learning accordingly, he can learn more effectively. What influence on continuity of learning for an individual child does continuity in a course of study have? Where would the bright child be after twelve years of schooling in a field in which he is gifted, if instruction had real continuity for him?

Unity and Totality

Learning is facilitated if teachers recognize that learning has unity.
What counts is the way the learner organizes his own experiences.
What he learns must have unity for *him*, not for the teacher, for
instructional materials, or for curriculum plans. The skilled surgeon
uses all the information that he has learned and organizes it in his
own mind when he performs an operation. In a similar manner, the
child brings various types of knowledge to bear on the solution of a
problem.

There is a unity in knowledge. In a genuine problems approach,
in a seminar that explores various avenues of knowledge, or in a learning center in which young children explore and create, unity of knowledge is recognized. There is unity between old and new learning.
Pupils can transfer best to a new situation what they have learned,
when their past learning and the new situation are related through
common features. The child can discover relationships and develop
generalizations which he can apply to another problem.

*Learning is a complex process involving the individual as a total
human being.* Any sharp distinction between intellectual and emotional learning is totally unrealistic. The child brings his total personality to the school. Although the activity may be primarily intellectual, the situation for the child is not. His entire physical, emotional, social, and mental being is involved. The mathematics teacher
cannot wisely be unaware of the physical condition of the child, nor
can the physical education teacher be unaware of the child's social
and emotional development. When a teacher fails to consider a child
as a social and emotional being, he may find himself futilely using
techniques to facilitate learning while at the same time so antagonizing
and disturbing the child that he cannot possibly learn the required
tasks. What is being learned by a pupil in any classroom is undoubtedly much more complex than we have ever imagined.

*Creating a good environment for learning means taking into con-
sideration the total situation in the classroom.* No teacher can safely
disregard the pupil's attitudes toward the subject, his own attitudes
toward the pupils, and the reaction of the pupils to his personality.
They are a part of the learning environment. The teacher's relation
to the pupils, the interpersonal relations among the pupils, the procedures used by the teacher, the content studied, the general physical
environment of the classroom, and the materials provided for learning
are all significant factors in learning, more than is generally acknowl-
edged. Studies suggest that the personal liking of a pupil for his

teacher is one of the more powerful factors in bringing about an effective learning relationship between teacher and pupils. Pupils strongly influence each other's likes and dislikes, attitudes toward others, and values.

Perception and the Self Concept

The quality of experience as perceived by the pupil determines the quality of learning. An individual perceives in terms of what the situation means to him and acts in accordance with his perception. Consequently, it is important for the teacher to try to understand how the pupil sees the teaching–learning process. Two pupils will perceive it in different ways; one may see the situation as dull and meaningless and the other as a challenging, exciting experience.

Teachers need to do more listening to children than talking. They need to find out about children's feelings toward them, the school, the society, and their parents. All of these factors affect the way in which they may perceive the learning situation in the classroom. To know why children perceive things as they do helps in planning intelligently future experiences.

Learning must satisfy a need as perceived by the child if it is to be of high quality.

A child's image of himself as a learner determines his learning performance. People tend to behave consistently with their image of themselves. Recent research in the self concept indicates that children with a high conception of their mental ability perform at a higher level in school than those of equal ability but with a low estimation of their mental ability. Pupils need to feel that they are capable of performing the required school tasks. They need to feel a sense of satisfaction with themselves. What meaning does this principle have for repeated failure in school?

Underachieving children of high ability tend to underrate themselves on such items as working independently, solving problems, thinking clearly, eagerness to learn. Such studies would suggest that a person's concept of himself is a basic factor in attitudes toward school and continued learning. Perhaps helping the child to see himself as a learner or, at a higher level, as a scholar, is one of the most significant contributions of the school.

Learning Environment

The quality of group process and relationships in a classroom affects the quality of the child's learning of school tasks. Research in group dynamics has confirmed the belief that the group process is an extremely vital one for learning. The climate in the classroom must be of such a nature that children feel a part of the group, accepted by their peers. Children who are looked down upon by their classmates because of family, social class, race, religion, or nationality tend to internalize these negative evaluations of themselves. Acceptance for oneself means as much to a child as it does to an adult. When the behavior of the group does not satisfy these needs for approval and affection, undesirable learning results.

The group itself motivates learning. Children will wear certain clothing, follow certain fads, or act in certain ways because of the pressures exerted by group opinion. When the quality of group relationships is good, the group can be an influential deterrent to undesirable behavior.

Children learn from each other. The classroom group provides important conditions for learning, especially if the teacher is aware of them. Any group reinforces an individual's need to learn since he must adjust himself to the particular society in which he is living. The child finds that he needs to know certain things to be accepted by others. His curiosity is stimulated by his relations to others. It is only through the group that a child can develop to his greatest potential; he cannot do it in isolation. The group provides the "field" for optimum growth.

Learning is more effective in an environment where the teacher guides and arouses new interests and helps pupils to clarify purposes and develop insights, than in one in which the teacher uses ridicule, fear of failure, and discrimination. Threats will invariably cause a person to behave unintelligently. The use of sarcasm, threats, and fear is the trait that pupils most dislike in teachers. This behavior on the part of teachers tends to produce anxiety instead of security in pupils. Anxiety or emotional upset that comes from insecurity and failure in school is just as effective a block to learning as the death of someone close to a child. Moreover, when a person feels threatened, the range of his ideas that he considers significant narrows. He develops a tunneled vision of thought. Yet, why is threat of failure so frequently used by teachers? Is it a means to satisfy their own desire to dominate?

An environment of overstrict discipline is associated with shyness, acquiescence, and conformity. Emphasis on individuality is incompatible with restrictive discipline. Parents cannot have both. Which traits does the typical teacher strive for? Contrast this atmosphere with one in which learning is an exciting adventure for children, where children are liked and respected.

Although the pattern of pupil–teacher relationships is unique for each child, teachers who know their pupils well, understand their interests, sympathize with their problems, and are in agreement with their purposes, have more effective relations with their pupils. The kind of teacher who produces a feeling of security on the part of the pupil helps the pupil to understand himself.

Learning is stimulated best in a rich environment. Not only is a material environment that offers many kinds of learning aids stimulating, but a rich environment also means one in which people are interested in books and learning. The depressing effect of homes that do not care is well known to teachers.

Reward and Punishment—Success and Failure

Reinforcement in learning should follow immediately the desired behavior and be clearly related to it.

Learning proceeds best when the individual can see results and is aware of his own progress.

Repetitive practice for learning skills should have meaning for the learner and should include some new elements in successive experiences. These three principles relate to reinforcement of learning. They can be seen operating in programmed learning, in which learning is reinforced immediately by knowledge of progress and in which small learning increments may involve repetition and the introduction of a new element as a sequentially higher step in learning.

They apply also to other types of situations. Repetition is necessary, but sheer repetition without improvement or knowledge of improvement is wasteful. Much meaningless drill might be eliminated as an inefficient learning procedure. Filling in forms in workbooks is a case in point.

Behaviors which are rewarded, from which the pupil receives satisfaction, are likely to recur. Much research shows reward is superior to punishment as an incentive for learning. Perceptual learning experiments show that subjects see or hear rewarded images but do not see the punished ones. Punishment is not an effective incentive to learning; yet there are many subtle forms of punishment, such as giving failing marks, assigning extra school tasks, and ignoring particular children.

The most highly documented learning principle is that cumulative success provides a far more effective learning situation than cumulative failure. Failure in terms of mistakes that can be corrected is not eroding, but constant failure produces a boy or girl with a poor image of himself who may turn against society and school, so that he becomes a rebel and a candidate for delinquency because of his frustration.

Success in a learning task motivates the learner to succeed in solving other, more difficult problems. In fact, for learning (of any permanency) to take place, the learner must get satisfaction from carrying on the desired behavior.

Is the fact that satisfaction from learning is its best reward applied extensively in classrooms? Who fails in the teacher–pupil relationship when the pupil fails to learn?

Theoretically, in programmed learning there is no failure in the sense that teachers have conceived of it, for the pupil learns a step before he goes on to the next one. What does this do to the concepts of testing? To the basis for determining marks? Are we wedded to the idea that pupils should necessarily fail to understand a certain number of items? Could instruction in elementary and secondary schools adapt to a genuine implementation of individual progress?

PRINCIPLES OF GROWTH

The literature in education and psychology is replete with information about the physical, emotional, social, and intellectual growth characteristics of children at various age levels, and is useful to the teacher in determining what experiences are most suitable to children at specific ages. There is also a great deal of helpful information on the psychological needs of children. In this chapter, selected principles are discussed in terms of their meaning for curriculum. No attempt is made to include the broad gamut of information about the child's and adolescent's growth and development.

The nature and development of the child are of themselves no single index of what the content and experiences of the school should be. Taken as a whole, they are a formidable guide to the child's experiences as he progresses through the various stages of his growth. They are clues to his worries, his needs, and his problems. If disregarded, the curriculum might be barren soil indeed on which to foster a child's growth.

Principles of growth and development become of even greater importance at a time when knowledge about human development is given less consideration because of the hurried scramble for academic achievement.

Unity and Continuity of Growth

Growth is a total, unified process. The child grows as an entity. He is not a mental, physical, or social human being at different times.

Longitudinal studies of the growth of individual children show there is a rather close relationship among the different types of growth. In cases where there is a lack of unity, the child tends to have problems of adjustment. Under conditions of deprivation children fail to realize their growth potential. In a rich environment, the child tends to select what he needs for his own growth pattern. In other words, the normal process of growth is unity. It is of a steady, stable, and continuous type.

The interrelationship of growth has special significance for the teacher. The child has to be dealt with as a whole human being rather than separated into parts. The child may become physically ill because of an emotional disturbance. In turn, physical growth can affect his emotional stability. The overly fat, overly tall, or pint-sized individual may develop compensating behavior that makes him a less effective individual. A girl who may be left out of games or parties because of being fat and homely grows aggressive, hostile, or shy. Social contacts are essential to normal development.

The notion of "brains vs. brawn" is a fallacy. Intelligent children tend to be well developed physically, have good emotional adjustment, and relate well to people.

There is no such thing as dealing only with intellectual growth in school. If the pupil's relations to his peers, his family, and his body, and his concept about himself are disregarded, achievement may be seriously impeded.

Growth is continuous and gradual, though irregular. A child in a favorable environment grows in a fairly orderly, sequential process. This continuous development applies to social and emotional growth as well as to physical and mental growth.

Growth may be uneven or irregular as a child progresses to adulthood. There will be plateaus when no progress is made. The most rapid mental growth occurs during infancy and early childhood. The age of puberty is accompanied by a spurt in physical growth. The development from screaming and tantrums to more subtle emotional reactions occurs gradually unless it is delayed by the child's environment. Development from a self-centered to a socially conscious being also follows a sequential pattern depending on the culture in which the child lives. Any severe setback in growth over long periods of time, however, spells difficulty.

Orderly growth has meaning for sequential development of the curriculum within the range of accomplishment of the individual, not the group. The precocious child, or the boy who is large for his age and awkward, but expected to behave like other boys of his size, are the more obvious examples of why group norms can have only general meanings for the curriculum.

Growth, while continuous, goes through stages; each stage of growth is recognized as a significant part of the life of the individual. Certain kinds of characteristics can be described for children of various ages. These are stages of growth through which the child passes in his process of development. Thus, a ten-year-old can be described as having good control of motor muscles, enjoying life, and not being overanxious; as being concerned with the specific and concrete, enjoying his family, and making friends easily. Or one can say that at twelve years of age a girl usually enters into the age of puberty.

Age characteristics are generalizations describing stages of growth that will be helpful in planning strenuous or light physical activities, intellectual activities suitable to the age, or social activities. They do not, however, occur on schedule. Children do not achieve a certain stage at the same time.

If growth is a continuous, unified process which cannot be pushed beyond the limits of the pattern of maturation, then a logical principle is to perceive each stage of the child's growth as significant in and of itself. The child lives in the present and needs to develop the skills, concepts, and attitudes that will assist him in living his life most successfully at his particular age. Teachers who realize that children at a certain age are likely to be uncooperative and rebellious will evaluate this behavior differently from others who have little or no knowledge of child development. The former teachers will not wish these children were different. Life is just as important for the seven-year-old as it is for the adult. What justification is there for having the child learn to do something only for the future, and completely disregarding his present life problems? Should the pupil's environment be a topic for study? Do we really accept children as individual human beings of importance if we disregard their own world? The world looks different from the vantage point of feet!

Uniqueness of Growth

Every child is a unique, rare human being with his own pattern of growth. In addition to being continuous and unified, growth is a highly individual matter. An "average child" is a misnomer. Even the use of generalized terms such as "slow learners," "gifted," "mentally retarded" hides the great variety of differences found among children. An individual child is himself, not a generalization. He has a certain pattern of growth that can be determined through measuring height, weight, ossification of bones in the wrist and hand, number of permanent teeth, strength of grip, and mental age over a period of time.

Children vary greatly in rate of growth, a range that is increased by good teaching. Part of the pattern of growth is the rate at which it proceeds. No two children are alike. They are not born alike, but their cultural heritage and their school experiences sharpen the differences.

Some children of seven are taller than others of eleven. Many at age twelve weigh more than others at age seventeen. There are well-known differences between the sexes in the rate at which they mature physically. In a group of some twenty-five six-year-olds, the range of achievement in the fundamentals is likely to be four years. In a group of twelve-year-olds the range is almost twice as great. Boys differ from girls not only in physical growth but in other ways as well. Four times as many boys as girls are non-readers, more boys than girls are underachievers, more boys have functional speech disorders such as stuttering, for example.

Good instruction increases differences in achievement. Outstanding pupils forge ahead to increase the span if they are given the help and encouragement to do so. Inversely, a narrowing of the range of differences is one clue to poor teaching. "Bringing all pupils up to the standard" is then a concept of mediocrity, not of quality. What does this evidence mean for traditional concepts of minimum standards?

Attempting to accelerate the rate of growth results in abnormal behavior. How the pattern of growth unfolds depends upon how nourishing an emotional, physical, and intellectual environment the child has. It cannot be forced without causing problems. Just as children cannot be pushed into learning to walk before they are ready to do so, they cannot be forced to learn other behavior beyond their development. Instead of producing early learning, such a strain results in frustrations, tensions, and aggressive types of behavior. Case studies of normal children without disabilities attest strikingly to that fact. How should today's emphasis on heavy assignments, competition for college admission, and "pushing" children be evaluated in terms of this principle of growth?

The three above principles taken together lead to one inevitable fact concerning the curriculum. Mass production methods based on grade standards inevitably conceal differences and do not stimulate individual children to optimum learning. The curriculum must have continuity for the individual. No other fact regarding behavior stands out as starkly, yet none has been more consistently ignored in instruction.

Developmental Tasks and Needs

Each child faces certain developmental tasks which he must learn to perform satisfactorily if he is going to meet his needs. These are tasks that the child must learn to do in order to make proper adjustments to his social group. Children face them as a natural course of their growing up. They include:

1. Achieving an appropriate dependence–independence pattern
2. Achieving an appropriate giving–receiving pattern of affection
3. Relating to changing social groups
4. Developing a conscience
5. Learning one's psycho-socio-biological sex role
6. Accepting and adjusting to a changing body
7. Managing a changing body and learning new motor patterns
8. Learning to understand and control the physical world
9. Developing an appropriate symbol system and conceptual abilities
10. Relating oneself to the cosmos.[2]

Each of these tasks may serve as a guide to centers of interest or problems in the curriculum. For example, learning to relate oneself to changing social groups is a developmental task of early childhood, and suggests types of social activities to plan for young children. If the school ignores developmental problems of sibling rivalry or striving for independence from the family, the child's success in school tasks may be affected. Children need to face these conflicts.

Such a classification should be helpful in planning learning experiences for pupils at different stages of growth. The teacher needs to go beyond planning for the group, recognizing that *each child's* own stage of growth and his background of experience determine which developmental tasks are important for him. For example, a child who has not learned how to get along with other children will have more difficulty in developing other essential skills and understanding

[2] Adapted from Association for Supervision and Curriculum Development, *Fostering Mental Health in Our Schools*, 1950 Yearbook, Washington, D. C.: National Education Association, 1950, pp. 84–87. In this reference, each task is traced for the periods of infancy, early childhood, late childhood, early adolescence, and late adolescence.

than a child in the same group who has already made that adjustment. The emotional conflicts resulting from possible teacher and parent expectancies will tend to block other learning.

These tasks are culturally oriented. They are not the same for the Negro, the Chinese, the child from a wealthy suburban area, or the Puerto Rican child; they are not the same for the child growing up in one of the new African nations.

The child will attempt to satisfy his basic needs and concerns in ways either socially approved or disapproved, through whatever means he finds available in his environment. There are a number of classifications of needs and studies of children's and youth's concerns and problems. Needs of children have been considered psychological needs, such as the needs for belonging, for security, for success, for love and affection, and for recognition; or as social needs determined by cultural factors, such as needs for making adjustments to different school groups, for selecting a vocation, for developing skills in conversation, and for attaining good health; or as purely physical needs.

Needs grow out of interaction between the personality of the individual and the demands of the culture. Teen-agers may want to become economically independent, but society imposes certain restrictions in the way of compulsory education and limited job opportunities. The concerns of children and youth deal with morals, finances, sex, getting along with others, getting along with their family, and making friends.

Whether or not teachers give consideration to needs, the child will still spend time working at his concerns and will endeavor to satisfy his needs through whatever means he can. He may meet them in ways that are not socially approved. Needs must be satisfied in ways acceptable to the child and to the culture in which he lives if he is going to develop a healthy personality.

Depriving the child of love, for example, can cause children to feel inadequate, warp their personalities, and create potential delinquents. A child who does not experience affection in early life may become an emotionally handicapped individual. The needs for security, success, and approval are essential to good mental health. Those who live emotionally starved lives cannot function effectively in human relations with others. Such deprivation has far greater effect on learning than most teachers assume.

The child needs to develop an adequate concept of self. Since the individual will act in terms of how he sees himself as a person, the feelings and ideas that children have about themselves, their estimate of their own worth, their ways of relating to other people, are governors of behavior. The child strives for self-realization, "to be somebody." These meanings about himself determine how he sees a situation.

The child who finds himself in an unreal world of "school," who is told again and again that he is a failure, who finds the handicaps of his cultural background too burdensome, soon develops a poor concept of self. Constant failure tells him that he is a failure, whether it be in academic assignments or in unsatisfactory relations with his peers. Teachers who understand child development try to find tasks at which a pupil can succeed. This, again, is one of the fundamental concepts of attention to individual differences. In what ways does the school give young people a chance to view themselves objectively?

Problems of Growing Up

In the process of growing up, children exhibit behavior problems that are caused by their previous experiences and the present social situation. In the process of meeting their needs, pupils come up against many frustrations resulting from differing standards of their peer group and adults. They are disturbed by the differences they see between the moral principles taught by their religion and the actual behavior of adults. They are sometimes treated as a child but expected to behave like an adult. Making adjustments to physical changes in the body at puberty is not easy. Behavior problems all have causes, many resulting from confusion of standards and consequent frustrations. Children are not just "naughty," or "bad," or "delinquent" because they want to be, as some teachers and parents seem to assume.

School experiences may tend to aggravate the causes of undesirable behavior. Children may steal. They may destroy school property. Or they may fight, skip school, or lie. It is not enough to condemn and punish this kind of behavior. Puritanical shock does nothing to alleviate the cause. Teachers are not psychiatrists, but with specialists' help if necessary, they must get at the cause of the behavior. The question is, how did the child get that way? Causes are not simple; they are always multiple.

There is evidence to show that teachers work more positively with children and seek behavior causes when they participate in child study.[3]

Some kinds of behavior are normal for children although not pleasing to adults. Many teachers are annoyed by behavior which may be

[3] Richard M. Brandt and Hugh V. Perkins, *Research Evaluating a Child Study Program*, Monograph of the Society for Research in Child Development, Inc., Vol. 21, Serial No. 62, No. 1, Lafayette, Ind.: Purdue University, 1956, pp. 77–93.

normal for children. Studies indicate that teachers tend to be more concerned with pupils who exhibit aggressive behavior than with those who are shy and retiring. Yet it is the latter child who is the more serious problem. The former is making more successful attempts to adjust to his environment. A group of elementary school teachers, for example, was annoyed most of all by behavior that violated the teachers' personal standards or challenged them as leaders or disciplinarians. Lack of completion of assignments, stealing, cheating, inattention, vocal aggression, careless work, and destructiveness headed the list.[4] Such behaviors usually are not deep-seated emotional disturbances. Is this because aggressive behavior constitutes a challenge?

The classroom in which absolute quiet is demanded is not a place where a child can grow up normally. Children use the classroom situation for social experimentation. It is normal for them to be noisy at times in their loyalty to their peers. At times they show aggressiveness and exhibit anxieties, fears, and insecurities. Aggression against treatment received from playmates outside of school or in the home may crop up in the classroom. To be unaware of these manifestations is to be psychologically naive.

The teacher who understands the roots of such behavior will consciously plan classroom experiences that legitimately allow children to conduct social experiments in learning how to get along with others. Group work and opportunities to work and play together with children of both sexes offer that type of an experience.

Children internalize the culture in which they grow up. Every child is a part of his culture, his family, his social group, his neighborhood, and his nation. His tastes, his religion, his dress, his attitude toward school, his conversation are all part of him, learned from his culture. He may value courtesy, success, money, independence, living for today, getting by, physical prowess, a square meal, or respectability, depending on the kind of neighborhood in which he grew up. Constant bickering, quarreling, infidelity may be his environment in a wealthy or a poor home. The way he talks and acts has become a part of him, which is accepted among his peers.

The school's task is one of understanding, correcting, substituting, facilitating acquired behavior. It is never an easy one. Wherever the cultural background is ignored, where children are not accepted but merely blamed for what they are, the school becomes something of little influence in the child's life. Its teachings are something apart

---

[4] Louis Kaplan, "The Annoyances of Elementary School Teachers," *Journal of Educational Research*, 45:649–65, May, 1952.

from living. Children either dawdle away time and become "under-achievers" because there is no challenge, or they wait for the day when they will be old enough to drop out of school and go to work.

ISSUES AND POINTS OF VIEW

Since principles of learning and growth have a social orientation, so do the issues and the controversies in this field. Those discussed here are the more practical types of questions of interest to the teacher and the curriculum worker.

1. *Should the school be concerned with academic learning only, or with the broad range of behavior necessary for living and working in a particular society?*

Some hold that the school's business is to teach the fundamental skills and disciplines. Attitudes, morals, character development, and emotional adjustment problems are the responsibility of the home, the church, boys' and girls' clubs, and other agencies of society. With all that has to be learned in the modern world, the school needs to be concerned exclusively with the intellectual growth of the child. Teaching is something done to the individual to get him to learn the facts, information, and skills needed to carry on intellectual activities. Laws of learning dealing with reward, punishment, forgetting, repetition, and spacing learning, discovered under laboratory conditions, help teachers most in what to do to pupils to get them to learn. Given the proper incentives, the child will be motivated to learn. Those who cannot learn should be dropped from school or put into vocational schools. This is what some rather vocal people seem to be saying.

Others believe that learning is a package in which are wrapped together the child's mental, physical, social, and emotional development. Thus, intellectual growth is only one fundamental concern of education since the child brings his worries, physical disabilities, and social deprivations with him to school. This is obviously the point of view taken in this book. There is enough evidence from learning and growth studies and from studies of learning disabilities to show that emotional blocks confound the teacher as well as the physician. Whether or not the school wants to be concerned with adjustment problems and physical and mental health, it has to be if the highest potential for achievement is to be reached.

2. *Are adolescent problems and children's present felt needs of concern for the curriculum, or are they of interest only to guidance workers and other specialists who deal with mental health?*

Studies of adolescent problems have found that young people are concerned about making new friends, being popular, wanting more self-confidence, securing more sex information, getting along with their families, and other personal–social problems. Young people of any age have concerns of their own. All have basic psychological needs for security, approval, success. These are all of importance for curriculum planning for they give important clues to what should be studied. According to one point of view, the problems of children should in and of themselves be content to be studied.

Others look with some scorn on that point of view. They speak condescendingly of the study of dating, boy–girl relationships, and the like, as "soft pedagogy" or "progressive." Much of this criticism is at the level of name-calling. However, others with a more scientific and objective viewpoint question the fact that security, love, creativity, have too much meaning in terms of the curriculum. These are abstractions that cannot be defined specifically, nor consequently can they be observed in order to relate these attributes directly to success in learning school tasks. They believe that such psychological needs may be useful to the pupil personnel worker who deals with mental health. Some believe, too, that pupil problems are of concern only to guidance workers. The teacher's job is to teach; he cannot also be a mental health specialist and should leave such concerns to those who have that specialty.

3. *What is the value of child study?*

The evidence indicates that teachers who have engaged in child study are more sensitive to underlying causes of behavior, have greater scientific knowledge about human development, show less negative behavior in handling discipline, improve in their human relations, are more cognizant of developmental tasks of children, and are more democratic in their relations with children.[5] Although teachers treat children differently after studying children scientifically, there is no strong indication that they make more curriculum adaptations to take care of individual differences especially as far as content, pacing, and materials are concerned.

Where does child study fit into current trends in curriculum improvement? Is it declining in importance? One needs to understand that child study as interpreted here is a scientific study of children's behavior to arrive at sound judgments about the causes of a child's behavior. Prescott describes such a procedure.[6] The sentimental kind

---

[5] Brandt and Perkins, *op. cit.*, pp. 23–90.
[6] Daniel A. Prescott, *The Child in the Educative Process*, New York: McGraw-Hill Book Co., 1957, pp. 447–81.

of approach which speaks of the whole child and love of children but with no depth of understanding has done more to set back any child-centered type of curriculum than to promote it. To the behavioral scientist or the scholar in the academic disciplines it represents slovenly thinking.

The more serious question concerns the future of the scientific study of children, whether it be through a case study approach or through research with children. Some believe that child study has suffered a severe setback because of the current emphasis on harder study, difficult subjects, and homework.

If mental hygienists and child study specialists are not listened to as much today as a decade ago, it may be that their voices simply have not been heard. The principles of human development have a great deal to say about forcing children to learn, about "overachieving" (an impossible term), and about some balance in a child's life activities. Important data could be gathered from the school setting to show the relationships between pressures of all kinds and mental health. Moreover, a negative approach will not do the job. Merely to criticize, without a positive program that is predicated on the current conditions, is not enough.

There is much in the current curriculum trends described in this book that indicates an excitement for learning and reveals a new kind of concern for the deviant child and for individual differences. If child study programs can adapt themselves, as all children have to do, to a modern environment, to the vastly changed circumstances under which we are living, no doubt they will continue to make a strong contribution to curriculum improvement.

6

KNOWLEDGE AND ITS NATURE

One of the seemingly obvious sources of the curriculum is the knowledge that man has accumulated, stored, and organized. The simple answer to what should be taught in the schools is what man knows. But the question is a complex, not a simple one. Knowledge in this period of history grows comparatively at a phenomenal rate; it will double in the period between 1960 and 1967. Concepts known as "laws" become obsolete before the child grows up. Some basis has to be used for deciding what knowledge should be taught to school-age children in the midst of the rapid changes coming about through advances in technology, discussed in Chapter 4.

Philosophers have pointed out that man knows "by way of truth and by way of beauty." Imagination and creativeness add to factual information, another dimension of the ways of knowing. Thus, what have become known as the fine and practical arts are important parts of man's knowing about himself and his world.

From this vast storehouse of knowledge that becomes more advanced and specialized every day, the curriculum maker must select what is most pertinent, most useful, and most enlightening and satisfying for children and adults to know in a certain culture and at a certain time. He must answer such questions as: What knowledge may be out of date within a decade or less? What should be taught by the home, by the church, by the marketplace, or by the school? What can be understood by children in different stages of development? Of what intellectual, cultural, and aesthetic value is the knowledge? What information, skills, and appreciations make a person a more competent citizen, a better neighbor, and an interesting person? What skills and competencies of a specialized nature are needed for the present-day world?

This chapter deals with the principles, concepts, and questions governing selection of what is to be taught, viewed in their more recent context of the nature and structure of knowledge.

THE OBSOLESCENCE OF CURRICULUM CONTENT

The Lag in Changes in Curriculum Content

One of the more difficult concepts to grasp about knowledge is that it is constantly changing. Partially this difficulty arises from the fact that knowledge in school subjects has been rather stable until recent years. Teachers could use textbooks published several years previously with some security in the fact that the basic facts had not changed. Knowledge tended to be regarded as something contained or stored in the brain for future use, as one would store knowledge in a computer, available for use at any time as needed. However, now scientists say that knowledge in science taught to the college graduate in 1965 is likely to be largely out-dated by 1975.

Then there are the psychological factors involved in admitting that what one has learned may no longer be true, especially if at least four years or more of college or university were devoted to learning what one was expected to teach in the school. This built-in type of psychological resistance to recognition of the weaknesses in one's learning has held back the needed revision of textbooks until recent years. Whether the promising revisions themselves become crystallized in a few years remains to be seen.

A typical example is found in the field of language. Although those scholars who have studied the subject scientifically have known for a long time that language changes and that rules governing grammatical usage are a relative matter, the textbooks used by English and other language teachers have in the past not given evidence of this knowledge. Thus, rules for the use of "shall" and "will" appeared in grammar textbooks long after the distinction in usage had ceased to exist among educated people.

Proliferation of Information

The explosion in knowledge has, however, referred even more to the proliferation of information brought on by new ideas, new concepts, new inventions, and an accelerating rate of research. Offshoots of older fields of knowledge, such as biostatistics, biochemistry, microbiology, fluid dynamics, space science, probability statistics, aeronautical engineering; the different specialties of medicine; computer science; social psychology; and African languages, Russian history and literature, have appeared on the scene in scholarly studies and courses in universities and colleges. Each has a growing amount of research and literature connected with it.

The applied branches of knowledge such as education, medicine, and other professions have all become more highly specialized, often in the face of resistance from the general public. In addition to the teacher, who in the early twentieth-century one-room school was the only person employed by the school board and was a combination of teacher-janitor-administrator, school districts now employ superintendents, principals, supervisors, counselors, school nurses, social workers, school doctors, school psychologists, attendance workers, visiting teachers, speech correctionists, the different specialists among teachers and supervisors, plus those from other specialties connected with running a school. Colleges and universities have planned programs preparing for each of these specialties. Each one—even the custodial services—has built up its share of techniques and information.

The explosion of knowledge is greater in its impact upon people than the explosion of population. In fact, the two are related. As knowledge about medicine, hygiene, and raising crops spreads into more areas of the world, the population that survives disease, hunger, and physical handicaps increases. This seepage of knowledge into areas where people have lived in more primitive fashion creates new knowledge, records new languages, new literature, music, art forms. More becomes known and written about areas of the world about which schools in other countries were little concerned in the past except for the study of geography.

Storage and Retrieval Problems

With more recorded knowledge from increased research, new fields, and new areas of the world, the problem of storage and retrieval of knowledge becomes a gigantic one. Many more statements, articles, and reports are preserved than ever before; even some of the more fleeting, such as conference reports, are duplicated and distributed in vast quantities. School systems contribute to these materials with increased numbers of curriculum bulletins. Libraries as storehouses have begun to bulge at the seams or find it an impossible task to keep up with all scientific knowledge. In the field of chemistry, for example, the Chemical Society's Chemical Abstract Service abstracted in 1960 some 150,000 articles and patents.

The technology of information, storage, and retrieval has developed as a phase of computer science to alleviate this problem. In fact, the matter of storing, retrieving, and transmitting knowledge is undergoing a revolution of its own. A librarian, almost overnight, needs to be a specialist in data processing as well as a specialist in all kinds of communication and storage media, such as magnetic tape, microfilm, and media that may be unknown at this writing but will undoubtedly be in use a few years hence. The whole process of managing and making accessible man's burgeoning knowledge becomes in itself a new field of knowledge!

Impact on Curriculum Development

The phrase "conventional wisdom" is an apt one that applies to trying to solve current problems by yesterday's truths, no longer true. A cultural lag can no longer be tolerated in a technological age. "We are now, by our new technology, compelled to live a century or more ahead of our established models of perception and judgment." [1]

Thus, it would appear obvious that curriculum content is not a frozen, static thing. It is and will be in the future in a changing, fluid state. This is surely one of the potent reasons for constant curriculum study. It is also one of the complexities that make selection of "the best" content a continuously more difficult task.

THE STRUCTURE OF DISCIPLINES

The interest of scholars in academic fields in the curriculum of the public school has led them into study of the nature of their own discipline and how it might best be communicated. Not all disciplines can clearly define or agree upon the structure of their field, but the inquiry of scholars into this topic has promise for the organization and teaching of school subjects.

Meaning of a Discipline

A discipline is usually regarded as a way of knowing, of learning, and of discovering knowledge. It is thought of as having a domain,

[1] Marshall McLuhan, "We Need a New Picture of Knowledge," chap. 3 in *New Insights and the Curriculum*, 1963 Yearbook, Washington, D. C.: The Association for Supervision and Curriculum Development, 1963, p. 63.

a history, and a set of rules of inquiry. Many will express, in simpler form, the learning of a discipline as a way of learning how a chemist or a mathematician or an historian thinks. The rules or methods of inquiry are the most significant features and vary for the different disciplines. Thus, how one studies a language or a scientific field such as anthropology; or a laboratory science such as chemistry; or the field of literature, in order to create new knowledge in each of these fields, is vastly different.

Broudy has classified groupings of disciplines by their role in knowledge. The bodies of knowledge which he includes are as follows:

1. Those that serve as tools of thinking, communication and learning. (i.e. language)
2. Those that systematize the facts about the world. (i.e. physics)
3. Those that show cultural development. (i.e. history)
4. Those that deal with future problems, or regulate activities of the social order, or guide dissemination of knowledge. (i.e. agriculture, economics, education)
5. Those that create syntheses or schemes of value. (i.e. philosophy) [2]

Each of these has its own unique type of structure. There is a wide range of knowledge that would fall under each of these classifications.

New Approach to Looking At a Discipline

The current interest of scholars in the nature and structure of their disciplines is new and quite different. It is not the stereotyped subject-centered approach. In fact, thoughtful scholars today reject as vehemently the idea of a curriculum based on isolated and insignificant bits of knowledge as did those who championed the cause of progressive education in the 1930's.

Nor can this new approach be used by teachers as an excuse for lesson-hearing, rote memory, or use of sterile, outmoded subject matter. For if there is one thing that scholars of different fields agree upon, it is that learning should be made exciting and that anyone who wishes to keep up with his field needs to be constantly learning. Teachers who wish to continue in their practices cannot look toward the scholars for any sympathy for mastering content that is handed down in "Moses fashion" from Mt. Sinai. Much of the current inter-

[2] Harry S. Broudy, "To Regain Educational Leadership," *Studies in Philosophy and Education*, 11:152–54, Spring, 1962.

est in the structure of the disciplines stems from a reaction against lifeless, passive learning, in favor of a view of a student as learning a mode of inquiry and a way of knowing, a healthy way of looking at learning as an active process. A structure thought of as something that can be contained, or as content lodged in the mind of a container, "belongs to the pre-electronic phase and to the era of Euclidean space and Newtonian mechanics." [3]

To learn structure is to learn how facts are related, for structure is a relationship of facts and phenomena.

The disciplines with their own mode of inquiry offer built-in suggestions for exploring and finding out new knowledge. Each has its own language, mode of thinking, ways of relating facts and principles, and methods of arranging phenomena. All of this has implications for school subjects.

THE SCHOOL SUBJECTS

In relation to the definition of a discipline, a school subject can be regarded as a translation of a discipline into subject matter to be taught in the school. While the academic scholar's task is to discover knowledge and to serve as the specialist in means of inquiry in the discipline, the educator's function is to translate scholarly knowledge and ways of working into a pattern of activities available for a pupil's learning. He should be the specialist in child growth and development, learning, school subjects, and society's goals and needs. For this task, he has a powerful ally in the academic scholar who is interested in keeping school subjects up to date and in modes of inquiry of the disciplines as they can be applied to school subjects.

Traditional View of Subject Matter

As viewed from the subject-centered approach to learning in school, subject matter is what is to be learned and stored for future use. Since a specific amount of subject matter is to be learned in a specified time or grade level, it is considered important that the book or course of study be covered. The emphasis is on factual, descriptive content and on learning information as a background to what a pupil will do or learn later.

The subject-centered approach actually represents a departure from

---

[3] McLuhan, op. cit., p. 66.

the scholar's view of a discipline. The features which make a discipline instructive include a simplification of understanding through analysis, a pattern of relationships, and the power to excite further learning. When knowledge is only to be stored and does not stimulate further inquiry, it is undisciplined knowledge.

Yet, the reason for the scholars' recent interest in school subjects is their recognition of the fact that subjects have for some time grown further apart from the discipline, both in the content taught and the way it is taught. Thus, Foshay has aptly said:

> We pedagogues have brought up a whole population that does not know the difference between grammar and composition, because we taught the one in the name of the other. Similarly, we have taught prosody in the name of poetry, thus killing poetry in our culture. We have taught places in the name of geography, thus almost losing this vitally important and interesting field to our schools. We have taught facts and canned interpretations in the name of history, thus betraying a basic discipline. We have taught computation in the name of mathematics, and facts and principles in the name of laboratory sciences.[4]

Contemporary View of Subject Matter

Actually, the current view of subject matter is closer to an experience-centered approach to learning. For it is the mode of inquiry that is to be learned, to be "contained," in order that the pupil may be enabled to inquire further into the subject. He is to become interested in the subject's rules, in ways of discovering knowledge, and in disciplined thinking as means of insuring that he will continue to be interested and knowledgeable in the subject, either as a well educated citizen or, for a few going deeper into the subject, as a scholar. Thus, the behavior of the pupil who "thinks like a scientist" is the focal point. If this idea were understood and implemented by teachers, it would truly lead to a revolution in the curriculum of the public school.

There is a technology or an art behind each of the so-called special subjects, such as business education, industrial arts, and home economics. Each is to be studied with particular emphasis upon the use of the technique or art for the discovery of knowledge in the field or for the applications of knowledge to practical situations.

Seen in its proper perspective, this contemporary view of subject matter can in no wise be an excuse for use of outmoded subject matter in a subject-centered approach.

---

[4] Arthur W. Foshay, "A Modest Proposal for the Improvement of Education," in *What Are the Sources of Curriculum? A Symposium*, Washington, D. C.: Association for Supervision and Curriculum Development, 1962, p. 9.

KNOWLEDGE AND METHODS

It is the very emphasis on reasoning, inquiring, creativity, and discovery that holds the greatest promise for a renaissance of pupils' interest in knowledge about their environment and their culture. These are the new basics of intellectual attainment and the hope for a citizenry of reasonable, thoughtful men and women who will put into practice the concepts and ideals of democracy.

Method of Discovery

The most important single fact that stands out in bold relief when one studies about knowledge is that the times have made it a vital necessity to attack subjects in a new way. The rapid obsolescence of knowledge creates piles of deadwood of content. The constant change and the vast amount of information make it difficult even for the specialist to keep up with all the discoveries in his field; hence the tendency toward greater specialization. These factors make it impossible for the non-specialist to know all that he ought to know in order to be intelligent about his world.

Today's first graders will be studying a new and changed science in high school ten years from now, and teachers who were educated five years previously and have not kept up with the expanding knowledge will be left behind the brighter students who have learned to educate themselves.

In the discovery concept for children in a classroom, they become active learners themselves, not passive recipients. If this concept can catch fire, if teachers themselves learn the methods of inquiry in the disciplines and translate the discovery method into the classroom, children can be helped to become perpetual self-discoverers. One can rightfully ask: How else can we cope with the advance in knowledge?

The ability to go on to learn more about a subject—and, of equal importance, the desire to do so—presents a reasonable means of solving the dilemma of what is to be learned. Adding more years of schooling, or more hours to the school day, or more months to the school year, or more homework will not do the task. The facts of learning reject the idea that more of the same—when the same is not good enough—will lead to any more significant changes in behavior. Such a solution is also in accord with the genuine meaning of a liberal education: to free the mind.

Unity of Content and Methods

The methods used to teach a subject most effectively are inherent in the content. If the subject matter has a means of inquiry that is indigenous to it, the idea of methods and content as two separate entities is untenable. The practice of teaching general methods, or how to study, apart from the content to be taught or studied has long been considered as an unnatural division by curriculum leaders. Most teachers who are attempting to provide the best possible experiences for pupils have come to the same conclusion. The concept is entirely compatible with the experience-centered approach, which focuses upon the quality of the pupil's total experience in school. When the pupil's experience is considered, separation of content from methods becomes entirely meaningless.

Once more then, as Dewey pointed out in different words,[5] the dualism of the method of scholarship and the method of instruction is revealed by scholars as inimical to good education. Scholars indicate that the nature and structure of a discipline suggest how it is to be taught. Experiences are to be arranged by teachers to help pupils discover principles of a discipline and the relationships of phenomena in a discipline. The experience is the focal point, experience with subject matter.

The shift suggested from the more typical means of studying content, which stresses the use of incentives to make the content more attractive, to one of suspended judgment, reasoning, and critical thinking is also in point. Pupils do critical thinking, that is, they approach the study of questions and problems in a certain way. They relate, analyze, formulate concepts, apply principles, and synthesize subject matter either from one or from a number of related disciplines. This is done in connection with significant problems. Problem-solving that involves these procedures can be vital and stimulating. But there is no difference between static knowledge taught by ritual and that taught by problem-solving that becomes stereotyped, ritualized, and as deadening as dry prose by a pompous writer.

SEQUENCE AND SCOPE OF CONTENT

One of the open questions that curriculum makers have struggled with continuously is what content to include in the limits of a course,

[5] John Dewey, *Democracy and Education*, New York: The Macmillan Co., 1916, chap. 13.

a grade level, or a field of study (the scope of the curriculum), and the ordering of these experiences and content in a sequential arrangement (the sequence of the curriculum). No one has been completely satisfied with the solutions. It has been relatively easier to develop sequential experiences in a skills subject or in mathematics and foreign languages. The social studies have presented a more formidable problem. There has been little research in this field to give any leads to the best sequential order and the scope for a particular age group. Should children of ages 10–14, for example, study their own state, community, and country, or other countries? The most typical solution has been to develop sequence on the basis of moving from the immediate environment of the child to the ever expanding community, and so into international relations. However, there is no evidence that another order would not be as effective in learning concepts about society and attitudes toward the social order and fellow men.

Scope as Related to Knowledge

The simple answer to the question of the scope of the curriculum is to use the scope of the subject itself. But this actually answers nothing. Each discipline is becoming broader in its own scope, splintering off into subdisciplines. The discipline does not resolve what to include for a particular level of development. Nor does it tell what to select, when it is obvious that school subjects cannot include all the knowledge of the discipline, even if it were stable enough in the future to be contained.

In addition, when knowledge is no longer contained, static, nor certain, the odds against the discipline itself giving the clues to scope are greatly raised. The concept of content as a mass of information to be learned holds no promise for selecting what should or should not be included. Covering, after all, is not choosing or selecting.

In the proposals made by scholars in the study of the structure of a field is contained a feasible solution to the problem. Where the stress is on learning of basic concepts, ideas, and principles through inquiry, the kinds of questions to be asked becomes a more important factor than the answers. One does not learn predetermined answers if he is after the discovery of knowledge. Taba believes that the approach through content as basic ideas holds a great deal of promise for defining the scope of school subjects; scope becomes the range of important ideas and the behavioral objectives to be learned.[6]

[6] Hilda Taba, *Curriculum Development: Theory and Practice*, New York: Harcourt, Brace & World, Inc., 1962, pp. 186–88.

Sequence of Learning

The idea of sequence that has prevailed in curriculum development is what experiences and content are to be placed at each grade level. Such organizing principles for ordering content have been used as: moving from the concrete to the abstract, going from the experiences closely related to the child's life to those in the larger community, moving from the simple to the complex, using chronological order, and following the logic of a subject.

This concept of placing content at grade levels has two limiting factors. One is the grade placement of knowledge and the other is the idea of scope as referring to content outside of the learner. It would seem that we need to move away from the prevalent pattern of thinking about scope toward a new view. If a discipline has not only a domain but a method of inquiry, if a discipline is a way of discovering knowledge, a way of knowing, and if school subjects translate this way of knowing into the classroom, then knowledge cannot be characterized as "placed" at a grade level. What if a child has already discovered or learned the concepts in previous grades or outside of school?

This gets us into the second limiting factor. Can content learned be viewed outside of the learner? For is not the central question what is learned? Have we not wrongly thought of coverage and learning as synonymous? If one wants to build sequential learning, he must look to what has previously been learned.

Teachers have long talked about "taking pupils where they are," and have in many cases done a better job of translating this concept into practice than have curriculum leaders. The use of children's needs, problems, abilities, readiness, and interests, their stage of development, and their social needs has yielded promising approaches to the problem of sequence. These are factors that determine when the child will best learn what is to be learned, or when he should learn it. However, they have not been widely used.

It took the development of programmed learning and the research studies in this area to indicate clearly that sequence is found in the learning process of the individual, that it is a matter of sequence of learning rather than of content which counts. These studies indicate that when material is arranged in sequential order and the child learns one step before going on to the next step, even slow learners can go much further in learning various concepts and skills. The obvious fact is that learning is sequential, that one learns new information, reorganizes his ideas, or relates concepts and principles on the basis of those previously learned.

This is a far cry from the usual pattern of covering materials, being tested on them for recall, and "failing" or "passing" on what has been learned. Success and failure take on a new connotation. There is no such thing in programmed learning as taking a course or a grade over again if the material has not been "learned," in order to "learn" over again what never has been learned in the first place. The sequential order is based on moving ahead as steps are learned. This is the very essence of individual progress, if teachers can only learn how to apply these same ideas of sequence in all their teaching. We do not yet know enough about programmed learning to say what it will do, but at least it has given us some valuable clues to sequence in the curriculum.

Taba has defined levels of knowledge as a helpful way to suggest the sequence of acquiring knowledge. These levels are as follows:

1. Specific facts and descriptive ideas, at a low level of abstraction, and specific processes and skills
2. Basic ideas and principles
3. Concepts, such as the concept of democracy, which are complex systems of highly abstract ideas
4. Thought systems and methods of inquiry.[7]

Readiness for Learning

In any group of children there is a wide variation in ability, maturity, and background. Since this tremendous variation in growth and cultural backgrounds affects readiness to learn, no grade standard, intelligence quotient, or course of study can tell a teacher what a child is ready for. This is an individual matter to be determined by studying the child through objective means. The concept of readiness psychologically, physically, and by virtue of previous learning is supported by psychological studies.

Studies in the area of creativity support the notion that readiness should be an individual matter. In fact, the idea of readiness as holding back all children until they are supposed to be chronologically or psychologically ready, is only a means of preventing a child from learning what he, by virtue of his maturity and background, is ready

[7] *Ibid.*, pp. 175–81.

to learn. Studies of creativity point out that preventing children from learning more than they are "ready" to learn may inhibit creativity.[8]

The study of the structure of knowledge in relation to sequential learning of a discipline has led to some interesting additions to the concept of readiness. The scholars in academic fields indicate that the structure of a discipline is highly suggestive of the way children learn the subject. There should be a similarity in what the school does and what the child does in approaching a subject for the first time. Teachers need to represent the structure of a subject in terms of the way a child views it; this is the task of translation of the subject into simpler terms. "One of the greatest barriers to progress in learning," Phenix holds, "is the failure to catch the vision of simplicity which the discipline promises." [9]

Bruner has proposed the hypothesis that "any subject can be taught effectively in some intellectually honest form to any child at any stage of development." [10] Good teachers have long known that effective teaching requires simplification. Good writers are the least erudite; they use simple, clear, expressive language, and a minimum of esoteric vocabulary. But still this proposal is resisted by some because it is a radical idea. The child, according to this hypothesis, can learn almost anything through materials simplified enough for him to understand.

Such a statement as Bruner quotes from a participant in a conference on the improvement of science in elementary and secondary schools would shock many primary grade teachers:

In view of all this it seems highly arbitrary and very likely incorrect to delay the teaching, for example, of Euclidian or metric geometry until the end of the primary grades, particularly when projective geometry has not been given earlier. So too with the teaching of physics, which has much in it that can be profitably taught at an inductive or intuitive level much earlier. Basic notions in these fields are perfectly accessible to children seven to ten years of age, *provided that they are divorced from their mathematical expression and studied through materials that the child can handle himself.*[11]

8 E. Paul Torrance, "Creativity," AERA–DCT Research Pamphlet Series, *What Research Says to the Teacher*, No. 28, Washington, D. C.: National Education Association, 1963, pp. 20–21.

9 Philip H. Phenix, "The Discipline as Curriculum Content," in Harry Passow (ed.), *Curriculum Crossroads*, New York: Bureau of Publications, Teachers College, Columbia University, 1962, p. 61.

10 Jerome S. Bruner, *The Process of Education*, Cambridge: Harvard University Press, 1960, p. 33.

11 *Ibid.*, p. 43.

The key to this hypothesis is in the italicized portion of the quotation, *"through materials that the child can handle himself."* Children, through concrete experiences, can be helped to understand concepts that they will learn to handle later at a more abstract level. Atkin and Karplus, working on a science curriculum improvement project financed by the National Science Foundation and with the help of experienced elementary school teachers, have taught scientific and mathematical concepts to primary grade children.[12]

The pupil's experiences before he enters school and outside his school environment are built upon. The child holds concepts that interpret his observations. He is helped to make discoveries with concrete materials that reinterpret and refine these concepts and teach him to look at natural phenomena from the point of view of science. These concepts are discovered, not presented in a definitive and final form.

For example, concepts dealing with objects are taught: the relation of objects to each other in a system, interaction between objects, their motion, equilibrium, and weight. Explanations are not made in abstract terms; children are led to understand the concepts by using concrete objects and words that have meaning to them. These studies demonstrate that children can begin to generalize and move from concrete to more abstract ideas.

The question of whether it is worthwhile for young children to learn these concepts is not answered by these experiments and demonstrations. This question relates to whether or not it is worthwhile for pupils at any age level to learn scientific concepts, when they can best learn them, and the important question of sequential learning. Curriculum workers need to answer, too, how pupils in elementary and secondary school can be helped to become scientifically intelligent in a scientific–technological world. The studies on creativity seem to point to the importance of an open, discovery method of learning in the early years, before the more rigid program tends to inhibit children's natural creativity.

Integration of Knowledge

One of the interesting developments in fields such as mathematics and science is the integration of knowledge that is occurring. This

[12] See J. Myron Atkin and Robert Karplus, "Discovery or Invention?" *The Science Teacher,* 29:45–51, September, 1962.

phenomenon is especially interesting in view of reactions in recent years against core curriculum and fused subjects such as social studies. Algebra and geometry become part of the same means of grasping fundamental principles of mathematics and the bigger ideas in the field. Materials have been rewritten in which the more pervading ideas are stressed and the dividing lines between subjects become blurred.

Thus, the scope of a subject changes to gather more breadth through its very purposes of teaching principles and concepts rather than descriptive facts. And as the concept of scope and sequence changes, so does the view of a subject. Sequential learning becomes related to the principles and ideas, which are expanded and may become more complicated and abstract. Sequence then, too, takes on the notion of developing an attitude toward learning that grows and deepens.

Narrowing the gap between elementary and advanced knowledge is part of this total development. If the concept of sequence is understood in this way, as an expanding and broadening of knowledge and a deepening of attitudes toward knowledge, the idea of continuity in what a child learns and what a scholar learns becomes clearer.

Within the framework of teaching principles and concepts, subject matter previously taught as distinctly separate subjects moves toward integration. The disciplines themselves show this trend, for example, in a union of biology and chemistry, of astronomy and mathematics, and of mathematics and various other sciences.

KNOWLEDGE AND QUALITY

The test for quality of knowledge lies in whether or not it can be communicated. Simplicity rather than obscurity, despite the esoteric technical jargon in which much research is reported, is the real test of quality. "Knowledge which is hard to teach is for that reason inferior."[13] Again, the notion is startling because somehow or other we have been led to believe that the more erudite, the more abstruse, the more hidden the meaning from the uninitiated, the more scholarly a work would be. Teachers do not read many scholars' works for the reason that these writers often speak another "language." A fact that linguists have long known, that the words which communicate best are the ones that are most effective to use, leads to a way out of the dilemma. Humble, direct, and simple words are needed to replace the vocabulary that befogs information.

[13] Phenix, *op. cit.*, p. 59.

The changes in content discussed in this chapter and elsewhere in this book also represent a change of emphasis and a rather profound change in methods. Meanings, concepts, ideas, relationships, discovery, issues, values, creativity, sequential learning, and the way a subject is structured and developed are stressed in the approach to the subjects. These approaches are all characteristic of excellence, of quality education. They are common to all subject fields. Neither excellence nor creativity resides in the subject. They are factors of the way a subject is viewed, analyzed, and studied by man.

Coming to the forefront is a notion, long overdue, that no subject has a monopoly on excellence. The skilled craftsman, the musician, the artist, the politician, the housewife can be excellent in his particular field. Quality education can be found in any field, any course, any place where teachers are skilled and knowledgeable in their craft.

Research in the behavioral sciences, in neurology, with handicapped children, with younger children, with the use of programmed learning, with creativity is beginning to point the way to the fact that there are probably no limits to learning if we only knew how to get beyond the supposed limitations. There are degrees of limitations, to be sure, for people differ, but the individual probably can learn far more than we have ever assumed. Labels of ability have dimmed our vision of his potentiality.

How will we adjust in the schools to this revolutionary notion? It is, of course, tied to the age-old notion of individual progress. What will we do in ninth grade with a youngster who already knows another language well? What will we do in twelfth grade with a boy who in ninth-grade industrial arts has experimented with transmitting data by light waves or with solar energy, constructed his own equipment, and knows all the principles of physics involved? Will we say that these students already know what is taught in high school or in college in that subject, and consequently they should take something else? Or will we have imagination enough and foresight enough to let such a student pursue the subject of his interest and "give him his head" so that he can run?

Quality education has no limitations nor any slums. It is only limited where the minds of men are limited.

ISSUES AND POINTS OF VIEW

There is no question in any educator's mind that knowledge is a source of the curriculum. The questions arise regarding what knowledge is needed and how it can best be taught. The curriculum specialists and the teacher cannot afford to be unconcerned about the updating of the content of the curriculum. This is one of the big tasks of curriculum improvement.

The recent inquiry into the nature of knowledge and the structure of the disciplines has placed subject matter in a new focus. This chapter has pointed out that the specialist in the disciplines is saying that there is a way in which inquiry is made to gain new knowledge and a way in which a discipline is uniquely structured with implications for how it is to be taught and learned. Many issues and questions arise in the teacher's mind when he reads about the new interest of the academic scholar in school subjects.

1. *Will the academic scholar in the discipline now replace the specialist in curriculum or child development as the person to take leadership for curriculum change?*

It is doubtful that any academic specialist wants to assume the role of working with teachers in the intimate way that the professional educator has. However, he does want to play a part in revising the school curriculum and in making curriculum decisions. Since, for various reasons, the academic scholars and the learned societies in the past have virtually been left out of curriculum-making, it is the curriculum specialist's responsibility to see that his colleagues in the academic fields become genuine partners in the mutual concern for curriculum improvement. No one is more aware than the curriculum leader that he needs all the allies he can muster.

If the specialties of knowledge of an academic field and its mode of inquiry, and of knowledge of learning, child growth and development, the school, and society are combined, there is real hope that programs and learning sequences can be developed that will make the school challenging and fruitful for all children.

2. *Will we wind up in a few years with a new stagnant knowledge, or will we keep the emphasis on inquiry as the central point of focus?*

This question is indeed a pertinent one. There is no guarantee that the use of the disciplines as a basis for school subjects will make the subjects more intellectually challenging or alive. Subjects live in the mind and skill of the teacher. If—and this is the big *if*—the teacher comprehends what the scholars are talking about and gives his pupils a genuine experience of discovering knowledge, the subjects that are now taught and how they are taught in the schools could be transformed.

But if the teacher has little imagination or flexibility of mind, he is likely to find a convenient excuse for adding more assignments, homework, and pages to be read. If vision and spirit are not there, any new knowledge will soon become old and sterile. In the approach that stresses open-ended questions and finding answers for oneself lies the possibility for keeping the subject continuously alive and new. Writing new content into new texts to be used for five years may only mean more gaps of knowledge created as the pace of man's inquiry accelerates.

3. *Should all subjects taught in school be drawn from the disciplines in order that understanding of the method and structure of a discipline be attained, or should some of the content be drawn from the problems of society and the problems, interests, and concerns of children?*

Some would argue that all curriculum content should be drawn from the disciplines per se. No other content is appropriate for school subjects; it is only peripheral to what should be studied in school. The rest must be learned in the home, the church, in the streets or the back alleys. Since a discipline is knowledge that is organized for instruction, it follows that such knowledge is the only kind that is instructive. This concept is but another way of saying that the organized disciplines are the only proper fields of study. It comes dangerously close to the idea of the study of subjects in a logical fashion as the only appropriate order. As a solution, it smacks somewhat of the untenable position that certain subjects in and of themselves, and for all people, are of a higher status order. Knowledge of a discipline is, however, not the same as disciplined intelligence.

Others hold that both the study of a discipline—emphasizing its mode of inquiry, its concepts, and its generalizations—and other ways of determining what is to be taught are useful and suitable for school subjects. There is a need for focusing on social problems and using data from many disciplines to solve these problems. The essential ingredients are that they be timely, crucial, and pertinent to the lives of the children of a particular age and the culture in which they live. The proponents of this point of view argue that pupils need to learn how to approach subject matter in different ways that will be useful to them in learning how to solve current and future problems that impinge on their lives. The method of discovery or scientific method (on which the disciplines themselves do not agree) and the problem-solving approach complement and reinforce each other.

The danger here lies in the quick resort to the all-or-none answer. We are either to have all disciplines as a basis for school subjects or all problem-solving or child interests or some other solution. If a proponent of one answer pushes for his point of view, he seems to drive the proponent of the opposite point of view into a rigid corner from which he refuses to budge.

4. *In curriculum planning for the elementary and secondary schools, is there need for a broader context than the individual disciplines?*

An oversimplification of the problems involved in curriculum planning would be to revise the subject matter in light of new developments and teach that subject matter to all children in sequential order. But what subject matter? Do balance of subjects and breadth of learning come merely from adding an equal amount of each? Someone has to decide what is most important in any one time, culture, or age. Someone needs to do learning studies to see what important subject matter is learned most effectively at what ages and in what sequence.

The recent years have seen a neglect of the humanities and social sciences and a continual emphasis on mathematics and science. Only a world in which no social and political decisions have to be made and in which all creatures are robots can afford to neglect a study of such social sciences as history, anthropology, political science, sociology, and economics. The question has been aptly asked: "Survival—for what?"

The curriculum specialist needs to work with academic specialists, teachers, and citizens of all backgrounds to determine what is to be the total scope of the curriculum of a school. This is a question of structure of the curriculum as a whole, not only of the individual disciplines.

The dilemma that faces the scientist and the scholar in other fields is the growing awareness, in an age of specialization, that nature recognizes no artificial boundaries such as exist between the sciences, for example. Solid-state physicists accidentally make discoveries in chemical spectroscopy. There is in science and in mathematics a reappraisal of the boundaries between subjects. Some blend into one as offshoots. Some leading institutions of higher learning offer graduate degrees in chemical physics. This dilemma is similar to the problem that faces the curriculum specialist in a time of ever increasing specialization of knowledge.

5. *Does the early teaching of a more complex concept in a simple way enhance a child's genuine interest in a subject and the probability of his continuing to learn it in some depth even into adult life?*

We have discovered that it is possible to teach the more complex ideas of a subject to young children in the primary grades, if the concepts are simplified and objectified for them. Any society has to answer first of all why it believes certain things should be taught in schools. If science is important to teach, then why should it not begin with as difficult concepts as can be learned? Yet, are these the concepts fundamental to children's understanding of scientific phenomena in their lives? Will such understanding help them to live richer, more interesting lives? (They will not necessarily become great scientists, although this is surely also needed.)

These questions still need to be answered through research in the use of more difficult concepts with the young child. If they do enhance his interest in things scientific or social or cultural, and such interest builds future understanding of greater breadth, then there is good reason for teaching some subject matter earlier.

SELECTED REFERENCES

Alexander, William M. *Changing Curriculum Content.* Washington, D. C.: Association for Supervision and Curriculum Development, 1964, 26 pp.
This pamphlet grew out of a conference of representatives of national curriculum projects and ASCD's Commission on Current Curriculum Developments. Examines the changing curriculum emphases in the projects, their impact on schools, and what needs to be done in changing curriculum content.

Association for Supervision and Curriculum Development. *Learning and the Teacher.* 1959 Yearbook. Washington, D. C.: National Education Association, 1959, chaps. 2, 3, and 8.
Applications of what is known about learning to teaching. These particular chapters discuss how personality, experiences, and environment affect learning, the control the teacher exercises over learning, and information on learning.

Association for Supervision and Curriculum Development. *Perceiving, Behaving, Becoming: A New Focus for Education.* 1962 Yearbook. Washington, D. C.: National Education Association, 1962, 256 pp.
Self-realization and the fully functioning person. Written from the point of view of the perceptual approach to learning.

Association for Supervision and Curriculum Development. *New Insights and the Curriculum.* 1963 Yearbook. Washington, D. C.: National Education Association, 1963, chaps. 1–4, 9–10, 13–14.
Some challenging statements by foremost thinkers in psychology, creativity, mental health, sociology, communications theory, anthropology, and education. Chapters are paired, with a curriculum specialist examining the presentation for its implications. An excellent source for Part II of this book.

Association for Supervision and Curriculum Development. *What Are the Sources of the Curriculum? A Symposium.* Washington, D. C.: National Education Association, 1962, 80 pp.
A helpful re-examination of the sources of curriculum by authorities in curriculum development, dealing with sources for identifying content, for determining structure and design, and for decisions on the curriculum.

Broudy, Harry S., *et al. Democracy and Excellence in American Secondary Education.* Chicago: Rand McNally & Co., 1964, chaps. 6–9.
A theoretical examination of readiness and knowledge and content of the curriculum.

Bruner, Jerome S. *The Process of Education.* Cambridge: Harvard University Press, 1960, 97 pp.
A much-discussed brief volume that presents some hypotheses concerning readiness for learning and the importance of structure of knowledge. Many thought-provoking questions are raised, for example, regarding intuitive thinking and the idea that young children are able to learn abstract ideas.

Burton, William H. *The Guidance of Learning Activities.* 3rd ed. New York: Appleton-Century-Crofts, 1962, Parts I and II.

One of the best explanations of how learning occurs in the school situation and the implications for teaching. A classic in its field, constantly revised and in use since 1944.

Chandler, B. J., Lindley J. Stiles, and John I. Kituse (eds.). *Education in Urban Society*. New York: Dodd, Mead & Co., 1962, Parts I and II. These sections identify forces influencing schools in large metropolitan areas and their implications for urban education.

Conant, James B. *Slums and Suburbs*. New York: McGraw-Hill Book Co., 1961, 147 pp. This paperback reports Conant's famous study of city slums and wealthy suburbs, focusing on such issues as de facto segregation and conditions that he calls "social dynamite" in larger cities.

Doll, Ronald C. *Curriculum Improvement: Decision-making and Process*. Boston: Allyn & Bacon, Inc., 1964, Part I. Deals with decision-making in the curriculum process on historical, psychological, and social bases, and on basis of subject matter.

Frazer, Dorothy M. *Deciding What To Teach*. Washington, D. C.: National Education Association, 1963, chaps. 1–2, 8. Discusses bases for making curriculum decisions and who shall make them. The report, prepared for the Project on Instruction, makes recommendations.

Frazier, Alexander (ed.). *Learning More About Learning*. Washington, D. C.: Association for Supervision and Curriculum Development, 1959, 88 pp. The sections of this pamphlet dealing with personality theory and its implications for learning, and perception and learning, give new insights into these areas.

Gagne, Robert M., and John R. Mayor, *et al.* "Factors in Acquiring Knowledge of a Mathematical Task." *Psychological Monographs: General and Applied*, 76: No. 7. Washington, D. C.: American Psychological Association, Inc., 1962, 21 pp. Also, Robert M. Gagne, "Learning and Proficiency in Mathematics." *Mathematics Teacher*, 56:620–26, December, 1963. Research studies at University of Maryland with programmed instruction in mathematics for seventh graders. A significant finding was that acquisition of new knowledge in mathematics depended on previous acquisitions of knowledge, indicating a sequence of learning, and that if learners are given time to complete the program, their performance at the end is independent of ability as measured by previous mathematics grades.

Goodykoontz, Bess (ed.). *Basic Human Values for Childhood Education*. Membership Service Bulletin, No. 8-A. Washington, D. C.: Association for Childhood Education International, 1963, 76 pp. A colloquium concerning the pressures on children in modern society related to learning and development, including a social anthropologist, a sociologist, a child psychologist, a pediatrician, and others.

Gross, Carl H., Stanley P. Wronski, and John W. Hanson (eds.). *School and Society*. Boston: D. C. Heath & Co., 1962, chaps. 2, 5–11. A book of selected readings in social and philosophical foundations. These chapters discuss educative agencies, democracy as a way of life, implications of democracy for education, and the social context related to purposes of education.

Havighurst, Robert J. *Developmental Tasks and Education*. 2nd ed. New York: David McKay Co., Inc., 1952, 100 pp.

An outstanding reference on the concept of developmental tasks, which are listed and discussed.

Havighurst, Robert J., *et al*. *Growing Up in River City*. New York: John Wiley & Sons, Inc., 1962, 189 pp.

A significant longitudinal study of children from ages 11 to 20 growing up in a Midwestern city, under the auspices of the Community Youth Development Commission, showing how background and personal characteristics of boys and girls relate to how well they perform their developmental tasks.

Huebner, Dwayne (ed.). *A Reassessment of the Curriculum*. New York: Bureau of Publications, Teachers College, Columbia University, 1964, 104 pp.

A relook at the curriculum in terms of the structure of knowledge, child development, society, and current developments.

Jenkins, William A. (ed.). *The Nature of Knowledge*. Milwaukee: School of Education, University of Wisconsin-Milwaukee, 1961, 95 pp.

Papers on the structure of knowledge presented by scholars in education.

Lantz, Donald, and Robert Scannon. "The Changing Discipline." *The University of South Florida Educational Review*, 1:1–67, Spring, 1963.

Articles on developments in the major trends occurring in some of the disciplines.

McIver, R. M. (ed.). *Dilemmas of Youth in America Today*. New York: Harper & Row, Publishers, 1961.

Pressures and problems faced by youth, analyzed by experts.

Miller, Richard I. *Education in a Changing Society*. Washington, D. C.: National Education Association, 1963, 166 pp.

This report of The Project on Instruction discusses the major social forces and values in our society and their implication for the school program.

National Society for the Study of Education. *Child Psychology*. Sixty-second Yearbook, Part I. Chicago: University of Chicago Press, 1963, chaps. 2 and 5.

A synthesis of findings of recent research in child psychology. These two chapters deal specifically with sociological influences on child behavior and learning. Any chapters valuable for those interested in research results.

Passow, A. Harry (ed.). *Curriculum Crossroads*. New York: Bureau of Publications, Teachers College, Columbia University, 1962, chap. 3.

The use of disciplines as curriculum content is discussed by Philip Phenix.

Passow, A. Harry (ed.). *Nurturing Individual Potential*. Washington, D. C.: Association for Supervision and Curriculum Development, 1964, 91 pp.

Papers drawn from psychology, psychiatry, and sociology examine aspects of nurturing individual potential: personality change, preconscious learning, productive thinking, teaching style, and social class.

Prescott, Daniel A. *Factors that Influence Learning.* Pittsburgh: University of Pittsburgh Press, 1958, 77 pp.

The biological, emotional, and cultural factors that influence learning, written from a wealth of knowledge in field of human development.

Prescott, Daniel A. *The Child in the Educative Process.* New York: McGraw-Hill Book Co., 1957, Part 2.

This book is helpful to the teacher in understanding his guidance function of gathering and interpreting data about the child. Describes child study programs.

President's Commission on National Goals. *Goals for Americans.* Englewood Cliffs, N. J.: Prentice-Hall, Inc., 1960, 372 pp.

A report of the President's Commission (first twenty-four pages) and accompanying chapters by noted scholars on such topics as American ideals, technological change, the age of science, and the quality of American culture.

Project on the Instructional Program of the Public Schools. *The Scholars Look at the Schools: A Report of the Disciplines Seminar.* Washington, D. C.: National Education Association, 1962, 63 pp.

Focuses on the ideas and methods of inquiry from different selected fields of study. Report of a seminar participated in by scholars in the academic disciplines and by educators.

Rockefeller Panel Reports. *Prospect for America.* Garden City, N. Y.: Doubleday & Co., Inc., 1961, pp. 337–464.

The two panel reports on the pursuit of excellence in education and a discussion of democratic ideals and principles. A significant group of reports written by distinguished citizens.

Smith, B. Othanel, William O. Stanley, and J. Harlan Shores. *Fundamentals of Curriculum Development.* Rev. ed. New York: Harcourt, Brace & World, Inc., 1957, Part I.

This part dealing with social diagnosis for curriculum development relates the culture, changes in social life, and value systems to curriculum development.

Taba, Hilda. *Curriculum Development: Theory and Practice.* New York: Harcourt, Brace & World, Inc., 1962, Part I.

An excellent analysis of society, the culture, learning theories, the nature of knowledge, and growth and development as the foundations for curriculum development.

Travers, Robert M. W. *Essentials of Learning.* New York: The Macmillan Co., 1963, 544 pp.

For the serious student of curriculum who wants to delve into the research on learning. Includes studies based on different theories of learning. To be sampled.

Waetjen, Walter B. (ed.). *Human Variability and Learning.* Washington, D. C.: Association for Supervision and Curriculum Development, 1961, 88 pp.

Articulates knowledge about individual differences and curriculum practices. Creativity and learning, personality influences on learning, and group influences on learning are sections written by a distinguished group of behavioral scientists.

Waetjen, Walter B. (ed.). *New Dimensions in Learning: A Multi-disciplinary Approach.* Washington, D. C.: Association for Supervision and Curriculum Development, 1962, 96 pp.

Insights of scholars in psychology, social sciences, and biological sciences into development and learning: physical growth, origin of achievement values, concept formation.

Watson, Goodwin. *What Psychology Can We Trust?* New York: Bureau of Publications, Teachers College, Columbia University, 1961, 19 pp.

Fifty principles of learning that the author of this pamphlet believes are grounded in a body of facts. A useful, brief pamphlet.

Woodring, Paul, and John Scanlon (eds.). *American Education Today.* New York: McGraw-Hill Book Co., 1963, Parts I and II.

Stimulating articles of a controversial nature dealing with the purposes of education and the changing philosophies of education, selected from *Saturday Review.*

III

PLANNING AND
ORGANIZING FOR
CURRICULUM STUDY

7

CURRICULUM PLANNING
IN LOCAL SCHOOLS

Curriculum improvement at the local level has the task of enlisting
and organizing in some workable and useful kind of program all the
forces that have influence upon the curriculum. The recognized leader
for curriculum improvement needs to ask himself: What kind of an
organization will make a difference in the experiences pupils have in
the classroom? Otherwise, he may find himself having a program for
the sake of being able to talk about it. What does curriculum study
really mean? Who defines the problems of study? What problems
should be selected? Who should participate? How can active support of the staff be secured?

Any curriculum improvement program must begin with teachers,
administrators, and parents, at the point where they are in their thinking and doing. The teachers' knowledge and orientation are significant factors, as are the community attitudes. Their leadership and
human resources, their willingness, insight, and skill in working with
people will affect where the program starts and expects to go.

The purposes of fruitful curriculum planning provide the focus.
Unless the study carried on by a school system has a broader purpose
than any single objective, someone's sights are too narrow. A number of changes are usually required to improve the quality of the
program for children. Note that the focus of these behaviors is on
ourselves, not someone else whom we seek to change. Curriculum
study that will result in improved programs for children can be expected to:

Help us to develop skills in planning together as teachers, administrators, supervisors, pupils, and laymen

Make us anxious to work with parents or with the school

Encourage us to seek for the causes of children's behavior and to learn how to study children

Cause us to demand a chance to take an active part in the program

Cause us to analyze the experiences we are providing for children in terms of the purposes we have in mind

Increase our knowledge of what we teach

Result in our attuning the curriculum to changes of behavior

Create good rapport between us and our colleagues

Create a desire for us to try out new ideas, to read, to question

Result in the improvement of children's experiences in the schools: experiences in being successful, in being understood, in being creative, in living with other children, in understanding the world about them, in understanding themselves, in gaining skills

Make a difference in the lives of children.

INITIATING CURRICULUM STUDY

Responsibility

When teachers want to get started on curriculum study in schools, who helps them get under way? Who provides the initial drive? In a few cases, groups of teachers have been successful in initiating curriculum study programs through the local education association or through voluntarily formed study groups. However, research in leadership and group process has indicated that, unless the responsible status leader is active in the study to improve a situation, the chances for improvement are slim indeed. The responsibility for initiating curriculum study rests squarely upon the shoulders of the leader.

The active support and interest of the superintendent, the principal, and the supervisory staff are needed. The principal as the main supervisory agent in a school building is the person to whom teachers look for leadership in curriculum study. He is actually the "curriculum director" in the building, unless that responsibility is specifically delegated to some other person. In a very small school system this person would be the superintendent since the principal ordinarily would be teaching full time. If a school system has a curriculum director, his main function is to give leadership to curriculum study for the total system.

The democratic leader takes positive action. He has ideas. He gets people together to discuss their ideas as well as his. Some make the mistake of waiting for teachers to initiate a program of curriculum study. Such a person is not exercising the leadership responsibility that is his. He will probably wait a long time before anything happens. Nor does the democratic leader tell the teachers that a particular study is going to be made; only the autocratic leader decides what is going to be studied and how the study is going to be carried on. The suggestions in this chapter are intended for those who wish to operate democratically.

This discussion refers to the leader as anyone who exercises the leadership function in curriculum study. The leader may be the committee chairman, the master teacher, the leader of a team, the department head, the supervisor, the principal, the curriculum director, or another teacher or administrator.

Identification of Problems for Study

The leader of a curriculum committee or a faculty may already have the problem for study designated for him. One cannot assume that curriculum study begins from scratch. In such a case, the leader's responsibility is to determine whether the problem is actually of concern to the group and what are the specific concerns within the scope of the problem.

Consider, however, the sources to which a faculty, curriculum council, or any organization for curriculum study and planning may look for problems of genuine concern to teachers. What are their potentialities?

1. **Surveys.** Surveys are made either by an outside group or individual or by the school itself. If they are made as self-surveys, the probability of a group's doing something about the weaknesses discovered are enhanced. Accreditation studies such as the National Study of Secondary School Evaluation combine self-study with a visiting team of school people. Questionnaires are used for survey of opinion of parents, teachers, and pupils to discover their dissatisfactions and concerns about the school program. Surveys of pupils' needs and interests and of community resources may give some leads.

2. **Problem census.** A problem census can be obtained in any kind of study group. Since teachers are often reluctant to confess that they have problems, only the accepted pattern of topics for study, one that holds no threat to the individual, may be stated. Thus, typical suggestions may be developing a course of study in English, language arts, or mathematics.

In one school at the beginning of a study of the secondary school curriculum, the teachers met for a full day in small groups to define the problems that needed to be resolved for the improvement of the curriculum. This was preliminary planning for the new separate junior and senior high schools that were to displace the six-year junior–senior high school. The problems were recorded in question form, compiled, and organized by a steering committee, which grouped them into larger categories for study by different committees. Committees were organized in three areas to study the problems and to make recommendations to the entire faculty.

3. **Workshop or committee reports.** In many cases a local workshop or a standing committee of the faculty may make recommendations for improvement of the curriculum. They may be in the form of recommendations for further study or for beginning a new program that requires consideration as to how it should be implemented. University or college workshops or institutes may be sources of leadership as well as of ideas for curriculum revision.

4. **Conferences.** Teachers gain new ideas through meeting in the numerous state and national conferences to discuss mutual problems with others. It is doubtful, however, that the impetus for local curriculum study could be traced directly to a general conference. Conferences that are called to deal with specific problems are probably more fruitful. No benefits generally come from asking those who attend a meeting to report to the rest of the faculty. The mistaken assumption is made that the individual can re-create all of the conditions that stimulated ideas for him.

5. **Testing programs and local studies.** Data from tests and appraisal of pupil aptitudes, achievement, and interests, are a source of study to determine some of the focal points of attack in a school program. Information on dropouts, attendance, or pupil population may reveal the need for curriculum revision.

6. **Funds from outside agencies.** A new phenomenon in American education that has become a rather powerful stimulator of curriculum study is a grant made by a public or federal agency or by a private foundation. Studies of the use of television, team teaching, pupil personnel services, and revision of content have been the direct result of these funds made available to school districts or schools in cooperation with colleges and universities. Funds for pilot programs are powerful incentives to curriculum revision.

7. **Problems of daily frustrations.** In cases where teachers have built up an antagonism toward curriculum study, perhaps one of the best ways of beginning cooperative planning and action is through looking

at some of the administrative routines that bother teachers. If decisions are arrived at and put into practice on immediate problems, teachers should become confident that the leader is sincere in his willingness to take their suggestions and to accept statements about their concerns without moralizing about them.

Criteria for Problem Selection

Under the concept of curriculum as the means or experiences that are planned to develop behavior changes, the problems studied can include any that affect pupil behavior. They include studying pupils, studying the community, developing new plans, revising content, planning experimental or pilot programs, planning cooperative research, writing curriculum materials, selecting materials and resources, studying instructional techniques and media.

The following criteria are suggested for situations in which there are no or few restrictions on what can be studied.

1. *The leader and the teachers participate as a group in selecting the problems.*

2. *The problems are those of the group.* Those problems that seem to be the most important and most pertinent to the group are selected for study.

3. *Problems are of such scope that tangible results of the study can be seen in the school program.* Changes may not be evident unless the study is carried on over a period of time.

4. *Only a few problems are tackled at a time.* One of the most frequent mistakes made in curriculum study is choosing too many problems for each to be considered adequately. Some groups set out on the impossible task of revising the content and organization of all subjects in a year or two. Others believe that all teachers' interests should be included in the final selection. Consequently, they take on too much work at one time. Every problem studied by committees is a problem of the whole faculty, and any suggested solutions should be submitted to the faculty for consideration. Frequent communication with the whole group takes time.

Resistance to Curriculum Study

Not all teachers are going to be eagerly waiting at the starting line to see curriculum study get under way. The leader who operates under this assumption will soon be disillusioned.

Why do these negative attitudes exist? To a certain extent, they grow out of an individual's reluctance to change: Why fuss around and cause problems? Or they may be a result of the teacher's concept of curriculum change: Curriculum change means changing a course of study and the one we have is good enough. In many cases, curriculum committees meet after school. This time is not regarded by teachers as the school day. For those who have families, it is an imposition on their time with their children.

Perhaps one of the dominant factors in the negative attitudes is a previous unfortunate experience. Much curriculum study has been juggling of content through rewriting courses. Little evidence of improved results has been indicated. In one school, for example, the teachers wanted no more of any curriculum improvement programs. Investigation through interviews with a few teachers uncovered the fact that they had spent the entire preceding year in developing a philosophy that might serve as a background to the beginning of curriculum study. They grew tired of philosophizing without getting any action. In other cases where teachers have recommended changes through committees and have never heard any more about their recommendations, they have become discouraged. Autocratic decisions make them justifiably suspicious.

If someone feels threatened, he does not ask questions that may reveal his ignorance. When teachers feel comfortable with their leader and are encouraged to ask questions, they soon begin to look for answers. There never was any magic formula that would overcome resistance to group study and planning. Unless the leader encourages frank discussion of gripes and problems, he has little chance of overcoming hostility already built up.

ORGANIZING FOR CURRICULUM STUDY

Curriculum study and planning take place at many levels. The school building, the school system, the state school system, colleges and universities, and national groups are all involved in curriculum improvement in the classroom. The organization is a facilitating factor for change in people. This discussion views the structure as a way of involving people in the working and decision-making process in order that such change may occur. Stress is placed on achieving as full participation as possible. No elaborate scheme is suggested. Special attention is given to workshops in the next section of this chapter. A later chapter is devoted to lay participation in curriculum study.

The Coordinating Council

One of the problems facing a school system which allows individual schools and teachers freedom to experiment is the achievement of some kind of system-wide coordination. This problem ought to be understood for what it really is: improving lines of communication between different schools and between individual schools and the central office. Coordination is not a matter of getting all the schools to study the same subject content at the same time. Nor is it one of seeing that children in one school keep pace with those in other schools. The larger the school system the greater the problem of getting teachers from all levels and buildings to work together.

Principles that apply to developing a coordinated program are these: (1) the organization should be as simple as possible in order to avoid the red tape of going through several channels to get approval for proposed curriculum improvements, (2) the organization should stimulate curriculum study at the local level, (3) teachers from various teaching levels and buildings should be encouraged to work together, (4) the central purpose of the plan should be to improve communication between the various teachers and school units in the system, and (5) the plan should provide a framework for formulating recommendations and policies for the school system.

School systems have varied means of achieving coordination among the units. One of the best known is the curriculum council or a similar coordinating body representing the schools in the system. The council ordinarily consists of teacher representatives of the school buildings, some principals, representatives from the central administrative and supervisory staff, and representatives of some of the special services. Members may be appointed or elected.

One suburban school system has a general curriculum committee composed of eleven teachers, four principals and deans of junior colleges, six supervisors, the superintendent, deputy superintendent, four assistant superintendents, a coordinator, and five lay persons. This committee coordinates the work of curriculum committees for the elementary division, the junior high division, the senior high division, the city college division, and the school for adults division, each of which has representatives on the general committee. Lay people are members of each of these committees, and two committees include student representatives. Recommendations for action are made from the divisional committees to the general committee.

In a smaller school system, the coordinating council consists of the chairmen of individual school curriculum committees, the lay chairman of the home and school council curriculum committee, the director of child guidance, the superintendent of schools, the chairmen of special area committees, and the director of curriculum and instruction—a total of thirty-four members.

Illustrative of the functions of coordinating councils are the responsibilities of the curriculum planning council in a large city:

Formulating a general, over-all policy for curriculum planning

Approving personnel for committees

Considering and recommending areas in which intensive curriculum studies need to be made within a given year or period of years

Recommending the use of school time for committee work as needs arise

Evaluating the curriculum program continuously

Approving curriculum plans and guides for recommendation to the superintendent

Approving committee work for in-service credit.

The Central Office Staff

Within the school system the responsibilities of various school leaders and the interrelationships of these responsibilities need to be clarified.

The superintendent, as the head of the school, usually delegates responsibility for curriculum leadership to an assistant superintendent or director and to principals. The assistant superintendent in charge of instruction is usually responsible for all phases of instruction including purchase of instructional materials and equipment, for the directors and supervisors of instruction, and for special services. He exercises administrative authority delegated to him by the superintendent. The principals are responsible to him for matters of curriculum and instruction.

School systems with several building units generally have a person in charge of curriculum improvement. In some systems, he may be the assistant superintendent. His title may also be director of instruction, supervisor of instruction, curriculum coordinator, or curriculum director. For purposes of simplification, he is called "curriculum director" in this discussion.

The duties of the curriculum director are to encourage schools to study the curriculum, to work with individual schools in improving their program, and to stimulate and launch curriculum study. His primary function is to facilitate curriculum improvement at the local school level. He furnishes resources from the central office in the form of curriculum study materials, instructional materials, and consultants. He makes contact with the community to assist in curriculum study. He develops in-service courses for teachers and arranges for courses to be offered by universities and colleges. He organizes summer workshops and often directs workshops for the school system. He assists in the selection of materials and makes necessary contacts with publishing companies. He may coordinate the work of supervisors. He supervises the curriculum committees and works directly with the curriculum council, giving leadership to it and serving as a type of executive secretary. Often, he is responsible for producing curriculum publications. In some schools, curriculum coordinators are appointed for individual buildings. Many of their duties are similar but involve more direct work with teachers.

The supervisor is a consultant who provides materials, information, assistance in committee work, and other services to curriculum committees and to school buildings. The supervisor should not have authority over principals nor teachers. Any attempt by the supervisor to rate teachers will weaken his effectiveness. One of the serious problems of coordination faced by school systems is the inclination of the old-line supervisor to work directly with teachers, assuming authority over them. The supervisor's proper role is that of serving as a resource person to the principal and the individual school. A number of school systems have subject supervisors who work from kindergarten through twelfth grade; others have special supervisors only for the secondary schools.

Special service personnel such as guidance directors, psychologists, psychiatrists, school doctors, school nurses, and school social workers may be responsible to the assistant superintendent or other central administrator. In the coordinated type of organization, which is gaining favor in schools, these service personnel are under a director of pupil personnel services. All of these specialized workers are available for assistance in curriculum study.

The Individual School

The principal, as the administrator and supervisor in the individual school unit, has the primary responsibility for working with the teachers in the building and for giving them leadership in curriculum study. He may delegate this responsibility to curriculum coordinators in the building.

The individual school building is the most effective unit for curriculum study. In some communities this means, of course, the entire school system. In larger school systems there has been a tendency toward centralization of curriculum study. At times, too, the state has been regarded as the primary unit. Such centralization may never get down to the basic problem of improving experiences for children in a particular school situation.

If the principles of group dynamics are to be applied, the individual school unit is the logical one for curriculum study. If change in human relations is the means of bringing about curriculum improvement, an opportunity must exist for school people to plan and work together. In large schools, the faculty needs to be divided in some way to achieve a workable group. One of the ways by which this is done is through the school-within-a-school idea. In high schools the departmental organization may serve this function although it has some disadvantages, particularly that of accentuating the division among subjects. The typical elementary school is small enough to furnish such an opportunity.

The chief advantage of the individual school building as the basic unit is that it constitutes a group of people concerned with the same children. They have a much better possibility of getting together and planning together continuously under the principal's leadership. In fact, many schools make provision for planning periods for teachers.

If all teachers are to participate in curriculum revision, a small enough unit is necessary. The concept of a course of study as something that is developed by a central committee, then given to different schools and "installed" by the teachers and the principal of each school, does not involve teachers, parents, pupils, and administrators at the grass-roots level.

In the elementary or secondary school unit, faculty meetings can be planned cooperatively and utilized as a vehicle of instructional improvement. In schools where these meetings are so utilized, they serve as the basis for discussion of curriculum problems, development of policy, coordination of committee reports, and planning curriculum experimentation.

Curriculum Committees and Study Groups

Curriculum study is often organized around committee work. Indeed, much of curriculum study is carried on with no more organization than committees of the faculty. The suggestions made here refer both to system-wide committees and to school building committees.

Some of these are standing committees and others ad hoc committees appointed to do a particular task. Committees that are formed for a specific purpose should be retained only until their work is finished. As the work proceeds, new members might be added if they are especially interested in the committee's assignment. Standing committees are of value only for certain types of functions that must be taken care of regularly. A steering committee for curriculum study is an example.

The selection and size of committees are important factors in their functioning. There should be no coercion to get people onto committees. Two procedures are recommended. One is to have the faculty elect representatives for its committee. This procedure offers a workable means for selecting representatives on central committees for the school system, but sometimes insufficient opportunity is given for careful deliberation in choosing members who are best suited to the committee's specific task. Another procedure is to ask people to volunteer for committee work with the selection made by a steering committee of the faculty. Some studies indicate that the use of sociometric choices for selecting committee members has possibilities for improving committee organization. Committees should not be too large to permit interaction within the group. Perhaps the optimum size is between five and fifteen, depending upon the function of the committee. For some jobs, committees of three people can do a task quickly and effectively.

Ordinarily, curriculum committees should have representatives from both elementary and secondary schools even when they may be focusing on only one level. The problems of coordination always need to be considered. In addition, interlocking committees, for example, from the social studies and English fields help to develop the needed relationships among departments. Often, the addition of some teachers from a related field will provide the necessary cross-fertilization of ideas.

Committees are merely a form of organization to do intensive study, gather data, and make recommendations to the faculty. Time in regular faculty meetings can profitably be spent on consideration of committee reports. The better part of an hour of discussion needs to be devoted to a committee report in order to permit full expression of ideas. Progress reports should be made periodically. Thus, when the report is finally accepted by the faculty, it represents the thinking and action of the total group.

In order to get faculty opinion other than that expressed in general meetings, committees can interview faculty members or use questionnaires. If the committee is one for the system as a whole, ample time should be allowed for the discussion of recommendations in faculty meetings in the individual schools. If there are committee representatives from the various schools, they are responsible for making reports and getting reactions of their faculty.

The study group, a more informal type of group than the committee, is formed by people who are interested in getting together to explore a particular problem. It has been a popular form of organization used by parents to study child growth and development. Study groups are set up in schools for teachers—probably a group of five or more—who wish to work together on questions of mutual concern. For example, in one school system voluntary groups have organized for in-service study "courses." Each group is sponsored by a member of the supervisory staff, but may choose its own leader. These groups define their own problems, meeting twelve times during a semester.

In-Service Education Programs

In-service education conducted by a school system represents its efforts to provide for its teachers' growth on the job. In most schools the growth of administrators and supervisors is also a matter of concern. There are many ramifications of in-service education programs, such as in-service credits and the program's relation to a salary schedule, that are not considered here. But the activities of these programs encompass many areas of curriculum improvement. If the individual grows in the process, he changes his ways of behaving and will in some way affect his pupils' experiences. These activities are vehicles for furthering the objectives of a curriculum improvement program.

1. **Comprehensive programs.** In one county school system the basic philosophy is to have every school develop its own in-service training program, with the county office offering guidance and consultant services. Administrators submit to the county office requests for teacher institute services, indicating the purposes and procedures for the institute, the number of meetings, and the number of teachers involved. A steering committee for the county acts on these requests. Each institute is held for at least ten hours. Curriculum committee work, outside consultants, regular consultation by supervisors, and meetings in the county office are other means of in-service education.

About half of the teachers in another county system work on instructional committees during the school year. Different central committees spearheading the curriculum and in-service study include a teachers' council of instruction, a parents' council of instruction, and a number of curriculum committees. The organization is based on the principle of the individual school as the unit. Parents are involved to a large extent in the total program. A number of workshops are held during the school year and the summer. One of these is planned as a preschool conference for teachers new to the system.

A medium-sized city school system conducts a number of workshops for its teachers during the summer. Over 500 teachers enroll in local workshops in a typical summer. Although a number are involved in developing curriculum guides, the majority participate in workshops that deal with new developments in content, method, and organization. Team teaching, flexible elementary school organization, creativity, programmed learning, and flexible scheduling for secondary schools have been some of the topics considered. In addition, workshops are held for the in-service education of principals. These are supplemented by spring and summer conferences.

2. **Programs for orientation of new teachers.** Many school systems have developed plans to assist new teachers in becoming acquainted with the school and its programs. Usually these have an emphasis on curriculum. One system has a plan of providing "helping" teachers who are released from their teaching duties for one month at the beginning of the school year to assist new teachers. The plan is regarded by the school system as a means of curriculum improvement. Another employs a full-time helping teacher who works exclusively with new teaching personnel. In that city the P.T.A. Council assists actively in the orientation program by entertaining new teachers and by finding permanent housing facilities for the teachers. A committee of teachers in another school system developed a plan of orientation in the form of a series of meetings beginning two days before school opens and continuing for five additional meetings in the fall.

3. **Preschool or postschool conferences.** In this type of conference, the school staff meets for a week or a few days before the regular school session opens or after it closes. Teachers and administrators have a chance to become acquainted with each other, with the school, and with the materials available, and to make plans jointly for curriculum study. Preschool conferences can be particularly useful if attention is paid to a discussion of ways and means by which the staff can work together most effectively during the school year. Postschool conferences also serve for intensive planning.

These conferences usually deal with the problems that occupy the attention of the school system in its curriculum improvement program. Thus, foreign language in the elementary schools, the new mathematics, ways of providing for gifted pupils, economic education, the new science courses developed nationally, vocational education, team teaching, and the ungraded plan have been included as topics in different school systems. Part of the time is likely to be devoted to grade-level meetings and building meetings.

4. **University and college programs.** The college courses offered on campuses during summers or in late afternoon and evening hours are still one of the typical means for furthering the teachers' or administrators' in-service education. One of the reasons is the rising interest of school personnel in securing advanced degrees. In a number of instances, certification or local requirements demand a master's degree or the equivalent, or an advanced professional diploma of sixty credits beyond the bachelor's degree.

Both state and private institutions of higher learning provide extension classes in the field. These classes may be in the nature of local workshops or courses in methods and materials, reading, audio-visual education, guidance, and other areas. One state university conducts curriculum laboratories in the local schools. These workshop-type courses use the experience-centered approach to curriculum development, centering the content entirely around the problems of the local school.

The campus institute or workshop supported by funds from a public or private organization is a relatively new phenomenon in education. The National Defense Education Act Counseling and Guidance Institutes and Foreign Language Institutes, the National Science Foundation Institutes, the Family Finance Workshops, and Economic Education Workshops are examples. Funds are provided for teachers who attend, usually in the form of tuition, board and room, or stipends that may include an allowance for dependents.

5. **Consultants.** State universities and colleges and state departments of education have staff members who give valuable assistance to local curriculum study. Special organizations, such as a bureau of research and field services, an institute, or a curriculum center, administer plans by which regular and special faculty are assigned, as part or all of their workload, to work with schools on research, child study, or curriculum study. Consultants are also engaged by local school systems from either private or public institutions of higher education or other school systems. The more traditional type of field service is the survey. More recently, universities have engaged in cooperative research projects with local school systems.

The use of consultants merits special attention. Most ineffectual is the practice of asking a person to come and talk to the group about some particular phase of the curriculum, especially if the topic is not related to ongoing study. Speakers are useful if a need for information grows out of curriculum study. The person invited should be informed ahead of time about the problems the committee is trying to solve and the kind of information it wants.

Consultants can be used effectively to assist the group in getting organized and in considering the procedure used for study. A consultant should work with the group over a period of time so that he may become acquainted with the faculty and be able to assist more effectively in the study. One curriculum service center found that a three-year period was the optimum time for working with a school system.

The consultant's responsibility is to give advice and assistance, not to direct the program. The group should give serious consideration to his suggestions; it should not feel that it must accept them. The consultant is there to help the group in its search for better solutions, not to provide answers. Unless this attitude is maintained, there is little hope for stimulating schools to do research on their own problems.

6. Support of in-service education. In a number of school districts, the board of education includes in the school budget funds for in-service education. These funds are used for consultants, for the purchase of professional materials, and for local in-service courses. One school system makes funds available for curriculum experimentation. Another provides a substantial amount in the budget for released time of teachers, local summer workshops, professional curriculum materials, salaries for summer employment of teachers working on curriculum projects, and consultants. Traditionally, schools have paid expenses of administrators and supervisors who attend professional conferences. More recently, this practice has been extended in some systems to teachers who have responsibilities in a program. The sabbatical leave plan to provide time for teachers' advanced study has been adopted by a growing number of schools. Some school systems pay the tuition and in many instances the travel expenses of teachers who attend summer workshops to study problems of particular concern to the school system. Others pay either full or part tuition for the local curriculum workshops. In one state, the county school systems underwrite in-service courses taught by the state university, guaranteeing a minimum amount for this self-support activity of the university.

Another means of support of these programs, including curriculum committee activities, is to schedule time for them during the school day. Some schools, particularly secondary schools, on one or two days a week begin the school day later for the pupils. On those days the teachers meet for in-service and curriculum study; on the other days there is an activity period for pupils.

In one junior high school, meetings of small and large teacher groups are scheduled every day from 8:00 to 8:45 A.M. Teachers not involved have small groups of pupils come in for help or for special activities, or use the time for preparation. A few major pupil activity groups may be scheduled regularly for morning meetings at this time. At a senior high school, teachers meet from 8:00 to 8:50 A.M. twice a week. During this time students accept responsibility for themselves with a minimum of supervision. Other schools dismiss students at noon or early in the afternoon once every other week or once a month or release teachers from their classroom duties, providing substitutes for them.

A less frequently used arrangement is the lengthening of the school year to twelve months. Teachers are employed on a twelve-month basis with one month's vacation. During the summer, teachers may work on local curriculum committees or in workshops, carry on study in some university or college, work with children in recreational or in other activities, or engage in educational travel. In a growing number of school systems, the teachers are paid for two weeks before school begins, to work in in-service education and planning.

State Curriculum Development Programs

Where does the state department of education fit into a scheme which considers the local school the primary unit for curriculum study? In times past it was quite common for a state department to issue courses of study which schools were expected to follow, a practice conceived of as leadership in curriculum improvement. The concept has changed radically to one of providing consultant services, spearheading curriculum committees, sponsoring workshops, and providing resource materials.

A number of state departments publish courses of study in the form of curriculum guides as a source of suggestions and helps. These guides are generally not written by the state office personnel but are developed by teachers and administrators from schools of the state, sometimes in summer workshops and sometimes in committees working during the school year. Informational bulletins dealing with school practices, procedures, and descriptions of programs may be developed to give assistance to the people of the state.

Rather comprehensive in-service education programs have been developed by a few states. One state department of education has organized a state-wide in-service program. The state provides basic school support money for five days during the year to any district or unit that wishes to develop an in-service program. A state committee has developed criteria for in-service programs and has stimulated such programs in the state. Many schools conduct under this program a week-long conference preceding the opening of school. Another state department of education in which there are a number of smaller school districts has taken the lead in developing a cooperative program for instructional improvement, in which voluntary associations of school districts are formed on a regional basis within the state. Through this organization, school districts exchange ideas about practices, plan joint projects, share resources, hold joint workshops and conferences, and avoid duplication of effort. The state department coordinates the program, providing consultant and secretarial services and securing the assistance of state institutions of higher learning and professional organizations.

Another frequent type of state service is that of sponsoring curriculum conferences. These conferences may be regional or state-wide in scope. One state department of education sponsors annual conferences in elementary education and secondary education. Another sponsors work conferences in a local area, which last for one to three days, sometimes longer.

County Services

The county school office, in states where the county is not the school district itself, supplements the services of the state department of education. In fact, in large counties in some Western states, extensive resource services are provided in addition to supervisory services. For example, one large county in this area performs the functions of a service agency to the schools of the county. It gives consultant services; produces and loans audio-visual aids and curriculum library materials; provides working space for curriculum committees in the curriculum laboratory; sponsors conferences and workshops; directs curriculum committee work through the curriculum planning committee for the county; prepares curriculum bulletins; publishes a curriculum journal; and assists the schools in other ways. These services are also provided on a large scale in the Eastern states where the county is the local school district. In fact, some large counties in this section of the country have far more supervisory and pupil personnel services than do many of the state departments of education in the less highly populated states in the Midwest.

Demonstration and Experimental Programs

The advent of funds available from private foundations and federal agencies has also brought some innovations to organizing for curriculum study and planning. One of these is closer working relationships among the academic departments of universities, the colleges of education, and the public schools, in combined in-service education and production of curriculum materials projects. The other is the provision of demonstration centers on a large scale.

Some of the new curriculum projects that focus on revision of content for classroom use have operated on the assumption that unless people change, little or no change in the curriculum can be anticipated. Instead of merely preparing curriculum materials with new content that represents a different approach, they have realized that the involvement of the teacher is essential. Thus, in one mathematics project, members of the faculty of the department of mathematics, the college of engineering, and the college of education; teachers and supervisors from the public schools; and members of the staff of the state department of education served as an advisory committee that met frequently to guide the project. At the same time that the new curriculum materials were being developed, teachers who were to use the materials met with the project staff in a weekly seminar to learn more about the new concepts and to assist in the development of the materials to be used in their classes. Following the completion of units of work, they were tested out in these teachers' classrooms and evaluated under the direction of the project staff. In the meantime, an extensive number of in-service classes in the new mathematics were conducted by the university in the schools participating in the project. During summer session, demonstration classes with children were conducted on the campus. As new schools requested purchase of the materials in order to use them in their classes, they were required to show evidence through former or present in-service activities that teachers had been prepared to use the materials intelligently. Subsequent to the development of these guides, many in-service classes have continued to be taught for new teachers coming into the school systems.

A few of the larger grants of funds have been for experimental–demonstration types of projects. This has been true for some grants for television and team teaching. School systems, or colleges working cooperatively with schools, have served in a real sense as experimental centers in which ideas were tried out under promising conditions.

They became demonstration centers where many school people came to observe the programs at work. The idea has caught on with granting agencies to the extent that some large grants of funds have been given for the purpose of making studies that specifically include demonstration centers where others can observe practices. These are pilot types of programs that stimulate other schools to make changes. In a sense they are a means of speedup of curriculum or instructional change.

WORKSHOPS

Participating in a curriculum workshop is a most fruitful opportunity for teachers to learn through illustrative experiences the principles being taught. The workshop is increasingly employed as an avenue to curriculum improvement and in-service education in school systems and on university and college campuses.

There is no *one* proved best way of workshop operation. However, experience and experimentation have indicated a number of principles and techniques that produce effective results and can be helpful to participants, consultants, and neophytes in understanding what a workshop is like.

Characteristics

A workshop can best be defined by describing its characteristics. The fact that the term has been used rather loosely, so that almost any kind of conference has been called a workshop, has led to criticism of workshops on college campuses as not being "respectable" courses. Certain principles govern the workshop process.

The workshop is based on the same theory and principles as the experience-centered approach to curriculum development. Of no little significance is the fact that the workshop utilizes procedures which people who believe in the experience-centered approach advocate for schools. In other words, through the workshop experience teachers can learn how to put this approach into practice. If any supervisor or college teacher is going to help teachers become secure in using an experience-centered approach, he must give them know-how in carrying it out.

The workshop has a flexible schedule planned cooperatively by participants and staff. A minimum of preplanned organization faces the participants when they first arrive, although the staff has done a great deal of preliminary planning. In some cases, the staff members may find that planning rather carefully for the first week will help give the participants security. In other instances speakers or consultants must be contacted ahead of time for definite dates, particularly if they come from other schools or colleges. However, even though activities may be planned for the group as a whole, participants need to have an opportunity to plan the activities that will help them promote their goals.

Participants determine their own individual and group goals. One of the functions of the workshop staff or consultants is to help the members define goals. Through conferences, the staff helps the members to clarify what they hope to accomplish during the workshop. Consultants also work with the total group to discover common interests around which small working groups can be organized. Sometimes schools send groups of teachers to a workshop to plan together for the school program. A very fruitful situation is one in which the administrator and a group of teachers come together to plan for curriculum improvement.

A workshop utilizes the best that is known about group procedures. Group process skills are applied in the workshop in order that it may function effectively. In addition to selecting problems and goals and planning how to accomplish those goals, the group constantly evaluates its procedures. In fact, one of the typical features is evaluation of the workshop itself, made at intervals throughout the time that the group meets. Participants are free to criticize and cooperatively change the plans for the good of the group. These are the essentials of cooperative planning.

Resources found within and outside the workshop are used to solve problems. One of the distinguishing marks of a workshop is that participants discover their best resources among themselves; they become well acquainted with each other and with the resources represented in the group. The members furnish information and help to clarify each other's problems through their own special abilities and backgrounds. Other kinds of resources are available outside the workshop. If it is held in a school, there are innumerable resources within the community. Community organizations, industries, and places of interest can furnish opportunities for field trips or resource persons. On a campus there are outstanding resources in the staff members who are specialists in various subject disciplines, and there may be summer classes in the laboratory school which can be utilized for observation purposes. A general library, a curriculum library, an audio-visual aids center, and experimental centers of various kinds are found on most campuses. A common practice is to establish a library of books and other instructional materials for the workshop itself, with students participating in organizing the library by bringing books of their own as well as gathering other materials.

A *block of time long enough to permit cooperative procedures is provided during each session and for the total workshop.* A workshop requires a longer period of time for each session than the ordinary class. For those held during the summer, full time is given to the workshop. Those held during the year in a school system are scheduled for at least three consecutive hours. Sometimes workshops meet from about four o'clock in the afternoon to about nine in the evening, with time for a social hour during the dinner period. If the group procedures are to be effective, groups must work together long enough to establish rapport among the members. A workshop needs to be more than two or three days long. Generally speaking, it should run from three to eight weeks during the summer or from fifteen to thirty weeks during the regular year.

Persons in the learning situation get to know each other. Much of the success of a workshop lies in the close ties of consultants and members. Consultants also get to know participants through individual conferences, small work groups, and social functions. Participants have many opportunities for informal conferences with the staff.

Preplanning

The purposes and problems to be studied or the general theme of the workshop need to be determined. Materials must be collected to be used as resources by the participants. Contacts need to be made with those who are to be in the workshop. It is a good idea to ask prospective participants something about themselves in order that consultants may use this information in their planning. Personal contacts are desirable between the staff, which may include supervisors from the central office or principals, and those who are planning to participate. The staff of the workshop will need to meet a number of times before the workshop begins. Demonstration classes may need to be set up. Usually there are publicity releases to be prepared and sent out to prospective participants. Consultants, whose services must be engaged ahead of time, need to be selected in terms of their specialties. In some workshops, such as those on family finance and economic education, speakers from the fields of economics, insurance, business, labor, and allied fields are scheduled for a number of sessions. All of this planning has to be done before the workshop begins. In local workshops, planning sessions with the consultant and a local planning committee of administrators and teachers will help to set the stage for the workshop and determine agreements with regard to policy.

Getting Under Way

One of the more difficult phases of a workshop is the beginning stage. At the first meeting, the director faces a group of people often unfamiliar with the workshop concept. They are wondering what this venture will be like. Some may come with a "show-me" attitude. If credit is given, many worry about the mark they will achieve.

The director first has the task of establishing some kind of rapport with the group. Time should be taken to get acquainted. At this point it is well to stress that the group should discover what resources they have among themselves. The members should tell enough about themselves to give a picture of their background. Sometimes this activity may take an hour or more. There will undoubtedly be those who object to consuming that much time on getting to know each other. They want to get to work as soon as possible. Some kind of a coffee hour during the early get-acquainted period is helpful. The consultants can mingle with the group, talking with the various members personally. As a part of the first session, participants can tell what they hope the workshop will mean for them. This procedure will indicate the participants' interests, and whether or not they have a definite goal in mind.

Then comes the troublesome problem of orientation to workshop procedures. Perhaps there is no satisfactory way of orienting a group except to give them actual experience in the workshop itself. Kelley, from his wealth of experience in workshops at Wayne State University, tells of an experiment that he has tried. At the opening session a staff member explains workshop methods and objectives; then at the closing session the speech is repeated. Yet, he has found that several people will invariably ask, "Why didn't you tell us this at the beginning?" [1] Their background of experience is too limited to understand the procedure until they participate in it. However, when evaluating workshops, participants indicate that they feel somewhat more secure at the beginning if they have been told what the workshop is going to be like and what will be expected of them. Probably the best way to define these expectancies is in terms of the various opportunities in the workshop for achieving one's own goals. If the

---

[1] Earl C. Kelley, *The Workshop Way of Learning*, New York: Harper & Row, Publishers, 1951, pp. 14–15.

director goes further and outlines in his opening remarks what is to be studied, he will to a large extent defeat the purposes of a workshop. It is useful to place on a table in the room several bulletins about workshops and reports of previous workshops. A danger is that groups sometimes feel that they must do the same things another workshop has done.

Small heterogeneous groups may be formed early to begin defining problems for group study. These groups are asked to appoint one of their members as chairman and to report to the entire group. The consultants spend time with the groups, helping them to clarify their problems and to arrive at some points of common interest, a task that may take more than one session. If the workshop is small, the director can serve as leader of the entire group in the problem-defining stage. Only committees that are really needed should be organized. The best time for getting committees under way is when the need arises. An alternate leader may be selected and potential resource persons identified.

There will be many discouragements in the early phases of the workshop. People may feel that it is moving too slowly and that they do not have enough to do. They will complain that because no definite assignments have been given they do not know just what is expected of them. There is a great temptation at this point for the leader to make assignments. About the end of the second week the members may find that they have too much to do; consequently, time needs to be spent on evaluating all of the activities and analyzing which of the individual's interests have caused him to be overburdened.

Organization of the Workshop

No one schedule can be suggested that will fit the needs of all workshops. This is the function of planning within the group. However, some illustrations are given here to indicate how certain workshops have been organized with flexible schedules that could be changed from week to week. In fact, it is an advantage that workshops have not crystallized into any standard or set pattern but are organized in different ways. Only through such diversity can knowledge about procedures in workshops be expected to grow.

The following description of a workshop that utilized a laboratory class is presented as an example. A workshop in secondary education at a state university had as an integral part a demonstration or laboratory class of junior high school students. Each year the workshop centered around a general theme broad enough to permit planning to meet the needs of the participants. The staff consisted of the director, a specialist in junior high school education, and a staff member who taught the laboratory class and served as a consultant to the participants. The group included both principals and teachers.

The schedule for the workshop was as follows:

9:00–11:00 A.M.	Laboratory class
11:00–12:00 A.M.	General session (preceded by a coffee break)
12:30– 1:30 P.M.	Lunch period
2:00– 3:30 P.M.	Meeting of interest groups, three times a week
	Individual conferences and individual work
	Free afternoon on Friday
3:30– 4:40 P.M.	Individual conferences
Late P.M. or evening	Social activities about once a week

Interest groups were formed one year around the topics of pupil participation in developing a good junior high school community, group methods and processes, and integrated English–social studies classes. Service committees included publicity, planning, recreation, and evaluation. Participants kept close contact with the children in the laboratory class, working with the different groups, assisting individuals who required special help, and utilizing the class as a means to meet their own objectives.

General sessions were devoted at least once a week to discussion of the laboratory class with the teacher. At one of the sessions each week, the committee on evaluation led the entire workshop in evaluating its experiences during the week. In these general sessions some time was spent on gaining better understanding of group procedures. Among the special resource persons invited were a principal from a junior high school with an outstanding core program, an assistant principal from a junior high school with another good core program, a director of instruction, and staff members from the university.

Another example of a general curriculum workshop was conducted in a large school system. The workshop, housed in a school building, was one of four held during one summer. Individuals from other local workshops served as resource people, and the director, a supervisor, and principals served as the staff.

In this particular case the workshop was an outgrowth of curriculum study carried on throughout the year. The five areas studied represented five curriculum committees that had been working during the year and wanted to continue their work during the summer with additional teachers to assist them. Any teacher could enroll if he wished. Considerable planning for the workshop was done ahead of time, and included the participants who could be identified.

The group met five days a week for six weeks, with a flexible schedule within this framework, including a coffee break in the morning:

8:00– 8:45 A.M.	Conference period
8:45–10:45 A.M.	Work groups
10:45–11:45 A.M.	General session
11:45– 1:30 P.M.	Lunch and social hour
1:40– 4:00 P.M.	Open for study, conferences, excursions, speakers, committee meetings

The instructional materials center, which was located nearby in the administration building, served as a valuable resource for the workshop.

In a workshop conducted during the school year in a school system with consultants from a private university, the following time schedule was arranged for daily sessions:

4:00–5:15 P.M.	General sessions: lectures, films, and discussion on problems, issues, trends, and practices in curriculum planning and teaching
5:15–6:00 P.M.	Work group meetings or continuation of general sessions: work groups on reading, citizenship education, science, arts and crafts
6:00–7:00 P.M.	Dinner and relaxation
7:15–8:30 P.M.	Work groups
8:30–9:00 P.M.	Workshop committee meetings, library books checked out, individual conferences, summary sessions, etc., as needed

In these examples, different phases of a workshop can be noted. Some of the following apply more to a continuous, all-day, summer workshop.

1. General sessions. The general session is a necessary part of any workshop, to give the entire group an opportunity to work and plan together. In these sessions, planning meetings are held, reports of the planning committee are given to the entire group for its consideration, and the schedule is outlined. (Some prefer to do the planning entirely with the group as a whole, without a planning committee.) This is the time when common problems are considered and speakers are invited to present information pertinent to the goals of the workshop. Evaluating and summarizing sessions can be held. At general sessions participants have an opportunity to ask questions, discuss common problems, and present information. Reports from the various interest groups can be given. Such total group activities are essential to form a real group and to achieve a unity in the workshop.

2. Interest groups. Ordinarily a workshop is divided into smaller groups to give participants an opportunity to pursue special interests that several members may have in common. These groups are formed through the cooperative planning of all workshop members. Each group chooses its own leader, recorder, and other resource individuals within the group. Interest groups are excellent laboratories for group procedures. The staff should assist each group in evaluating the process by which it works. Staff members serve these groups as consultants, not as leaders.

Leaders may be appointed by the workshop director ahead of time from among principals or supervisors in the school system. In some cases, they are consultants who are regular members of the workshop staff. In the case of interest groups that are formed from specific school systems, and in other instances as well, the election of the leader by the group itself is accepted procedure.

3. Individual objectives. Provision should be made in the day's schedule for individuals to work on their own objectives. They need time for individual work, study, reading, and conferences with consultants. Provisions should be flexible enough so that the creative individual does not need to follow all of the routine procedures if he has some objectives to pursue that might be hampered by a fixed schedule.

If change of behavior is the objective of the workshop, participants should not be required to write a paper. The individual's goals may be found within the workshop itself. For example, a participant may find that he wants to learn to do role-playing, learn about evaluation, or learn about group procedures. He can utilize the workshop as a laboratory, or if there are children's laboratory classes he has even greater resources at hand. A participant may learn how to work with small groups of pupils in a classroom by assisting the laboratory class teacher.

For some, individual work may mean study and thinking about problems that bother them, having frequent conferences with consultants, other participants, and resource people. They may wish to present their thinking to the group as a whole for criticisms and suggestions. Others will have definite planning to do for their work for next year—units, other instructional activities, or a course of study.

In other words, the goal of the individual in the workshop should be to solve some problem that is important to him. The emphasis is on the individual's goals rather than on projects. Early in the workshop, the consultants should begin exploring goals with the individual participants, helping them to reach a definition. For some people this may take a week or more, but it is better to work with such an individual until he clarifies what he wants to do than to suggest a project for him merely to get something under way. In local workshops individual objectives often will tend to be a part of those of the group, decided upon by the small group of which the participant is a member.

4. Service committees. In every workshop there are materials to be taken care of, plans to be made for recreational activities, general planning to be done, and other kinds of services to be performed for the whole group. Service committees to assume these responsibilities ought to be formed rather early in the workshop, as soon as the group discovers what services are needed. Examples of such necessary committees are a library committee, a resource committee, an evaluation or reviewing committee, a social or recreation committee, a coffee committee, a luncheon committee.

5. Social activities and housing. In the formation of a cohesive group structure, the value of socializing activities should not be underestimated. The "living-in" workshop, where the group lives together in a campus dormitory or in a camp at a lake, has the advantage of enabling participants to plan all of their activities together. If the participants commute to a campus, or if a workshop is held during the school year when other activities compete with it, there is a distinct limitation to carrying on social activities. The group can meet together for luncheon in an all-day workshop and for dinner in a local workshop that meets in late afternoon. Many workshops have found it successful to schedule a coffee break in the middle of the morning or afternoon. In local workshops that begin after school, it is a distinct advantage to begin with a coffee hour. In summer workshops, activities such as picnics, summer theatres, field trips, square dances, salmon bakes, and steak fries have been found popular. Needless to say, there should be no forced activities. The participants themselves should plan their recreational and social activities. It is an advantage to have a social get-together early in the course of the workshop.

Socializing activities are related to informal, comfortable housing. On campuses, some workshops are housed in a dormitory by themselves, with lounges used for meeting rooms for committees and other small groups.

6. Laboratory classes. A demonstration or laboratory class is a distinct asset to a workshop. Teachers and administrators have the opportunity not only to talk about teaching procedures but also to see them in action. These classes are a very definite part of the ongoing activities of the workshop, not an adjunct for observation purposes

only. There are many opportunities for participants to take part in the laboratory class itself and to assist the laboratory teacher. They come to feel an identification with the class, participating in the recreational as well as the instructional activities of the children. In one university, laboratory classes of children with different kinds of handicaps and of different ages, as well as groups of gifted children, are held in connection with special education workshops in cooperation with the county schools.

Time needs to be allowed in general or group sessions for laboratory teachers to explain what they are doing, the purposes they have in mind, and the reasons behind the activities of the class.

Evaluation

Perhaps more evaluation has been done of workshops than of any other kind of course. The different types of evaluation that can be used are: evaluation carried on cooperatively throughout the workshop by participants and the staff, personal evaluation by participants, follow-up studies, and research studies, especially action research.

Workshops conduct constant evaluation of procedures and of the progress that the group is making. The weekly evaluation session presents an opportunity for the staff and the participants to talk over ways in which the workshop can be improved. An evaluation committee can facilitate this objective by devising ways and means of evaluating the workshop. On the days set aside for evaluation, the committee presents a report compiled from information gathered from the participants. Evaluation throughout the workshop can be made by a process observer in the general sessions or interest groups. Evaluation is also made when the consultant discusses with individual members the progress they have made toward their goals. The staff holds meetings at which it evaluates how it functions and how it can improve its services.

Data gathered from the participants and from careful observation are important kinds of objective information. Immediate personal reactions given frankly and sincerely express feelings accurately in a permissive situation. The remarks people make to each other voluntarily during a workshop and the statements on an unsigned, open-ended evaluation form developed by the participants can be relied upon as being fairly accurate descriptions of feelings. They represent a newer kind of evaluation that probes interpersonal relationships in a group and attempts to understand the dynamics of the group. They express what people feel about the particular experience that they have had.

If it is true that curriculum change occurs as relationships among individuals change, then it follows that workshops have been important factors in changing the curriculum. These observations apply only to the workshop that meets the criteria discussed. By no means would all workshops be so evaluated.

There is some evidence from follow-up studies, observation of behavior in workshops, and statements made by participants on evaluation forms to indicate that significant changes are taking place. Seemingly, attitudes are changing toward the use of such procedures as class participation in planning, pupil participation in problem-solving, teacher–pupil evaluation, group work, and the handling of discipline cases as adjustment problems. Many teachers participating in workshops change their attitudes toward the experience-centered approach when they have both observed and experienced its use. Frequently, evidence of reading done appears to be greater and more selective than that done for a regular course. One of the most conclusive bits of evidence that workshops serve their purpose is that they meet the individual needs of participants.

In general, a workshop is much more expensive than any other kind of class because the number of students per staff member is much smaller. The ratio of students to staff members should be no greater than ten to one if the principles of a workshop are to operate most effectively. The budget of the workshop needs to provide for bringing in outside consultants, secretarial services, teachers of demonstration classes, and other costs. By no means should a workshop be evaluated in terms of the income it brings to an institution or school.

ISSUES AND POINTS OF VIEW

The issues which relate to ways of organizing for curriculum improvement are neither as sharply drawn nor debated as those which deal with the experiences of pupils or the ends of the improvement program. In a sense, the issues discussed here are a part of the larger question of group process and leadership.

1. *Should all of those concerned about curriculum decisions be organized to participate in curriculum study, or should only those especially concerned and willing to experiment and change be involved?*

In a way, this issue is a question of a solid-front vs. a broken-front approach in curriculum development, but it looks at the problem from a different perspective. The question is not whether we attack the problem in all groups or only in a few. Rather, do we begin with those who are really concerned enough about the problem to be willing to change?

There are those who believe curriculum study should achieve full participation on the part of all the faculty in any school unit that tackles curriculum study. The pros and cons should be debated by the whole group to arrive at some type of consensus. The principle that those involved in change should be consulted about it is cited as supporting this position.

Others ask whether any kind of curriculum study can ever achieve full participation. What of the recalcitrants? Will they not be a drag on progress? Not everyone wants to be organized into a working group. Also, to be able to argue a point is a far different type of participation from being willing to take the risk of experimentation with a new approach. The one who argues places himself in a rather safe position without any hazard of changing his ways. Besides, who has sufficient vision and competency to do the job? The proponents of this argument hold that far greater progress in thinking will be made if the few who are really concerned enough to want to do something are encouraged and helped to make the change. How could 100 per cent participation be achieved anyway? What about pupils and citizens, to say nothing about all teachers?

2. *Should the organization for curriculum study be centered on committee work within a broad framework, or upon the individual teacher and his freedom to experiment?*

The typical pattern for curriculum study is some type of committee structure, with committees responsible to an over-all steering committee or to the faculty as a whole. Much curriculum study under this process consists of making revisions in courses, recommending some changes in content or procedure, or dealing with some organizational changes.

A different pattern, which is discussed more fully in Chapter 9, consists of the teachers' involvement in searching for and testing out new ideas. Experimentation, research, and demonstration are ways of working at curriculum change in which the teacher becomes the researcher, the experimenter, and the demonstrator.

The difference seems to lie between an emphasis on an organizational pattern that sometimes acts as a barrier to creative approaches, and the individual's own involvement. Committee consensus often means a common denominator rather than any breakthrough to demonstrate and try out new ideas. The former may freeze rather than free.

It is of interest to note that some of the newer types of programs that involve experimentation with new content have involved individual teachers from the beginning. Yet, they had no elaborate structure, but gave to teachers who wanted it the opportunity to be a part of a study.

The fundamental question is which type of approach will really promote change in an individual's thinking, feeling, and doing; in human relationships; and in the individual's perception of himself.

3. *Are workshops an effective means of changing behavior, are they adapted to meeting the individual needs of participants, or are they less respectable than other types of courses, suited to in-service work but not to college programs?*

The layman would think this a silly question. He would say, "Why don't you find out?" But curriculum questions are generally not argued out on any rational basis. All the emotional attachments to a point of view, personal feelings, folk tales, and self-images are entailed. The question of effectiveness can be asked of any type of course or curriculum study.

However, this is a real issue on campuses. The workshop grew out of the progressive education era and, consequently, is suspect. Its precepts violate some of the hoary concepts of respectability of courses.

The workshop needs to be examined rigorously as a means of providing experiences that change behavior—that is, if change of behavior is important. Since it is more experimental than other means of college campus instruction, it more readily comes under scrutiny. Since it takes more time of students and instructors, its value should be questioned. So should courses: lecture courses, seminars, and other types. But college courses are sacred ground and are rarely subject to evaluative studies.

If an analytical study could be made of the kinds of behavior both instructors and students exhibit in different kinds of teaching–learning situations, perhaps we could come closer to the answers to these questions.

8

CITIZEN PARTICIPATION
IN CURRICULUM STUDY

The upsurge of interest in citizens' advisory committees and lay participation in curriculum study is of relatively recent origin. In the curriculum field, one of the earlier publications devoted to this topic was *Laymen Help Plan the Curriculum*, published by the Association for Supervision and Curriculum Development in 1946. The National Citizens Commission for the Public Schools (now the National Citizens Council for Better Schools) was formed in 1949. No major publications on the topic appeared for about half a decade after the middle 1950's. In the early 60's the clamor of voices from the critics became louder. Since then the public's interest in its schools has been more widespread than ever.

PRINCIPLES OF CITIZEN PARTICIPATION

Principles of curriculum development discussed in the first part of this book have applications in the school–community cooperative process. Out of the experiences of schools and field programs of institutions of higher learning have emerged other guiding principles for effective teamwork.

The community has a right and an obligation to participate in defining the school's program. Not only does the citizen have a right to participate in curriculum study, but he also has a duty to do so. This country's splendid public school systems could not have been developed if devoted citizens had not felt it was their obligation to serve on boards of education and had not sacrificed their time and energy to promote and improve the schools. The public school could not long exist as an institution if the community were not interested in its schools and had no way of showing that interest.

The public schools are a cooperative venture of citizens and the educators that the community employs to run this important enterprise. Where close cooperation exists, there is better understanding of the school's program. In turn, the community has a means of expressing its wishes concerning the school. The close cooperation of school and community, where educators and citizens respect each other, means better schools for the children of the community.

Well organized two-way channels of communication are essential. Communication between the school and the public is a two-way street. The school needs to obtain the opinions and other kinds of information the public can furnish just as much as the public needs to have information about its schools.

Sometimes the school centers its efforts on telling the citizens what the school is doing through public relations media, such as radio, television, newspapers, and school bulletins. This concept does not involve interaction. Nor does it assume that there are mutual benefits to be gained from cooperative efforts.

The school that wants to strengthen its program organizes ways by which citizens and parents can regularly communicate their ideas, their questions, and their opinions.

The citizens of the community should be the ones who defend their schools against ignorance and calumny. The forces of economy, self-interest, and ignorance are usually well mobilized. It is relatively easy to promote a cause *against* something. Educators cannot be expected to battle these forces alone. It is the community's responsibility to protect its schools from these regressive forces. The destructive attempts of opportunists, sensationalists, racketeers, individuals and groups with biases, and foes of public education, to get into school affairs result from having no regular participation by citizens. Well organized channels of communication between school and community are a bulwark in times of irresponsible attacks upon the schools.

The community should cooperate with the school in constant evaluation of its program. Not only is it the citizen's function to help determine the purposes and experiences of the school, but it is also his responsibility to share in the evaluation of the school program. He should know what the school is accomplishing for the children in the community.

Citizen participation in evaluation of the school's program is a great advantage to the educator. As curriculum committees working with lay participants make plans for change, they should set up methods of evaluating the changes they suggest. There is little danger, if citizens participate actively in evaluating change, that they will consider changes "radical" or find them convenient points of attack. If they are involved in the planning and appraisal of curriculum improvement, these citizens will be among the strongest supporters of changes that prove successful. Lay participation is a means of strengthening curriculum improvements that are made.

Effective citizen participation requires school leadership. No strong program of school–community cooperation in curriculum study is likely to exist unless the school leaders take the initiative. The superintendent, principal, curriculum coordinator, or other leader is responsible for seeing that lay advisory councils are started or that citizens are invited to participate in curriculum committees and local workshops. The leader who believes in working with the community will undoubtedly use various means for establishing channels of communication with the community. The school activities described in this chapter did not just happen to occur.

Any lay advisory group should have the guidance of school leaders. The practice of lay committees working by themselves without school representation violates the principle of cooperative action that results in mutual understanding. It is exactly the situations where citizen groups organize by themselves which make teachers and administrators fearful of lay participation in curriculum affairs.

Citizen participation in curriculum study is useful and productive only if it involves fact-finding, seeking evidence, and reading. When lay persons participate in curriculum committees, councils, or workshops, they should be involved in some real, hard study of the problems under consideration. There is no point to inviting citizens to serve on committees to air their prejudices and argue for their point of view. Instead, the curriculum leader would be far better off to schedule hearings where the public can have their say.

This study should not be of the casual kind. It means an obligation and a willingness to seek better answers. It means participation from the beginning in defining a problem, gathering information, reading widely, evaluating on the basis of evidence, and drawing conclusions. When citizens become an integral part of the total study in this manner, they will both contribute to the program and learn about it.

Committees studying the curriculum should include lay persons.

This principle is valid only if the assumption is made that the citizens will engage in study of the committee's problem as actively as teachers do. One has to assume also that they have something valuable to contribute. We should not sell parents short nor underestimate their potential contributions to curriculum improvement. In fact, in some instances the parents are far ahead of the teachers in their thinking, and would make changes more rapidly. Incidentally, this may be one of the reasons why some teachers are reluctant to include parents in curriculum study. Moreover, since school–community cooperation is an excellent means of adult education, the mutual gain from the process makes it important not to miss such an opportunity.

Lay persons involved in curriculum study should be broadly representative of the community. They should be spokesmen for different points of view on the problem studied, different geographical areas in larger communities, and different socio-economic levels. Even though it may be more difficult for the factory workers and the store clerks to come to committee meetings, they should be included in curriculum study. The leaders of unions can be asked to suggest participants. It is expected that the citizen-members will seek suggestions from others in the community and will publicize what the school is doing to improve its programs. Consequently, wide contacts are needed from various groups.

One means for the selection of citizens in order to secure a representative group is to invite certain individuals to work with the committee. Inviting people who teachers believe can help will aid in allaying teachers' fears about citizen participation. Practice indicates that inviting persons broadly representative of the community is more successful than asking community organizations to send representatives. An organization may send its president, secretary, or some other official who is already a busy person or who may not be the one in his group most interested in the study. Another procedure is to ask community groups to suggest or nominate possible participants. School leaders and community group leaders can confer in making the choice on the basis of definite criteria jointly agreed upon.

Recommendations made by lay advisory groups should be channeled through the board of education. The board of education as the legally constituted body for the school district is the lay group which represents the community. Advisory bodies expand the community's participation in its school affairs. These groups are, thus, responsible to the board. If any new policies are involved, they must be acted on by the board. In some cases, where the advisory body is a separate group from the curriculum council of the schools, the council, as the coordinating body for curriculum study in the schools, should first consider these recommendations.

There should be a clear understanding of the roles and responsibilities of citizens working with the schools. This principle is fundamental to successful school–community cooperation. Where citizen groups want to take over functions of the board of education or dictate to the administration, lay participation will be of negative value. The only change that may result is likely to be a backward step. Dissident minorities can capitalize on lack of coordination, confusion of role, and poor leadership by the school. Lay participation seen in its broader sense includes many types of involvement, from room mothers to committee membership. In each instance, the role of the lay person is a different one. This question is explored in the next section.

THE ROLE OF THE CITIZEN

What then should be the citizen's function in curriculum improvement? What are the specialties that he can contribute to curriculum study? These questions need to be examined in the context of a broad scope of participation.

Principles Governing Role

Citizens should participate in both the determination of the school's purposes and of the experiences provided for pupils. There should be no quarrel with the idea that citizens should participate in determining the purposes of the school. This is the area in which they can make their greatest contribution. They are very much concerned about the kind of person they want their children to be. They can also make invaluable contributions toward determining the total framework of experiences children should have.

The subject-centered approach to curriculum development, which identifies purposes with subject matter to be learned, regards content and method as separate entities in the teaching–learning process. Thus, it is easy to say that the community should participate in the determination of objectives and content but have nothing to do with the methods and evaluation of teaching. A considerable argument can be made for excluding the public from participating in decisions concerning methods of teaching or in the selection of content, since it requires years of study for the teacher to attain professional competency in both subject matter and methods.

In the experience-centered approach to curriculum development, no sharp distinction is made between method and content. If the curriculum is regarded as experiences provided for pupils to change their behavior, the whole process becomes a unified one. Under this approach, if they participate at all, it is logical that citizens should take part in making decisions about the curriculum as a whole.

If the premise that the schools belong to the public is true, then citizens have a right to be concerned about the kinds of experiences that pupils have in the public schools. Only if we separate means from ends can we uphold the point of view that citizens should be concerned about purposes and content but not about methods and evaluation. Both content and methods enter into determining whether purposes have been achieved. The purposing–evaluating process goes on throughout the learning situation.

It does not make sense to say that parents should know nothing about the methods of teaching reading. This attitude only alienates parents. Parents need to understand the concepts behind modern procedures in teaching reading. They do not "decide" how reading is to be taught or how the teacher is to function in the classroom. The procedures that a teacher uses are generally left to his own decision.

The particular contribution that the citizen can make depends upon his special competence in relation to the situation. In advisory bodies in which a broad representation from the community is wanted, the competency needed is the ability to communicate one's own opinions, survey opinions of others, and in turn communicate to the citizenry the school's purposes and program. The process is always a two-way one. Those who in past performances have shown no ability or desire to rise above prejudice and work for the good of the school have no place on advisory bodies either through election or appointment. This by no means infers that all who participate must be those who agree with "the establishment." They need to represent different opinions but they also need to be able to listen to others' opinions and to work toward rational ends.

It is in the study of specific curriculum problems by committees where some greater specialization of competency may be demanded. The committee studying the advisability of inaugurating a program of foreign languages in the elementary school can use lay persons who have some understanding of language, for example. Yet, even here, it would be a mistake to assume that all need such a specialty. It is more necessary to secure persons who can look at the question objectively.

There are a number of situations in which citizens can be unusually helpful. For example, in the study of improvement of a social studies program, the question of community resources invariably will arise. The group will be concerned with resource people and all kinds of fields trips that can be taken by the school. Citizens have often given invaluable assistance to committees in a survey to determine the available resources. In one committee study dealing with the development of a cumulative record for the school system, the parents' knowledge of children's after-school activities was helpful in deciding the kind of information to record.

Other types of participation require special interests, hobbies, backgrounds, and talents.

Citizens should participate in the committee deliberations from the beginning of the study. They should help to define the goals of the study and the ways of attaining the goals. They should be considered as fully participating committee members who work through the problem to its solution. At times, teachers engaged in curriculum work will say: "We want parents to work with us, but let us wait to invite them until we have clarified what we want to do and how we will do it." In other words, they want to make some preliminary decisions and agreements before the citizens are brought in. They are reluctant to admit that teachers have differences of opinion, not realizing that such differences may be valuable sparks for the study itself and that clarification of thinking can be done with parents in the group as well as without them. They fail to understand that defining the problem and procedures is a significant part of group process. Someone who joins a group after these decisions are made will find it difficult to become a part of the group.

Citizens' roles may be as regular committee members, consultants, or as a purely advisory group, depending upon the situation. When citizens participate as members of a school–community council or as invited members of a curriculum committee, they are in effect bona fide members of the group, assisting in making decisions. At other times, a school committee may wish to invite citizens as consultants for a series of meetings. In that case, their role is different. They are called upon to furnish the information or opinions wanted. Lay advisory councils serve in the role of a group that advises educators concerning school problems. The function of the lay participants should always be spelled out at the time they are invited.

Citizens' Perception of Their Role

Obviously only a few citizens in a community will be able to participate on intensive study programs, whether they be surveys, workshops, or curriculum committees. Many others will have different kinds of contacts with the school. But how will the total group of citizens, including the many who have no direct involvement, see their role in curriculum change? This is probably as crucial a question as one of definition of role. For the citizen's perception of his role in relation to the school will determine how he acts toward the school.

Perhaps it would help us to try to place ourselves in the role of a citizen in order to understand how he feels about his school. How does he see himself in his relationship to the school, especially in terms of his part in or knowledge of curriculum changes? The following are some typical statements citizens make with reference to their schools, which describe the way they view these relationships.

1. "About the only time that I am invited to the school is for events for which I am asked to pay an admission charge."

This perception typifies a situation in which there exists a low level of relationships between school and community. But these situations do exist, as some parents can testify. When a parent has no contacts with the school other than basketball games, plays, or special events in which he is a part of a mass audience, he has no way to communicate with the school except indirectly. This he may do by expressing his hostility in the way he talks about the school or in his actions when he is called upon to vote on some question relating to needed increased funds for the school.

2. "I am invited to the school for open house, for conferences with teachers when my child is having some difficulty, and for parent–teacher meetings."

This parent sees himself as having little opportunity to become a part of a real community school. There is actually little opportunity for communication in which the school can capitalize on the parents' ideas and information. These activities are confined largely to parents. The other citizens are left out of most of these activities. If a parent feels this way about his role in school–community relationships, it is doubtful how much correct information he has about the school's purposes and programs, or how much he can be counted on for support of any curriculum changes that are made. Parents with this concept of their role do not feel that they are contributing much to the improvement of the school program.

3. "I am asked by the school to give of my time, express my views, or help the school only when a new bond issue is before the people, when higher salaries are needed for teachers, or when the school is attacked by some anti-public school group."

The citizen who sees his participation in this light may be a supporter of the school, he may feel that the schools are doing a good job, but it is just as likely that he will express his resentment by some act inimical to the interests of a good school program. More than one community has had the experience of having a drive for finances turned down when the school leaders and school board fully expected the community to support their requests. Citizens resent being called upon for their assistance and opinions only when money is needed, and never being asked their counsel concerning the school program. Educators cannot afford to bring citizens in only during times of crisis.

4. "The school is none of my affair; let the busybodies who want to meddle in school matters do so."

There always seem to be some who indicate no interest in the school. They show an apathy that is difficult to explain. Some may not come to the school for parent–teacher meetings or for conferences with teachers because they feel out of place or unwelcome. Others simply do not seem to care. But these might be the very ones who are most easily swayed by rabble-rousers and self-appointed critics who spread falsehoods to suit their own purposes.

5. "This is *our* school."

This brief statement says a great deal. People who have a part in the school and who work closely with it identify themselves with it. There are schools throughout the country where parents and other citizens assist in children's programs, serve as room mothers, cooperate on field trips, assist in the lunch program, come to school for conferences and meetings with teachers, work with school curriculum committees. Many of these are in rural communities and smaller schools. The public feels that it is *their* school.

In order for the citizen to assume a new role, he must gain some greater satisfaction in it than the one that he now plays. It is the school's responsibility to see that it is possible for him to communicate with the school in some way that is satisfying for him and supportive of good school–community relations.

CHANNELS OF SCHOOL–COMMUNITY COOPERATION

Granted that citizens should participate in curriculum study, how then shall we go about it? How many lay people should be asked to work on such a study? How can we use them most effectively? In what ways can parents participate in the school program?

Curriculum Councils and Committees

The central curriculum coordinating councils of larger school systems often include in their membership lay persons who have been invited to serve. In some cases, they may represent the school areas or regions in the city, county, or consolidated school district.

Although not an extensive practice, the inclusion of citizens on curriculum committees to study certain problems has proved to be a practical means of involving the community in curriculum study. The committee may have the responsibility for updating the content in science, for studying the dropout problem, or for selecting materials and resources to use in a social studies program. On each of these problems, citizens have something to contribute and to learn. In a suburban school system, parents are members of a committee whenever major policy is of concern, such as the committees on moral and spiritual values, reporting to parents, and homework.

Probably more women will be available for committee work than men, but usually some men are willing to give their time if the study seems important to them. Committee meetings need to be scheduled at times when citizens can meet with the group. In one community, a number of lay men and women participated in a study of the improvement of the science program in the school. They came regularly to committee sessions after school. During the summer, when the committee decided to go to the state university for a brief workshop, a number of them spent two weeks on campus.

One unfortunate tendency of some teachers, particularly those who do a good deal of talking in the classroom, is to preach to parents who work with them on committees. They tell the parents what ought to be done. They see this opportunity as a means of educating parents and education is "telling." An important principle in curriculum committee work with parents is to listen to what they have to say.

Parents, as well as teachers, may feel superior and *know* they are right. There is no guarantee that in community–school cooperation in curriculum study everything will run smoothly. There will be times perhaps when lay persons will refuse to listen and will adhere dogmatically to their opinions. But this is also true of teachers. The selection of individuals who come to assist and learn, not to "sell" the school on some pet idea, should be the criterion kept in mind by school and community people. The calculated risks are fewer if the community is adequately represented than if it is on the outside.

Lay Advisory Councils and Citizens' Committees

In order to have more citizens involved in curriculum study, some school systems have organized lay advisory councils which serve in an advisory capacity to the coordinating curriculum committee. There may be an advisory council for each school unit or for the system as a whole. The councils have their own organization and hold their own meetings. They may or may not be studying the problems that are being studied by the curriculum council or school faculty. However, they receive reports from these other groups, carry on studies of their own, and report to the school on what needs to be done. Their function is entirely advisory.

A potentially embarrassing situation may arise when an advisory committee makes recommendations that are ignored. What is the effect upon the citizens when this happens? Doubtless it is as disconcerting and irritating as instances in which reports of teacher committees are disregarded. Cooperation between citizens and school people makes such occurrences less likely. Advisory committees should have regular communication with school leaders' committees. To have citizens' committees work alone without teacher representatives or consultants is as much a mistake as to have teacher committees work without lay representatives. Teachers and principals should use advisory committees only if they are willing to work with them and to accept their recommendations insofar as possible. Educators should neither dominate nor remain aloof from these advisory groups.

Citizens' advisory councils and committees can serve a number of useful functions. They can diagnose community needs, in vocational programs for example. They can assist in evaluative studies of the school program. They can make studies of community opinions concerning the schools and school practices. Inventories are available that can be used to secure the opinions of citizens in a systematic way. Through these and other means, they can assist school leaders in ascertaining and allaying parents' anxieties. "What will this new method mean for my child?" "Do these experimental practices mean that my children are being used as guinea pigs?" "Will they not be better off under the old program?" These thoughts represent normal anxieties of parents.

Different modes of organization of councils have developed. In a suburban community on the West Coast, an educational advisory committee composed of approximately 140 members representing community organizations of all types serves as a communication medium. The board of education, school administrators, and teachers invited as guests for a specific session, meet with the committee. An agenda is planned by the officers to include questions that the lay committee members wish to have discussed. Information regarding these questions is presented by the school administrators and teachers, and questions are raised by the members.

In one Eastern city, the home and school council curriculum committee is composed of a representative from each individual school's association of parents. The council curriculum committee meets a number of times a year. The director of curriculum and instruction and other educators are invited to attend meetings as resource persons. This committee functions as a study and parent education group. It selects important curriculum problems for study and in many instances organizes discussion groups, panels, and conferences in the individual schools. It has also planned city-wide conferences for laymen. In a New England state a governor's fact-finding commission established a local citizens' committee in every town interested. Thousands of citizens in the state participated in the study of school problems. There were studies of school population, school building needs, salary schedules, and curriculum and instructional problems.

Workshops

Local workshops offer another avenue for interchange of information and for using the talents and ideas of lay persons. In a study of the problem of reporting to parents, the parent–teacher associations in the schools in a large Western city cooperated during the year with a school committee. During the summer, a workshop growing out of the year's work included several parents in the four weeks' deliberation.

In the curriculum laboratories or workshops conducted locally by a university in one state, citizens participate in the majority of cases. They serve as regular members of the committees in the workshop, are present at general sessions when the group discusses the progress reports, and help to determine the final conclusions and recommendations. Cooperative planning with the citizens in the workshops has given teachers an unparalleled opportunity to become acquainted with parents and their thinking. The social activities in which teachers and citizens in these workshops participate are of importance in helping the two groups to get acquainted. These common activities help break down teachers' fear of working with the public.

Teachers and administrators have indicated through their evaluation of local workshops what they felt lay members of the group contributed. Some ways mentioned include:

Offered different points of view
Asked questions that made it necessary for us to clarify our own thinking
Contributed ideas which represented public attitudes about school affairs
Called attention to certain basic needs of young people
Showed us the cause of some pupils' attitudes
Opened up new possibilities for school–community cooperation
Broadened our vision concerning the community's needs.

Study of the Community

Another way of working with citizens in curriculum improvement is the study of community life, agencies, and activities by groups of teachers or by committees or councils of teachers and citizens. One of its direct purposes is to make teachers aware of the community's historical, economic, sociological, and industrial backgrounds, potentialities, and problems. The ultimate purpose is to improve the school program.

In a large city's community study program, the aims are child acculturation, curriculum revision, and community action. Excursions into slum areas, visits to churches of various faiths, meetings with racial groups, exploration of community resources, research projects in measuring community feelings, and studies of housing and governmental activities are some of the undertakings in which the teacher groups participate. Teachers assist community agencies in such action programs as improving community recreational facilities. They work closely with the Council of Social Agencies, The National Conference of Christians and Jews, the Citizens' Planning and Housing Authority.

A joint community study by lay and school people is illustrated by an area study in a Midwestern city. The study included a survey of community organizations, community–school conferences, and questioning of teachers and parents regarding opinions and problems of recreation and health. The general purpose of the study was to explore all possible opportunities to work together. Outgrowths of the work of the study were an area health council and a community-center lay advisory committee.

State or regional councils on economic education have been organized in many areas. Composed of members from school, industry, business, and labor groups, these councils have helped to develop mutual understanding about school programs, alert teachers and administrators to economic problems of the community, and promote first-hand contacts of teachers with community leaders. They have encouraged experimentation in the area of economic education. In a metropolitan area council in the East, fall conferences of three days in length are sponsored, and representatives of labor, management, and education are participants. Economic problems of community growth, economic aspects of metropolitan problems, and human factors in economic relationships have been discussed. Through summer workshops and a series of meetings during the year, educators and laymen have together grown in understanding of economic and educational problems.

School Surveys

In the traditional type of school survey, a consultant from a college or university is employed to conduct the survey with his staff and to give a report to the board of education. Sometimes these reports are compiled in rather voluminous form and published. Such surveys have some value. However, the trend is to have the survey made largely by the administrators, teachers, and people of the community, sometimes under the direction of an outside consultant. In the survey, the parents and teachers form committees to analyze the phases of the school program. They collect data and make recommendations based on the information they acquire. This procedure involves citizens directly in the study of school problems, including the curriculum.

An illustration of the effectiveness of such involvement occurred in one rural school system. A committee of citizens was formed to study the school, with the school staff acting as consultants. For years the supervisor had attempted to get new equipment and new teaching materials for the classrooms, but the board of education had turned down each request. When the citizens' group studied the program and surveyed the kinds of equipment and materials in the classrooms, it recommended that these needed items be purchased. Its recommendation was heeded by the board of education.

Parent–Teacher Associations

The work of the National Congress of Parents and Teachers and its many affiliate Parent–Teacher Associations is a common means of school–community contacts. In communities where the energies of the organization have been devoted to gaining mutual understanding and to studying the school problems, the P.T.A. has been an effective organization for furthering school–community relations. Where the organization has become a fund-raising and entertainment group, it has failed in accomplishing its purpose.

The school–community association in a suburban community is an example of another local organization of this nature. This organization is interested in improvements in both school and community. The central board of directors, under an executive president, has as its members the president of each individual school unit of the association. Among its activities are establishing a student loan fund, sponsoring activities for children, conducting open house at schools, bringing speakers to the community, establishing a youth center, and maintaining committees to work with existing organizations concerned with young people.

Many schools use to good advantage meetings of teachers and lay people. For example, in a regional high school, a dinner and evening conference dealt with building the best educational program possible to meet the children's needs. Discussion groups of lay citizens, teachers, and students met for two hours to consider ways of improving the school program and to clarify such questions as: "What is adequate training in basic academic skills?" "What help should the school give graduating seniors?" "What student activities should be provided for all?" The conference was planned by a parent committee under the leadership of the school. Meetings with parents of kindergarten or first-grade children are a rather common procedure. Conferences of this type can be of value for promoting school–community understanding and for hearing citizens' suggestions about the curriculum.

Parents Working Directly with Teachers

The more direct way of bringing parents into the process of curriculum development is to utilize them in the classroom as resource people. In many small rural schools, parents take as a matter of course working closely with the school, especially in elementary schools. They assist with programs that are put on for the community, helping the teacher to direct the program, furnishing transportation, and providing equipment. They help the teacher and the children in fund-raising activities for trips. They furnish cars for field trips and act as chaperons.

Close school–community contacts that go on day by day are some of the best types of ways of using citizens in curriculum development study.

In some schools the parents work directly with the teacher. The room mothers organization is common in the primary grades. Mothers of the children in a particular room meet frequently with the teacher to discuss the school program. Mothers may be invited to see the class in progress and to assist with small groups. However, the purpose is not to lighten the load for the teacher but to help the parent gain understanding of the school program. In one elementary school, teachers and parents hold meetings of room mothers during the morning, with the children meeting in the assemblyroom, lunchroom, library, or gymnasium under the direction of the high school student members of the Future Teachers Association. Mothers send the invitations and serve as hostesses. The meetings are held in the classroom where the teacher can explain the children's work. The teacher presents information on the characteristics of children of the age group, what is expected of them in school, and the nature of the program.

Other Channels

Actually, there are numerous ways by which the school contacts community people to inform them about the school or to determine their opinions. Some are not as organized as those discussed above, nor are they the most direct ways of involving citizens in curriculum study, but they represent avenues through which contacts can be maintained. One of the important aspects of the Great Cities Projects, discussed in Chapters 11 and 13, is the close contact of teachers with the community and the work that is done to bring the parents into educational programs to increase their understanding of their children and the value of education.

1. **Adult education.** One of the ways to familiarize people with the school and make them feel more a part of it is through adult education classes held in the school. Classes dealing with child development are especially useful in parent education on school problems.

2. **Bulletins for lay people.** One of the recent developments in curriculum bulletins is the type written especially for the parent. Bulletins to parents of young children starting school are published by many school systems. These bulletins are written in a simple, interesting style, are well illustrated, and avoid the use of "pedaguese." In fact, they are a considerable improvement in style and make-up over the typical curriculum bulletin.

3. **Parent–teacher conferences and reports.** The parent–teacher conference is supplementing report cards in an increasing number of

schools, especially at the elementary level. Letters to parents, from both children and teachers, are other newer means of reporting. The personal contact is undoubtedly the best means of making a report on the pupil's progress as a process of communication.

4. Use of community resources. Field trips to study the community, committees of pupils making community studies, and community resource people invited to talk to pupils are means of utilizing the community in the curriculum. Interviewing community leaders in classroom studies of local problems is an effective way to make contact with the community.

5. Opinion polls. Written opinionnaires or questionnaires to get citizens' opinions about school issues and practices are used to gather information in curriculum studies of various kinds. They are especially helpful in finding out whether a vocal group actually represents public opinion in the community. The *Illinois Inventory of Parent Opinion* has been used extensively by schools. Others construct their own opinionnaire forms.

ISSUES AND POINTS OF VIEW

While there seems to be only one fundamental issue in lay participation in curriculum improvement, it has different facets. It is not simply a question of whether citizens should take part. Curriculum improvement occurs day by day in the classroom as well as in curriculum committees. It comes about through experimentation and research. There are strong opinions against as well as for active lay participation in these activities.

1. *Do lay persons have something to contribute to curriculum improvement, or are they more of a nuisance than a help?*

The opinions on this question range from almost complete exclusion to inclusion in any curriculum improvement activities. The attitudes found among educators are as follows.

Citizens should have very little, if anything, to say about the school program; it should be left to the experts. The ivory tower concept of the school represents the attitude of some administrators and teachers. They believe that what the school does is none of the parents' business. School-teaching is the teachers' business. They feel that their attitude is justified in view of the parents in their communities who want to run the schools.

Where these conditions exist, the school is likely to be highly traditional. Perhaps failure to work with the public is a subtle means of avoiding change, which always means more work and upsets one's routine. On the other hand, schools that make no curriculum changes and continue in the old patterns are less subject to public criticism. Consequently, failure to keep up with the changing times has gone unchallenged in many communities.

Barriers to good school–community relations are embedded in this concept. Lack of knowledge of the facts concerning school policies and practices leads to rumor and speculation. Any change or experimentation with new ideas becomes fertile ground for criticism. Under ivory tower practices, there is no channel of communication from community to school. Parents' opinions about the school are never solicited. Similarly, there is no way to inform parents about the school's purposes.

If citizens participate in school affairs, they will "take over" decisions that rightfully belong to the school staff. In some cases, teachers and administrators are reluctant to bring the public into curriculum study because they feel uncertain about what might happen or how they can handle the situation. It is unknown and unexplored territory for them. For many of them, the only contacts they have had with the community with respect to the school program have been the complaints or inquiries of parents concerning failures or discipline problems of their children. Aside from these not particularly pleasant contacts, they may have had little chance to get to know parents as people.

Citizens who form groups of their own outside of any school auspices in order to influence the school program are a distinct threat. This attitude may well reflect an unwillingness to work with citizen groups, a lack of comprehension of what face-to-face discussions may accomplish, or a concept of the citizen committee as an undesirable pressure group.

The school should decide its program and then enlighten the public about it by "selling" it to them. This represents the more traditional public relations point of view, undoubtedly taking as its model practices in the business world. The assumption is that the school staff will develop the best possible program and then sell it to parents and other citizens. It is an idea quite similar to that of a small committee's developing a course of study and then convincing the rest of the teachers in the school system that they ought to use it.

Some administrators and teachers regard school–community relations as a one-way street, with certain points stressed and some information withheld. Witness the many annual reports to the public that deal only with the positive phases of the school program and never mention the problems that the school faces. They seldom include any pictures of the buildings, facilities, or equipment that are substandard for a good educational program. The concept of selling the public does not involve discussion and interaction. It is based on the idea that one group knows what should be done and the other group does not.

Citizens have much to contribute to the school program and their cooperation should be welcomed. School leaders who take this point of view have little fear that inviting the public to cooperate in the study of curriculum problems may get them into difficulty. They are convinced that citizens have a contribution to make in improving the school program. Perhaps some will say they are foolhardy; others that they are courageous and wise leaders; but certainly no one can call them "scared hired men."

Many school personnel welcome citizens' advisory councils, citizen study groups sponsored by the school, and frequent meetings to which citizens are invited to discuss school problems. They have found that once regular contact between the school staff and the public has been established, fears are dispelled. They believe that curriculum development is a social process involving in different ways those concerned.

Most citizens also welcome the opportunity to work with the school if they are made to feel that their contributions are important. True, all who are invited to participate will not accept. Many will have valid reasons. Some will not want to spend the extra time necessary on such concentrated study as curriculum improvement. But the larger portion of the public will cooperate in some way.

2. *Do close working relationships with the community entail hazards that may cause difficulties in operating the schools, or do they produce improved working conditions?*

All cannot possibly be unruffled harmony and pleasant cooperation in close school–community working relations. There must be some hazards involved. There are. The question is, "Are the results worth the risks?"

The opponents of lay participation point out that lay committees may become pressure groups, they may attempt to take over the responsibilities that are not rightfully theirs, they may cause headaches for the administration of the school since they do not agree with the administration's policies, or they may delay decisions.

Others believe that citizen participation aids in adopting, understanding, and accepting improved policies and new programs. They believe with Alfred North Whitehead that "It is the business of the future to be dangerous." They are glad to take the risks entailed in order to move ahead. They believe that improvement in the quality of experiences that children have in school will result from an understanding of the child, his home situation, and his problems, all of which the parents can help to clarify. Improved relationships with the community result from mutual understanding and common purposes.

Those who take the position taken in this book believe that leaving out lay people from curriculum study is the greater risk. Citizens become less informed about what is going on in the school. If citizens cooperate with the school in evaluation of programs, they become partners in the great enterprise of education.

9

CURRICULUM EXPERIMENTATION AND EVALUATION

Experimentation and evaluation are integral parts of the process of curriculum improvement. Schools and teachers experiment to try out new procedures, content, or organization of the curriculum. When the improvement process is genuinely experimental, systematic evaluation is a part of it. The process of evaluation involves (1) clarification of objectives, (2) determining and gathering the evidence needed, (3) interpreting the evidence, and (4) using the information gained to make decisions. It is far broader than measuring, counting, or determining what proportion of pupils achieved beyond a certain score. The principles of evaluation define its scope.

PRINCIPLES OF EVALUATION OF CURRICULUM IMPROVEMENT

The principles governing evaluation of curriculum improvement programs are similar to those basic to evaluation of pupil progress. The two are interwoven since change in pupil behavior determines the efficacy of a curriculum change.

Evaluation of the program is based on its objectives. Focusing upon objectives is the beginning point of evaluation. Objectives provide the only accurate guide to appraisal. Any form of evaluating instrument is used blindly unless changes sought are first specified. Changes in pupils are stated as specific behavior changes. Changes in the curriculum are stated as changes in pupil behavior, in teacher behavior, in materials used, in school–community relations, in school organization, in classroom environment, or in relationships among people.

The specification of changes they would like to see occur is the first step to be taken by a group that wants to experiment. These changes then must be stated in terms specific enough so that the behavior or phenomenon can be observed. Thus, evaluation must follow, not precede, the establishment of objectives.

Evaluation needs to be consistent with objectives. If the program seeks to develop attitudes that deal with human values or to change community conditions, evaluation only by standardized tests would be entirely inconsistent with purposes. Appraisal of growth in ability to do critical thinking requires different kinds of instruments from those used to test the amount of information acquired.

Evaluation is a continuous, cumulative process with systematic gathering of data. If evaluation is for the purpose of appraising progress toward goals or for determining whether one procedure is more effective than another in fulfilling the goals, it needs to occur throughout the process of learning or experimenting. Foresight rather than hindsight is called for. Unless baseline data are gathered at the beginning of an experiment, there is no possibility of measuring the growth of pupils involved.

Evaluation should go on continuously as a part of the curriculum improvement process. It is never an isolated process nor a mere end point, something to be done only when one finishes testing out a new aspect of the curriculum. Rather, it is cumulative. Evidence of pupil growth is gathered throughout the span of experimentation with reference to the goals established.

A systematic plan for gathering data means looking at the various kinds of objectives and the different facets of the school's program, facilities, and staff to see what kinds of evidence need to be collected about pupils, teachers, teaching–learning operations, and resources. When teachers try to help pupils develop understanding, functional skills, and desirable attitudes, evaluation must be planned as broader in scope than appraising growth in intellectual achievement. When the school sees its function as stimulating continued interest in a cultural, scientific, or political area, evaluation takes on a longitudinal dimension as well. For no end-of-the-year measurement yet devised can foretell whether a pupil will behave in the future in the manner of one who has acquired a keen sense of responsibility to his school (or larger) community or a profound desire to explore further the mysteries of science.

Evaluation is comprehensive in scope. When a teacher evaluates the growth of a child toward the objectives of the school, his task includes what the school has stated about understanding, skills, attitudes, and other kinds of behaviors. Evaluation has breadth as well as depth.

Evaluation of mastery of information and skills is relatively easy for the teacher and the school. Consequently, little else may be done. It may seem too difficult to evaluate other outcomes. No instruments are available, or they are not valid. Thus, the objectives are narrowed down to those that concern achievement only. Even important studies of national scope often display the same weakness.

The Commission on Evaluation of the Association for Supervision and Curriculum Development has attempted to define a comprehensive evaluation program that includes data on pupil achievement, on factors affecting learning, on teaching methods, and on teaching–learning operations.

MODEL FOR A COMPREHENSIVE EVALUATION PROGRAM

1. Deciding what kinds of evaluation data are needed:

A. *Objectives and Evidence Pertaining to Them*
   Thinking abilities
   Attitudes
   Skills
   Creativity
   Concepts
   Levels of perception
   Etc.

B. *Factors Affecting Learning*
   Class culture backgrounds
   Peer culture influences
   Social learning
   Initial level of subject matter mastery
   Motivational patterns
   Special abilities
   Feelings
   Etc.

C. *Teaching–learning Operations*
   Nature of assignments
   Procedures for maintaining control
   Patterns of teacher response to pupil behavior

D. *Teaching Methods*
   Telling
   Discovery
   Laboratory work
   Recitation
   Discussion
   Use of problems
   Demonstration
   Etc.

2. Selecting or constructing the needed instruments and proce-
   dures. These may include:
   Objectively scored tests
   Essay tests and other written exercises
   Sentence completion tests
   Tape recorder techniques
   Attitude scales
   Social class scales
   Interest inventories
   Behavior check lists
   Sociograms and participation flow charts
   Questionnaires
   Interviews
   Performance tests
   Rating scales for performance and products
   Anecdotal records
   Etc.

3. Analyzing and interpreting data to develop hypotheses regarding
   needed changes. The broad patterns of relationships to be studied
   are as follows:

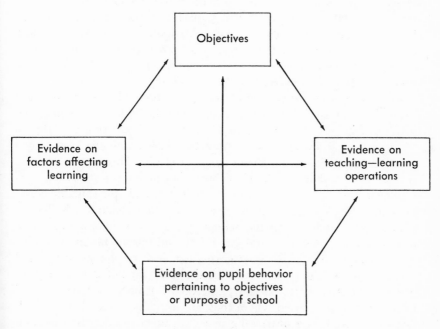

4. Converting hypotheses into action.[1]

[1] Hilda Taba and Enoch I. Swain, "A Proposed Model for Evaluation," *Educational Leadership*, 20:57–71, October, 1962. Copyright © 1962 by the Association
for Supervision and Curriculum Development. Also, Hilda Taba, *Curriculum
Development: Theory and Practice*, New York: Harcourt, Brace & World, Inc.,
1962, pp. 328–29.

The process of evaluation should involve those who are concerned with the educational program. Until the 1930's the predominant concept of evaluation of a school's program was the survey done by specialists from outside the school system. These experts studied the conditions and made recommendations for improvement. In most cases of state and local surveys, the thick volumes of the findings were the only evidence of the survey's having been made. Seldom did the program change.

The gradual trend in accreditation and other evaluative studies has been toward including in the study the persons who would be affected by any change. Basic to this procedure is the principle that people change as they change their perceptions, ideas, and relationships to others. Evaluation of a curriculum improvement program becomes a cooperative job for administrators, teachers, supervisors, citizens, pupils, and outside consultants.

Each one can contribute information or judgments concerning the program, to the extent of his expertness and his willingness to be objective about results. Besides, the process from clarification of objectives to setting up hypotheses, gathering data, and judging results is an educative one. Those who participate in the planning and decisions know and understand the purposes of the change. Thus, cooperative evaluation has its own built-in channels of communication to teachers and citizens of the community.

Evaluation, as an appraisal of practices, should be as rigorous and objective as possible. Personal involvement in evaluation of practices involves risks. The personal biases and emotional ties to either a traditional or a new and exciting practice with which one is identified may make objective judgment most difficult. This is one of the reasons why supervisors and teachers who are not a part of an experiment, and lay persons who may be impersonal, are valuable assets to a study that seeks to evaluate practices. The consultant who has no personal connection with the school system plays an important role in systematic gathering of objective data and interpretation of results.

It is imperative that the information secured be as valid and reliable as possible. Instruments used should be suited to their purposes. Objective data can be gathered by trained observers; valid instruments can be used where they are available. Yet, there will always be a need for constructing new instruments under the direction of someone competent in measurement and research. For example, when the new mathematics program was being tried out experimentally in schools, the standardized examinations in mathematics were not useful for testing understanding of many of the new concepts in the program.

If teachers can become more objective in day-by-day evaluation, more skilled in using different means of observing behavior changes, more skilled in research techniques, there will be greater hope for objective evaluation of practices. Some will become skillful in doing curriculum research of a more formal and fundamental nature, a real need in education. But the need is just as great for the majority of teachers and administrators to move from prejudice and bias to more objectivity. That is the essence of this chapter.

Evaluative data need to be interpreted in light of the types of pupils and the community involved. Survey examinations or state examinations may compare children from the schools in the economically and culturally deprived areas with those from the wealthy suburban communities. National norms are often used as a basis for judgment in particular school environments that have not the slightest resemblance to a national "average." Both intelligence and achievement tests have been found to be biased culturally. Groups with cultural handicaps may be achieving more, for them, than other groups with a rich environment, even though scores of the former group are lower by comparison. The learning environment and the disabilities or advantages it has caused are important factors to consider in the interpretation of data for evaluative purposes.

Growth can be appraised only by use of the previous growth as baseline data. Evaluation is a measurement of individual growth of pupil or teacher. It is a process of finding out how far a person has progressed from the point where he started. One of the basic principles of evaluation is to find out a pupil's present status in learning by giving tests at the beginning of whatever study is being conducted.

A cross-section of the individual's work or scores at any one time may show very little about progress unless one has reference points to use. Most evaluation has been of the cross-sectional type. Anecdotal records, progress in growth in work habits, study habits, and attitudes over a period of time require evaluation of a longitudinal nature. Some kinds of objectives require follow-up into postschool experiences to determine whether they have been accomplished. For example, if we hypothesize that a certain type of program will prevent pupils from dropping out of school or will assist them in making better progress in college, follow-up studies need to be made.

Evaluation should be a planned part of changes in the curriculum. Change is constantly taking place in school systems. Some of the changes and experiments described in this book have been carefully evaluated, some include a rather superficial evaluation, and some have not been evaluated at all.

The time to plan means of evaluation is during the consideration of what changes will be made and how they will be made. Thus, baseline data can be collected and used for comparison. Curriculum committees have been adept at proposing changes but few have recommended well-conceived plans for the evaluation of those changes. A plan should have written into it the hypothesis as to how the changes will affect learning or the people involved, what data need to be collected, what instruments are to be used, and how judgments will be made. Otherwise, curriculum change operates on the basis of guesswork.

CURRICULUM EXPERIMENTATION AND RESEARCH

A Modest Goal

Experimentation may vary from simple tryout of a new procedure to highly controlled experimental designs. Most school administrators and teachers use the term to refer to procedures which are new to the school, to the classroom, or perhaps to educational practice. While teachers should be encouraged to experiment with new ideas, a haphazard trial-and-error method can scarcely be called experimental. Some kind of evaluative measures need to be included. While a great deal more controlled experimentation and curriculum research needs to be done, teachers cannot be expected to do studies of the magnitude, controlled conditions, and scope that even a majority of college professors do not attempt. The purpose here is to encourage going beyond a casual, informal appraisal to one in which the school and the teacher make plans for testing the innovation.

At this stage of the development of curriculum research and of research sophistication of school people, it would be foolhardy to expect more. Only the larger school systems have research directors, and many of them are kept busy by the superintendent's office in gathering information about pupils and teachers and in conducting testing programs. In the study of practices in educational experimentation and change conducted in New York State, it was found that: "Instructional innovations are almost always evaluated by observing the reactions of students while they are receiving the new instruction. In the eyes of the practitioner, no other evidence outweighs student reaction as a measure of success. More complex evaluative techniques are rarely used." [2] This is scarcely a picture of rigorous evaluation

[2] Henry M. Brickell, *Organizing New York State for Educational Change*, Albany, N. Y.: State Education Department, 1961, p. 33.

of experimental change. Undoubtedly, it could be duplicated in any other state.

Yet, at the same time, there are more instructional innovations, more experimental plans, and more funds available to encourage schools to innovate than at any other period of the history of education in the United States. Television, team teaching, ungraded schools, flexible scheduling, radical revision of content, programs for the gifted, programs for the culturally deprived, programmed learning, independent study—all discussed in this book—are but some of the experimental plans that have occupied the attention of educators in recent years. Thus, the need is greater than ever for the school practitioners to look at innovations with a critical eye, to give evaluative measures first priority for curriculum change, to look at the pitfalls that face them, and to use whatever instruments and talents are available for doing the evaluative job that needs to be done.

Experimentation with Built-in Evaluation

When proposals are developed for curriculum changes and plans are made at the same time to study the effects of the change, the procedure for evaluating the change becomes a part of the plan, is built into it, so to speak. It is not an afterthought, nor a means of justifying the change.

In twenty-eight carefully selected school districts known to have emphasized evaluative procedures, the National School Boards Association and the American Association of School Administrators sponsored case studies of how evaluation was conducted in these schools. One of the characteristics often noted in the schools that had made strides toward comprehensive evaluation of their programs was that specific provisions for evaluation were included in program changes and new procedures.[3] Although these school districts are in the minority, they set the pace for what others can do.

A number of examples of what could be defined as built-in evaluation of experimentation were found. In a large city district, careful study and analysis of a problem are followed by testing the plan or recommendation in operation, using as research approaches comparative studies, opinion surveys, and other means.[4] A large city district

[3] Lewis E. Harris and Clyde R. Moore, "Keys to Quality," Booklet No. 14 of *Quest for Quality* Series, Washington, D. C.: National School Boards Association and American Association of School Administrators, 1960, p. 43.

[4] National School Boards Association and American Association of School Administrators, *Quest for Quality* Series, Booklet No. 1, Washington, D. C., 1960, p. 16.

established an experimental program for gifted pupils in a special sixth-grade class, evaluated through pupil and parent questionnaires, conferences, and a survey of pupil progress.[5] An experimental plan for the teaching of arithmetic utilizing special experimental tools and teaching methods was tested by a small industrial city district by a comparative study using control groups.[6] In another instance, a suburban district experimented with the teaching of Spanish in grades 4 through 8 of an elementary school. It was planned to follow the children through high school over a five-year period in order to ascertain how the study of language affected their subsequent progress in language and other questions. Both standardized tests and tests developed by the school system were used in measuring progress.[7]

Cooperative Research by Schools and Universities

The advent of funds being made available by the federal government and by foundations for research in education has stimulated cooperative research by universities or colleges and school systems. Some of this research has been in the nature of action research and some has been more highly controlled.

The U. S. Office of Education Cooperative Research Program was inaugurated in 1954 under a law which authorized the Commissioner of Education to "enter into contracts or jointly financed cooperative arrangements with universities and colleges and state educational agencies for the conduct of research, surveys, and demonstrations in the field of education." [8] This program has done much to encourage research in education. The first appropriation of funds, not made until 1957, was for approximately one million dollars. In eight years, the appropriation had increased to over fifteen times that amount.

Studies in the curriculum area have dealt with such problems as mental retardation, underachievement, attitudes and values, classroom environment, concept formation and development, cognitive processes, creativity, dropouts, the gifted, group dynamics, individual differences, programmed instruction, cultural deprivation, language, mental health, parent–child relations, self-concepts, spelling, reading, emotional development, student characteristics, teacher effectiveness, vocational education, and many others.

[5] *Ibid.*, Booklet No. 13, p. 17.
[6] *Ibid.*, Booklet No. 10, pp. 12–13.
[7] *Ibid.*, Booklet No. 3, pp. 12–13.
[8] *Research Projects of the Cooperative Research Program: A Five-Year Summary, July 1, 1956–September 30, 1961*, U. S. Office of Education, Washington, D. C.: Government Printing Office, 1962, p. iii.

Types of research conducted have encompassed controlled experiments, survey, correlational, methodological, case study, developmental, and historical. In 1963 the nature of the program was expanded in scope to include basic and applied research, curriculum improvement, demonstrations, research and development centers, small contracts, and developmental activities. Translating research findings into practice; pilot studies; development of new experimental devices, models, and theories; and demonstrations are among the more recent emphases in the expanded program.

Curriculum improvement projects emphasize the following purposes:

1. To clarify or redefine the nature and aims of a content area.
2. To develop sequential patterns in a content area based upon factors of human growth and development and on the teaching–learning process.
3. To develop instructional materials and methods that will achieve general and/or specific aims within a content area.
4. To evaluate the effectiveness of the materials and methods that have been developed.
5. To disseminate the most promising materials and methods to interested individuals and groups throughout the country.[9]

Considerable expansion has occurred in the number of bureaus of educational research and field services that have been established by universities and colleges. State departments of education and larger school systems have also developed research bureaus. The most notable trend among these agencies is that they are becoming more actively involved in research projects rather than engaging chiefly in counting and survey studies and testing programs.

Research and demonstration projects as the new mathematics and science programs, Project English, Project Social Studies, and the Interprofessional Research Commission on Pupil Personnel Services study are examples of cooperative efforts joining school systems and universities in solving persistent educational problems.

Computer science has made possible the processing of research data at phenomenal speeds and comparisons of data never before attempted because of prohibitive costs in time and funds. Newer statistical techniques of multivariate analysis and variance analysis have helped educational experimentation by providing a means of studying cause and effect on interacting variables. Non-parametric statistical

[9] Francis A. J. Ianni, "USOE Cooperative Research," *School Life*, 46:28, October, 1963.

analysis has helped to convert qualitative to quantitative data for analysis and interpretation.

Difficulties and Problems

In spite of promising beginnings and a definite trend toward research-oriented solution of educational problems, carefully evaluated curriculum changes are still few and scattered. Curriculum research has largely failed to modify practice. What are some of the difficulties that face curriculum experimentation and evaluation?

1. Need for development of sound theory for curriculum research. Much of curriculum research consists of the counting variety or status studies without any attempts to test hypotheses related to theoretical frameworks. Others have hypotheses that may not be based on an adequate frame of reference. Often the only theory that is given consideration is in the statistical design and in the analysis.

2. Fragmentary nature of curriculum research. Little attention has been paid in graduate schools and in doctoral studies to a coordinated type of research where several people may be working together on the same problem. In fact, this idea has often been discouraged as inimical to independent thinking. As a result, the scattered efforts of hundreds of dissertations attack small aspects of some particular problem. Integrated curriculum research and interdisciplinary cooperation in research are virgin fields now being pioneered by research bureaus or research programs supported by grants. Most of the research has been done once rather than repeated to test a theory.

3. Need for skill in evaluation and research. Many school leaders have not been trained in evaluation procedures and research techniques. Leaders in school systems must first of all *want* to do serious, objective evaluation of the program. They also need skills and understanding to help teachers in carrying on such evaluation. It is not always easy to get assistance from colleges and universities since the demands in any state are heavy. Little time is generally allocated in the college professor's schedule to work with schools on a consultant basis. State department consultants with research skills are relatively few in number compared with the need for their services.

4. Teachers' and parents' apprehension about research. Few teachers have been trained to do research of any kind. They exhibit fears toward research procedures and statistical techniques, fears which may have had their origin in unhappy childhood experiences with arithmetic or algebra. To them, these procedures are something which sounds formidable indeed. When teachers begin to see, through experience, their potential contribution in cooperative research and evaluation, these fears tend to dissipate. Parents' apprehensions are of another kind. They do not want their children to be "guinea pigs." Research is a test-tube term to many of them. Cooperatively planned research done to improve practices is a new concept to them.

5. **Lack of time on the part of teachers.** Conscientious teachers carry a heavy load of responsibilities. They find it difficult to reduce the time spent with their many other responsibilities to do the exacting kind of work that is required in objective evaluation or research. As evaluation is regarded as more of an integral part of curriculum study, it will be seen not as an "extra," but as the very heart of the study. Under grants for research, funds can be obtained for released time for those who will participate intensively. Some school systems provide funds for this purpose in their budget.

6. **Reliance on subjective judgments.** In many curriculum improvement programs, the evaluation is mainly in terms of subjective judgments of individuals in the group, not even systematically gathered. Too many studies depend upon the reaction of pupils and teachers as the only evaluative data.

7. **Subordination of the importance of the study.** In at least some cases, the more intricate the design of the statistical research, the more highly the research seems to be regarded. The most important aspect in research is whether a study of a problem is of real value and will add important knowledge in education by testing well-reasoned theory. Unless the findings of a study are of special importance, no amount of statistical study of the data can make it any better. Statistical techniques are only one set of tools for studying problems. That they have an important place is not questioned.

8. **Fitting the measuring instrument to the purpose.** Instruments for measuring achievement and skills have been used more extensively in research than have other types of evaluation because they have been developed in more highly standardized form and have lent themselves to producing data that could be treated statistically. Even the measurement of understanding has not kept pace with that of factual information. As research has been done on newer developments such as the core, the researcher has often used tests of subject matter skills to evaluate an idea that depends for its strength on emphasizing the all-round growth of the pupil. Consequently, the range of objectives which are evaluated is limited. The value question is: What is to be evaluated? Is it to be the facts, the principles, the concepts, the skills, the attitudes, the interests, or some other factor?

Different means will need to be used for evaluating different outcomes of instruction. Testing can only measure the results of some of the outcomes.

9. Types of problems studied are limited by techniques available. Innumerable studies in curriculum research use the questionnaire technique. Instruments to measure group interaction, attitudes, values, and appreciations are still far behind those for measuring skills and academic achievement. Consequently, the scope of studies has been limited by the dearth of evaluative instruments for some types of goals. We have been satisfied to use techniques that have already been developed. Creativity in research includes the ability to discover new ways of gathering and analyzing data.

10. Underestimating the role of the public school person. Most of the curriculum research has been done by persons who hope that others will put the results into practice. The role of the teacher, administrator, and supervisor in the planning and conducting of curriculum experimentation in the actual school has been underestimated. Education is unlikely to make the progress it should unless the school problems are studied by people within the school in the environment in which they occur, as is true in the recent emphasis on cooperative research done by universities and public schools.

11. Lack of study of interrelated factors that operate in the school situation. Curriculum research is concerned with the means by which specific ways of behaving are brought about. Consequently, interrelated factors in the school environment need to be studied. No single factor can be properly understood apart from its interaction with other factors operating in the field. In other words, the environment should be seen as a dynamic situation, not as a static one. This suggests more cooperative research among the different disciplines, looking at the total environment, with the use of the newer statistical techniques.

12. Evaluation regarded as an end product. Probably one of the most widely spread current misconceptions concerning evaluation is the fact that it is done at the end of a unit or a study, the assumption being that there is no need to evaluate during the ongoing process of the teaching–learning situation in the classroom. Another result is that the process by which curriculum improvement is secured receives little attention.

13. The Hawthorne effect. Researchers have discovered that the stimulation of being involved in an experiment and the attention and

recognition received by the people involved exert a positive influence toward improvement. Thus, teachers and pupils engaged in experimentation are more likely to succeed, and any type of innovation may show improved results. This phenomenon makes it difficult to make judgments concerning the effect of the experimental factor. Yet, it also has definite implications for experimentation as a means of securing improvement in programs, aside from the research difficulties involved.

14. Misrepresentation of research findings. In hundreds of studies, the failure to find a significant difference has been interpreted falsely to mean that there is or was no difference. In others, this has been interpreted as failure. If a research study is well conducted, either negative or positive results are just as significant. Otherwise, it cannot be dignified with the respectability of "research."

15. The bandwagon complex. School administrators tend to want to get on the bandwagon of something new, to be able to say that their district is in the forefront of curriculum improvement. Yet, this may be one of the major handicaps to knowing whether the curriculum has actually been improved, for it often means a disregard for evaluation of the type that seeks to answer objective evaluation.

16. The failure to translate research findings into action. Perhaps this is the greatest deficiency in curriculum research. The next section on action research deals with alleviating this problem.

ACTION RESEARCH

Action research as a new orientation for curriculum research is probably the single most significant development as a technique of curriculum improvement in the last decade. As evaluation of curriculum change in schools is conducted with greater care, as evidence is more systematically collected, as hypotheses are developed to be tested, and as more careful controls are exercised in the situation, then the evaluation takes on the nature of research.

What Is Action Research?

Action research is actually a method of curriculum study with evaluation as a fundamental component. It is a form of curriculum experimentation and evaluation.

Corey, who has contributed substantially to the thinking regarding this type of research, defines it as follows: "Action research in education is research undertaken by practitioners in order that they may improve their practices." [10] It is a type of research undertaken by school people in order to study their problems scientifically and, as a consequence, improve their own procedures. It is a new orientation given to research, placing it in a different kind of setting. Not all projects that have been called action research can meet the standards for objectively gathering evidence and studying a problem.

One of its functions is to close the gap between practice and knowledge. Foshay and Goodson state that it is "an attempt to make what we do consistent with the way we believe." [11] Putting our beliefs into practice can be facilitated by testing them in actual school situations. That is what action research attempts to do. As in all research, evidence is systematically sought, gathered, recorded, and interpreted to test hypotheses. Probably the most important feature about action research is the stimulus that it is giving to teachers, supervisors, and administrators to move from casual evaluation of results to gathering of various kinds of evidence to test out ideas.

Traditional formal research and action research are related. The former is often an important preliminary step to the latter in developing theory and conclusions that need further testing in an ongoing school situation.

There are some distinctive features to look for, however, when a person asks: Is this action research? The important factor is that some action is taken in the situation to test the hypothesis. Gathering data to discover what some conditions are like at the present time in a school is not action research. This is a type of status study, which may be very important as a preliminary to determining the kind of action that is desirable and to developing hypotheses to be tested. But unless some action is present that is tested in the school situation, it is not action research. In other words, action research looks forward rather than backward. It is not done to discover what has already been accomplished but to test new ideas that may or may not change practices, depending upon whether or not they are found to be successful.

[10] Stephen M. Corey, *Action Research to Improve School Practices*, New York: Bureau of Publications, Teachers College, Columbia University, 1953, p. 141.

[11] Arthur W. Foshay and Max R. Goodson, "Some Reflections on Cooperative Action Research," *Educational Leadership*, 10:411, April, 1953.

Characteristics of Action Research

Certain characteristics distinguish action research from traditional research.

1. *Those who do action research have in mind the improvement of their own practices.* This is a rather revolutionary principle in research. In traditional research, the people who carry on the research are making discoveries that will be put into practice by someone else, not by themselves. They do not feel any obligation to put their findings into operation. When their research is accomplished, their responsibility is over. It must be granted that it is much more difficult to carry on research with the idea of improving one's own practices, for it is always easier to suggest that someone else should change. In addition, it is more difficult to be objective under such conditions.

2. *People who carry out the findings participate in the total research project.* In action research, the school people are involved from the very beginning. They cooperate in defining the problem, working out the hypothesis, determining the ways of gathering data, and making generalizations from the data. This is not a casual type of participation, nor is it an afterthought where people are brought in to discuss how findings can be put into effect.

The persons who carry out the research select and develop the problem to be studied. This practice is consistent with the principle of learning that individuals must have a real purpose of their own in a learning situation. The purpose is to try to change something about one's own environment and one's own practices.

Those who plan and do the research are more likely to carry out the findings. Innumerable reports of research have been presented in journals. Attempts have been made to disseminate research findings more widely. However, one important fact has been overlooked: people will not easily change their practices unless they themselves are involved in some way in study of an evaluation of those practices. Thus, action research is a means of speeding up the process of curriculum change.

3. *Action research is carried on in an actual school situation.* The school may be an elementary school, a secondary school, or a college. The research is done in a realistic teaching–learning situation involving one or more teachers working with a group of children or an administrator working with a group of teachers. The school is its laboratory.

4. *Teachers, administrators, supervisors, or university and college faculty members cooperate in the research.* Action research is usually a cooperative affair among a number of persons. It may, however, involve only the teacher and the principal. More often it includes more than one teacher and consultants from a university. The consultants may spearhead the research but they work cooperatively with school personnel in the process. Often the term "cooperative action research" is used to indicate this kind of teamwork.

5. *Generalizations from an action research study are applied to the particular situation.* Since the research studies a practice in a certain school, the generalizations apply to that situation. However, evidence indicates that pupils in any class constitute a random sample of the cumulative population of a teacher's future classes in the same school.[12] In other words, predictions can be made for the school itself, providing that the conditions do not change considerably. Just as pupils of one class represent a random sample of future classes, so does that class represent to a degree a sample of all other classes similarly constituted in the same school.

The findings in one action research study in a particular school or class will furnish hypotheses to be tested in other places. If the same findings have been verified in several studies in a number of situations, generalizations can be made with greater confidence for other similar groups. It is possible to generalize for the particular school with a greater degree of confidence, if the research was done in that school, than it is to generalize from a single experimental study for schools as a whole. In experimental research, generalizations are made from a situation in which all variables except one are held constant, to a class environment where none of the factors is controlled and the dynamics of the situation are ever changing.

6. *Action research, carried on in a social setting, does not try to control all variables but one.* Nor does it essentially try to compensate by statistical means for those that it cannot control. Instead, it regards the total environment as an integral whole and looks at all the factors that influence the situation, such as the teacher, the other pupils, the physical environment of the classroom, and the morale of the school. These factors are not to be ruled out, but are to be considered as significant because they are present in any school situation. They are described carefully and objectively, so that others can understand the conditions in which the research takes place.

7. *Action research attempts to determine the amount of growth of*

[12] Corey, *op. cit.*, pp. 134–39.

the group with which it deals. It does not necessarily have a control group with which to compare results, as in an experimental type of study. In action research, the concern is to find out how much growth the pupils have made in a specific situation when certain action is taken. If the research group is studying its own procedures, the concern is how much growth it has made.

8. *In action research the whole rather than the sample population is usually used.* The question of sampling is not a great problem in action research, since predictions are made only for the particular group that is studied. When a group of children are studied in a classroom, the total group are the subjects of the research. Consequently, predictions can be made more safely for that particular group than predictions from sampling populations, if adequate controls are used.

9. *In action research, purposes may change as the research develops, and new hypotheses may be developed and tested as a part of the study.* Since it is a part of an ongoing teaching–learning situation, as the group gains new insight it may refine or develop new hypotheses. For example, a group of teachers doing an action research study may find that as they explore and study together they get new leads that would suggest altering the procedure after a period of time. Since their purpose is to improve their own practices, they can shift the procedure or "begin again." It must be remembered that the chief aim of action research is one's own curriculum improvement, not data to be used elsewhere. Thus, there is no major catastrophe when a group changes its direction during a study, if it finds that its original hypothesis is too narrow.

10. *Action research usually begins where other curriculum study leaves off.* In most curriculum study, the group collects data, gathers information concerning practices, reads what others have done or recommended, and arrives at its own recommendations for the school. This is precisely the point at which action research begins. As a part of the curriculum improvement process, the recommendations are then tested and evaluated in practice.

Usefulness for Evaluating Curriculum Improvement

Action research is a valuable means for evaluating curriculum improvement. Since action research is a testing of curriculum theory and practice in operation, it is by its very nature an evaluation of curriculum improvement. No theory or practice would be tested unless it were thought to be an improvement.

Teachers see its value as something related to improving what they are doing. Alexander and Saylor present evidence to show that there is satisfaction among teachers with this kind of cooperative research.[13] Teachers evidently overcome their fear of research when they find that their participation is worthwhile.

We cannot assume, however, that it is an exclusive pattern, or that all teachers will accept it with open arms. There are threats to teachers' security in action research. Many kinds of anxieties make it difficult to get under way. Action research, like any research, is a severe discipline, socially and intellectually. It may be status-eroding for the insecure. If supervisors presume that all will be delighted with it, teachers may participate because it is the thing to do.

Administrators, teachers, and parents can, through action research, systematically appraise the new procedures developed for a school. Information is gathered as evidence for school and community alike to share. Bringing teachers, parents, administrators, and college and university staff together to study problems is of significance to educational progress.

In the school in which action research is conducted, conditions need to be conducive to carrying on this kind of research. School administrators, supervisors, and teachers must be interested in testing their practices. There needs to be an atmosphere in which new ideas are accepted as important. In a rigid, inflexible climate where teachers are required to follow a prescribed course of study, there would be little chance for the growth of action research. Teachers, too, must look upon their procedures not as something determined for all time as "right," but as open to testing. The whole school climate should be one that encourages the experimental approach.

Role of Participants in the Process

From the time of determining the problem to that of looking at the consequences of the study, the teachers are the main participants, with the administrators and supervisors of the school as leaders and with community leaders and pupils as assistants. The community is brought in to participate in the same way that it does in other types of curriculum study. Pupils also are a part of this kind of study. When the focus of the problem is the improvement of the experiences of pupils, they can assist in gathering descriptive data. For example, logs or recorders' notes kept by pupils are useful in obtaining a com-

[13] William M. Alexander and J. Galen Saylor, *Curriculum Planning for Better Teaching and Learning*, New York: Holt, Rinehart and Winston, Inc., 1954, pp. 525–26.

plete picture of what happens in the classroom. They furnish information through interviews, fill out questionnaires, and supply information about the classroom relationships.

The role of university and college or state education department staff members is to contribute their expert knowledge to public schools in carrying on research. Although they may suggest problems, they do not determine the problem nor the procedures but suggest ways of studying the problem, help the group think through the problem, and give consultation throughout all of the steps of action research.

Action research may also be a cooperative project on the part of a number of school systems. This plan has the advantage of bringing together people from different schools to exchange their experiences, to discuss how they are conducting the study, and to develop useful instruments. It also makes possible the testing of the proposal in a number of different situations.

Steps in Carrying On Action Reseach

Several steps are necessary parts of action research.

1. **Identification of a problem.** The first step in action research is the identification of problems that the faculty faces. Problems need to be pointed up and sharpened; they cannot be hazy statements of general problem areas. The problem identification is done through a discussion of the difficulties involved in reaching the school's goals. In an alert faculty that constantly works together, these difficulties have undoubtedly been discussed before and are now brought into a new focus. In other instances, it may be more fruitful to talk over what people would like to do. As the problems are identified, it is helpful to state them in question form. From the variety of those proposed, the group concerned selects a particular one for study, agreed upon by the group as being significant for the changes in ways of working or changes in pupils' behavior.

As in all curriculum study, the definition of the problem is a cooperative task shared by teachers, supervisors, and administrators. There may be cases where a teacher determines a problem with the principal and studies the problem by himself, but such a practice has obvious weaknesses. The research may well become an isolated island in the school.

2. **Discussion of proposals for action.** The selection of the problem is only the beginning. The group must then consider what it can do about the problem—the proposals for action to be taken. These are the means of bringing about changes in practice.

At this point, the group needs to look seriously at the values inherent in the proposals. Is the proposal consistent with the values that are held? Is it consistent with desirable social values? It is also the time to determine what beliefs are being tested through the proposal.

3. Selecting the course of action and developing the hypothesis. Following a thorough discussion of the possible actions that might be taken regarding the problem, the group has the responsibility for choosing a course of action. This should be a group decision after all the different proposals have been discussed. It can be assumed that under such conditions the action to be taken is the best that the group believes it can find for its particular situation.

One of the ways that action research differs from the usual form of curriculum study of a problem is that it has a statement of a hypothesis to be tested. In action research, the hypothesis should include both a *goal* and the procedures or *action* to be taken. For example, a group might state a hypothesis: Including lay persons on all committees that carry on curriculum study will make the community better informed about what is going on in the school. In this statement are a goal (a community better informed concerning the schools) and a procedure (including lay persons on all committees that carry on curriculum study). Another example of a hypothesis would be: If a variety of materials are used in every class (procedure), the quantity and quality of reading will improve (goal). A faculty may be concerned about the use of community resources. It has studied how different schools go about getting teachers to use to a greater extent the community as a source of experiences in instruction. It believes that a guide to community resources will do the job. However, it wants to do more than just prepare such a resource guide; it also wants to test out the idea. Consequently, the group develops the hypothesis: A well prepared guide to the use of community resources will result in greater use of those resources by the teachers. These are quite simple examples of the kinds of curriculum study that go on regularly in schools.

In addition to the statement of the hypothesis, there should be a more careful and detailed description of the goal. This description should show how the goal relates to the total teaching–learning situation. Furthermore, there needs to be a detailed description of procedures so that others will understand what procedures or action are tested.

4. Planning for the collection of data. In an action research project, the data to be collected at the beginning and during the study are

determined before the study gets under way. This point is obvious with regard to testing achievement. However, it also holds true in getting other kinds of evaluative data. For example, a teacher may want to find out whether planning with pupils in the classroom will affect their attitudes toward school. In this case, having the children recall toward the end of the study whether they felt differently toward school than they did five or six months ago is not so accurate a method as getting their opinions at the beginning of the study, throughout the study, and at the end.

Teachers need to make careful plans for collecting data throughout the study. For instance, pupils may keep records or teachers may keep logs of the activities that go on. When evaluation instruments need to be constructed, such as forms for getting opinions of pupils and parents, they will have to be developed ahead of time. One of the features of cooperative action research rated high in value by a group of teachers was reaching of agreements, prior to observation, as to the meaning of categories for recording and interpreting behavior. Foshay and Wann's study indicates how important it is for the group doing action research first to test out the collection of data in order to develop categories that have a common meaning and to arrive at mutual understanding of terms used.[14]

If the action is to be studied in a specific kind of situation, there must be a complete description of that situation. In other words, abundant descriptive evidence, obtained in many ways, is needed. No single device will suffice as a measure of change in a social setting.

The kinds of data that can be obtained to study a situation and evaluate progress in curriculum improvement are many and varied. They include data obtained from the classroom and school records, from the pupils, from teachers, from parents, and from the rest of the community. Some of the means of obtaining data for action research include the following:

Opinionnaires or opinion polls on school practices
Structured questionnaires
Inventories of values and beliefs
Follow-up studies of pupils and of teachers
Tape recordings of staff meetings
Records of group evaluation sessions
Group process analysis
Informal evaluative comments

[14] Arthur W. Foshay, Kenneth D. Wann, and Associates, *Children's Social Values: An Action Research Study*, New York: Bureau of Publications, Teachers College, Columbia University, 1954, pp. 209–11.

Free response evaluation
Interviews with pupils and teachers and parents
Sociometric techniques
Classroom observation records
Anecdotal records
Information from permanent records
Daily logs of activities in the classroom
Diaries
Minutes of meetings
Group tests
Case studies
Rating scales

In evaluation of curriculum improvement, the group is concerned with means as well as with ends. The process is subjected to constant evaluation, and improvement in the process is actually one of the important goals besides being a means toward other goals.

Instruments are often specially constructed for the research. Illustrations are those used by Bush in action research in teacher–pupil relationships: What Do You Think of Your Teacher?; What Is Your Judgment Concerning This Teacher?; A Test of Teacher–Pupil Relationships; What Do You Think of This Pupil?; Purposes Rating Scale.[15] Examples of those used by Foshay and Wann in the action research study of children's social values include: Check Sheet Used to Study Considerateness and Popularity; Things About Me; Who Would It Be?; Things I Wish; My Problems of Growing Up.[16]

5. Taking action and gathering evidence. Proposed action is then put into practice. Without it, research can be in no sense called action research. The hypotheses are tested out in the classroom, in the faculty meetings, in the school–community relations, and in other kinds of settings in which people are working together to discuss, plan, or execute learning activities. The group meets periodically in order to discuss the collecting and recording of the necessary data and to exchange ideas about the kinds of action being taken.

This whole process is a learning process, a factor that needs to be considered as a part of the total condition and not ruled out in studying interaction between pupils and teachers, pupils and pupils, teachers and teachers, and teachers and parents.

[15] Robert N. Bush, *The Teacher–Pupil Relationship*, Englewood Cliffs, N. J.: Prentice-Hall, Inc., 1954, pp. 203–45.
[16] Foshay, Wann, and Associates, *op. cit.*, pp. 300–5.

6. Drawing conclusions from the data. When the action has been tested, the group looks at the consequences. What have been the results of applying the particular procedures? If data have been carefully collected throughout the study, the many types of information will need to be organized and analyzed. The group is now ready to draw generalizations regarding the relationships between the action and the goal that it had in mind. These generalizations are for its own school. Whatever conclusions are arrived at apply to the population in that school. Like other types of research, action research is of high quality only if it is objective, is planned carefully, includes valid data systematically collected, and draws reasonable conclusions based on the evidence available. Those conducting the research must be extremely careful in interpreting findings since they are directly involved in the situation that is being studied.

In the study, there may be other findings that were not necessarily a part of the original intent. For example, a faculty that has kept careful records may find out through the data that it has improved its ways of working together.

If the community and members of the school staff have been involved, the question of implementing the findings should not be of any concern. The practice will already have been put into effect: it has only to be continued and improved. If a few teachers have been carrying on the experiment, but all have shared in the planning and evaluating of the study, there will be an easier transition in implementing the results in other classrooms.

7. Communicating findings to others. If the total school faculty has been involved in some manner, the communication will be an integral part of the whole study. If not, communication with other faculty members ought to be done through face-to-face contacts, where the participants explain the procedures and the findings. A plan will need to be formulated for informing the community about the results, even though some community members have participated in the study. The community members can play an important part in giving the information to others through parent–teacher association meetings, meetings of other organizations, special meetings called for that purpose, and individual contacts.

The question arises as to what is being done in action research in other school systems. Teachers in other schools are interested in how the research is conducted and what the results are. Consequently, those who carry on action research have an obligation to report through professional journals and conferences.

ISSUES AND POINTS OF VIEW

In the effort to move curriculum evaluation and experimentation from informal and incidental kinds of appraisal to more exact research, several issues arise.

1. *Should the evaluation of practices in a school be done by an outside agency or by the school staff?*

Some believe that if evaluation of practices is ever to be done objectively and impersonally, it must be done by disinterested persons from colleges, universities, state departments of education, or other agencies. The survey by an outside group has been a popular means of evaluating a program. Yet, surveys could not be classified as having any of the elements of experimentation or research. Others hold that school administrators, supervisors, and teachers should do the evaluation assisted by outside experts. The main direction of accreditation evaluations has been toward self-evaluation. They point out that involvement in the enterprise is directly related to willingness to change conditions found unsatisfactory. Those who advocate action research as a means of curriculum improvement point out that it has the advantage of its own integral evaluation.

2. *Should evaluation of a program or procedure be based upon pupil achievement in school subjects, or should consideration be given to other aspects of pupil growth and development?*

The temptation is great to collect the easily collectible. Readily quantifiable information has been used almost exclusively in the evaluation of many experimental programs even where they have purported to change pupils' behavior in other ways. Those who feel that the school's business is only to develop the intellectual side of the child are satisfied with this evaluation. Those who think otherwise want a broader appraisal of what happens to the child if given certain kinds of experiences.

However, if research on school programs is ever to come into its own, the easy way out is not the solution of the problem. As long as the school's goals continue to emphasize international understanding, civic interests, democratic commitments, mental health, and values, ways for quantification of data that deal with behavior expressing these atittudes and beliefs must be found. No evaluation is respectable unless it is related to purposes.

3. *Are demonstrating and trying out new ideas in pilot programs consistent with principles of evaluation, or are they means of further-*

ing a new program without the proper controls demanded by evaluation?

New programs in teacher education, television, and team teaching, for example, have seemed to some educators to have the zeal of the missionary rather than the caution of the researcher. They appear to have set out to prove something that the sponsors who have the funds for these experimental programs already believe. Schools have joined in these projects because funds were available for doing something that would advance their programs in new techniques and procedures. Others hold that these experiments are promising means for developing new programs in education, long overdue. They say that most changes have come about in education through the long process of the test of time, that practices are so firmly rooted that something needed to happen to jar loose the traditional practices.

In one sense, the latter are justified in their arguments. Few, if any, traditional practices in the curriculum have been subjected to careful evaluation. They are accepted in the same manner that the results of demonstrations are accepted. For the practical-minded, they work.

Perhaps the dilemma lies in the fact that demonstration and research have been intertwined. Can evaluation ever be objectively applied to a situation in which someone sets out to show how something is done? After all, research begins with asking good questions and then moves to testing out possible answers. The distinction has not been clearly made between finding out what is good and illustrating what is good. The one involves evaluation; the other, dissemination.

If evaluation is to move from guesswork toward research evidence, the dominant idea of establishing norms through finding out what other schools are doing and then evaluating one's practices against those norms cannot continue to prevail. Norms become standards, frozen into the structure of school practices. Curriculum improvement is not fostered by judgments based on current practices.

4. *Does action research have any value as research, or does it have little value in solving curriculum problems?*

Much argument has been expended upon the question of whether or not action research is research. The question is of academic interest only. If one holds to the position that anything called research must be done under rigorously controlled conditions, as in the sciences, then 95 per cent of what is reported in professional research journals fails to qualify as research. A reading of almost any summary of research in the *Review of Educational Research* reveals that in many of the articles reviewed the conclusions drawn are questionable because of faulty research or statistical techniques or small number of cases. Some are from articles giving opinions.

The useful question seems to be how we can move from a non-research-oriented program of curriculum improvement to one with greater commitments to research and experimentation. This chapter has pointed out that most curriculum study ends where action research begins. Action research is a means of curriculum improvement, a way to build evaluation into so-called experimentation.

Much that has been written up in periodicals and pamphlets as action research is not high quality research. Some is not research at all in that it does not follow the rather rigorous discipline of defining the problem; setting up hypotheses; obtaining baseline, continuous, and end data; and drawing generalizations based on the ideas tested in the conditions described.

5. *Can a person disengage himself sufficiently from action research to arrive at unprejudiced evidence, or are the individual's perceptions a legitimate part of the research process?*

The traditional point of view in research is that the researcher must disengage himself from any personal involvement in the research. If knowledge is to be furthered, he must be entirely impersonal about the findings. Some advocates of action research take the position that the research process is as much a process of feelings and behavior as it is a process of logic. If people are to be involved in research in order to change their own behavior, how can feelings be left out?

The difference stems partially from lack of a clear distinction between basic research and applied research. Basic research in education is research into human behavior that underlies school practice, in learning, in human development, and in all facets of the behavioral sciences. These results then need to be tested in the school situation as applied research. In a sense, action research is a form of applied research but not the only form. Action research must look to basic research as well as to theory and opinion for ideas that need to be tested in practice. This is the type of research in which most teachers are free enough and competent enough to engage. Basic research has nothing to do with practicality, costs, acceptance by the public, and instructional procedures. Action research does.

SELECTED REFERENCES

Association for Supervision and Curriculum Development. *Research for Curriculum Improvement.* 1957 Yearbook. Washington, D. C.: National Education Association, 1957, 350 pp.

Gives an excellent picture of research in improvement of curriculum practices, how it is conducted, and how teachers are involved.

Brickell, Henry M. *Organizing New York State for Educational Change.* Albany, N. Y.: State Education Department, 1961, 107 pp.

A descriptive study of the processes of curriculum change in New York State's school systems, including the role of the state department and the colleges and universities.

Corey, Stephen M. *Action Research to Improve School Practices.* New York: Bureau of Publications, Teachers College, Columbia University, 1953, 161 pp.

An earlier statement on action research that contains helpful examples of two action research studies and outlines some of the basic principles of such research.

Cronbach, Lee J. "Evaluation for Course Improvement" in Robert W. Heath (ed.), *New Curricula.* New York: Harper & Row, Publishers, 1964, chap. 12.

Suggestions for collection of data to evaluate new courses.

Doll, Ronald C. *Curriculum Improvement: Decision-making and Process.* Boston: Allyn & Bacon, Inc., 1964, Parts II and III.

The process of curriculum improvement, including initiating activities, participants' roles, and promising strategies. Has a chapter on evaluation of curriculum improvement programs.

Doll, Ronald C., Harry Passow, and Stephen M. Corey. *Organizing for Curriculum Improvement.* New York: Bureau of Publications, Teachers College, Columbia University, 1953, 77 pp.

Compares the centralized, decentralized, and centrally coordinated types of organization.

Harris, Lewis E., and Clyde R. Moore. *Quest for Quality.* Booklet No. 14, "Keys to Quality." Washington, D. C.: National School Boards Association and American Association of School Administrators, 1960, 48 pp.

A series of fourteen booklets of about 30 to 40 pages each which describe how a selected group of school districts evaluate their educational programs. Published under the general title *Quest for Quality.* The approaches used in evaluation are described by means of case studies of schools in different sizes and types of communities. This booklet is an over-all summary of procedures used by these schools.

Herzog, Elizabeth. *Some Guide Lines for Evaluative Research.* U. S. Department of Health, Education, and Welfare, Children's Bureau Publication No. 375–1959. Washington, D. C.: Government Printing Office, 1959, 117 pp.

A discussion of evaluative research dealing with social-psychological change, addressed to such questions as: What kind of change is desired? How trustworthy are the categories and measures employed? What is the evidence that the changes employed are due to the means employed? Should be helpful to the curriculum worker.

Jones, J. Charles, et al. The Upper Susquehanna Valley Program: Three
Years of Cooperative Research. Lewisburg, Pa.: Bucknell University,
1963, 52 pp.
    Describes the research projects conducted cooperatively by a univer-
sity and school systems to attempt to discover defensible answers to
the acceptance of curriculum proposals.
Kelley, Earl C. The Workshop Way of Learning. New York: Harper &
Row, Publishers, 1951, 169 pp.
    Still one of the best brief, readable references on workshop procedures.
Krug, Edward A., et al. Administering Curriculum Planning. New York:
Harper & Row, Publishers, 1956, chaps. 1–9.
    Much practical information for state-wide and local curriculum plan-
ning, teacher and lay participation in such planning, curriculum ex-
perimentation, and the use of workshops and consultants.
Lawler, Marcella. Curriculum Consultants at Work. New York: Bureau
of Publications, Teachers College, Columbia University, 1958, 212 pp.
    A helpful account of how consultants worked with six school systems,
their successes and their problems.
Leese, Joseph, Kenneth Frasure, and Mauritz Johnson, Jr. The Teacher in
Curriculum Making. New York: Harper & Row, Publishers, 1961, chaps.
13, 15, 16.
    Three especially pertinent chapters dealing with practices and prob-
lems of organization for curriculum study, community participation in
the study, and curriculum research.
Long, Harold M., and Robert N. King. Improving the Teaching of World
Affairs: The Glens Falls Story. Bulletin No. 35. National Council for
the Social Studies, Washington, D. C.: National Education Association,
1964, 92 pp.
    A significant story of how one school and community went about im-
proving international understanding. Has been termed "one of the
most significant projects in international understanding ever developed
in this country."
McNally, Harold J., and A. Harry Passow. Improving the Quality of Public
School Programs. New York: Bureau of Publications, Teachers College,
Columbia University, 1960, chaps. 5–11.
    Case descriptions of seven local and state curriculum improvement
programs.
National Society for the Study of Education. Citizen Co-operation for Better Public Schools. Fifty-third Yearbook, Part I. Chicago: University
of Chicago Press, 1954, chaps. 3–9 and 11.
    Contains many examples of citizen cooperation with the schools and
a chapter on the citizen's participation in evaluating a school program.
National Society for the Study of Education. In-Service Education for
Teachers, Supervisors, and Administrators. Fifty-Sixth Yearbook, Part I.
Chicago: University of Chicago Press, 1957, chaps. 5–6.
    These two chapters concern principles of how a faculty works together
productively in in-service education and the role of the teacher in
these programs.
O'Rourke, Mary A., and William H. Burton. Workshops for Teachers.
New York: Appleton-Century-Crofts, 1957, 100 pp.
    Much useful material for conducting and evaluating workshops.

Parker, J. Cecil, et al. Curriculum in America. New York: Thomas Y. Crowell Co., 1962, chaps. 15, 17.

Evaluation of the school's curriculum by school people, lay persons, and the critics. Good information on curriculum research by schools.

Pritzkau, P. T. Dynamics of Curriculum Improvement. Englewood Cliffs, N. J.: Prentice-Hall, Inc., 1959, chaps. 1, 15–17.

A challenging concept of an approach to curriculum improvement by the teacher in the classroom, with such interesting ideas discussed as developing an environment of ideas, the intangibles of anger and fear, and developing high level concepts of learning.

Shumsky, Abraham. The Action Research Way of Learning. New York: Bureau of Publications, Teachers College, Columbia University, 1958, 210 pp.

A helpful discussion of action research for the teacher, including both practical and theoretical analyses of the concept. The author holds that attitudes and personal perceptions of the researcher do and should enter into the study.

Spears, Harold. Curriculum Planning Through In-Service Programs. Englewood Cliffs, N. J.: Prentice-Hall, Inc., 1957, chaps. 2, 4, 7, and 13.

A comprehensive account of how teachers participate in curriculum improvement and other kinds of in-service education, with illustrations from school systems.

Stratemeyer, Florence B., et al. Developing a Curriculum for Modern Living. 2nd ed. New York: Bureau of Publications, Teachers College, Columbia University, 1957, Part V.

This section deals with planning for curriculum change and doing curriculum research and experimentation.

Taba, Hilda. Curriculum Development: Theory and Practice. New York: Harcourt, Brace & World, Inc., 1962, chaps. 19, 23.

Discusses evaluation of curriculum change and the strategy for making curriculum changes.

Taba, Hilda, and Elizabeth Noel. Action Research: A Case Study. Washington, D. C.: Association for Supervision and Curriculum Development, 1957, 58 pp.

Descriptions of action research conducted by teachers.

Taba, Hilda, and Enoch I. Swain. "A Proposed Model In Evaluation." Educational Leadership, 20:57–71, October, 1962.

A model for evaluation of curriculum programs proposed by the ASCD Evaluation Commission.

IV

CURRICULUM
DEVELOPMENT
IN ELEMENTARY AND
SECONDARY SCHOOLS

SOCIAL STUDIES
TO UNDERSTAND THE WORLD—

10

TRENDS IN THE ELEMENTARY SCHOOL CURRICULUM

In the early history of our nation, the focus in education was upon the elementary school. The purpose for the establishment of schools was clear-cut and widely accepted. Education represented a dream of the founding fathers who cherished the opportunity for their children to acquire skills in reading, writing, and ciphering. Men of fortitude and courage who braved the perils of exploring a new world believed wholeheartedly that with these skills an individual's opportunities for social and economic mobility were unlimited. If one could read, write, and cipher he was equipped to be a teacher, a preacher, a lawyer, or to have some other professional career of his choosing.

With the schools taking on the responsibility of helping the young acquire certain academic learning, the home and community accepted the responsibility for the development in children and youth of the related skills, attitudes, and values essential for effective participation in the society of that particular time. As boys became of appropriate age, they took their places alongside their elders and learned through first-hand experiences the chores with which they had to help at home and in the community. They became skilled in such jobs as plowing a furrow, building a stone fence, and caring for cattle. They soon joined their elders in roof-raising bees and other adult community activities. Later, as apprentices they learned by doing the trades they were to pursue. Likewise, under the tutelage of their mothers, the girls learned how to spin, to cook, to weave, to quilt, and to perform the many other duties which were the lot of women at that time. The goals of education were clearly defined and the responsibilities of the home and school were accepted and kept separate in the education of the young.

THE NEED FOR REVAMPING THE GOALS

Just as the elementary schools of pioneer days rose to meet the demands of the society that maintained them, they have continued to redefine their goals and adjust their programs to meet the needs of a society which continues to change through the years.

Yet, it is not difficult to find one elementary school after another in which the programs appear to be determined, in spite of the evidences of change on all sides, to meet the objectives of education of a bygone day. The goals or objectives stated by educational leaders in 1900 can no more fit the needs of today than the horse-drawn carriages or gas lamps of that era can fit the transportation and lighting needs of today.

New Forces and Pressures

The elementary school is the seed bed for the growth of democratic learning. A democratic society is not a static society nor does it have a manifest destiny. It must be born anew in each individual in every generation.

In a democratic society the setting is constantly changing. What might have seemed certain today is likely to be one of the uncertainties of tomorrow. In 1900 only a visionary would have dreamed of the automobile replacing the horse and buggy, and the airplane replacing the automobile. There is an air of legend about the individual who was born in the carriage era of 1900 and who now at 65 years of age is contemplating the possibilities of traveling into nonatmospheric space.

Unprecedented advances in sciences and technology, the struggle of people throughout the world to realize new ways of living, bureaucratic development, and population growth have been important factors in the radical change our society has undergone since the turn of the century. Along with these, there have been other forces such as more leisure time for workers, the development of materialism, the incidence of crime and immorality, less association of children with parents in the home, urbanization, and interdependence between people and among nations.

We have been a nation on the move, even if that move is no far-ther for some than from the metropolitan area into suburbia. The growth of suburbia is only a part of the picture. Each year during the past decade a million children have moved from one geographic area of the country to another; ten million have moved from one state to another; two million have moved from one part of a state to an-other; and five million from one community to another. In one year ten million of forty million school children have moved to new schools.

Add to the adjustments children have to make when moving into a new community, the tensions being transmitted to them by the adults as they seek to find their place and as they speculate as to whether or not they have made the right move. As adults live in fear of the uncertainties which lie ahead, they frequently feel respon-sible for the shortcomings of society. In an effort to make certain that these shortcomings will not continue to occur again, they begin to pressure the children. They want the children to achieve in areas in which they think they have failed.

The conquest of space, with all its ramifications, has thrown the nations of the world into renewed competition with each other. Each conquest by one nation threatens the status of other nations. The times have become electric with the race for superiority. Pressures for achievement are felt on all sides. These pressures from the home, the community, and the nation at large are being directed at education —as if education had failed somewhere along the line and there is need for a change in emphases.

Changes in Goals

The goals of education have evolved in terms of the needs of society and the needs of the individual. The over-all goals tend to remain constant. These goals are related to knowledge and understanding, skills and habits, attitudes and values in the areas of physical, social and emotional, and intellectual growth. At different times one area of growth has been emphasized more than the others.

There is no question that one of the major goals in elementary schools today is intellectual prowess or academic achievement. This is in contrast to the social emphasis that permeated elementary class-rooms a decade ago. Along with this major goal there is still em-phasis upon such long-term standing goals for the individual as maintaining and improving his physical fitness; understanding his world; acquiring basic skills, problem-solving ability, and rational thinking; expressing himself creatively; and living by democratic values.

Modern elementary schools serve society and the individual by accepting certain responsibilities. Through the process of education the school strives to develop boys and girls who place a high premium on healthy bodies and sound minds; who are curious to learn about and understand the physical, social, and scientific world of which they are a part; who are interested in acquiring the skills essential to effective participation in the modern world; who value creative expression; and who resolve to develop behavior patterns in harmony with the principles of democratic living.

Physical Fitness

The elementary school accepts as far as possible the responsibility of helping each individual maintain and improve his physical fitness. This is achieved in various ways.

Many elementary schools have mandatory physical examinations before enrollment in kindergarten, with complete physicals at fixed intervals, usually at the third and sixth grade. Likewise, eye screening and hearing tests for each individual are given in the first, third, and sixth grades, and at other times upon the recommendation of the teacher and/or parent. Parents are encouraged to have regular dental examinations and dental care for their children.

In special cases more intensive examinations and diagnostic treatment are provided through clinics. Home instruction is given children with particular illnesses. Nurses and physicians are part-time or full-time members of the school staff. Public health departments cooperate with the school and make their facilities and personnel available.

Instruction in healthful living is stressed throughout the grades, and good health habits are encouraged. The importance of nutrition is emphasized and encouraged as a part of daily living. School health programs are made an integral part of health instruction.

The physical education program is made up of games of a wide variety, rhythmic activities, alternating activity and rest, and in many schools, swimming. The National Physical Fitness Program has become an integral part of the physical education program in the majority of elementary schools. Self-testing activities are used as the basis for evaluating and planning programs in terms of individual needs and interests.

Mental Health

The modern elementary school considers the individual's mental health of extreme importance to his total well-being. The great increase in mental illness in recent years has made this objective all the more important. Statistics from the National Institute of Mental Health indicate that one out of every ten children in the classrooms of the nation at the present time will spend some time in a mental institution. The elementary school is sensitive to the ingredients that make for good mental health. Love, experiences with success, feelings of belonging and worth, and a wholesome concept of self are readily recognized as some of the important essentials to mental well-being. The family, the school, and the community share responsibility in this important area of an individual's development. The school cannot make up for lack of love or damaging personality practices in the home, or subjection to discrimination in the community. However, through child study, teachers become sensitive to the needs of particular children. When necessary, the schools weight the scales in favor of those ingredients essential to good mental health which are lacking in the other areas of an individual's life space.

The teacher uses many techniques to help him deepen his insights into child behavior and to understand the motivation of children. He requests the help of psychologists and psychiatrists when problems appear to be serious and deep-seated, services described in Chapter 11.

World Understanding

The modern elementary school realizes that the extent of an individual's participation in his physical, social, and scientific world will depend upon his understanding of it and his relation to it. The elementary school accepts the development of this understanding as one of its major responsibilities. To meet this responsibility, experiences are provided which help children acquire knowledge and grow in understanding of the basic needs of all human beings, wherever they may live in the world, the activities in which man engages to meet his needs, the ways in which he uses science to control and improve his environment, the institutions he has developed to perpetuate and improve his way of life, and the ways in which he has enriched his living through the arts. Knowledge and understanding related to man, his world, and his activities are basic to the development of good human relations. The elementary school recognizes the importance of good human relations in the world today and stresses learning in this area throughout the elementary grades.

Creative Expression

There is more need today than ever for an individual to express himself creatively. The modern elementary school recognizes the importance of creativity in the wholesome personality development of each girl and boy. It is cognizant of the contributions that the arts and crafts, music, bodily rhythmic movement, and literature make to full, rich living. It provides experience that insures wholesome emotional development. A variety of media are made available so that individuals may find those most suited to them. The various media provide the channels by which individuals find release and redirection for their emotions.

Teachers in a modern elementary school are sensitive to the potential for creativity which is innate in each individual. Teachers are also sensitive to the therapeutic values in creative experiences and their contributions to good mental health. They see them as essential to balance in the curriculum. These experiences are in addition to helping children enjoy the creative efforts of others.

Self-Control and Self-Direction

If the goals of education are to be realized, the modern elementary school has the responsibility of guiding boys and girls in ways which will help them to develop behavior patterns in harmony with the principles of democratic living. It is important that each individual be helped to grow in self-control and self-direction. The teacher works to establish a classroom climate that is friendly and accepting. The discipline in the modern classroom is not imposed by a teacher who dictates and then has to turn policeman to see that the dictates are carried out, but it is imposed rather by the tasks in which the children are engaged. Opportunities are provided for the children to participate in planning the activities of the day. As partners in the planning, they then hold themselves responsible to see that the plan works.

CHANGES IN EMPHASES AND CONTENT

It is only natural to expect that with the changes which have occurred in the goals of education and in the expectancies placed upon elementary school pupils, the emphases and content of the curriculum should change. Some of the changes represent efforts at experimentation. Many are the results of pressures from parents in particular and society in general. A few are innovations for innovation's sake. Although some of the changes have been slight, many have been radical.

Broadening the Subject Matter Base

In an effort to help children understand and adjust to the social and scientific world in which they live, there has been a discernible trend in recent years to broaden the subject matter base in nearly every area of the elementary school curriculum, and particularly in the social studies.

Previous to the appearance of social studies in the elementary school curriculum, geography and history were taught as discrete disciplines. They became the subject matter content of early social studies programs. The remnants of this limited content are still to be found in many schools, particularly where a textbook determines the subject matter content.

As the purposes of the social studies have become more clearly defined, it has become evident that there is need for extending the scope of the subject matter. The understandings, skills, and attitudes defined as social studies objectives require for their realization subject matter from more of the social sciences than those formerly relied upon. It has become necessary to draw subject matter from economics, sociology, anthropology, philosophy, history, and social psychology, as well as geography, political science, and the physical and natural sciences, in order to give pupils more help in understanding this rapidly changing world.

The curriculum is moving away from such limited studies as holidays, birds, minerals, the zoo, transportation, the circus, and national parks. Frontier thinkers in the field tend to select a broad area of human experience—conservation; communication; transportation of people and goods, and the producing, processing, distribution, and use of goods; recreation; and government—with subject matter from all the social sciences feeding into the study. The limited studies mentioned earlier are incorporated into the broader areas just described. The broader studies are concerned with the functioning of a particular area of human experience, not only in the nation but also in the world complex, including the long-established and the newly emerging nations. The tendency is away from memorizing the boundaries, names of rivers, and heights of mountains of regions and nations studied, and toward a focus upon the people, the ways in which people meet their needs, and the *why* of their development and living conditions. Emphasis is placed upon different cultural, national, and ethnic groups that make up the world's population, the relations of these various groups to each other, and the roles they are playing in the expanded world.

A movement that is gaining momentum is exemplified by the joint effort of curriculum leaders and social scientists to improve programs in the elementary schools. It is interesting to review the programs of state-wide, regional, and local conferences called by state departments of education, county offices, and local school districts, and to note the frequency with which social scientists are appearing with curriculum leaders, elementary school teachers, and principals in giving attention to the social studies. The programs are planned in a variety of ways; however, a common pattern seems to emerge. The social scientists generally present the structure of their particular discipline. The curriculum leaders then meet with the teachers by grade level to analyze the studies carried on in their respective grades and to explore the ways in which the larger ideas presented by the social scientists can be incorporated into the studies in progress.

Resource units are being prepared to help teachers carry on the new studies suggested, particularly those related to the emerging nations. Old resource units are being studied and revised to insure a broader base of subject matter content.

Emphasizing Basic Skills

There has always been a marked emphasis in the curriculum of elementary schools upon the goals in the language arts: listening, speaking, reading, and writing. Reading and writing especially have persisted in holding the spotlight for worry on the part of educators and criticism on the part of the public.

In spite of the emphasis which has dominated curriculum development through the years, some educators and a segment of the public appear to be dissatisfied with the results which have been achieved in the area of the language arts, and particularly in reading. These expressions of dissatisfaction and criticism have led educators to renew their efforts to improve the language arts program as a whole and the reading program in particular.

Teachers are placing a high premium upon the oral language expression of children in all grades, but especially in the kindergarten and primary grades. Opportunities are provided for the children to talk about their interests and activities. Situations are arranged in which the children can acquire word symbols for their experiences. Beginning reading is built upon the child's experiential background. Formal approaches to reading are not limited to one method. Instead, teachers may use a variety of methods geared to the abilities of the children.

As far as possible, teachers individualize instruction by grouping on the basis of needs and achievement. Efforts are made to insure success for each child. Reading experiences are not limited to a single series of readers. The abundance of reading materials available today makes it possible for the teacher to choose from a wide selection of reading series. The role of phonics in the reading program is being examined and evaluated. In most places it is being introduced as a method of word attack as soon as the child's sight vocabulary warrants.

Many schools are introducing individualized or self-selection programs in reading. In these programs a variety of reading materials with a wide range in difficulty and interest is made available. The individuals pace their reading in terms of their needs, interests, and abilities. Researches related to these programs report high interest and wide reading by individual children. Evaluations are based on an individual's growth and not on a mythical national norm.

Introducing a Foreign Language

Along with the trend to bear down on all aspects of the language arts in general and on reading in particular, a radical extension of the language arts is occurring in many elementary schools through the widespread introduction of a foreign language to the curriculum. Until recently, foreign languages were taught only in secondary schools and institutions of higher learning.

The teaching of a foreign language in the elementary grades was the exception rather than the rule. A few states, such as Louisiana and Texas, had state courses of study for use in their public elementary schools. Likewise, several of the larger cities had courses of study and teachers' guides. For example, one large city school system on the West Coast had a course of study for the teaching of Spanish. In the first grade the children learned greetings and leave-takings. Several new words and phrases were added each year.

In some schools, during or as a part of a culture or life study in the social studies, some of the vocabulary of the people studied was learned. As an illustration, when the children engaged in a study of China, resource persons who spoke Chinese were brought in to acquaint the class with the Chinese language. The characters of the Chinese language were presented and the boys and girls learned words and phrases in Chinese. There was no attempt, other than to provide experiences in language, to have the children acquire fluency in the use of a second language.

Although what may be called incidental learning of a second language may continue to be the objective in many elementary schools, the real push of the foreign language programs in the elementary grades at the present time is for fluency in the use of a second language. In an effort to insure fluency, some programs are starting in kindergartens. Others start at any grade above kindergarten. In most situations the classroom teacher, who is likely to be ill prepared, teaches the foreign language. However, specialists are being used wherever available. Intensive in-service programs are being carried on to develop competency in classroom teachers. Television is playing an important role in providing in-service education for teachers and direct classroom instruction. TV films from FLES (Foreign Language in Elementary Schools) are used. Some states are solving the teacher recruitment problem by employing after careful screening refugees or emigrants from other countries who are now living in the state, who are or can become qualified to teach.

The impetus for the tremendous increase in the number of elementary schools in the nation that include a foreign language in the curriculum is due largely to the National Defense Education Act, which make funds available for conferences and institutes at the national, state, and local levels for in-service education; the preparation of materials and development of procedures as well as research studies and consultative services. Education and language departments at a number of institutions of higher education are collaborating in the development of instructional materials and television programs.

The Evolving Area of Communications

The emphasis on communication skills and the introduction of a foreign language into the elementary school curriculum have turned the spotlight on the total language arts program. In the past the different phases of the language arts—listening, reading, literature, oral expression, written expression, spelling, and handwriting—were kept in separate compartments with little recognition of the relation of one to another. Now, with the emphasis on communication, which embraces all these forms, they are more likely to be treated as a whole and the interrelatedness among and between them is stressed. In the modern elementary school where teachers see their job as one of helping children grow in their power to listen, to speak, to read, and to write, the language arts provide the dynamics for moving through the entire program. The vitality of living in the classroom determines the quality of the language arts program.

Problems arise in relation to the study in which the children are engaged. In order to solve the problem it might be necessary to read to secure information. Notes may be taken on the reading and an outline prepared. An oral report based on the outline might be given to the class. A written report might be prepared for the class record book. It is also possible that the solution of the problem might involve writing a letter, engaging in an interview with an adult, introducing a speaker, listening to a speaker, thanking a speaker. It is difficult to think of any part of living in the classroom in which some aspects of the language arts do not function.

Considerable impetus for pushing out the frontier in the area of the language arts has come from Project English, a part of the Cooperative Research Program in the U. S. Office of Education. Through this program, several curriculum development centers in English or the language arts and demonstration centers have been established. Projects initiated previously under the general cooperative research program are now considered part of Project English if they represent any phase of the language arts. Two projects of this nature which have significance for the language arts in elementary schools are the Strickland Project and the Loban Project.[1]

The Strickland Project involved children from grades one through six who lived in and around Bloomington, Indiana. They attended rural schools, small-town schools, and the laboratory school of Indiana University. At intervals during one school year, the natural, informal language of children in each of the grades was taped. To get at the structure of current textbook material, samplings from four series of reading textbooks were made at the same time the children's language was being taped. A formula set up by a committee of linguists was used to analyze and compare the children's speech with samplings from the textbooks. The results of the study showed, among other things, that children's oral language is far more advanced than the language of the books with which they are taught to read.

The Loban Project was also concerned with children's spoken language. The study involved kindergarten children who were followed year after year through grade six. Of the 338 children who started in the kindergarten, 241 were still in the study in the sixth grade. A

[1] Ruth Strickland, *The Language of Elementary School Children: Its Relationship to the Language of Reading Textbooks and the Quality of Reading of Selected Children*, Bulletin, Vol. 38, No. 4, Bloomington, Ind.: Bureau of Educational Studies and Testing, School of Education, Indiana University, July, 1962, 131 pp.

Walter Loban, *The Language of Elementary School Children*, Research Report No. 1, Champaign, Ill.: National Council of Teachers of English, 1963, 92 pp.

recording of each child's spoken language was made each year. Each conversation was about one of a series of six pictures and the same pictures were used year after year. Many different kinds of evidence were collected about each child and used to analyze the characteristics of the child's oral expression from year to year. One of the significant findings from the study indicated that the child's progress in reading, in writing, and in oral language showed positive relationships with each other.

In the modern elementary school, teachers are being encouraged to study the oral expression of children for both content and quality and to examine carefully the materials the school provides for their work in reading and language.

Educators are conscious of the need for reading material suited to the needs and interests of children and written at their level of language development. This is particularly true of children who are culturally disadvantaged. To meet this need several large city school systems have undertaken to prepare their own materials which will be more closely related to the experiential backgrounds of particular pupils than the present reading material.

Another significant development in the language arts program is the emphasis on linguistics. Language arts specialists are speaking and writing about the influence linguistics may have on the content of school readers as well as on the study of spoken and written language. Numerous school systems are experimenting with linguistic approaches to reading as suggested by such linguists as Bloomfield, Barnhart, and LeFevre.[2]

Linguistics is concerned with the structure of a language and with the translation of oral speech into written symbols. The position of a word in a sentence, rather than a definition of it, determines its classification. Schools are experimenting to test the effectiveness of a linguistic approach not only to reading but to speaking and writing.

Emphasizing Experimentation and Discovery

In contrast to the old objective of gathering facts and attempting to store them in a mythical brain box to be drawn out for use sometime in the future, the modern elementary school has children acquire facts for use in experimentation, discovery, and concept building.

---

[2] Leonard Bloomfield and Clarence Barnhart, *Let's Read: A Linguistic Approach*, Detroit: Wayne State University Press, 1961, 470 pp.

Carl A. LeFevre, *Linguistics and the Teaching of Reading*, New York: McGraw-Hill Book Co., 1962, 252 pp.

The value then shifts; instead of placing the premium on the facts acquired, it is on the use made of them.

Elementary school pupils experiment to find the solutions to many problems that arise in the social studies. As an illustration, children in the kindergarten often plant a garden. They perform simple experiments to find out the best conditions for raising their vegetables and flowers. The experimentation may be related to the germination of seeds, the effect of sun and shade on growing plants, or the need for water.

When children in the fifth grade study about the westward movement in the early history of the United States, problems often arise related to the food supplies of the pioneers. The pupils may experiment to find ways of preserving foods. In a study in the sixth grade on one of the Latin American countries, the pupils may have a problem related to distances from one place to another in South America. The solution of the problem will require the application of certain mathematical principles and processes.

A procedure to help children discover principles, used by Suchman of the University of Illinois, is termed "inquiry training." [3] It is a method of instructing children in the process of inquiry. Emphasis is on the pupils asking the questions rather than the teacher, whereas in the typical classroom the teacher asks eight to ten times as many questions as the pupils. Intermediate grade children are shown a film of a simple physics demonstration and are asked to explain why the demonstration had the result that it did. In order to obtain information, the children ask questions that the teacher can answer by "yes" or "no." It is an inductive type of inquiry, with no physical manipulation of the materials and with a minimum of verbalization on the part of the child. The inquiry is guided by the teacher, who has in mind the general principle to be learned and guides the pupils through inquiring about an example, helping them in developing a plan of inquiry and in gathering data and constructing an explanation. Children first ask questions to verify the facts of the demonstration, then set up imaginary experiments to determine relevant variables, next identify through questions the conditions necessary for the demonstration, and finally determine why these conditions are necessary, in order to discover the principles.

The learning procedure uses both the principles of reinforcement and feedback. Each week a new film is shown and the pupils receive guided practice sessions. Subsequent films involve principles that

[3] J. Richard Suchman, "Inquiry Training: Building Skills for Autonomist Discovery," *Merrill Palmer Quarterly*, 7:147–69, July, 1961.

have been presented in previous films, plus a new principle or a new application. The one film builds on the other. Each session is tape recorded and teacher and pupils in this way can evaluate the sessions.

In inquiry training, more attention is paid to process than in the usual classroom procedure. Since children do the questioning, there is little pressure on them and they are encouraged to explore and take risks. The pupil operates differently if he realizes that truth is to be discovered by him, not revealed to him. In a sense, the process is not unlike the way a creative individual operates.

New Directions in Elementary School Science

Scientific advancement, technological development, and national and international events have focused the attention of the public upon the critical role of science education in today's world. Science instruction is relatively new in the programs of some of the elementary schools. The emphasis on science and the amount of time devoted to it has varied from state to state and from school to school within the states.

The passage of the National Defense Education Act of 1958 by the 85th Congress has been a real incentive for educators to re-examine the place of science in the educational program and to plan and provide new educative experiences for children. The availability of funds has made possible an increase in materials for use in science instruction and a variety of programs directed toward the improvement of science education.

Over a period of years, persons and institutions responsible for developing science programs have been the recipients of grants from associations and foundations. The American Association for the Advancement of Science, the National Science Foundation, as well as other foundations such as Ford, Sloan, and Carnegie, have made grants of various sizes which have made possible the planning and operation of institutes and workshops at teacher education institutions. Earlier in the foundation programs, the grants were largely for the purpose of improving science programs in the secondary schools. These have been extended to grants to teacher education institutions for the establishment of summer workshops for elementary school teachers.

In classrooms across the nation, one finds evidences of science programs in action: bulletin boards prepared around science problems, exhibits of science work prepared by the boys and girls, children sharing interesting experiments or other science activities with other classes, assemblies based upon scientific developments, articles related to science in the school paper, class record books describing science activities, a science center, and above and beyond all these evidences, a science table equipped with all the paraphernalia necessary to perform experiments.

An examination of the objectives of elementary school science, as presented in recent courses of study and teachers' guides, reveals a heavy emphasis on helping boys and girls behave as scientists in their search for verifiable knowledge. Such objectives are stated frequently as follows:

> To help children acquire skill in the processes of inquiry—hypothesizing, investigating, probing, experimenting, checking, exploring, thinking, reasoning, and analyzing
>
> To help children develop attitudes consistent with the methods and content of science, such as open-mindedness, critical thinking, withholding judgment until all the facts are known, and willingness to change an idea when new evidence is discovered
>
> To help children develop a sense of responsibility for the wise application of science to the problem and situations of everyday life and to the modification and control of environment for the improvement of human welfare.

The growing emphasis appears to be upon those objectives related to the scientific method and attitudes, personal discovery, and functional use of scientific findings. The modern objectives differ from previous ones which implied acceptance on the part of the pupil. They preclude the tendency, so often found in elementary school science programs, of reading about science experiments and accepting generalizations arrived at by other people. Rather, they encourage the performance of experiments by the children themselves so that science becomes an experience in discovery and application of scientific findings.

The tendency is to define the major ideas which constitute the content of science. Then, rather than slicing the content into layers and allocating a layer to each grade, experiences are provided in the primary grades related to these ideas. At each subsequent grade level, experiences are built upon experiences with a cumulative effect. The spiral widens as it moves through the grades. Thus, individuals are able to arrive at generalizations which have meaning for them.

Modern Mathematics

One hears about the "new mathematics" or the "modern mathematics" in the elementary school more often than he hears about arithmetic. It is quite logical that this change in nomenclature should occur since certain mathematical concepts permeate the arithmetic program from the grade school through high school. This does not mean that the old arithmetic, as it were, is being replaced entirely by the "new mathematics." The elements of arithmetic are still an integral part of the "new mathematics."

The change from arithmetic to mathematics has been so dramatic that many mathematicians refer to it as a revolution. The revolution is attributed to three causes: (1) advances resulting from mathematical research, (2) the automation revolution, and (3) the introduction of the large-scale, high-speed, automatic digital computer.

At its highest level mathematics in the elementary school is becoming more and more a study of form or pattern. The concern is with the language used in describing the structure of these forms and the methods of reasoning by which conclusions are derived. Attention to structure is being extended to the study of arithmetic, the most elementary branch of mathematics. This is a shift in emphasis. Previously, the main province of arithmetic was computation. The emphasis now is upon inductive learning, identifying and comparing recurring elements among similar kinds of problem situations, discovering principles, and the thinking process characterizing logical argument or reasoning.

Although computation and skill development are still necessary and reinforcement exercises are provided to fix skills, it is the *why* of computing that is emphasized. It is assumed that if an individual has a grasp of the basic principles involved and he uses an approach that is meaningful to him, he will cut down on the amount of time he will need to devote to reinforcement exercises.

The modern mathematics program revitalizes and updates the former arithmetic program. It adds much that is above and beyond limited learning in arithmetic. Individuals are helped to discover that there are a number of systems instead of *a* number system. They are helped to discover that there is more than one geometry, and that there is a high correlation between algebra and geometry; they are helped to acquire a precise mathematical language. They learn about the significant contributions of high-speed electronic computing devices and gain some understanding of the mathematical operations of these machines.

The bases for this understanding and many of these discoveries begin in the kindergarten and primary grades. The child has experiences which will help him to understand such principles as the commutative, associative, and distributive laws, the closure property, and order. A pupil increases his understanding of the meaning of the fundamental processes of computation—addition, subtraction, multiplication, and division; fractions; and negative numbers—when he has the opportunity to explore these ideas with the help of the numerous teaching aids available. He learns to work with the number line, the abacus, the counting frame, Cuisenaire rods, and magnetic discs and boards.

INNOVATIONS IN STAFF UTILIZATION AND ORGANIZATION FOR INSTRUCTION

Accompanying the applications of technocracy and automation to learning experiences have come changes in the organization of the elementary school for instruction and staff utilization, and the introduction of various ways of grouping children and classes for instruction. These changes are attempts to modernize education and to improve learning experiences for children.

Among the innovations during the past few years are television, team teaching, and programmed instruction, discussed at length in Chapter 14. Elementary schools throughout the nation are experimenting with the use of new media and different forms of organizing for instruction. These innovations have received wide publicity in recent years. In some instances camps have been set up and battle lines have been drawn for attack and defense.

Use of Television

At the present time there are two types of television programs in which elementary schools are interested. The first is educational television—types of educational programs having general community interest and value. These programs may be related to almost any facet of living. They may be concerned with the dissemination of information, the explanation of various phenomena, or provision for personal cultural growth. The second is instructional television, which refers to programs designed for in-class viewing during school hours, or in-service education programs for teachers, administrators, and supervisors. The most frequent use of television in the elementary schools is in science programs and in the teaching of foreign languages. In these programs there is an extensive use of video tapes.

The following is a description of the use of instructional television for elementary schools as observed in a large school district.

The studio was flooded with light. Television cameras were being moved into place. Eight fifth- and sixth-grade pupils were seated behind flat-topped desks, each with his sketchbook open to a blank page. A large bulletin board to the back and right of the girls and boys displayed artistically arranged art prints by well-known artists. To the front and right was an old-fashioned lamp post with a potted rubber plant at its base. The stage was set. At a signal from the director, eight pairs of eyes were focused on a lectern at the left and front of the stage. With a small microphone around her neck and a long extension cord trailing behind her, the art supervisor advanced to the lectern. She smiled at the children. The children smiled back.

"This morning you are going to have a lesson in sketching," the art supervisor announced.

The broad smiles of the children indicated that this announcement was no surprise to them. Their sketchbooks were open and they were ready to go. The art supervisor moved through the steps in a good sketching lesson. The eight pupils responded in ways that would bring joy to any teacher's heart. This was the eighth in a series of sixteen art lessons being taped for use in the fifth and sixth grades of the city system.

At 9:15 on the Monday morning following the taping of this eighth lesson in the series, 4,896 girls and boys in 152 fifth- and sixth-grade classrooms in the city sat with their sketchbooks open on their desks. The 152 teachers stood in front of their classes each holding a copy of the "Teacher's Guide to Art Lessons," which had been prepared by the art supervisor who gave the demonstration lesson on television. Each teacher had followed the guide in preparing the pupils for "A Lesson in Sketching." Art prints were arranged on the bulletin boards, and lamp posts with rubber plants at the base took shape and form in 4,896 sketchbooks between 9:15 and 10 o'clock that Monday morning in 152 classrooms in the city.

This situation presents a synthesis of the use of television, team teaching, and programmed instruction. The art supervisor might be thought of as the master teacher, the classroom teachers as assistants. The art supervisor and the classroom teachers, making up a teaching team, were the givers. The 4,896 fifth- and sixth-grade girls and boys were the takers. The learning experience was programmed in a central office.

As research and experience continue to add to the potentialities of television and to a knowledge of skills required in utilizing television in elementary schools, its use will be rapidly extended.

Team Teaching

Team teaching is perhaps one of the most controversial issues that has appeared on the educational horizon in the last decade. It is a term used to describe some kind of innovation in staff utilization. It has come to mean different things in different places.

Team teaching, or teaching teams, as some prefer to call any innovations in staff utilization, has appeared in various shapes and forms through the years. In a one-teacher school the teacher and the pupils are the team. A person from the community might be brought in to aid the team, or a county or district supervisor of instruction might be on the team at different times. In a two-teacher school, the two teachers usually relate themselves to the total school population at some time during the day through assemblies, recreation, and other total school activities. However, in the elementary schools where some type of team teaching has been introduced it is a much more loosely organized arrangement than that advocated by the NEA Commission on the Experimental Study of the Utilization of the Staff in the Secondary School, as discussed in Chapter 12.

There are numerous variations of staff utilization labeled team teaching in elementary schools. In general, the pattern is to have a head teacher or master teacher, a number of classroom teachers, student teachers, and teacher aides making up the team. The procedure generally followed is to have a teacher with a particular competency related to the study in progress present material to a group of children that might range from 50 to 150 in size. The large group is then broken into as many smaller groups as there are teachers in the team to pursue problems and to engage in related activities. These groups might then be broken into still smaller groups in which individual and group study might be pursued.

Programmed Instruction

Programmed instruction is a teaching method in which materials and procedures are used to provide a self-instructional program. Typical programs take the pupil through a set of specific behaviors. These are designed and ordered to make it quite certain that the learner will behave in a certain way in the future. These materials are described in Chapter 14.

Changes in Elementary School Organization

Early in the history of education in this country the elementary schools were organized for instruction by grades. This organization became the tradition and the large majority of elementary schools today are organized on a grade basis.

Some frontier thinkers in elementary education have never seemed particularly happy with this administrative device for grouping children. Dissatisfaction has grown through the years as teachers and administrators have become more and more sensitive to the differences that exist in human beings in all areas of development.

As deeper insights developed in relation to individual differences, there was an awareness of the need for individualizing instruction. It became apparent that it was unrealistic to place the same expectancies in physical, social, and intellectual development for every individual. A grade has come to mean a place where a group of children of approximately the same chronological age but with wide differences in mental age, academic achievement, needs, interests, and abilities work together in learning situations under the guidance of an adult.

In an attempt to improve learning situations and to individualize instruction as far as possible for elementary school children, various proposals regarding organization have been put into operation.

The *ungraded school* organization has been in operation in a large number of elementary schools for the past several years, particularly in the primary grades. In a few districts the ungraded organization has moved up into the middle or intermediate grades.

In an ungraded primary, an individual is in a group of six-, seven-, or eight-year-olds where he paces his own learnings. Instead of being in a grade, he is in a specific teacher's group. The expectancies are placed in terms of the individual's interests, needs, and abilities rather than in terms of a grade norm or standard. Some children may take the usual three years to go through the primary grades, some may take more, others less. This same arrangement may carry on in the ungraded middle grades. The philosophy of the school determines what constitutes the program in the ungraded school. As is to be expected, there are different interpretations of an ungraded school and wide variations in the program.

The *multigraded school* organization has some of the earmarks of a two-or-three-teacher rural school where a teacher is responsible for teaching three or more grades and is similar to the ungraded organization. A six-year-old may be reading with a group of nine-year-olds, whereas a nine-year-old might be reading with a group of six- and seven-year-olds. Although an individual may be working in groups of older or younger children, he continues to be identified as a first, second, or third grader.

The graded, ungraded, and multigraded schools describe the outside structure of elementary school organization. There is also an inside structure which relates to instruction. The inside structures are commonly referred to as the self-contained or semi-self-contained, and the departmentalized or the semi-departmentalized classrooms.

A *self-contained classroom* is the well-known typical organization in which children have the same teacher for the major portion if not the total day. In a semi-self-contained classroom the group might have a teacher for the major portion of the day and then one or two other teachers for particular subjects. These are often physical education, art, music, reading, or science.

In a *departmentalized classroom* the day is usually divided into a certain number of periods. Each period is devoted to a different subject with a different teacher teaching each subject. In a seven-period day the pupil meets seven different teachers. A semi-departmentalized situation is one in which one teacher has a group for a larger block of time than one period. It may be two or three periods back-to-back. The social studies and language arts are usually taught in the larger block of time. The rest of the periods are devoted to different subjects, each taught by a different teacher.

Other Organizations and Groupings

Numerous efforts are being made in elementary schools throughout the country to provide for more flexible organization and staff utilization to improve instruction. This is demonstrated by the Eugene, Oregon, Project which is partially supported by a grant from the Fund for the Advancement of Education. One phase of the project is directed largely toward meeting individual differences and individualizing instruction.

A district policy has been established which permits children to enter school early if a psychological evaluation and a summer trial period in a preschool class "verify" his ability. This predicts a change of organization, at least in the primary grades. Certain schools in the district are moving into non-graded primary programs to individualize instruction further.

Some grouping is being done on the basis of interests. Provision is made for children with common interests outside the regular program to work together. These pupils come largely from the middle grades. Some groups are structured for work in specific areas of the curriculum. Large or small groups are organized to make better use of a teacher's particular strength or time.

ISSUES AND POINTS OF VIEW

There is a climate to every year of living that makes each year different from the one before. The years following the mid-century mark may well become known as The Pressure Years. There seem to be pressures on all sides: on government, on communities, and on individuals.

Education is particularly sensitive to the pressures of today. Schools seem to be living in a kind of "hurry up," "produce more" climate. Whatever the problem, there is an attitude on the part of some educators that they must hurry up and get something done, make some change. Change and progress seem to go together in people's thinking. Innovations are introduced which are accepted by some educators and rejected by others. The changes or innovations become issues on which persons both in and out of the profession disagree and upon which they take stands. The years ahead will tell if the issues have been weighed in the scales and found wanting. If they stand the tests of experimentation, research, and experience they will become an integral part of the programs in elementary schools; if not, new changes will be tried.

Some of the issues being weighed in the areas discussed in this chapter are described in the following pages.

1. *Should certain subject matter such as reading and mathematics involving abstract learning be taught earlier, or should it be taught when the individual has need for the learning?*

Subject matter which formerly was taught in the middle and upper grades is now being taught in many kindergartens and primary grades. This is particularly true of formal programs in reading and mathematics.

Advocates of organized reading and mathematics programs for very young children appear to be influenced by sensational and often misleading news stories which have been appearing in the press.

These advocates point to the fact that today's children are literally drenched in the various media of mass communication. The amount of time preschool and primary school children spend looking at television has had an impact upon their behavior. This is particularly noticeable in their oral language expression. The language precociousness of young children is interpreted by the advocates of earlier reading and mathematics instruction to mean that children arrive at readiness for these experiences at a much earlier age.

The advocates reason that if children learn to read early they will work at an advantage throughout their school careers. They also present the point of view that if children are taught reading and mathematics in the kindergarten it will give more importance to kindergartens.

Many educators will not go along with this point of view. They stress the physical, social, and intellectual differences that are characteristic of young children. They point to the lack of eye development required for reading. They also adhere to the research findings that reveal the need for a mental age of six-and-one-half to insure success in learning to read.

The opponents to these early programs hold to the theory of learning which has to do with biological maturation. According to this theory, certain concepts cannot be learned until there is a biological readiness. The individual moves from concrete to abstract ways of learning on a fourteen-point continuum. Reading is fourteenth on the continuum. An emphasis on the concrete ways of learning is advocated before abstract learning is introduced. The facility in the use of language on the part of very young children is interpreted by the opponents to early programs in reading and mathematics to be verbal precociousness. This verbal precociousness or facility in the manipulation of words is frequently misleading. Children often verbalize without having any meaning for the word symbols they are using.

Many leading educators feel that kindergarten and first-grade children have many involvements more closely related to their needs than learning to read or to study mathematics. In a good program for five- to eight-years-olds they are having learning experiences integrated around broad areas of human experience such as transportation, communication, and the production, processing, and marketing of goods. They are acquiring concepts in the physical and biological sciences appropriate to their maturation. Through daily practice health habits are being learned or reinforced. They engage in suitable games and use play equipment to develop muscular coordination. They are learning to listen, to express their ideas, and to dramatize stories. Opportunities are provided for them to have experiences in art, music, and bodily rhythmic movements. Living in the group provides many opportunities for counting, grouping, comparing objects and numbers, playing number games, and measuring. Probably the most important learning of all is related to social relations with age-mates, with younger and older children, and with adults outside the home, these proponents hold.

All this sounds like heavy school diet for little children. But this is early childhood. The question that educators need to come to grips with is what learning should be given priority during the child's first years in school, and to resist temptation under pressure to stampede superficially to a passing excitement.

2. *Should a foreign language be included in the elementary school curriculum, or should the time and effort devoted to it be used to improve the pupils' use of the English language?*

To teach or not to teach a foreign language in the elementary school is a relatively new issue in education. The move to introduce foreign languages into the elementary school came shortly after the end of World War II. Following the war, the people of the United States were more conscious than ever before of the extension of everyone's life into all parts of the world and the need to improve international relations. The geography of the war took more people from this country into more parts of the world than had migrated during the entire history of the nation. Both civilians and soldiers had acquired smatterings of a second language—or more—from living in foreign countries where they were stationed.

As our international involvements increased rapidly, some educators began to feel that if individuals were to participate effectively as democratic citizens in a world order, they would need to be equipped with more than one language. Need also was felt for revitalizing the foreign language departments of secondary schools where enrollments before and during the war had fallen off noticeably.

Pros and cons have developed among educators in relation to the inclusion of a foreign language in the elementary school program. Those favoring the teaching of a foreign language feel that it will build an appreciation of people of other countries. It will be possible to understand them better through a reading of their literature. Ability to speak another language indicates a person's interest in people of other countries. The use of other languages will help to further and improve international relations.

The supporters contend that many private schools teach foreign languages. They argue that many students in foreign countries are fluent in several languages. In addition, they claim that the study of a foreign language cultivates the more precise use of English and provides a tool useful in other pursuits. If pupils continue study of the language through the elementary grades and the secondary school, they will be able to learn to use it well.

Those opposed to teaching foreign languages in elementary schools express grave doubts as to its value to the elementary school pupil. They argue that the curriculum is already overcrowded. Only a small portion of the day or week could be spared for instruction, whereas it takes hours of concentrated effort over a long period of time to really become proficient. Unless fluency in speaking is acquired there is little use in spending time on a foreign language. If a child has no opportunity for using the language he has learned, it is soon lost. If a foreign language is taught in the elementary grades, there should be assurance that there will be opportunity to study it in succeeding grades.

The opponents raise the question as to what language should be taught if it is to be related to the people with whom we are most involved in our international relations, and following quickly upon that question they raise another: "Who shall teach the foreign language?"

In spite of the pros and cons, there has been a tremendous increase in the number of elementary school children studying a foreign language. In the past few years the number has grown from 145,600 in 1953 to about 1,277,000 in 1959–1960.[4] It is not unlikely that this number will continue to increase as materials are developed, teachers become available, and teaching techniques improve. Experience is showing that achievement is negligible in the majority of schools because of poor teaching and the little amount of time devoted to it.

3. *Should one teacher take major responsibility in a self-contained classroom for a single group of elementary school children all day long, or should different teachers teach the different subjects that make up the curriculum?*

The advocates of the self-contained classroom contend that the teacher can get to know each individual in the group in an intimate way so that his guidance becomes one of the important factors in the pupil's development. The individual is able to build a feeling of belonging and security because he can attach himself to an adult and adjust to one group. The program can be flexible and the teacher and different groups can be working on more than one goal at a time. The advocates stress the point that with one teacher, activities in one area of the curriculum can give purpose to activities in another, and learning in the different areas can be integrated. The group in a self-contained classroom can identify itself with other groups in the school and with the total school through assemblies and other all-school activities.

The advocates of the self-contained classroom contend that it is

---

[4] Marjorie Bruenig, *Foreign Languages in the Elementary Schools of the United States, 1959–1960,* New York: Modern Language Association of America, 1961, p. 1.

impossible for a teacher to know the large number of boys and girls he meets in a departmental situation well enough to give them any kind of guidance. As a result, the boys and girls live through a day feeling unknown, unrecognized, and unloved. This makes it possible for some of them to live anonymously and it tempts them to develop techniques for "getting by," since nobody knows and nobody cares.

The curriculum is fragmented and the children are left to their own resources to integrate their learnings. Instead of an individual adjusting to thirty or so children in a self-contained situation, he has to adjust to any number from one hundred and fifty to two hundred children.

In defense of departmental situations, the advocates say that there is so much new knowledge to be taken in that one individual cannot become a specialist in all the areas that make up the elementary school curriculum and they believe that specialization is basic to a quality program. Teachers are relieved in one or two fields in order to lighten their loads. They claim that through cooperative planning teachers can acquaint each other with the work in progress in their specialty and at times implement or supplement each other's programs. In the same way, they hold that the teachers can share their observations of the pupils and give more guidance than if the pupils were alone with one teacher.

A number of schools are settling this issue by finding a happy medium. Two subjects with the periods back-to-back are taught by one teacher. The subjects taught under this arrangement usually are social studies and language arts as a block and mathematics and science as another block. This arrangement cuts down on the pupil–teacher and teacher–pupil contacts. It also makes it possible to integrate the learning in the different subjects. Other solutions are combining in different ways self-contained and departmentalized plans or using team teaching and the ungraded plan as described in this chapter.

11

PROVISIONS FOR INDIVIDUAL DIFFERENCES IN ELEMENTARY SCHOOLS

The basic responsibility of the public school is to attempt to educate each pupil in all areas to the extent of his capacity. In order to implement this philosophy, it is often necessary to provide special opportunities and programs for children with aptitudes, skills, interests, and problems which cannot be served within the regular classroom programs.

Ideally, these pupils would be identified and instructed in the regular classroom by proper grouping and instruction. However, this is rarely possible. For many of these children, it is necessary that special programs be available at the elementary level to supplement or replace the regular program. Emphasis is placed upon early and accurate identification and placement in the proper program in order to insure maximum growth and to prevent an individual's problem from becoming too complex.

With the unprecedented yearly increase in the numbers of children attending the public schools, the heterogeneity of the student body has become more marked and individual differences more sharply defined. Schools have striven to provide for the differences found among the pupils of their system through course selection, through employment of methods of grouping within the grade and within classes, through wide choice of activities within a course of study, through extra or especially designed projects, through individual work with a

teacher, and through clubs and pupil organizations. Programs of study have been built to meet the needs and interests of all pupils. The increase of numbers in the schools makes it administratively possible to open new opportunities for improving the ways by which public education can bring each pupil closer to his fullest potential. Science also helped to this end, for it has recently produced new instruments and techniques by which educators are able to analyze the differences found among pupils, measure them, define their relation to the learning process, and use the results to improve instruction.

No one pupil would give evidence of all characteristics in one category or another. There may be evidence of overlapping characteristics in individuals; for example, a generally superior child may be deficient in writing or in organizing his work, while a child who is generally slow may give evidence of leadership in an area in which he has some particular talent. Differences are usually differences in degree rather than kind. The "average" individual may be strong in some characteristics, weak in others, and have shades of in-between in still others.

This chapter describes some of the programs and provisions that the elementary schools are introducing in an attempt to provide for these individual differences. Some of the provisions for special education and services apply also to secondary schools.

THE CULTURALLY DEPRIVED

Public schools are becoming increasingly aware of their responsibilities to the children described or labeled as "disadvantaged," "culturally deprived," "underprivileged," or "disabled." These pupils often demonstrate insecurity, emotional and social instability, and underachievement, and are high risks as potential delinquents.

There is no simple cure for these children from poverty stricken homes and unhealthy surroundings. Schools cannot do the job by themselves. The problems and conditions can only be resolved by an all-out community effort. However, in some communities, the schools are becoming the focal point of local action. The nature of the programs in elementary schools and two examples of programs are described in this section.

Objectives and Nature of Programs

In a study of the characteristics of programs for the disadvantaged in forty-two local districts, many similarities of special projects were noted. No two school systems listed the same objectives or purposes, but a study of the description makes it plain that most of the programs aim, among other things, to raise the achievement levels of the children, recognizing that a deprived child's I.Q. is not likely to indicate his full potential; to discover latent talents and develop them; to motivate each child so that he will want to do his best; and to build strong ties and understanding between school and home.

Effectiveness of the specific procedures and activities depend to a large extent upon six key factors.

1. Understanding, competent teachers.
2. Well staffed pupil personnel services, with emphasis on counseling and social work.
3. A remedial reading program geared to the language and experience limitations of the children involved.
4. A flexible and varied program of special education.
5. Effective means of involving parents and securing their cooperation.

6. Enthusiastic and sustained help from community agencies and civic organizations.[1]

Higher Horizons Program

The New York City school system has many programs for its wide range of pupil ability and background. Provisions for slow learners and culturally disadvantaged pupils frequently overlap, as do these two categories; therefore, it is difficult to establish what provisions are applicable to which program. The Board of Education has labeled a number of elementary and secondary schools as Special Service Schools. Schools designated in this category receive increased financial and professional aid in a concerted attempt to raise the level of educational opportunity for their pupils. It should be pointed out that each school is a comprehensive school, one that offers a variety of programs for gifted pupils as well as for slow learners and mentally retarded pupils.

One school in this program enrolls 1,900 students with an average class size of twenty-five pupils, and reveals a representative sample of provisions for slow learners. There is a pupil–staff ratio of seventeen to one and pupils are sectioned according to interests and abilities. The slow learner classes are held to a small class size, usually of twenty pupils or less.

There is no special set of criteria for determining slow learners; but once the slow classes are determined, these sections receive specialized remedial help according to their needs. Here a specially designated master teacher, known as a program teacher, is brought into play. A program teacher is usually an expert in English, reading, social studies, or mathematics. He works and plans closely with the regular teacher of the subject for a given section. After planning the work, the program teacher takes the poorer half of a slow section into a classroom and teaches them according to the previously determined plan. The regular teacher teaches the remaining half of the class. This practice is repeated as far as six program teachers can spread themselves over this particular school. Grouping for exposure to the program teacher is flexible, according to the needs of the group. In effect, the program teacher gives in-service education to the regular teachers of mathematics, English, reading, and social studies. Naturally, program teachers are carefully selected for their ability, prepara-

---

[1] National Education Association and American Association of School Administrators, Educational Research Service Circular, *School Programs for the Disadvantaged*, Washington, D. C., February, 1963, p. 3.

tion, and effectiveness. In addition, department chairmen supervise and give leadership to teachers in preparing them for their tasks.

Curricular offerings vary with the type of group and its needs. There is a minimum program expected of pupils by the state and by the city in subject areas. Slow learners receive remedial instruction in reading, mathematics, and English skills. A typical weekly program would include eight periods of English (including reading), one period of assembly, one period of group guidance under a guidance teacher, five periods of social studies, five periods of mathematics, two periods of science, three of art, two of health education, one of music, and four of home arts or shop arts.

Teachers are selected as carefully as possible and trained to work with these low ability classes. They largely determine the nature of their subject offerings under the guidance and supervision of the program chairman or program teacher.

As a whole, the school has adopted the thesis of the Higher Horizons program which promotes community cooperation, cultural experiences for the pupils, parent education, a wide variety of field trips and other techniques of lifting self-esteem among pupils.

Central staff personnel work with the school providing occupational information, job placement, resource personnel in establishing parent workshops, promoting P.T.A. work and other school–community liaison help.

In this one school there are four counselors plus two counseling teachers per grade. Counseling teachers are non-certified guidance counselors.

Project Springboard

An increase in the number of disadvantaged children brought serious problems to a particular area of New York State. Low student achievement levels and high dropout rates were directly connected with the cultural deprivation, poor motivation, and low socio-economic status of immigrant families. In an effort to cope with this problem, Project Springboard was initiated in one of the elementary schools. The project was approved for special state aid under the New York State Education Department's Project ABLE. It offered to the community pupil guidance, remedial reading, ungraded primary classes, and after-school and evening enrichment programs.

Its objectives were similar to the Higher Horizons concept—mainly to provide some of the cultural experiences lacking in the home environment and to identify and encourage pupils with special abilities to make the most of their potential while in the elementary school.

The project staff reported that P.T.A., after-school, and daily pupil attendance increased; vandalism decreased; and achievement scores were encouraging.

THE SLOW LEARNER

It is common practice to classify pupils as slow learners when they have scored between 75 and 90 on repeated intelligence tests. There are many other factors which affect the performance of pupils, including cultural deprivation.

Slow learners are those pupils who are not mentally retarded but definitely are below average in academic ability. They are capable of achieving a moderate degree of scholastic success but may progress at a slow rate with less than average efficiency. On tests of mental ability their scores will fall in the lowest 20 per cent. The results of mental ability tests and standardized achievement tests along with teachers' estimates of school achievement are valuable in identifying these pupils. Teachers' observations, anecdotal reports, and health records also supply valuable information. Whenever possible in schools with the necessary resources, an individual intelligence test is administered; and there is an examination by a school psychologist who can rule out factors such as brain damage, mental retardation, and severe emotional handicaps.

Even more than other children, slow learners desire and need security, a feeling of adequacy, and opportunities for growth and self-realization. Likewise, the general objectives are the same for all children, the ultimate goal being worthy membership in a democratic society. These pupils are potentially able to assume this role in society, and they should be systematically and specifically prepared for effective citizenship. Since our culture is increasingly demanding a higher degree of intellectual competence, the slow learner's potential value to society should be a basic factor in determining the amount and quality of education provided for him during his formative years.

If the slow learning pupil is considered to be the child who is below average in measured mental ability but not mentally subnormal, the implications for planning a curriculum to coincide with his needs become important. Slow learners need a realistic program that is commensurate with their level of maturation and readiness. Educational adjustments in both content and methods must be provided.

Designated groups of slow learning pupils may often include pupils of average or better ability who are currently functioning as slow learners. In working with these functioning slow learners, the program of instruction and supportive services aim to help them realize their true potential so that at least some of them can eventually function effectively in the regular instructional program.

The Higher Horizon programs and Project Springboard are examples of effective programs for the slow learner.

THE UNDERACHIEVER

The Underachieving Reader

A number of years ago educators realized that a total school reading program must involve three kinds of readings: developmental, corrective, and remedial.

1. Developmental reading. The developmental phase involves systematic instruction at all school levels and in all content areas for those who are developing language abilities commensurate with their general capacity levels. This developmental phase is the responsibility of every teacher, affects all the pupils, is provided for in the regular curriculum and is a continuous on-going process.

2. Corrective reading. The corrective phase of reading deals with those pupils who are able to comprehend the assigned material only after a great amount of laborious effort, if at all. Many difficulties involved are those common to all pupils in reading, but are greatly accentuated. These cases do not usually require clinical instruction unless the retardation is compounded by continued inattention to correction and attendant emotional complications.

Most of the corrective instruction is the responsibility of all teachers in their daily class activities. In an increasing number of school systems, a special reading teacher provides systematic instruction in small groups. If a school system is fortunate enough to have special teachers to work with the corrective cases, one of the following approaches is usually taken.

Each school is staffed by a corrective teacher. The teacher is an experienced classroom teacher who has additional preparation in the reading area and works with these "retarded readers" in small group situations at their proper instructional level without worrying about the course of study. The pupils come out of their regular classroom and meet with the reading teacher a half-hour to an hour a day, three to five times a week. Usually there are five main planks in this corrective program: parent education, teacher education, individual small group instruction, individual small group testing, and research. The corrective reading teacher takes part in these five areas depending upon the needs of the local school. Modifications of this type of program are conducted in Maryland, Pennsylvania, and Florida.[2]

In the second type of corrective program the pupil does not receive instruction in his home school, but is transferred from his own school to the nearest school having a reading center. There he is placed in a classroom on his grade level for all work but reading. For one period a day he goes to the reading center for instruction in reading on his instructional level. A large Eastern urban school district offers this type of service.

Another type of corrective instruction is demonstrated by a Midwestern school system. Pupils are assigned to the clinics two or three (occasionally four or five) times a week for forty-five to sixty-minute instructional periods, dependent on individual needs. Pupils pay their own carfare to and from the clinic. Most pupils are given individual instruction when they first enter the clinic, but work in very small groups after they become independent in word perception skills. Pupils are usually held for clinic instruction until they can perform independently with books in their home classrooms.

3. Remedial reading. The procedure known as remedial reading, as contrasted with corrective reading, applies to a small clinical group showing severe symptoms of reading retardation. Children in this group differ from those in the corrective group by the etiology and the degree of their deficiency. The cases are frequently characterized by associative learning disability, inadequacies in memory span, deficiencies in concept formation, and neurological or emotional complications. Pupils with these problems demand individual and small group instruction on a clinical basis by specially trained personnel. It is often in this last group that reading difficulty may result in real damage to the personality. A child who cannot read well is every day embarrassed and discouraged. It is very difficult for even a skilled classroom or corrective reading teacher to develop the pupil's confidence in himself since his classmates and worried parents often magnify his deficiency.

This remedial reading program is a clinic type program designed for the retarded reader with a slightly below average, average, or superior intelligence who cannot profit from the pedagogical tech-

[2] John Money, et al., Reading Disability, Baltimore: The Johns Hopkins Press, 1962, chap. 4.

niques that are used in the regular developmental or corrective programs. A large county school system in an Eastern state has attempted to develop this type of program in its elementary schools. A pupil attends the clinic for three hours in the morning and then returns to his regular school for the afternoon session. Whenever possible, the programs are structured in the local schools for these youngsters so that they attend classes and participate in activities that require only limited reading and writing skills. The clinic program is geared to the immediate needs of each individual. The educational program centers around the use of basal readers and experience stories. The psychological approach utilizes all sensory pathways—visual, auditory, kinesthetic, and tactile—to reinforce weak memory patterns. During the clinical period some of the pupils visit the psychologist for individual or group counseling. A pupil is dismissed from the remedial reading clinic when the staff feels the pupil has received maximal benefit from the program. Parents of the children in the remedial reading program accept the responsibility for providing transportation to and from the clinic each day and are also expected to attend P.T.A. and Parent Life Discussion group meetings.

The Underachiever in Arithmetic

Children differ greatly in intelligence and background of experience necessary for effective learning in arithmetic. Since their capacities vary, all children cannot be expected to reach the same degree of mastery in the same period of time. Some children may never develop ability in a given number operation at the abstract level. However, all children with the capacity to learn should have experience with all of the major mathematical concepts before leaving elementary school. It is therefore imperative for the teacher to organize instruction to take care of the differences in rate of learning and the level of development found in his class.

Differentiating instruction in terms of levels of learning seems to offer an effective method for adjusting to individual differences. This means the grouping of children should be flexible and based on their level of operation. The level of operation employed by a child may differ from concept to concept and from time to time. A child may be in the group working at the abstract level in subtraction but in division he may need to work in a group using a modified form of the algorism.

One elementary school in an Eastern state takes care of underachievers in arithmetic by dividing the class into two groups: children who require some explanation of basic arithmetical concepts and children who need some reteaching. After identification of the cause of the problem, and some explanation from the teacher, the first group may help decide or be assigned the type of practice they should follow. While this group works independently, the teacher is free to give her attention to the children who need reteaching.

Many school systems employ a modification of the Joplin Plan in attempting to remediate the underachiever in arithmetic. At a designated time during the school day, children leave their regular classrooms and assemble for the arithmetic period in homogeneous achievement groups for specific help and instruction.

THE EXCEPTIONAL CHILD

Special education is the modification, adjustment, or extension of the regular school program for pupils whose needs cannot be met wholly or in part within the four walls of the regular classroom. The children participating in the program of special education are often called exceptional children. An exceptional child may be thought of as one who deviates significantly from the so-called average or normal child. In short, there is a difference that makes a difference. The entire purpose of a program of special education is to make provision for the significant differences among these exceptional children, while capitalizing on and emphasizing the ways in which the exceptional children are like other children.

For convenience, exceptional children may be divided into three major categories: (1) physically handicapped, including crippled, epileptic, tubercular, cardiac cases, impaired hearing, partially sighted, speech handicapped, aphasic, other brain injured children; (2) mental deviates, including mentally retarded (educable and trainable) and the gifted; and (3) emotionally disturbed and socially maladjusted.

Programs for the Physically Handicapped

Children with physical anomalies may need special educational facilities and services. The programs vary within different school districts. However, some plans should be developed in every local district to service these pupils.

1. Sight-saving. Children become eligible for sight-saving programs when they are recommended for participation in them by an eye specialist.

Children are placed in a regular school and come to the sight-saving teacher for assistance and close work. The sight-saving teacher serves as a resource person and prepares material for regular classroom teachers, as well as being available on an itinerant basis to all schools where pupils need sight-saving materials (large-print books, talking machines, optical aids, etc.).

2. Speech therapy. Speech is considered defective when it calls attention to itself, is unpleasant to the listener, or causes a person having such a defect to become maladjusted. Speech therapists are itinerant personnel who are assigned to two, three, or four schools. Their responsibility is to work individually and with small groups of pupils who have communicative problems. Nearly all speech defects are diagnosed by the speech therapist, although specialists in allied fields often are called upon for specific help. The speech therapist, therefore, has training in dealing with children who substitute, omit, or distort sounds where the condition is often a functional one; with those whose problem has an organic basis such as the cerebral palsied, hard of hearing, or cleft palate; and with those who have a strong emotional involvement and social maladjustment as in the case of the youngster who stutters.

3. Aphasia. An aphasic child is one who shows marked inability to express or understand language symbols as a result of some defect in the central nervous system. Although he often acts as though he were deaf, retarded, or emotionally disturbed, his condition does not result from damage to the peripheral speech mechanism, ear, or auditory nerve, or from a lack of general intelligence, or severe emotional disturbance.

The primary goal in this program is to prepare children, through specialized speech and language training, for entrance into regular or special education classes as near to the appropriate age and grade level as possible. While the primary objective with the beginning pupils is to develop speech and language skills, teachers also have the responsibility for teaching the academic subjects when there is sufficient language facility to make it possible.

4. Brain injured. A brain injured child is a child who before, during, or after birth has received an injury to or suffered infection of the brain. As a result of such organic impairment, defects of the neuromotor system may be present or absent; however, such a child may show disturbances in perception, thinking, and emotional behavior either separately or in combination.

There exists, in many school systems, a considerable number of these children who are in need of classes which utilize special methods devised to remedy these specific learning disabilities.

5. Orthopedically handicapped. Some orthopedically handicapped children are served through the home teaching program; others, whose physical handicap will permit, are enrolled in regular classes, special classes, or special schools. Those who require a special physical environment, who need to be taught by qualified teachers, and who are in need of occupational, physical, and speech therapy are currently enrolled in a variety of programs. Several school systems have opened special schools for these handicapped children. The nature of multiple handicapped children dictates the need for a variety of educational, medical, and socio-psychological services, coupled with a highly individualized school program.

6. Hard of hearing. A few school systems have an organized program for the deaf or severely hard of hearing. Children who have a mild to moderate loss are placed in a regular school program. Often they require preferential seating, hearing aids, and the supportive help of speech therapists in order to make normal school progress.

Programs for the Mentally Retarded

For many years the great impetus for establishing classes for the mentally retarded came from principals of the secondary schools, since large numbers of retarded children were passed on to the junior high school on the basis of social promotion. At this level, their inability to handle academic work beyond third- or fourth-grade level was evident. They often showed concomitant deficiencies in the area of emotional and social adjustment.

Some classes for educable retarded children have developed a sequential program which permits a child to enter a primary special class and progress through intermediate, junior high, and finally the terminal senior high program.

Most school systems furnish a bulletin describing organizational policy, admission procedure, and eligibility requirements which give a thorough treatment of the entire subject of developing the special, ungraded class for the educable mentally retarded.

A definite effort is made to integrate the special class and pupils into the school in which it is housed. Whenever possible these handicapped children are placed with their peer groups; for example, in recreational and lunch programs and if there is an opportunity for success in music, art, and social activities.

While there are many specific objectives which educators try to accomplish in the program for the educable mentally retarded, the main goals are: (1) to provide educational experience which will enable each individual to advance as far as his capacity will allow, (2) to assist the individual in making a maximum adjustment in the home and in the community, so that he may assume his role as a contributing citizen in society, and (3) to provide the individual with the necessary skills and social competence to become employable in semi-skilled or unskilled jobs that are appropriate for him.

Some school systems have special schools for the trainable retarded pupils with very limited potential. These schools usually are staffed by classroom teachers, speech therapists, an arts and crafts teacher, a health nurse, teacher aides, and a non-teaching principal. The major objectives of the program for trainable retarded children are to teach the child self-care; to help him make a maximum adjustment in the home, school, and community; and to give him necessary training to become partially self-supporting under close supervision.

Programs for the Gifted

Elementary school teachers have three major responsibilities in meeting the needs of highly able pupils: identifying these pupils in a systematic and continuous process throughout the grades, making recommendations for the placement of these pupils in high ability groups, and providing a program that will challenge the unique abilities of these pupils. In extreme cases, the very gifted student presents a much different problem from the child who is "just superior." It should be remembered that although gifted and superior pupils may have high potential, they are still children and do not have the breadth of experience of adults. Achievement and intelligence tests, classroom performance, conferences, and the cumulative records are further aids to understanding them.

Certain criteria have been established for the selection of superior and gifted children in the elementary schools of a large county school system. Special provisions are made for pupils with unusually high intellectual capacity (130+ I.Q.); those with superior intellectual capacity (120–129 I.Q.); those with unusual talent in one or more academic areas; those with strong motivation for academic work; and those with a school history of high academic achievement.

The present method of grouping in many school systems places emphasis on reading ability and academic achievement. However, in whatever way bright pupils are grouped, they remain individuals with varying interests and aptitudes. A pupil may be outstanding in only one or two special abilities such as word meaning, numerical facility, memory, logical reasoning, and social leadership. These differences are taken into consideration when planning the program. Grouping is flexible in order to provide for the varying abilities of pupils in different subject matter areas. Constant study of both the curriculum and the characteristics of the pupils helps the teacher answer the question of how to provide for the individual differences of pupils. Provisions are made for a variety of learning experiences that will place each learner at an optimum rate of advance.

There are many different approaches to helping gifted children, but for all practical purposes they all are based on three administrative arrangements—acceleration, grouping, and enrichment in the classroom.

1. Acceleration. Any system that allows a pupil to move more rapidly and complete a prescribed school program in less time or at an earlier age than the average peer may be called acceleration. This concept is based on the philosophy of not holding back the highly able child but instead moving him on to more challenging work. This is one of the oldest techniques and procedures employed in American education and can occur at any point in the educational process from kindergarten through college.

The actual process of elementary school acceleration as an administrative device may occur in such forms as grade-skipping, early admission, and combining two years of work in one, or three years in two. Acceleration in a subject area is discussed in Chapter 13.

Skipping is one of the oldest methods of acceleration. The rationale is that bright children can skip the learning experiences of their peer groups. However, many authorities frown on this method because of learning gaps and possible emotional and social difficulties, and it is used rarely now.

In many school systems a pupil may be accelerated one semester in the elementary grades. A unified school district in a Western state attempted to accelerate approximately 25 per cent of the gifted pupils who would benefit from (and whose social and physical maturity warranted) such acceleration. This type of acceleration allows the pupil to complete the standard amount of academic work in less than the usual time. If the pupil has great ability and is not being challenged adequately by the work offered at his present grade level, he is given the opportunity to advance one grade.

Another acceleration method combines two grades into one. Through specially planned classes, bright pupils can complete the full educational program in a shorter time than their peers. For example, in a few mid-Atlantic public school systems a rather small percentage of the gifted youngsters in the elementary age groups are offered this type of program.

Most educators hesitate to approve an early admission program. They feel that a four- or five-year-old child is not matured enough to benefit from the educational experience. However, in the past, schools in different countries have started to teach children to read at different times. In fact, some countries begin earlier in their schools than the typical beginning time in the United States. Northern Rhodesia, for example, recognizes a sex maturational difference and starts girls at the age of six and boys one year later.

In 1931, Morphett and Washburne concluded from their study that the percentage of children who learned to read satisfactorily is greatest at the mental age of six years and six months. If this magic figure were interpreted literally, a bright child of 140 I.Q. would have the appropriate mental age to start school at the chronological age of 4.6.[3]

2. **Grouping.** An increasing number of educators feel that the best way to provide for the needs of all pupils is to bring together children of similar abilities for all or part of their educational experience. This method reduces the range of individual differences in the particular factor by which the children were grouped and facilitates instruction in groups where ability and interests are comparable.

Elementary classroom teachers are familiar with grouping for curricular work such as reading and special projects. However, there are several special grouping organizations for gifted children.

1. *Specialized schools.* This program calls for a separate school for the gifted where the pupils are placed in a special type of school in an atmosphere where the academic requirements are stiffened.

2. *Special class in regular school.* This plan differs from the specialized school in that it involves special classes for gifted pupils within the regular school. The highly able pupils are separated for all except recreational and extracurricular activities.

A Western school system has developed a cluster plan in grades 1–8. Under the plan, the children who have been identified as gifted at each grade level in any school building are grouped or clustered in one classroom. At the same time an equal number of children at the other end of the mental range are removed from the classroom. This plan provides for a nucleus for working with the

[3] Mabel V. Morphett and Carleton Washburne, "When Should Children Begin to Read?" *Elementary School Journal,* 31:496–503, March, 1931.

gifted at each grade level and allows the teacher more time for concentration and preparation for the gifted group.

In some school districts outstanding gifted children from several schools are brought together to a centrally located school where a gifted class has been established.

3. *Special grouping for part of the day.* The most common and popular method of grouping is to cluster gifted students into specialized groups for part of the day. These children spend a part of the day in the regular classroom with peers of varying abilities and the rest of the school day in special classes of highly able pupils.

Generally, grouping for the special areas has been in art, music, dramatics, and crafts, and grouping in the general areas usually centers around reading and arithmetic. Most of the elementary schools in the United States practice such a form of grouping.

3. **Enrichment in the classroom.** The most popular technique for providing for the highly able student is to offer him an educational program richer than the one offered to the other pupils in the same classroom. The bright pupil remains in the classroom with other children of less ability and theoretically at least is given special attention either individually or in small groups.

The classroom teacher may make changes in the instructional programs in two ways in order to challenge the gifted child. First he can provide opportunities for the pupils to explore more deeply any subject being studied by the class. Or the teacher can provide breadth by assigning subjects that are not normally covered in the classroom. Enrichment does not mean a program of more of the same thing; it may mean less. Enrichment does mean that in the same classroom with children of varying abilities and interests, the gifted child is provided with a greater variety of new learning situations, materials, and activities in order to supply him with the depth and range of educational experiences that he requires for the fullest development of his unusual abilities.

In some schools, interest club programs offer enrichment both during and after school. In other schools, children serve on all-school projects such as art, hobby, and talent shows, science and social studies fairs, and school publications.

A Far West elementary school system offers special enrichment programs for pupils gifted in reading, arithmetic, and science. Those who are achieving above their grade level in reading are excused from the formal reading program for two or three days a week in order to carry on individual reading projects.

Advanced groups who show complete understanding and skill in mathematics are given opportunities for broadening their learning. They may learn shortcuts, do more advanced work in mental arithmetic, work with more complex number situations, engage in special projects, or carry on other enrichment activities.

Extracurricular activities are provided for pupils with interest and talent in the study of science. The programs include experimental activities, field work, discussions, films, individual projects, and talks or demonstrations by guest speakers.

Programs for the Emotionally Disturbed and Socially Maladjusted

Very few school systems have organized classes for emotionally disturbed children. Most of the more severely emotionally disturbed are housed in residential treatment centers; others receive private psychiatric help; others receive out-patient therapy from mental hygiene clinics. A few receive psychotherapy from school psychologists.

Emotionally disturbed children are those who have more or less serious problems with other people or who are unhappy and unable to apply themselves in a manner commensurate with their abilities and interests. These children often have to be taught and directed in special ways. Unfortunately, although there are many existing resources for these children, few stress education or attempt to combine the educational or social–emotional consideration for the most severely disturbed. Child guidance clinics, residential treatment centers, and the treatment of children in the private offices of psychiatrists, psychologists, and social workers cannot supply the needed help to educational problems. The guidance services in the public schools act as a screening and limited help program but do not offer sustained help in the manner needed.

Several years ago one large county school system in an Eastern state began exploration of different classroom settings, teaching methods, and materials in search of appropriate educational environment for children with central nervous disorders. The state school system had previously conducted an experiment in nine elementary schools. The children in the study were moderately to severely emotionally disturbed and had reflected their disturbances in a wide range of behavior symptoms. In a well designed experiment, a small group of emotionally disturbed children was placed in a highly structured classroom environment with brain injured children. There were three groups of emotionally disturbed children. Group I was presented a highly structured special class environment with a prepared sequence of academic tasks; Group II utilized a regular classroom setting for teaching emotionally disturbed children; and Group III had a comparatively non-structured, permissive special-class setting.

For the first time in their educational experience, the emotionally disturbed children began to show academic gains and to adjust to the classroom situation. The controls imposed by the carefully controlled structure, the steady routine, and the specialized techniques of teaching made it possible for the children to develop gradually greater adaptability within the classroom setting and also to improve their educational status.[4]

The results indicated that from a practical point of view the children who were placed in the structured, academically programmed special class showed an increase in academic achievement and behavior adjustment. The study also showed that a teacher can successfully teach a class of the type of youngsters studied herein, provided she has instruction, direction, and support from experienced psychologists, special educators, and principals.

AESTHETIC SUBJECTS

Many educators realize the valuable contribution that the aesthetic subjects, art and music, can provide the individual child.

Music

Classroom teachers are encouraged to use music daily as a socializing experience, as an aesthetic experience, as an emotional release, and as a change of pace from the academic subjects.

Remedial work is usually offered to the uncertain singer. The problem most of the time is due to the child's inability to focus listening on pitch differences. Educable and trainable education classes need a greater emphasis on the rhythmic area in music. These pupils should be exposed to songs with easier texts and to a greater variety of activities. When working with orthopedically handicapped children, the teacher must be able to adapt the participation in music to the limitations of the individual child. Choral groups and vocal festivals, in which the best singers from the various elementary schools are combined, are often available for pupils who have a special interest in singing.

[4] Norris G. Haring and E. Lakin Phillips, *Educating Emotionally Disturbed Children*, New York: McGraw-Hill Book Co., 1962, pp. 62–84.

Many school districts offer instrumental instruction in all elementary schools, grades four to six. In some of these schools, lessons are given during the school day; in others they are given after school. Several elementary schools in a large industrial city have introduced an experiment involving seven elementary schools. Every child in these schools has the opportunity to explore the string, woodwind, brass, and percussion instruments by learning to play a simple three-note tune on a representative instrument of each of these. Presented for the most part in the fourth grade, this experience is withheld until the fifth grade for slow classes. Experiments in sound and the acoustical principles under which they work are made. The evolution of instruments is also presented.

Several school systems in an Eastern state present educational concerts by the local symphony orchestra. This is operated on an area basis. Every school in the area has an opportunity of sending a representative number of children to these concerts. Some schools are given one opportunity to attend, others have two opportunities. These concerts are given in high school auditoriums and are administered as field trips. Programs are discussed with the associate conductor of the orchestra. Program notes are distributed to all schools so that some advance preparation may be made.

A "Young Musicians Series" of concerts held in some elementary schools are concerts presented by small ensemble groups. The programs are prepared to appeal to the elementary level. These groups, ranging from two to five musicians, singers, or dancers come from New York City, or local members of the city symphony orchestra or the local conservatory. The cost is carried by the local school P.T.A.

Art

Most special art programs are enrichment courses. One county school system has developed a wide variety of experience for the pupil interested in art. The elementary schools have a circulating "library" of one hundred and eighteen frame reproductions to which about twenty new prints are added each year as the budget allows. This collection allows each of the forty-three art teachers to have three or four prints for study and exhibition for a period of three months. Each teacher then sends these prints on to another scheduled teacher by station wagon and receives three or four more from another teacher in the same way. Each print is laminated in plastic and framed in a narrow aluminum frame for durable transportation. Each print has a brief study of the work and the artist laminated to its back.

Many school libraries are building files of reproductions of artists' works. Local artists often have an opportunity to demonstrate and discuss their styles of work with the children of the school. Some schools have traveling exhibits of contemporary artists' works on display.

Individual schools plan gallery and museum tours. The evaluation department of an art gallery in a Northeastern city, for example, offers guided visits of the collection, slide talks on art, and a loan service of a variety of materials on art.

School classes may arrange for a guided visit of the gallery's collection. Since nothing can replace actual encounter with original works of art, the visit emphasizes outstanding examples of painting and sculpture in the collection. Through guided observation and discussion of about ten or twelve objects, pupils gain an understanding about art and its significance today as well as for times past.

If, for good reason, it is impossible for a school class to make such a visit, a special slide talk on painting and sculpture in the gallery's collection may be arranged. A gallery staff member visits the school, giving the talk in the classroom. The department offers special slide talks to supplement class work. For example, a French class could request a slide talk on French art; a social studies class might have need for a discussion of Egyptian, Greek, or Roman art, or the art of the Middle Ages; an art class might need a particular phase of creative art discussed historically.

SUPPLEMENTARY SERVICES

Most educators agree that supplementary services are most helpful and necessary for many exceptional children to profit most from their school studies. An inter-disciplinary approach may mean the difference between success or failure in understanding and adjusting to the exceptionalities of atypical pupils.

Guidance Services

The counselor plays an increasingly significant role in the total educational program as the educational opportunities for the academically able, the slow learner, the underachiever, and other children with specialized needs have been increased. Present-day understanding of the self-concept as a prime factor in learning has given impetus to an increased emphasis on counseling with a correspondingly greater depth and breadth in the professional preparation of the counselor.

The counselor at the elementary level observes the development of the child's self-concept, his feelings of personal worth, and his sense of values. Also, the counselor notes beginnings of unrealistic self-concepts, feelings of inferiority, or distorted values, which may lead to underachievement. In working with these children through individual and group counseling, he may help to prevent serious maladjustment in the educational process.

At the elementary school level, the counselor can be helpful to administrators and teachers in planning learning experiences suitable to the needs of all children. By his interpretation of accumulated data, the counselor aids in the placement of children in groups and assists administrators and teachers in setting up realistic educational goals for each group.

Health Services

The health service department is responsible for screening tests to find pupils with hearing, vision, and other health problems. It also helps in keeping children with health problems in school and providing for emergency care for them if they become sick or injured at school. It assists teachers regarding health education and sponsors health careers or future nurses' clubs.

Testing Office Services

The test program is designed to help in understanding the differences and varied patterns of abilities, achievements, and interests among the children and thus in providing a sound basis for the differentiation of learning procedures.

This program also aids in evaluating the effectiveness of the instructional program. It is flexible in that it reflects the changes in the instructional program and keeps pace with the ever increasing mass of psychometric theory and the improved test materials constantly being produced.

Psychological Services

The school psychologists are providing important supplementary services to many school systems. The psychologist's basic responsibility is to provide diagnostic and evaluative services to individual children whenever factors or situations contributing to poor academic progress or to poor school adjustment need to be given individual study. Such exceptional children may include the gifted, the mentally retarded, and the emotionally disturbed.

Visiting Teacher Services

The visiting teacher works closely with the parents or guardians of those pupils who need special understanding and help in order to derive the most benefit from the school program. The visiting teacher meets pupils whose needs may be expressed in terms of behavior difficulties, emotional stresses, socio-economic problems, or irregular attendance. He uses all available resources to locate the cause of the problem and to bring about a solution.

Some of the responsibilities of the visiting teacher include planning home teaching programs for physically handicapped and emotionally disturbed children; arranging special transportation to school for handicapped children; making recommendations on special cases involving admission to school, withdrawal from school, and transfers.

Library Services

The gifted child needs some experiences which are different from those provided for the average or below average child. Increasing the volume of expected reading without changing the nature of what is read can result in extreme boredom and eventual dislike of books. The teacher or librarian who works with the gifted should try to provide books that meet the pupils' interests and challenge their abilities. This does not necessarily mean books which are harder to read, but books with ideas that stimulate the child's imagination, make demands on his ability to interpret, or require checking of facts.

The low ability pupil or the mentally retarded child needs the help of both teacher and librarian if he is to make much use of books. Close cooperation between the teacher and the librarian is essential, the teacher providing information about individual children and the librarian locating books to match needs. The two most important factors in serving children in this group are interest in and information about the individual child; and material suited to his ability, his interests, and his span of attention. The librarian should know the characteristics of books enjoyed by this type of child: books about animals, other boys and girls, home life, and simple adventure stories; books with many pictures and little text; open pages with short sentences and easy vocabulary. He should know also that these children cannot listen to reading aloud or storytelling for more than a few minutes at a time; that they will probably not take very good care of their books; and that they may need help in getting started.

In an experiment conducted in a special class in a county school system, the teacher made a brief interest inventory for the librarian and briefed the librarian about each child's reading level and personality. Based on this information, the librarian made a special reading list for each pupil. When the class came to the library, the librarian taught a simple lesson in the arrangement of the library to which the children responded with unusual enthusiasm and interest. Later, they were allowed to find their own books, which most of them did very successfully. Both the teacher and the librarian talked with each child about his book and gave him whatever help he needed.

Even children in schools or classes for the trainable retarded are capable of enjoying books and using them under the direction of an adult. Aphasic groups enjoy going to the library with their teacher to look at books, to read, and even in some instances to tell a little about the stories.

Physically handicapped children usually need no special materials, but they do need a library designed for their own use. Ramps for wheel chairs, low shelving which can be reached from a seated position, and other modifications of the library room are necessary if the physically handicapped are to derive full benefit from the library period.

For the child with impaired vision, there are editions of the *World Book Encyclopedia* in Braille and in very large type. Also, lists of other books in large type are available. Many stories about children with physical handicaps help to give both the afflicted child and his more fortunate friends a better understanding of the fact that there is a place in the world for all kinds of people.

ISSUES AND POINTS OF VIEW

Today there are many controversial issues and points of view with respect to adapting elementary education to the individual learner. For the most part, research has been spotty and unsophisticated. Educational researchers have been searching for the common syndrome or answer. Instead of cooperative, organized, scientific studies we have had a profusion of small cults, all proclaiming their discovery of the magic curriculum or pedagogical procedure. Pity the school teacher who tries to absorb and conscientiously practice the numerous "antidotes"!

1. *Should the school delay the institution of corrective programs until the third grade or later, when the true retarded reader will have*

segregated himself from the "late bloomer," or should there be a concentrated effort to develop a program of early identification and remediation so that the child will not be exposed to several years of frustration and failure?

Recently educators have taken the time to evaluate some of the merits and weaknesses of corrective reading programs. One of the major concerns appears to center around the early identification of reading disabilities. Results of a four-year survey involving over 10,000 pupils indicate the tremendous advantage of early remediation.

It appears that pupils with reading disabilities identified as early as the second grade have over ten times as great a chance of being remediated in a prescribed period as a comparable disability detected in the ninth grade.

Of even greater concern is the apparent lack of "skill maintenance" that many secondary pupils demonstrate. The latest research indicates that many junior and senior high pupils, having been discharged from special reading programs as being remediated, tend to "slip back" when returned to the regular classroom program.

As the non-reader ascends through the primary grades, his problems multiply, for all other subject matter is conditional on reading. Thus, he cannot solve the problems in arithmetic or social studies, even though he may have the skill to do so, because he cannot read the examination questions. The impression is one of general academic failure. He is likely to be considered as mentally retarded or as a lazy child with the view that "he could if he would." It is difficult to imagine a more chilling indictment of a confused child bewildered by his inability to learn despite earnest efforts to do so. Failure by teacher, parent, and physician to recognize the key problem will have devastating results. The child soon is attending a class conducted in what is for him almost a foreign language.

At home he may be surly and unwilling to do his homework. Or he may be of concern to his parents because of low self-esteem, withdrawal, and general apathy. Frustrated by his inability to learn, bored by class exercises he cannot follow, coerced by parents and teachers to do what he cannot, the non-reader has both the inner turmoil and the lack of constructive outlet to become a major problem at home and at school.

However, in most school systems it has become customary to delay the institution of corrective programs until the third grade or later. Many educators feel that additional reading instruction imposed on the immature child can only result in compounded frustration and failure. These reading experts contend that since our public school systems are overcrowded and remedial reading is costly and often unavailable, special remediation should be delayed until the true retarded reader has segregated himself from the "late bloomer." This undoubtedly effects an economy from the standpoint of the administrator in that special instructions are not needlessly provided for children who are in any event going to learn.

But this economizing may be accomplished at a heavy cost to the low achieving child. For by the time the remedial program is offered to him, he has had several years of failure, with a consequent development of aversion to reading and related activities as well as of emotional problems related to feelings of inadequacy.

2. *Should the school provide some of the cultural experiences lacking in the child's home environment, or should the school only consider its academic responsibilities and leave the cultural development to the home and other community agencies?*

The total responsibility of the school to its community has never been clearly defined. Most educators agree on the academic role of the school but disagree on their cultural and social responsibilities to society.

Proponents of an increased activity of the school insist that the American society, through its schools, must reach out and extend itself. The erratic pattern of the pupils' home and social lives leaves an indelible imprint on their personality. They yearn for something on which they can plan, some moderate degree of success which they know will be theirs. The teacher and the classroom thus become the stabilizing influence in a very unstable environment.

The successful teacher in the slum area must have a big bonfire of love for all the children in his class. This is what these children lack most in their unenviable plight. It should not be saccharine-sweet in its application but should have the warmth of sincerity coupled with genuineness of mutual respect.

Some proponents of school participation in community activities believe that the school should even provide breakfast and lunch for some of these deprived children. It is said that a growling stomach often prevents a hungry child from hearing the class discussion.

However, some educators insist that the school concentrate entirely on its academic responsibilities. They feel that the addition of special non-academic subjects has a tendency to monopolize the time that should be reserved for the traditional "three R's." In addition, many believe that the teacher is there to teach, not to be a parent substitute involved with the emotional or physical needs of each child. This, in their opinion, should be left to the home or to social agencies.

3. *Should special enrichment programs be provided for gifted children, or should these highly able elementary school pupils be accelerated in their grade placement?*

An increasing number of educators feel that acceleration is the best way for students to progress academically in relation to their ability. The proponents of this point of view feel that the gifted student should be encouraged to advance at his own rate rather than at the pace of other pupils of lesser ability of the same age. Another argument for acceleration is that fewer school years means less expense to parents, schools, and the community.

Educators who oppose acceleration fear that students who mature early intellectually may not be as mature socially and emotionally. Other opponents feel that acceleration results in serious learning gaps in academic areas. On the other hand, enrichment within the regular classroom requires few additional expenditures or administrative alterations. Also, the enrichment program allows the gifted pupils to stimulate the other pupils intellectually and even to assist in the teaching process. Another argument for this type of organization is that it does not segregate the gifted child, but enables him to develop in real life situations among those of differing abilities.

4. *Do children learn more when they are grouped homogeneously according to ability, or do they profit more from heterogeneous grouping?*

An examination of research on the relative merits of different grouping procedures for pupil learning and achievement may raise as many questions as this same research attempts to answer. Some studies seem to show achievement gains in favor of ability grouping and some in favor of heterogeneous grouping. Still others show little or no statistically significant differences among grouping methods in pupil achievement as measured by standardized tests.

A survey of grouping practices in thirty-five schools in the North Central states brought these findings:

11 per cent used ability grouping as a controlling factor
18 per cent used social maturity as a controlling factor
32 per cent used chronological age as the basic factor
39 per cent used a composite of all factors.[5]

Ability-type groupings include grouping according to mental maturity rating, I.Q.'s, levels of reading achievement, teacher evaluations, or a combination of these.

[5] Baltimore County Public Schools, *Practices in Grouping for Organization and Instruction in the Elementary School*, Baltimore: 1955, p. 4 (NEA Research Division data as of March, 1954).

Proponents of ability grouping feel that in a democratic society the chief concern of our schools is to direct the growth and development of each pupil along desirable lines that will help him to become a well-adjusted, contributing member of society. The school should recognize varying interests, needs, abilities, aptitudes, and levels of learning capacity of each individual and place him in the group which will promote his optimal development. In addition, if a school program is organized on the basis of homogeneous grouping according to ability, it is assumed that the range of ability is considerably reduced so that the same or similar learning activities suitable for the whole group may be selected. Many teachers do not know how to identify or how to plan for the bright and the dull.

This point is strongly contested by the opponents of ability grouping. They contend that although the range of mental age scores may be somewhat less than the average range at the time when children are assigned to a group in accord with homogeneity of mental ability, the relative rates of growth are not likely to be the same. The most likely result is movement toward increased heterogeneity, since evidence indicates that changes within individuals are continually taking place.

Acceptance of ability grouping is in part based on the assumption that a child's ability to learn can be adequately measured. New knowledge regarding the nature of intelligence and the ability to learn is continually coming to light. Many dimensions of intelligence recently identified are not included in commonly used intelligence tests. In view of the many and varied elements that make a difference in each individual's ability to learn, the opponents contend that it seems unlikely that homogeneous grouping according to generalized learning ability can actually be accomplished except in a very limited sense.

12

TRENDS IN THE SECONDARY SCHOOL CURRICULUM

This chapter is concerned with trends of today, not those of a decade ago; for the secondary school curriculum is changing as a result of social and scientific change. The accelerated pace of change has caused investigation of outmoded practices. Everywhere, secondary schools are experimenting with new content and procedures. These are exciting times in secondary education, which is proving to be surprisingly responsive to the needs of the times.

CHANGE IN FUNDAMENTAL CONCEPTS

Some Contrasts

Over the years since the early part of this century, changes in secondary education have not been inconsiderable. For many members of the preceding generation, going to high school was only a dream. Today that dream has become a reality for most children of secondary school age.

A backward look reveals that there was formerly a great deal of rote memorization. Lesson-learning was the order of the day and the pupil who could guess when his turn came up and recite well had "learned" the lesson. "Teacher" was someone who stood in front of the room and asked questions out of an open book; the good student was the one who knew "what the book says." Teaching was recitation, and learning was knowing the answers wanted, a process of answering rather than questioning.

The poverty of offerings in the high school curriculum was in sharp contrast to what we find today in the modern, comprehensive high school. A generation ago, many secondary schools were small, and English, history, mathematics, science, a foreign language, and perhaps manual training and domestic science constituted the program. Today's rich and varied offerings in art, music, social studies, industrial arts, home economics, business education, and vocational subjects were unavailable to most high school youth. If the student had a chance to play in a band or orchestra, he was indeed fortunate. (Actually, it was not too long ago when extraclass activities came into the high school curriculum by the back door. One of the vestigial remains of that bygone era is the term "extracurricular.")

In the twenties and thirties, the high school classroom, with its screwed-down seats, was often located on the top floor of a red brick mausoleum of a building in the center of the village, conspicuous for its ugliness. Its library was a cubbyhole. Audio-visual aids consisted of the blackboard, maps, and globes. Textbooks were drab com-

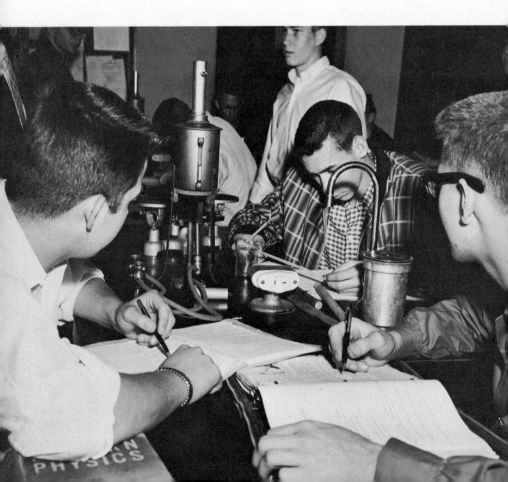

pared to the artistry in make-up and illustrations found in modern ones.

There were dire predictions in the 1930's, the days of WPA and the Civilian Conservation Corps, that some new institution would have to be invented to replace the secondary school. Youth studies revealed that for many young people, school had little or no relation to their lives. Secondary education was in the doldrums. Meanwhile, educators proceeded with their huge task never before undertaken by any country—the provision of secondary education for all the children of all the people.

Renaissance in Secondary Education

During the last decade we have been witnessing a world-wide renaissance in secondary education. Most nations, including the new ones, regard education of youth as the major instrument of economic, social, political, and industrial advancement. Fundamental changes are being made in content, in teaching methods, in materials, and in facilities. These are not transient changes which will disappear like many fads in education.

There are several factors that make the situation quite different from that of previous decades. Foremost among these is the inexorable fact that there will be in the foreseeable future a greatly increased number of children to educate. Another is the rate at which knowledge increases. Furthermore, we must face the fact that there will be fewer well-prepared teachers to instruct children for a world that demands a higher level of knowledge and skill than ever before.

DEMANDS OF THE 1960'S

Demands are being made on the secondary school curriculum as a result of the technological revolution and explosion of knowledge. They are the manifestations of an age of specialization, in which it becomes more important for a person to be truly cultured; of an age of mass production, in which it becomes increasingly difficult to be an individual; of an age of social revolution, in which social stability is a prominent goal; of an age of uncertainty, in which a person has more need than ever for security.

Quality

Reports from a number of eminent organizations have called for increased quality in secondary education. Many have used the term "excellence." There has been a surge of interest in quality education on the part of scholars in all disciplines. In addition, the proponents of excellence have emphasized that it takes excellence in teachers, excellence in materials, excellence in facilities, and excellence in method and content to have a high quality product. The public has come more and more to realize that it cannot obtain quality with a policy of niggardly penny-pinching for its schools. Nor can parents discourage children who are outstanding students from going into teaching, for they will get in return exactly the quality of the young people that they educate to become teachers.

Concern for quality education should be mindful of the quality of experience that every pupil has in secondary school—the slow learner as well as the fast learner, the disadvantaged as well as the advantaged. Excellence in any task, whether it be performing at a high level in a complex research problem in science or being the best craftsman possible, should be the goal. We should not equate excellence with academic subjects, for excellence resides in the individual, not in the subject.

Intellectual Attainment

There is no doubt that the modern technical age evidences a vastly increased need for high intellectual attainment, the use of the mind for both general and specific knowledge. There is more to be known in order to be an intelligent citizen. The advancement of knowledge in different fields requires more highly trained specialists. Medicine, for example, has advanced beyond the powers of a general practitioner to keep up with new developments. The problems of world order, transportation, human relations, space exploration, urbanization are so complex that specialized knowledge is required to deal with them. To survive as a nation, intellectual status is needed in government, business, the diplomatic service, industry, education, the military, the research laboratory, and innumerable other phases of life.

By and large, the community sets limits upon the intellectual interests and achievement of its children. Where inane, cocktail-party small talk takes precedence over good conversation, where football has priority over a dramatic event, where television overshadows books, or where the "egghead" is someone different and queer, there is little nourishment for scholarship. Fortunately, intellectual and scholarly achievements are more highly regarded today than even a decade ago.

But it is a mistake to identify the pseudo-intellectual with the genuinely stimulating intellectual environment. This demand sometimes takes strange turns. Getting "tough" with students or piling on long assignments is not the answer. A teacher without interests in depth in a number of fields and without scholarly attainment in the subject he teaches cannot provide the kind of atmosphere that excites the intellect.

Individuality

One of the dilemmas of our times originates from the numerous pressures for conformity. A worker who does the same thing as hundreds of others finds it hard to be an individual. He has the same coffee breaks, sees the same shows, bowls once a week as his neighbor does. Or as a business or professional man he goes with the "right" crowd, votes for the acceptable party, yearns for a Cadillac, and swears by rugged individualism.

In spite of mass production of goods and services and the subtle drives toward the orthodox, there is a desire for individuality. Witness the great interest that has developed in do-it-yourself projects, in crafts, in painting, and in home decorating. These desires are reflected in what parents want for their children as well as for themselves. The surge of interest in creativity in education is a manifestation of this demand.

Special Attention to the Able and the Talented

During the early part of the century, only the more able and the economically privileged attended secondary school. As the proportion of youth attending secondary school increased, those who were unusually able learners were neglected in the process of democratization of the American secondary school. Amidst the failure to individualize instruction as high schools grew in size and classes became larger, the good student was quite capable of taking care of himself, adapted readily to mass instruction, and usually made top scores on examinations. Why be concerned about someone who was already the best?

The fallacy of this type of reasoning became apparent as society placed a greater premium on scientific research and technical competency. The "best" had not been good enough. Often, it had failed to challenge the bright pupils to live up to their capacity. Moreover, the discovery that there are probably no limits to learning exposed the weakness of common lessons, common class activities, and the use of the same books by all members of a class—practices which leading educators had long argued against.

One of the distinguishing marks of the secondary school curriculum in the last decade has been the attention given to the academically talented. The great majority of publications dealing with the gifted and talented student have been issued since 1950. The National Education Association Project on the Academically Talented got under way in the late 1950's. Such noted reports as the Rockefeller Report on *The Pursuit of Excellence: Education and the Future of America* in 1958 and Conant's *The American High School Today* in 1959 were influential in making the public aware of the need in American education.

But talent is not confined to those who are academically inclined. Creative talents are found in any field of endeavor: in speech, in art, in politics, in music, in science, in writing, in technical skills. Creativity in these fields has not had as much emphasis as academic ability. The findings that highly intelligent students are not necessarily creative and that creativity is often opposed to the traits that make a student strive for good marks, should lead to greater emphasis on any type of giftedness and the development of unusual talent in any field.

Meeting the Needs of Disadvantaged Youth

In the midst of the clamor for greater attention to the student of unusual ability, one finds the disturbing fact that many young people of potentially high ability are no longer in school. The total loss of trained manpower is reflected in the fact that one of three of the nation's youth drop out before they finish high school. The dropout from high school is likely to be found wandering the street, in the courts, or getting himself into some kind of difficulty.

In some large cities, where the problem is especially acute, around 60 per cent of the youth ages 16 to 21 are out of school and unemployed. Studies in some areas indicate that about half of the boys who drop out become laborers in industry or on the farm. Yet, within the next decade it is predicted that only 5 per cent of the total labor force will be engaged in unskilled labor.

The concern for disadvantaged youth has risen sharply. These are young people who are disadvantaged because of living in slums, knowing only poverty in their lives; who are often members of minority groups that are discriminated against; who are from homes where there is no family solidarity or perhaps no family, from migrant groups that have no community roots. Conant has called this situation in city slums "social dynamite" in his *Slums and Suburbs*. Other titles appearing in publications in recent years evidence the recognition of this group of youth who need special help: "The Culturally Deprived Child," "Disaffected Children and Youth," "Education and the Disadvantaged American," "Fugitives from Failure." The National Education Association began in 1961 its Project on School Dropouts and large cities have their own projects such as those described in Chapters 11 and 13.

Minimizing Social Distinctions

The American secondary school set out to be a common leveler of all men, where the plumber's son could attend classes side by side with the industrialist's daughter. The fact that the goal has never been completely achieved does not dim the importance of the ideal. Even severe critics of American education, such as Hutchins, recognize the merits of free, universal public education through the secondary school. He contends:

> The conception of a people all devoting the early years of their lives to study with a view of attaining the maximum development of their highest powers is surely one of the grandest that history can show. Nor does the fact that this ideal has not yet been realized, except in quantitative terms, in any way diminish its vitality or validity.[1]

We have our blots upon the brightness of this ideal: our "separate but equal" policy in the South, where schools have been separate for Negroes but never equal, our elite schools in suburban areas and deprived schools in slum areas, our small high schools with a sparse curriculum in rural areas. Few would say that they are proud of these. The movement in some sections for special schools, "tracks" which emphasize social distinctions more than they provide for individual differences, and any kind of segregation that demeans the individual may be trends which we shall also live to regret.

Yet, the school that is segregated on the untenable basis of race is doomed in spite of the dying gasps of the Wallaces and Faubuses. The fact that the segregated school for Negroes is no longer acceptable to the majority of the American people is a trend that must be recognized as one of the most significant for secondary education in the latter half of the twentieth century.

[1] Robert M. Hutchins, *Some Observations on American Education*, New York: Cambridge University Press, 1956, p. 22.

More Education

Higher education in the United States used to be a privilege of the few. Now it is a goal of all Americans who want a better life for their children. Some senior high schools send approximately 90 per cent of their graduates on to college. The National Defense Education Act student loan program, state scholarships, and merit scholarships of various types, supported by foundations and industries, have made it easier for the children of families of average or poor economic circumstances to achieve a college education.

This zeal for higher education has not been without its vexing problems. The stiff competition to get into college and the high ambitions of parents for their children have caused some secondary school students to break under the strain. Testing programs for scholarships, rather than a good education, have become the goals toward which some teachers work. False notions about engineering occupations may cause youth to be entirely unrealistic about their capabilities and interests.

DEVELOPMENTS IN CONTENT

These demands of a technological age have resulted in some rather pronounced changes in the secondary school curriculum. Content is being updated but the approach to the teaching of the new content is also quite different. In such fields as the sciences and the humanities there are fewer absolutes. Rules and truths propounded through the years have been found wanting. Actually, these changes represent a profound revolution in method as well as content. Studying English or mathematics to derive meanings is a significantly different way of attacking the subject than learning the rules of grammar or the computational skills. Most important of all, these transformations mean a greatly improved quality of experiences for students. This is the true meaning of excellence.

Developing Meanings, Ideas, and Relationships

In the sciences and mathematics, where some of the major changes in content have occurred in recent years, emphasis is placed upon understanding the basic concepts. Students seek principles and generalizations in the new courses in physics, chemistry, and biology. In the elements of modern mathematics, the move is away from manipulating symbols and toward an awareness of abstractions denoted by the symbols. The newer courses stress, for example, the concept of a mathematical system, properties of numbers, set theory, and the ability to use principles of mathematics to explore new situations. Computers are faster than hand calculation by a millionfold, and the world of tomorrow will require understanding of basic mathematical principles far more than it does computation. Emphasis on structure and the "big" ideas is one of the fundamental changes in mathematics as well as in the physical and biological sciences.

But no subject has a monopoly on meanings. In the social studies, generalizations and basic concepts come to the fore in the proposed revisions. Fragmented knowledge, isolated facts, and descriptive information are being replaced by cohesive sets of ideas in the curriculum projects under way. The study of foreign languages as well as the English language is pointed toward knowing the characteristic of the language, its structure, and its changing nature. The whole idea of linguistics substitutes meaning and relationships for memory and repetition.

Furthering Discovery and Experimentation

One of the most remarkable developments in the fields of science, mathematics, industrial arts, and the social studies has been the unqualified commitment to discovery and experimentation on the part of scholars who have developed new course materials. The idea that secondary school students are to discover principles and generalizations for themselves is indeed a radical change. If one could be assured that teachers would understand how to lead young minds to discover truths for themselves, rather than hand them the answers to learn, he would indeed have good cause for expecting a renaissance in secondary education.

In mathematics, emphasis is placed on learning through discovery by inductive and deductive methods. The logic of mathematics and mathematics as a way of thinking are prominent in the new programs. Laboratory experiments in the new biology, chemistry, and physics are the open-ended type, in which students are led to discover the answers for themselves. No more cook-book type of laboratory manuals are to be used. More attention is paid to laboratory experiments.

Although it has touched fewer schools than the changes in either the mathematics or science, which have powerful national bodies or funds to promote them, just as noteworthy a change is occurring in the field of industrial arts. The approach uses an industrial arts research laboratory in which the student selects a problem, builds the equipment needed, and solves it through methods of experimental inquiry typical of modern industry. The laboratory is patterned after research in industrial processes; ninth-grade students perform complex experiments on testing radio amplifiers, experimenting with high-frequency induction heating, and testing missile design for drag.

Social studies projects attempt to have teachers guide students to discover generalizations and to use independent study skills and the modes of inquiry of the social scientist. Students are given some experience with the research methods of the social sciences. Sociology and psychology, for example, become the avenues for introducing students to quantitative analysis characteristic of these fields.

Decompartmentalizing of Subjects

There are some peculiar contradictions to be noted among the trends in the curriculum of secondary and higher education. At the same time when the core curriculum seems to have reached its peak and is now declining in use, new interdisciplinary subjects are springing into prominence, especially at the college level. Geochemistry, cybernetics, general systems theory, bionics, computer science, space age technology, biochemistry, and physical chemistry are but a few examples of newer specialties in which scholars carry on research. While the vast amount of materials an individual must learn before he can be considered proficient in his field continues to mount, there is a growing awareness that nature recognizes no such artificial boundaries as those which supposedly exist between the branches of the sciences. While these fields represent new specialties, they also portray the trend toward fusion of content from different fields. The core was based upon psychological principles; the new integration of subject matter derives from the recognition that subject boundary lines may hinder expansion of knowledge and that, as one looks at the structure of a subject, the differences become less and less distinct.

Modern mathematics courses in the secondary school emphasize the relatedness of various aspects of mathematics. There is no artificial distinction among algebra, arithmetic, and geometry in many of the new courses. In some schools the unification of the different branches of mathematics is exemplified by the titles of courses offered, such as Mathematics I, II, III, and IV for the four-year sequence.

At the same time, an opposite trend is evident in the social studies, where forces are at work to break up the unified subject into its separate disciplines, such as sociology, world geography, economics, and American government; there is also some tendency to divide up a subject among several teachers.

Improving Communication Skills

One of the realizations of the modern world is that people who will come face-to-face more often need to learn how to communicate orally as well as in writing. The classroom for teaching a foreign language has become a live laboratory where the language is spoken, instead of a place for laborious translation of passages in a book. The audio-lingual approach with its emphasis on hearing and speaking has given a complexion to language teaching greatly different from that of the period previous to World War II.

Both in classes in our native tongue and in foreign language classes, new ideas about the fundamental nature of language as expressed by linguists have affected instruction. The changing nature of the language, the descriptive analysis of the structure of a sentence, and the presentation of language as a system of patterns are aspects of the linguistics approach found in a few English classes.

Composition, or the communicating of ideas in writing, is coming back into its own. It is recognized as one of the fundamental skills that contribute to success in college. To be able to say something precisely, to say it simply, and to say it well is an art which seemingly few people master. It is a significant goal for its own sake. Somehow or other the erudite and the esoteric have got mixed up. The initiated, whether they be in the club of education, psychology, mathematics, or any other specialty, unfortunately tend to form an in-group whose purpose is to keep communication from crossing its borders.

In addition to teaching listening and writing skills, secondary schools are recognizing that a person does not reach his zenith in reading at the end of the sixth grade. Organized reading programs are found more frequently in junior high schools than in senior high schools, but the majority of all secondary schools offer some kind of work in reading. The reading laboratory for assisting both good and poor readers in improving themselves on an individual basis is quite popular.

Promoting Freedom of Inquiry

The notion of freedom is a powerful one—so powerful, in fact, that some people cannot stand the thought of youth's being exposed to "subversive" ideas. They must be given "safe" materials to read, that is, the non-controversial kind. Consequently, they will grow up with the "right" opinions. But who is to determine what is right?

A swing away from this position of shielding youth from the ugliness of the world can be noted. Study about communism is being urged upon the schools even by the more conservative community organizations. The ability to attack issues and problems analytically is recommended by scholarly groups in the social sciences. Even the study about religion seems to have possibilities as a controversial issue.

The classes that deal with the really controversial issues are growing. In high schools where students are encouraged to arrive at their own independent conclusions, and more important, taught how to do so, they examine such questions as sit-downs, anti-Semitic practices, corruption in local elections, censorship of books and movies, civil rights, and oil depletion allowances. In these schools, values that youth hold are admitted and examined objectively.

Focusing on New Areas of the World

Until a few years ago, the objective of international understanding was still largely a subject for discussion at conferences. Only intercultural education as it relates to ethnic, religious, and racial groups in the United States had made considerable headway. A changing world has caused a surprising transformation.

The world, rather than America and Europe, has become the source for content to be studied. World literature holds a larger place in English classes. The Russian, Arabic, Chinese, and Japanese languages have been added to the traditional languages studied in high school or college. Native informants are used in connection with language study, and the understanding of cultures different from our own has become one of the important objectives of foreign language classes. The economic and political systems of other countries, their manner and standard of living, their religion, and their music are studied more frequently. Cross-cultural understanding, issues of foreign policy, and the geography and history of newer nations are receiving attention in revised social studies programs.

Asia, Africa, and Latin America are recognized as important areas of the world for the citizen to be acquainted with. A major portion of a recent state bulletin on teaching about world cultures is devoted to non-Western cultures, such as the Soviet Union, China, Japan, India, southeast Asia, the Islamic world, and Africa. The surge for freedom among the former colonial areas makes these newer nations increasingly significant in world affairs.

Developing Realistic Vocational Education

Along with other areas of the secondary school curriculum, vocational education has been affected by the technological revolution. The proportion of farm workers and unskilled laborers in the labor force has been steadily dropping. Automation has taken its toll of both of these. The changes in occupations, new ones, and new details in older ones, have caused dislocation. Unemployment has been rising, especially in areas where new technology, along with shifts in consumer needs and defense needs, has resulted in some industrial plants becoming obsolete. Youth without skills have felt the unemployment trend keenly.

Yet at the same time, skilled craftsmen, clerical workers, workers in service occupations, teachers, engineers, doctors, nurses, and many other fields have had a shortage of qualified workers.

Probably one reason why vocational education has not been as adaptable to the changes in an age of automation is that it has been firmly ensconced behind the fortification of federal legislation, beginning with the Smith-Hughes Act in 1917. Yet it seems perfectly clear that the splendid programs in vocational education developed in the past forty years could not have come about without these federal funds.

Suddenly, industrial states have found themselves with funds for programs in agriculture, departments to administer them, and colleges to train for agricultural occupations, when their crying need was actually for funds and programs for technical education and for retraining workers in new skills. Even the non-subsidized vocations such as business education are just waking up to the fact that computer science will undoubtedly change radically the skills needed by an office worker. The typical commercial high school program of typing, shorthand, and bookkeeping is not geared to tomorrow's world.

Many important new occupations, such as those related to electronics and the growing area of service occupations for which little or no formal preparation has previously been available, demand the attention of the public schools, whether comprehensive secondary schools, vocational and technical schools, or community colleges.

One of the really promising trends in vocational education has been the part-time cooperative education programs, only some of which are supported by federal funds.

The Vocational Education Act of 1963 provides funds for broadened vocational education programs for youth in high school, in junior college, and in vocational and technical schools; for unemployed and out-of-school youth; and for youth with academic or socio-economic handicaps. Work-study programs and residential schools are included. Vocational agriculture programs are expanded to include increased emphasis on management, farm mechanization, forestry, transportation, processing, and marketing of farm products.

One large city has a plan for all students attending comprehensive high schools in the ninth and tenth grades, where the emphasis would be on general education and where they would take exploratory occupational courses. Those with the needed interests and aptitudes would then be put in specialized schools, including vocational and technical areas and advanced academic programs, on an individual basis and returned to the comprehensive high school when they have learned the vocational or technical skill, if previous to graduation. The pupil would remain in the specialized school from six weeks to two years.

Another city has a recently developed secondary school to provide terminal job training to low-ability pupils in such fields as custodial services, food preparation, family service aides, lawn and garden care, painting and decorating, shoe repair, valet service, and small appliance repair.

DEVELOPMENTS IN ORGANIZATION OF THE CURRICULUM

What have the demands of the technological age of the 1960's done to the way students and teachers are organized in secondary schools as to size of groups, time schedules, working relationships, and other conditions for learning? These broader aspects of curriculum organization provide the setting within which the curriculum is developed by teachers working with students.

Perhaps in no other aspect of the secondary school curriculum has there been as much change. Uniformity—one period a day for classes, the same length of time for each period, and twenty-five students to a class—has been challenged.

No evidence has existed that any one of these forms of organization is superior to another. The question now facing secondary schools is: Which is superior for what purposes? Large classes, small classes, independent study groups, flexible schedules, and utilization of teachers in different ways need to be tested for the appropriateness of the setting for specific kinds of learning activities.

These organizational forms will be discussed in relation to their evolution, meaning, and future potential. They all have one highly important ingredient in common—a built-in flexibility.

The Core Curriculum [2]

Although the core is not a recent innovation, it is one of the forerunners of the idea of a flexible organization for the curriculum. In fact, it represents another era of vigorous innovation in the secondary school curriculum.

The core grew out of a period of experimentation in secondary education during the Eight-Year Study of the Progressive Education Association in the 1930's. At that time the experimental secondary schools were freed to revise their programs since agreements had been reached with colleges to accept students without any certain pattern of courses. There was also a healthy atmosphere for experimentation. Many had become dissatisfied with the secondary schools' failure to provide adequately for the needs of all youth.

Although a longer block of time than the typical school period is one of its distinguishing features, the concept of the core represents a more fundamental reorientation of the secondary school curriculum. It is, first of all, a way of organizing common learning experiences around problems, drawing from content of different subjects, and focusing upon the opportunity for students to deal with issues and questions vital to a democratic society and to personal development. But it is more than that. It is also a growing, dynamic, and experimental concept of curriculum which represents a revolt against the rigidity and extreme compartmentalization of the curriculum.

It is this dynamic quality that can be traced as an evolutionary process to the present developments in curriculum organization.

If one were to look at the block of time feature of the core, certain trends can be noted. The evidence shows that the proportion of junior high schools having block-time classes (scheduled for more than one period) increased from 15.8 per cent in 1948–1949 to 31.4 per cent in 1956–1957 and to 40 per cent in 1959–1960.[3] A similar upward trend was noted in junior-senior high schools. Thus, the block-time

[2] See Vernon E. Anderson, "The Evolving Core Curriculum," in Harl R. Douglass (ed.), *The High School Curriculum*, 3rd ed., New York: The Ronald Press Co., 1964, chap. 13.

[3] Grace S. Wright and Edith S. Greer, *The Junior High School: A Survey of Grades 7–8–9 in Junior and Junior-Senior High Schools, 1959–60*, U. S. Department of Health, Education, and Welfare, Office of Education, Bulletin 1963, No. 32, Washington, D. C.: Government Printing Office, 1963, pp. 18–20.

classes almost tripled in this period representing slightly more than a decade. Other surveys made of nation-wide samples and state schools from 1955 to 1960 have indicated that from 40 to 60 per cent of the junior high schools had block-time classes. It is almost wholly a junior high school movement.

If one looks at another feature of the core, the unification of subject matter around problems, known as the experience-centered type of core, the picture is quite different. In 1950–1951, 42.8 per cent of the secondary schools having core programs reported the use of the experience-centered type of core. In a follow-up study in 1956, of the schools that reported using block-time classes only 12 per cent had the experience-centered type.[4] The percentage was approximately the same in 1959–1960.[5]

While the evidence shows that the core curriculum as a form of organization with definite characteristics [6] is declining, and the name "core" is no longer used in many such programs, the external format of a block of time that includes more than one subject is on the increase. Yet, has this basic concept of the curriculum entirely lost its influence on the American secondary school curriculum? Have the dynamism, the experimental force, and the flexibility, which represented its greatest contributions to curriculum development, disappeared from the scene? Although it is doubtful that they have, we are in danger of losing these powerful ideas. Let us see what has happened.

Research evidence indicated that core programs of the experience-centered type were superior in gains in attitudes and values, while few significant differences in academic learning were found between the experience-centered core and the traditional program. Other types of student behavior, such as better relations with teachers and improved attendance, were found in favor of the core.[7] However, much of the effort toward evaluation of the core was centered on showing that it did as well in preparing students in the conventional skills, when its original purposes went far beyond the skills.

Few teachers were ever well prepared to teach the core. The ones who were had largely been prepared for this quite different approach by the school systems through their in-service and curriculum development programs. The greatest handicap came from the fact that few teachers were prepared equally in depth in two subject fields.

[4] Anderson, *op. cit.*, p. 253.
[5] Wright and Greer, *op. cit.*, p. 23.
[6] See Anderson, *op. cit.*, pp. 248–52, for a statement of these characteristics.
[7] *Ibid.*, p. 254.

Moreover, many core classes became as routine and mechanical as any other class might be. The greatest enemies of the core were those teachers who did not understand the concept and spent endless time in fruitless activities such as dull class reports by committees.

The crystallization process was also exemplified by the tendency to think of *the* core. It had finally "arrived" and some of its proponents wanted it to remain in their image. They, too, had lost sight of the essential experimental ingredient of the core.

Although the pressures are for long required assignments and for "solid" subjects taught separately, the idea of the core is not dead. There are manifestations of its original purposes in programs that have evolved from the core. Teachers who have the same ideals are using the core approach effectively in their teaching. One kind of program that lends itself to a core approach is team teaching.

Team Teaching

One of the popular ways of utilizing the strengths of teachers, yet permitting them to work with students in periods of greater length in order to achieve flexibility of learning activities, is team teaching. The increase in the use of teams of teachers has been most marked in the large secondary schools, where the percentage employing these teams jumped from four in 1955–1956 to thirty in 1960–1961.[8] It has continued a steady growth since that time.

Encouraged by the studies of the Commission on the Experimental Study of the Utilization of the Staff in the Secondary School (A National Association of Secondary-School Principals project), secondary schools experimented with the teaming of teachers for instructional purposes. Teachers of different competencies in different subject fields or phases of a subject are scheduled to work together with a group of pupils usually varying from 60 to 150, although a group may run as high as 400. Two to four teachers are generally scheduled for a block of time consisting of from two to five periods.

There are several types of organization of teams. A physical science major and a biological science major may team up to teach a general science type of course. Or, the social studies teacher and the English teacher may work together in what formerly may have been the seventh grade core. Teams may include a broad span of subjects such as mathematics, science, social studies, and the language arts, but more frequently include two subjects such as Ameri-

[8] National Education Association, *The Principal Looks at the Schools*, Washington, D. C., 1962, pp. 17–18.

can history and American literature. The varying competencies may also be in terms of preparation and experience. For example, a neophyte, an experienced teacher, a teacher aide, or a clerk may work together.

The group of students is then scheduled for varying periods of time within this block, part of it being used for lectures or instructional activities with the whole group, part for small group discussion, and part for conferences and independent study.

The Claremont Teaching Team Program, one of the better known and evaluated team teaching experiments, in which the Claremont Graduate School cooperates with several school systems in the southern California area under Ford Foundation support, began in 1959. In the secondary school phase of this program, the team is an instructional unit within a school. In this unit are from 90 to 180 secondary school students assigned to a faculty team of three to six teachers with complementary talents. They work as a team with a leader, have a daily conference and planning period, and have for their assistance a teacher aide and a roster of citizens. The team is responsible for the guidance of the student group.

The plan allows teachers to work together for coordination and unity in teaching different subjects, for flexibility in grouping students for instructional purposes, for greater use of community resources, for improved guidance of students because of knowing them well, and for greater use of a variety of materials.

These are recognizable characteristics similar to the core. The utilization of these opportunities, or a problem-solving approach, may or may not occur but the chances of its occurring are greater than in the conventional classroom situation. The fact that team teaching may be traditional in nature should certainly be no surprise. The unmistakable evidence from studies of the core programs was that most of these programs were of the same nature.

The team approach in many cases has been opposed to unifying two or more subjects and has gone in the direction of fragmentation of the curriculum, with less stress on individual–personal relationships. However, that trend is no more inherent in the concept of team teaching than it is in the core. The imagination, vision, and perception of the teacher as to what is important for adolescents of secondary school age are the fundamental factors in whether core or team teaching utilizes its potential for integration and understanding of relationships among subject matter from different fields.

There is evidence that in a number of team teaching situations these core procedures are being applied. Evaluation of programs in the Claremont Project indicated that the reasons most commonly reported by secondary school students in favor of continuing in the team were as follows:

Knowledge and appreciation of teachers
Special large-group programs, outside speakers, trips
Same teacher for two years
Emphasis on making students think
More interesting subjects and learning
Enriched activities, variety, flexibility
Teacher coordination and cooperation
Integration of material.[9]

Teachers and parents listed similar types of reasons. In some schools studying these aspects of student behavior, team students had fewer suspensions, fewer disciplinary referrals, and less tardiness than non-team students in control groups.[10]

There are some advances of team teaching programs over core programs as they existed in schools. One is the fact that individual differences in teachers are used to advantage. Buildings are being designed for use of the flexible-sized group in team teaching and to provide for independent study. Greater utilization is being made of newer instructional media and of flexible kinds of grouping. But neither core nor team teaching is any guarantee of teacher–pupil planning, problem-solving, integration of subject matter, concern for pupil problems, or adapting of subject matter to capabilities and aspirations of students.

Variety in Class Size

The trend in secondary schools seems to be toward scheduling classes of different sizes for different purposes. No longer is the standard class size of twenty-five to thirty pupils accepted by all educators as the infallible rule.

Studies conducted some thirty years ago indicated that students attained conventional learning as well in large lecture groups as they did in the usual size classroom. Yet, educators shrugged off these studies as dealing only with achievement. Completely overlooked was the fact that this is exactly what the majority of teachers dealt with exclusively.

In recent years, different questions are being asked, leading to some

[9] Adapted from *Claremont Teaching Team Project, Annual Report, 1961–62,* Claremont, Calif.: Claremont Graduate School, 1962, p. 32.
[10] *Ibid.,* p. 27.

different directions. What size group is most appropriate for what kind of learning activity? If the classroom is a place to dispense information, then it might as well be done to large groups as to small. Yet, this approach leads to just as stereotyped a situation. Pupil–teacher contacts and kinds of learning other than pure achievement are important.

What has been called the "Trump Plan" has been studied by the Commission on the Experimental Study of the Utilization of the Staff in the Secondary School.[11] The Commission suggests that the curriculum of the secondary school be examined with these questions in mind: What can students learn largely by themselves? What can students learn from explanation by others? What requires personal interaction between students and teachers? When this approach is taken, the size of the group becomes a variable to achieve instructional purposes.

Spurred by experimentation in secondary schools working with the Commission, schools have scheduled some large classes of 100 or more, some small classes of 15 (more or less), and some normal-sized classes of 30 or so. The first is used to impart information and may use television or live lectures and demonstrations. The second is used for small group discussion purposes or for seminars of various types. The other is for the more typical class activity. However, if the principle of purpose is applied, there will be no such thing as a "normal-sized" class.

Team teaching relates to the flexible-sized group, in which students may easily be regrouped, within the block of time provided, into any size group needed. More teacher aides are needed in a flexible type of programming.

New secondary schools have been built in recent years to provide classrooms for groups ranging from 15 or less to as many as 300 students.

Independent Study

In 1961, the report of the aforementioned Commission stated that "the organization of instruction in tomorrow's schools will provide many opportunities for individual students' *independent study*." [12] This was not a reference to more study periods or more homework. (Yet many schools are doing just that.) It referred to independent

11 J. Lloyd Trump and Dorsey Baynham, *Focus on Change: Guide to Better Schools,* Chicago: Rand McNally & Co., 1961, 147 pp.
12 *Ibid.,* p. 26.

research, experimentation, and reading done by the individual student who wished to explore new avenues opened up to him in his courses or to study a field in depth. Trump has proposed that a student spend 40 per cent of his time in independent study, 40 per cent in large group instruction, and 20 per cent in small group discussion.[13]

A few secondary schools have caught the spirit of this notion of self-directed study. Students use the library, the science laboratory, the language laboratory, and learning laboratories that feature programmed learning and computers to pursue independently non-assigned projects of their own. The school is a learning resource center. There are reading rooms, listening rooms, and viewing rooms.

The Humanities Center for the secondary school in the illustration on page 326 provides facilities for instruction in English, social studies, and foreign languages. The large group lecture area accommodates 300 students or two groups of 150 each, where they can view films, hear presentations, and listen to community resource people. The facilities enable students to meet in small groups of fifteen or less to question and discuss in a seminar setting. Independent study is provided for in an area containing study and writing cubicles and private viewing and listening areas, supported by a wide variety of reading and resource materials. These facilities are consistent with provisions in the other buildings on the same campus. They are also consistent with the principle of sequential learning made possible through the newer technology.

Emphasis on going to college puts emphasis upon independent study rather than on study in classrooms, as was encouraged under the supervised study plan in which there was a decreased amount of time spent in study halls and the library.

Scheduling for Individuality

The use of electronic devices, programmed learning, team teachers, different-sized classes, and the concept of individual progress in a subject have brought about changes in scheduling classes and students. All of these developments have a common element of flexibility. A rigid schedule of sixty minutes a day for five days a week for each subject no longer suffices.

One of the ways to achieve flexibility in scheduling has been to divide the school day into time blocks of shorter length than the usual period, called "modules," which can then be added together in different combinations. Fifteen-minute modules are frequently used.

[13] *Ibid.*, p. 41.

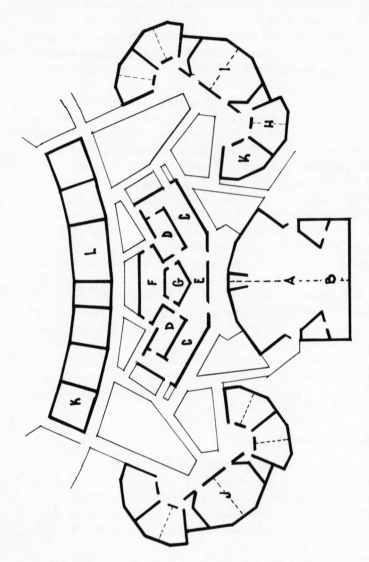

(A) Large Group Presentation Area — 300 Students — Dividable
(B) Stage
(C) Individual Study Spaces
(D) Teacher Offices
(E) Departmental Library
(F) Teacher Conference and Preparation Area

(G) Teacher-Aide Workroom
(H) Dividable Regular Classroom
(I) Regular Classroom which can be combined
(J) Language Laboratories
(K) Regular Classrooms
(L) Reading Laboratory

A school day may be divided into twenty-six modules which can be combined in different numbers to make a schedule of varying length for different classes. Thus, in grade eight, five modules daily may be assigned to English, two modules a day to foreign language, four modules twice a week to some laboratory-type courses, and so on.

At the same time, senior high schools have more frequently offered courses four times a week instead of five, with the same amount of work being done as previously in five; extra periods are created for certain classes; and rotating schedules are used. In an increasing number of schools, sections for bright pupils meet four times a week. In some schools, a computer is used for scheduling the entire student body, and each student has an individual schedule. The table of schedule changes in six states (see page 328) shows some of the different trends in scheduling.

Team teaching, with its longer block of time, provides a built-in type of flexibility for scheduling and regrouping as desired. For example, within a three-hour block, a team of teachers who teach a group of 75 students in English, social studies, sciences, and mathematics in the seventh grade can plan the schedule within these three hours week by week or even day by day.

ISSUES AND POINTS OF VIEW

This chapter looks at the secondary school curriculum as a whole and synthesizes some of the trends that appear to be of significance. The questions discussed in this section present some of the foremost issues over which sharp arguments often flare. They go beyond some of the trends. The next chapter includes the issues especially related to individualizing instruction.

1. *Should the common part of the secondary school curriculum center exclusively around knowledge from scholarly disciplines and traditional skills, or should it also focus on social, civic, aesthetic, and vocational objectives?*

Probably no debate in the history of twentieth-century education has been as heated as the one dealing with this issue, especially in the last two decades. The Council on Basic Education, a number of leading scholars, and persons from other fields such as the military have taken a position that the schools should be concerned only with intellectual objectives. The advocates of this point of view feel that much of the fuzzy discussion about citizenship and character training takes on the guise of life adjustment. The schools should get on with their business of teaching academic skills and disciplines.

Schedule Changes *

Questionnaire Items	Subject Area (A—Operating; B—Contemplated)															
	English		Social Studies		Math		Science		For. Lang.		Pr. Arts		Fine Arts		P.E. Health	
	A	B	A	B	A	B	A	B	A	B	A	B	A	B	A	B
Definition: Schedules are more flexible because of modifications which affect the length and/or number of periods, lengthen the school year, or provide for new types of activities.																
1. Classes are scheduled for longer than normal periods, but for fewer times per week.	76	36	71	41	56	33	72	47	47	20	51	36	65	32	52	22
2. Extra periods for specialized large-group instruction have been created.	43	22	34	31	20	17	35	24	18	9	21	10	22	8	18	6
3. The school day is divided into 15-, 20-, 25-, or 30-minute time units with classes scheduled for different numbers of units. (modules)	7	13	9	16	9	12	10	15	15	10	6	12	7	12	6	10
4. The regular schedule may be changed for an individual student on any given day.	139	10	120	8	118	7	123	10	100	7	92	7	97	6	105	4
5. A summer school is operated to provide special opportunities for all students who wish to attend.	624	47	579	50	598	59	508	56	441	54	332	31	281	24	175	17

* Ira J. Singer, "Survey of Staff Utilization Practices in Six States," *Bulletin of the National Association of Secondary-School Principals,* 46:9, January, 1962, Table IV. The figures represent the number of schools carrying on or contemplating the practice from a total of 2,177 schools surveyed in six states.

Many proponents of this point of view consider European schools as the epitome of good education that prepares one to be a scholar and a cultured individual.

Others hold that the education we decide is good for our children must be judged in terms of American goals. No educational system can be viewed outside the culture in which it exists. Those who advocate stressing only intellectual objectives are concerned largely with those children who are fortunate enough to be academically endowed.

No one has ever questioned whether or not the schools should stress intellectual objectives. The question is, have we done this task well enough? But the two purposes—intellectual achievement and responsible citizenship—are not necessarily the same. Intellectual training per se does not necessarily improve the individual as a citizen. Depth in specialization is one kind of need; breadth in understanding, commitments to democratic behavior, and some reasonable understanding of oneself and one's fellow man are others.

Restriction of opportunities through a curriculum for the academically talented alone is a negation of a fundamental principle in which we have long believed. Equality of opportunity does not mean that everyone gets an equal dosage. If we believe in equality of opportunity, we must also believe in provision for individual differences, giving each person a chance to develop his own talents and capabilities to the maximum. Large numbers of students need a curriculum in some aspect differentiated from that of students who will specialize further in a study of a profession or in a logically organized discipline. For each, the experience should be fruitful in order to be of the highest quality.

Nor can we afford to deny young people an equality of opportunity to explore the arts and the humanities, at the expense of specialization. The arts and the humanities contain some of the basic knowledge and interests which make life worth living; the sciences, it is hoped, will help people to enjoy these aspects of living more fully.

2. *Should the secondary school curriculum be geared to immediate, pressing needs or to long-range goals?*

In a sense, this is the question of specific vocational education vs. a more comprehensive type of general and vocational background. But it is more than that. In recent years, the pressures upon the secondary school to prepare technically trained individuals and scientists for an arms, space, or what-have-you race have been considerable.

Most thoughtful persons today would say that the curriculum should change to meet the needs of a technological age. However, the tough question is how any school program can prepare for needs that change so constantly. It is important to remember that young people in the beginning years of secondary school will not be taking their place as workers and citizens in a community until at least ten years hence, and more likely they will not be the community leaders until their 30's, twenty or more years from now.

It may well be that when the children now in school go through college and into civic and professional life some skills will no longer be as essential as they are now. Continuous assessment of the trends and changes in American life as related to the world-wide situation needs to be made in order to develop long-range aims for the school program.

It is disturbing to find some who interpret the need for more technically trained individuals, such as engineers and scientists, as providing a license for neglecting the matter of general education. For, certainly, the problems of the future lie not only in keeping up with or surpassing other nations in technical know-how, but even more so in surpassing them in insight in adjusting people's ways of living to the rapid technological expansion and in insight into the skills of human relations. As Norman Cousins so aptly put it, the biggest problem facing us today is to be able to settle conflicts without a war, to seek "alternatives to violence." General education that stresses values, attitudes, and understanding necessary to deal with complex issues of the world today is a solid base of secondary education from which specialized learning stems in order to provide for individual interest and skills.

3. *Should programs for secondary school students be planned individually or predetermined according to some vocational or educational objectives?*

This question is quite different from one which asks whether or not students should be grouped. It concerns, instead, how much flexibility there should be in developing a program of courses for an individual student. Should he, for example, not be allowed to take industrial arts, art, or homemaking because it is not in the college preparatory curriculum?

One of the ways by which secondary schools have attempted to provide for differentiation within the curriculum is by means of multiple curricula, such as the college preparatory curriculum, the general curriculum, the vocational curriculum, and the like. There is a good deal of discussion over the value of the multiple curricula or tracks, as they are sometimes called. The danger seems to lie in the inflexibility or the lack of adaptation of a program to an individual's needs. There is no need for such curricular divisions where good guidance services prevail, in which the student is counseled each year concerning the program that he should take. Differentiation in the curriculum is certainly important, but fixed curricula may tend to make people fit into a single mold where there probably should be several molds.

One problem is that the greater the difficulty in breaking across curricular barriers to fulfill special needs, the more the risk of accentuating the socio-economic class differences within a particular school. School leaders are questioning practices that strive to enhance these social distinctions. With the increased number of subjects carried by high school students, there is a possibility of following a vocational curriculum and preparing for college at the same time.

4. *Will a change in the organizational structure or framework for the curriculum improve learning?*

This is a question most difficult to test. Yet, it is one of extreme importance since team teaching, different-sized class groups, new forms of schedules, and other forms of organizing a student body or faculty for working together are advocated as panaceas for all that ails the secondary school curriculum.

Care should be taken not to substitute the form for the substance. No form of manipulation of organization can make an incompetent teacher competent. Changes in forms of patterns for teacher–pupil contacts may facilitate understanding of students, using one's competencies, planning learning activities, and the like, but it is doubtful that such changed contacts will alone improve learning experiences. We should remember what happened to the core curriculum in the hands of some teachers who had neither affinity for it nor the slightest idea of what its fundamental concepts meant.

Team teaching will permit teachers to plan together. It will facilitate taking field trips, redeploying pupils into different groups, providing for independent study. But the skeptic who believes teachers ought to give assignments and then hear them will only be a bungling misfit in such a situation. He will do better in his secluded classroom dispensing his assignments.

In any organizational setting, chemistry may be a series of formulas; mathematics, an exercise in memory and repetition; English, a stilted treatment of forms; and language, a study in how to translate words—all devoid of the human touches, intellectual stimulation, and insights so necessary to learning. Grouping of any kind is of no value if adjustments are not made in the curriculum and materials.

13

PROVISIONS FOR INDIVIDUAL DIFFERENCES IN SECONDARY SCHOOLS

Provision for individual differences among pupils is one of the axioms in the life of a teacher. For some it is a well understood goal toward which they work zealously. To others it is a slogan from the textbooks but a real puzzle in its application. Schools may turn to administrative and organizational devices to do the job. However, the essence remains within the curriculum and the kinds of differentiation of experiences provided in the classroom.

Children may be thought of as belonging to somewhat discrete or at least different categories for purposes of emphasis or discussion. Thus, we have books and articles written about the gifted, the academically talented, the creative, the slow learner, the mentally retarded, the culturally deprived, the educationally disadvantaged, and the underachiever. Such classifications are convenient for discussion of children with common problems. But within any such group, individuals are far from alike.

Unless we regard pupils as individuals no matter what kind of a home or cultural background they come from, and no matter what intelligence tests may show, we fall into a trap that can easily lead to accepting administrative palliatives for the real cure. Reaction among educators and the public is directed against undue attention to the deviates at both ends of the scale. For the great majority of pupils are often labeled "average" (another misleading term that hides

differences) and the majority of children are in fact in the middle group. But such categorizing can lead to the teacher's and the school's doing something special only for the deviates and regarding all others as alike. Thus, grouping, tracks, special classes, and special programs are provided for certain groups of children but the big middle group is regarded as mythically alike.

Although the discussion in this chapter is divided into five main headings that describe similar characteristics in secondary school pupils, the focus is on the fact that *individuals are more or less gifted or creative or slow, that they differ not only in this trait but in many others,* and *that true provision for individual differences helps children to make progress according to their own potential and to develop that potential to the fullest.*

THE GIFTED AND ACADEMICALLY TALENTED

Experts disagree on what percentage of the top group academically are talented or gifted. Undoubtedly, there can be no sharp dividing line. Fortunately, the I.Q. score is no longer considered sufficient to identify these groups. The proportion for the nation as a whole identified as academically talented varies from the top 10 to 15 per cent, and for the gifted from 3 to 10 per cent. Some make the distinction of calling the upper 1 per cent extremely gifted and the upper 10 per cent gifted.

Since any test used to establish aptitude is not infallible, no sharp distinction can be made. The data gathered by a U. S. Office of Education study showed that academic records of the upper 25 per cent in academic ability in comparison with the lowest 25 per cent were not as different as differences in academic ability indicate they might have been.[1] Moreover, no single high school could use percentages with any degree of confidence. A Maryland study of academically talented students in secondary schools (upper 10 per cent) revealed that variation was from less than 1 per cent to more than 22 per cent of the total graduating class in different secondary schools.[2]

Moreover, the term "gifted" is used here to mean superiority in any kind of talent, including general intellectual ability; ability in a special area, such as mathematics, foreign language, human relations, or mechanics; and talents in creative arts such as music, crafts, writing, painting, and dramatics.

More to the point is the degree to which any pupil in secondary school has characteristics identified as exhibiting talent. Thus, the more academically talented individual would tend to have greater facility for perceiving relationships, for retention and recall, for learning facts and principles independently and rapidly; he would have more unusual intellectual drive and more curiosity about ideas. In other words, it is a matter of degree, in that one person is more capable than others in certain specifically definable talents.

Rapid Progress Plans

The term "enrichment" refers to broadening and deepening the experiences pupils have in an area of study. "Acceleration," as used frequently in professional literature, refers to some speedup in the pupil's work or progress through school. A different analysis is used here, identifying two categories both of which may involve enrichment and acceleration.

The first type is acceleration through school by shortening the time taken to complete a certain number of grades or credits. A rather

[1] Edith S. Greer, "The Academically Talented," *School Life*, 45:9, March, 1963.
[2] Thomas G. Pullen, Jr., "What the Academically Talented Study," *Public Education in Maryland*, Vol. VII, No. 3, February, 1959, 4 pp.

large—and increasing—number of students are carrying five or six subjects. It is becoming more common for bright students to complete the full six-year program of secondary education in five years. (In other instances, students graduate within the customary number of years with an increased number of credits.) The Advanced Placement Plan permits secondary school students in their senior year to take courses for which they will receive credit at some colleges and universities and possibly even enter college at the sophomore year. An increasing number of students are receiving such advanced standing. In some school systems, eighth-grade students in junior high school are permitted to take some courses in senior high school, and seniors may take some courses in junior college. Summer school courses are also offered by secondary schools to speed up the time needed to accumulate the needed credits for graduation. Credit by examination is also used for the same purpose.

There is no evidence or data to indicate that taking work a year earlier in college by completing high school in fewer years is superior or inferior either to acceleration in college itself or to acceleration within specific subject areas.

A more promising means of rapid progress is acceleration within the subject itself. Sometimes this means of acceleration has erroneously been described as pushing high school subjects down into the elementary school. Actually, it involves continuous progress in a subject from year to year, so that a superior student in any subject moves at his own pace and is not held back by his slower classmates.

Some of the more common ways that are believed to facilitate acceleration within a subject are altered grade placement of subjects, such as algebra in the eighth grade, grouping by ability, the ungraded school or class, and placement examinations given by colleges to entering freshmen in order to place them in a higher level course if they indicate they have the necessary background. None of these ways necessarily guarantees more rapid progress although each may expedite it. Grouping makes possible different and accelerated learning experiences but is of no value unless adaptations are made by the teacher to the individual pupil's background and previous learning. Most programs for the gifted involve ability grouping of some kind.

The crux of the matter is continuity of learning in a subject (or more specifically, in understanding and skills) which makes it possible for the more talented or gifted to progress at his own accelerated pace. The subject of foreign language best illustrates this concept. If a language is begun in the early grades and continued on through elementary school, junior high school, and senior high school, the pupil proficient in language will have, at the end of the twelfth grade, a knowledge advanced far beyond that of most college sophomores in language classes. Should there be a break in language study for three to five years in upper elementary and junior high school, however, the continuity of progress would not be evident and what had been learned in elementary school may be forgotten.

Special Classes

Seminars, honors classes, and advanced classes are special types of classes to which academically talented students are admitted on the basis of achievement tests, previous records, and teacher recommendation. The distinction among the three is not always clear-cut. They are generally characterized by opportunity for study of a subject in depth, wide exploration through reading and library research, and discussion and writing about more advanced and abstract ideas. These courses represent a definite form of grouping by ability because of the selectivity factors.

1. **Seminars.** These classes are likely to be small and informal and tend to draw a wide area of subject matter. In a number of respects, they employ the principles of the core curriculum. They are modeled after college seminars, which generally involve extensive student participation. The most common seminars in the Midwest are college level courses. Flexibility is a significant characteristic suited to the more talented student. Sometimes logic, psychology, philosophy, literature, music, art, and drama are subject fields more frequently drawn upon for the content. Some senior high schools offer seminars in the social studies, organized around great ideas and issues or on the basis of the historical approach to contemporary problems. Most seminars define their own problems. Often they serve to relate subject matter from other courses pupils are taking and to advance the pupil beyond these courses.

2. **Honors courses.** The honors courses are special courses offered for the academically talented or for those talented in a particular field. They may be advanced elective courses in subject areas or highly enriched required courses. In some secondary schools, the high-level ability group is called the honors section.

Honors English pupils may engage in an advanced study of English literature or literature of some other country; write short stories, poetry, and drama; and emphasize logic, organization, and style in writing. In one secondary school, an honors course in American history is offered for a double period. In another school, pupils in the 90th percentile in the eleventh and twelfth grades are offered honors courses of ten weeks each in four subjects: advanced composition, science, mathematics, and social studies.

3. **Advanced courses.** It is obvious that one would be hard put to distinguish between what is "advanced" or "honors."

Advanced courses of any type give the pupil with specific talents an opportunity to study a subject in further depth and to go beyond other pupils. Where the selection of students is based not only on ability but on previous achievement and understanding developed in the subject, the principles of continuous progress operate. Such courses as microbiology, ecology, cytology, genetics, geophysics, electronics, humanities, world literature, calculus, probability and statistical inference, astronomy, and earth science give these opportunities.

In another sense, these courses may be exploratory both at the junior high school and senior high school levels. Courses in Russian, Chinese, problems of human behavior, great issues and ideas of western civilization, junior research science, creative writing, non-Western studies, Pan American history, and computer technology permit pupils to explore fields in which they broaden their perspective of the world, its languages, literature, history, and discoveries. They make the secondary school curriculum a place both to advance one's knowledge and to challenge one's thinking.

Independent and Special Study Opportunities

Only in recent years has the secondary school offered to the talented student the privilege of pursuing independently some projects, research, and study. One of the characteristics of the academically talented individual is the ability to learn independently. Actually, it is the responsibility of the school to develop independent thinkers, who can make and execute plans on their own initiative and power.

For youth with this potential, the principle of relative uniqueness of the curriculum needs to be applied, considering the uniqueness as their competency to pursue studies on their own. They need to have a different as well as a similar kind of experience.

Yet, opportunity for genuinely independent study planned in the program is still quite rare in secondary schools and even in colleges. Such opportunity relates to and grows out of what is studied in classes or discussed with teachers. It does not mean a pupil entirely takes care of himself. But it does mean that an inverse ratio of classroom teaching and learning is needed, that this kind of student needs to be freed to explore and do research, and that somehow the school must create opportunities for him to have the stimulation of good minds both within and without the school.

The activities described here are those which schools have structured for their talented and gifted students. They involve credit and non-credit groups; the availability of laboratory, shop, and library facilities; use of summer, after-school, and Saturday; use of community resources and facilities; and independent projects and research. Some of the activities overlap in various categories.

1. **Use of non-school time.** Secondary schools have made imaginative use of summers, Saturday mornings, and after-school time for the enrichment of the program for talented pupils. Summer school programs for enrichment and acceleration are increasing. Summer camps serve for activities in drama, music, art, outdoor education, and science study. Special institutes, demonstration classes, and research projects are developed in summers in connection with universities and colleges. Or, students may attend evening lectures or take early-morning television courses. Special experiences are arranged in the community for after-school hours and Saturday mornings. Small discussion groups of the "Great Books" may meet after school, for example. Even scholarship trips to other countries, such as the newer nations in Africa, are arranged for by some schools to study conditions in other lands.

2. **Use of community resources.** Universities, colleges, community cultural centers, industrial plants, distinguished people in different fields, and the school itself furnish a laboratory for extending the experiences of the talented. One secondary school holds weekly seminars beyond regular class hours, using speakers, field trips, and resource persons from the school faculty. Another holds ninety-minute after-school sessions with community leaders. Talented art students take Saturday classes in several art centers in one large city. Another large city district uses its special high schools with shops or science laboratories on Saturdays for pupils from the comprehensive high schools. Another holds a series of evening lectures in museums, art galleries, and other community centers. Students with leadership talents are given special preparation as well as opportunity for leadership positions in the school.

The university or college furnishes rare opportunities for intellectual and research experiences for pupils in secondary schools of the area. One university conducts a science institute for high school seniors, followed by independent laboratory research. Many universities have developed plans under National Science Foundation grants to give talented secondary school science students summer experience in working with scientists on research projects. (The same type of plan has been developed with research laboratories in some industries.) Some colleges schedule on Saturday opportunities for secondary school juniors and seniors to listen to lectures and to discuss topics with professors of the sciences, the social sciences, the humanities, and mathematics. Not all of these are federally supported projects.

3. **Individual research and study projects.** Independent research projects permit pupils to carry on research in the school or community. The project may be related to class work or grow out of interests developed by talented pupils through class, reading, or discussions with teachers and scientists. In one school system, for example, pupils with high ability in science are assigned during the last two periods of the day to work in scientific laboratories in the community. In other schools, pupils are programmed certain periods to do independent study and group experiments.

The quality program that permits and encourages independent study for capable pupils actually frees them for part of the day to work in laboratories, the library, learning centers, shops, and other laboratory-type areas. The program provides time when these facilities are free from scheduled classes and when librarians, teachers, and other resource persons also have time scheduled for conferences and individual assistance as requested by pupils. This concept really means freedom to explore one's own interests, not supervised study nor projects that have to be "handed in." Foreign language laboratories, laboratories with programmed learning, and computer-based devices are available for outstanding students.

Differentiation Within Classes

Adaptation of the curriculum to individual differences should be a part of all classes whether grouped homogeneously or heterogeneously. Grouping and regrouping within regular-sized classes and within large classes for team teaching is one way of making adaptations to groups. Another way is to allow pupils time to work as individuals part or all of the time when the group meets.

Differentiation for those pupils who have greater intellectual or other giftedness means more alternatives for pupils in the learning act and an absence of rigidity and prescription on a group basis. Pupils make critical and analytical reports orally and in writing. They interpret ideas, generalize, make comparisons and contrasts, deal with relationships, analyze philosophical ideas. They examine the dynamics behind events and analyze the historical and sociological processes that have shaped events, the times, and literary figures. They do library research and research papers. They are allowed to try out new ideas, new styles of writing, new techniques of craftsmanship. Emphasis is placed on the experience of phrasing good questions, the right questions in order to probe into something. Much field work and survey work may be done in the community.

The experience of being objective and scientific in one's approach to questions characterizes classroom work for the talented. Objectivity in observation, exactness of definition and meaning, developing hypotheses, the testing of ideas, identification of fallacies in thinking, deductive reasoning, doing controlled experimentation, and arriving at conclusions based on evidence are essential ingredients. In all of these experiences, the more gifted the pupil, the more he may work with greater abstractions.

Basically, these high-quality intellectual experiences are possible in relation to any subject matter that is not composed of just a relatively simple skill. Subjects such as business education, art, and music are certainly no exception to this generalization. It is the limited concept placed on these subjects by teachers and administrators that has created the slow learner image for them.

THE CREATIVE

Studies in creativity have caused educators to take a new look at the high achiever and the highly intelligent pupil as measured by I.Q. Will he necessarily be the inventor, the outstanding artist, the imaginative architect, or the researcher who breaks through knowledge barriers? Does working for high marks or high achievement as measured by examinations given in schools and colleges promote such original thinking? Evidently not, according to the research findings.

Creative Behavior

If creativity is defined in terms of behavior, one does not have to argue whether or not "creativity" is a vague term that does not lend itself to research, any more than one argues the same point about "intelligence." Adaptability, originality, imagination, inventiveness, and non-conformity can be defined in terms of what the pupil does, how he writes, tackles problems, reacts to what he reads, and puts together in different forms. A teacher can look for certain clues in spotting creative behavior. For example, the creative tend to be more open, less hemmed in, in their feelings and emotions. They tend to prefer perceiving rather than judging. They ask irritating, probing questions. They are keen observers and interpreters of experience. They tend to be independent in thought and action, refusing to agree with flat statements, often getting bored with routine classroom assignments leveled at the mythical average. They play with words, ideas, music, and materials to try to come up with new combinations and forms. They prefer the unconventional. Even an unconventional career choice can be a clue.

The investigations of creativity by Torrance, Getzels and Jackson, Barron, Calvin Taylor, Guilford, and others provide some other leads to the teacher if he is willing to accept them. The academically talented, the highly intelligent pupils, are preferred by teachers over the highly creative. The former tend to receive the higher marks in school; yet, both groups score equally well on standardized achievement tests. In other words, their academic achievement is equally superior, even though the more creative average lower scores on intelligence tests. (Intelligence tests miss identifying about two-thirds to three-fourths of the creative.) Most pupils have been taught to look for correct and "right" answers. The divergent thinker has survived this experience and rejects what convention in ideas or forms says is right. The pupil may exhibit bizarre behavior in clothing or dress, a form of superficial non-conformity or perhaps a rebellion against being allowed to be different in thought and actions. He may rebel against what to him is stupid "correctness," such as the ritual of protocol. Most disturbing to teachers should be the clue that children are penalized in school for being different.[3]

Adaptations in the Curriculum

The problem then is not only to help gifted children become more creative, to act in the manner described above, but also to help all children act more creatively. Every child has some creative ability, often latent, perhaps never developed. Again it is a matter of degree; a child has more or less of what is defined as "creative."

Nor is creativity measured by absolute, adult standards, for absolutism is the very antithesis of creativity. It is a relative term in more than one way. Children who give of themselves, who create some-

[3] See evidence for statements in this paragraph in Jacob W. Getzels and Philip W. Jackson, *Creativity and Intelligence: Explorations with Gifted Students,* New York: John Wiley & Sons, Inc., 1962, 293 pp., and research references of the other authors mentioned on pp. 278–84 of this reference.

thing of themselves that is unique and satisfying for them, are creative not in the sense of world-stirring products but in a highly personal sense.

The adequate, totally functioning person is creative not because he avoids conflict and is always happy but because he can deal with conflict. In fact, he accepts himself for what he is and will often have to create conflict for himself in order to function properly. If he succumbs to convention, he narrows his own range of creativity.

These concepts have meaning for the curriculum. But we know more about how creativity is stifled than how it is promoted. Actually, the whole idea of creativity is annoying as a gadfly to both teachers and researchers, since it refuses to be confined to numerical symbols, or to be easily codified, classified, and processed. The human, the beautiful, and the artistic products of man are not so neatly arranged.

A number of conditions or actions of teachers, parents, and other adults tend to stifle creativity. Among these are setting mediocre standards for one and all, giving inflexible assignments, demanding quiet and orderliness to the point of suppressing spontaneous expression or enjoyment, overvaluing authority of the book, considering mistakes in learning as wrong rather than as a process of learning, asking pupils to fill in blanks, using force or threat.

Asking a pupil to do an assignment because "I told you to" is a form of behavior that values non-thinking pupils. They do not need to know the reasons. They need no purpose for what they do. In other words, they are being prepared not to cope with but to fit into an age of automation.

The dispenser and enforcer of rules, the person for whom rules are made for rules' sake only, is likely to be a non-creative teacher himself. These are managerial rather than human considerations. He sees the need for formality and correct behavior, but he does not see what an overdose of correctness does to the individual's creative healthiness. Concern for minutiae, the details, and correctness of usage characterizes small rather than expansive, open minds. Moreover, such actions are not in accord with scholarly research in linguistics. Pigeon-holing, classifying, and tunneling mark the demands of a teacher who tends to restrict original, imaginative behavior and fantasy. Any action that resembles these more extreme behaviors on the part of teachers might dampen curiosity and creativity.

The experiences that foster the development of the potential creativity of the pupil are closer to autonomy in learning. The individual is encouraged to explore, write, experiment, read. He lives in a school that shows that it values differences by providing richness in laboratories and libraries. His teacher shows that differences in ideas are valued. He feels free to question or challenge the teacher's statements if they appear unsound, dogmatic, or wrong. He perceives the classroom as a place where experimentation, brainstorming, and imagination are possible. He has the skills, the experiences, and the tools of knowledge with which to do the experimenting and imagining.

The teacher who encourages creativity of mind, spirit, and hands is a well-educated person as well as a flexible individual. He must be, to feel secure enough to be challenged; a teacher who knows little would find questions a threat to him. He welcomes argument. He stresses alternatives in solutions, answers, and books. He makes it clear that pupils have the freedom to raise questions about anything; he does not hesitate to show that he too is a constant, inquisitive learner and the more he knows the more he questions what he knows. He stresses the affective, sensory experiences as well as the cognitive. He prefers individual to mass activity, abhors awards and prizes as tinsel reasons for learning. He demands good questions rather than answers and frees the pupil from too much external evaluation, always a threat to the unique. He discusses with pupils any ideas they may have and shows that he relishes such discussion. He emphasizes problems that require seeing relationships and restructuring. Learning readiness is not a holding-back operation with him. Above all, he places a premium on self-initiated, independent learning, and catches the moment when the spark of originality, the questioning and curiosity appear.

The difficulties a teacher faces in giving opportunity for experiences of this nature are both external and internal. The schedule may be confining. Pupils have no place to explore outside the classroom, or the regulations may prohibit it. The teacher may be unable to let his own imagination go or to free himself from previously learned concepts. He may find that he tends to analyze rather than synthesize, judge too quickly, furnish the answers, and make conclusions before he has all the facts. He may find, as some studies show, that the teacher with creative traits is rated below average in teaching ability.

The nature of the newer developments in content which accent open-endedness lend themselves to nurturing creativity. These developments are a far cry from some interpretations that are placed on learning academic subjects. Actually they open up new avenues of exploration. They do not confine any pupil to a mediocre base but, in the hands of creative teachers, serve as a medium for further learning.

Learning Centers

Since the opportunity to be creative parallels the opportunity to be oneself and to develop one's latent powers, the secondary school should be the laboratory for individuality. In a school that values differences, there would be laboratories of various kinds: the natural laboratory of the community, of the shop, of the farm, of science, of research in industrial processes, of the Peace Corps type both abroad and at home, of the school community, of reading, of available centers of information, of programmed instruction, and other kinds of laboratories where students can experiment, practice, or study, often on their own under only as much guidance as necessary. The laboratory work in many instances would grow out of or relate to classroom work.

A number of new secondary school facilities have well-designed learning centers. A laboratory school, for example, is moving toward a continuous progress plan where students move at their own rate and spend one-half of their time in independent study. The independent study is done in the instructional materials center, which is equipped with auto-instructional materials, monaural tapes, videotaped lessons, teaching machines, tutorial devices, reference books, and study kits. The teacher is a guide of learning activities, assisting students in investigations and experimentation. A number of secondary schools have been designed in similar fashion to a junior high school in a Far Western state, which has individual study spaces combined with workshop laboratories in two main centers, a communications arts center, and a science–mathematics center. Included as a part of the latter are listening–viewing conference rooms and graphic arts space.

Two illustrations of learning laboratories are given here.

1. **Laboratory for study of human behavior.** The secondary school pupil has much to learn from the areas of psychology, sociology, anthropology, and the general areas of human growth and development. The study of human behavior is the key to mental health, to human relationships which spell success or failure on a job, and to the solution of the conflicts among people whether on a local or international scale. Knowledge can be selected from the behavioral sciences, such as economics, psychiatry, political science, and biology.

Children are already in school. Teachers do not need to seek a place to observe and study children's behavior and growth. This kind of a laboratory is furnished by any group that meets and works together, including the very classroom in which students meet.

But there may well be a place in the school in which students will have available written materials, audio-visual materials, research studies, and expert assistance to delve into these studies. This would be a central focal point for studies of human behavior in the other laboratories available in school and community.

2. Laboratory for study of communication skills and international understanding. Such a laboratory would deal with a variety of communication skills and media: television, communications and electronics systems, language skills, speech skills, and language of behavior. There would be opportunity through the laboratory not only to improve one's skills but also to do experimentation on communication problems and to study the nature and evolution of language.

Language would be regarded in a broader perspective as a means of understanding other cultures and the problems facing new nations. The Peace Corps exchange idea would be practical for bringing native college students from other countries to the United States to serve as aides in laboratories of this nature. With the growing numbers of opportunities for exchange students, this laboratory could extend into foreign countries. The phenomenal growth in possibilities for travel can make it quite common for the young American to have been abroad by 1974. The schools have a responsibility to educate ambassadors of goodwill rather than obnoxious souvenir-hunters and thrill-seekers. Our youth have already demonstrated they can carry this responsibility well when they feel they have a mission to perform for their country and for international neighborliness.

Exchange studies of other cultures is an idea that countries abroad might eagerly enter into, an arrangement that places no one on an inferior basis. A little imaginative thinking such as some private organizations and public secondary schools have been doing would make possible first-hand, fruitful communication with other cultures for a greater number of our youth.

THE CULTURALLY HANDICAPPED UNDERACHIEVER

Beginning in the 1920's sociologists became interested in making studies of social classes in the United States, describing the class attitudes and ways of living, and relating these to schooling. In the 1930's, the Depression furnished a laboratory for the study of youth who were out of school, unemployed, unwanted, and unloved. A number of these studies were published under the National Youth Administration.[4] Educators were also concerned about early school-leavers, holding power, and retention. Most of the youth discussed in studies of this nature were from lower-class homes with distinct cultural handicaps.

With the concentration of minority groups in large cities and in the slum areas that breed juvenile delinquency and crime, the interest of educators in the 1960's again turned to children who suffer from cultural deprivation. Youth in these groups are still out of school and unemployed in large numbers. The terms used to describe these young people are legion: culturally deprived, disadvantaged, disaffected, alienated, underprivileged, and different; or reluctant learners, underachievers, slow learners, migrant children, and dropouts.

The first impression one gains is that these terms describe different categories of children. However, the more one reads the clearer it becomes that these are no sharp distinctions. The salvaging programs that have been developed for potential dropouts, for the culturally deprived, for the underachievers, and for slow learners have many common features. The lines become blurred. Social class, ability, and economic limitations are interwoven. In fact, the child who comes from a poor home with few cultural advantages is much more likely to be a dropout, a failure or slow learner in school, and one who achieves below his potential, than a child brought up in a home with many cultural advantages. To be sure, he may only appear to be a slow learner, but then any slow learner may potentially be an average to good student. The I.Q. identification is not infallible.

The studies made of intelligence tests that minimize the cultural disadvantages, the change in scores on tests that measure intelligence when the child's environment is changed, and the use of such concepts as "talented underachievers" and "the slow gifted child" emphasize the idea presented early in this chapter, that creativity and giftedness are relative matters.

Similarities and Differences

This section concentrates on the young person of secondary school age who is handicapped culturally and who is also an underachiever in school. The child who has an inadequate home and community background tends to have low achievement; to be over-age; to have a high failure rate; to be erratic in attendance; to have reading diffi-

[4] See Vernon E. Anderson and William T. Gruhn, *Principles and Practices of Secondary Education*, 2nd ed., New York: The Ronald Press Co., 1962, p. 102, for a list of references.

culties, poor motivation, unrealistic vocational goals, and an inadequate concept of himself. He may seem to be "non-verbal" but actually he is not. He can communicate well in a different quality language. He is likely to have negative attitudes toward school, and his parents' attitudes are not supportive of schooling. True, he is often a "reluctant" learner but this does not mean that he has low intelligence.

If, on top of the cultural deprivation of his living in slum conditions, the child is also from a migrant family of Spanish-Americans or Puerto Ricans, or from the Southern Appalachian region, he has even further handicaps of a lack of continuity of schooling.

These children are likely candidates for dropping out of school at as early an age as the law permits. For every school dropout from the upper and upper-middle classes there are more than thirty from upper-lower classes. Studies of dropouts tell that they are generally retarded in school and in reading, fail in one or more subjects, are underachievers, come from families where neither school attendance nor achievement is considered of much value. There are more non-whites than whites among dropouts, they are twice as likely to be unemployed as graduates, and later in life will probably be engaged in unskilled or semi-skilled jobs when at work. Before these pupils drop out of school, counselors report that they are often withdrawn, defiant, antagonistic toward school. Their reasons for dropping out are likely to be lack of interest in or dislike of school. In many cases, they reflect their parents' attitudes. But they are not all from the lower socio-economic classes. Some come from emotionally inadequate homes, in another sense just as "poor," broken homes, or homes where there is little love or respect for children. Culturally handicapped underachievers are not all the same nor one class of children.[5]

Juvenile delinquents are also individuals with individual problems. Although it is estimated that 95 per cent of the seventeen-year-old delinquents are school dropouts, not all dropouts are delinquent. Nor do they all come from slum areas. The coddled youngster who is indulged with a souped-up sports car that he is allowed to drive as he will, may also end up as a delinquent. His home environment is not necessarily "better" than his contemporary's in the city slums.

Studies of pupils who underachieve in school, those whose school progress belies their potential as measured by intelligence or other prognostic tests, reveal some, but not all, similar deficiencies. The one factor these studies reveal most often is the negative attitude

[5] "Graduates and Dropouts in the Labor Force," NEA Research Bulletin, 41: 120–21, December, 1963.

toward school. Research studies show that attitudes toward school, achievement motivation, social status and adjustment, parent attitudes, and identification with adults are related to school achievement. Some underachievers are "psychological dropouts" who sit in school seats but do not contribute much to class work. Many are also likely to have poor notions about themselves, for either they have been threatened with failure or some may have been failed so often that they assume they are non-learners. It has been estimated that from 15 to 30 per cent of able students are underachievers.

In 1960, about 40 per cent of the top third in intellectual ability did not go on to college, at a time when almost one-half of the high school graduates went to college.

The most persistent common thread that one finds in studies about dropouts, culturally deprived, or migrant children, unemployed youth, and juvenile delinquents is the parents' attitudes toward school. It is essentially negative (where there are no identifiable parents, this is still true of relatives or adults who are a part of their environment). Parents' attitudes are in turn influenced by their experiences in and with schools.

But these children are of a variety of types. We seldom hear of those who survive slum conditions to become good students. They should really be the cause for wonderment, surviving the seemingly insurmountable handicaps that are just as much of a burden as physical handicaps. Children from families that are poor economically can be scrupulously clean, morally strong, intellectually alive, and highly motivated by their parents toward an education. Any equating of these "groups" does a rank injustice to individuals. It may be helpful in developing programs and in dramatizing the situation to categorize children as "culturally deprived" or "potential dropouts" but we have to be extremely careful so that we do not think that anyone so categorized is like any other child. They are different, just as gifted children are different. In fact, some have unusual talents, often undeveloped.

Common Elements of Special Programs

A number of programs for children with cultural handicaps have been developed with the aid of foundation funds, such as the Great Cities Program in thirteen major cities, Higher Horizons in New York City, the Dropout Project in Chicago, The Job Upgrading Project in Detroit (some of these are a part of the Great Cities Project supported by Ford Foundation), The Project of School Dropouts of the

National Education Association, and others. Most of them are in urban areas. Although these programs usually include kindergarten through twelfth grade, it is at the junior and senior high school levels where most of the work is done. Many of these generalizations apply to the children of all ages and grades.

1. **Additional school personnel.** In these programs the pupil–teacher ratio is usually lower and classes are smaller because of added teachers. Moreover, specialists in remedial reading or other remedial work, health service personnel, visiting teachers, and counselors are added to the school. Especially noticeable is the addition of counselors to lower the counseling load of teachers.

2. **Careful selection and in-service preparation of teachers.** A common feature of the programs is that workshops, in-service programs, and planning sessions are held for teachers in order to help them understand the children with whom they work and to develop the skills needed. Teachers are rather carefully selected in the first place in terms of their sensitivity to intergroup relations and their human relations skills. In-service programs stress the intercultural interaction between teacher and pupils.

3. **Additional financial aid.** Many of the programs are supported by foundations, but schools may give added support. For example, in one large city school system, 10 per cent is added to the regular per capita costs for instruction in the special program.

4. **Modified organizational patterns.** Team teaching, block time, core programs, innovations in grouping, summer and work experience programs are typical of these projects. One Western state has a full-time employment–forestry project combined with study of conservation and biology in summer camps. Summer programs are frequently operated for migrant children.

5. **Modified curriculum and materials.** One of the major characteristics of the Great Cities Program is the willingness to experiment with a variety of types of materials and instructional media. All of these programs have adapted the curriculum and materials used, at least to some extent. For example, books dealing with familiar background have been written, units of study have been related to job opportunities, corrective and remedial reading has been included, intraschool cultural programs conducted, and an attempt has been made to build on the strengths these pupils have, such as the idea that slowness is an asset in many cases.

The national crash program of the summer of 1963, aimed at bringing dropouts back to school, was not a striking success since the former pupils came back to the same dreary curriculum that had previously only spelled frustration and unreality.

Even more important, perhaps, was the fact that the damage had been done earlier in school and at home. Most dropouts did not learn to read well in the earlier grades. They may have been placed in heterogeneous classes where they were unable to keep up. From many unfortunate experiences came the resulting deep-seated fears and attitudes toward self, school, teachers, and other adults.

6. **Direct parent–teacher relationships.** More visiting teachers have been added to work with parents, parents may be brought to school for afternoon and evening adult classes, or parents are reached through some other means of school–community coordination. These projects have recognized that unless parents' attitudes toward school and education are changed, the influence the school might have on the youngsters will be diminished. Consequently, the parents have been involved a great deal.

7. **Use of the community.** At the same time, other community persons are used to assist in the program, sometimes as aides for after-school recreation groups, for home study tutoring, and in similar ways. Field trips into the community are frequently a part of the curriculum. Welfare agencies, business establishments, and industries are also involved.

8. **Work–study programs.** One of the more significant community involvements is the work experience programs combined with school study to develop skills and work attitudes and in order to help the young people become economically independent. These programs are described in a following section.

Community–School Projects

The community–school cooperative features in the projects for the culturally deprived underachievers take the form of work in the community, community service, teacher–parent cooperation, and the use of community agencies and persons. These are not the exclusive features but they are prominent parts.

One of the best known of the broad programs involving the school and the community is the Higher Horizons program of New York City, described in Chapter 11, which includes pupils in junior high schools, and was established to reduce the waste of talent in low socio-economic neighborhoods.

A visit to a junior high school in Brooklyn in an area that is considered culturally deprived and is part of the Higher Horizons program reveals the nature of possible programs for slow learners.

Of significance is the allotment of additional staff members to the school in addition to those that are assigned on the basis of pupil–teacher ratios as determined by the Board of Education. In this particular school, approximately five additional people are assigned to work solely in the area of remedial instruction. These people work with the classroom teacher and during regular sessions each week take one-half the class while the regular teacher takes the other half. There is a close coordination between the two teachers. The remedial teacher trains the regular teacher in the skills needed for this type of instruction. The school has found this plan to be of value in raising the achievement level of the students by reducing class size and improving skills in remedial instruction.

Another part of this program is extensive cultural enrichment through experiences that are not a part of the children's everyday living: field trips to theatres, concerts, museums, and libraries, as well as trips to a business or industry. Teachers voluntarily take the pupils on trips even on Saturday because they feel the response from the children is so appreciative.

A particular type of class that exists in the school is the career guidance class. These classes are organized to supply suitable group guidance to junior high pupils who are potential dropouts. Most of them would be considered slow learners or pupils with serious retardation. Classes are held to fifteen. The class organization is on a ratio of approximately one professional person to twelve students. A guidance counselor is assigned on the basis of one for every six classes, or one for every ninety pupils. An interview, concentrated on helping the child in terms of vocational goals, and later placement in an occupation, is held weekly with each child. This counseling is supplemented by a job placement adviser at the Board of Education, who assists in looking for job opportunities as well as in providing vocational information. At present, only boys are included in these classes and the objective is to get them into the main stream of the population or the regular programs where possible.

Teachers of the slower youngsters teach one period less per week than other teachers as a compensation for their more difficult task. The career guidance program is in the process of developing a curriculum. In this school, pupils operate their own car wash business to provide them with some experiences of a very functional nature.

Job upgrading in which schools and local employers cooperate in work–study programs, often coupled with vocational classes, is found in many of the projects of the larger cities especially.

The School for Employment Program (STEP) in New York State is a work experience program for potential dropouts in the state's largest cities. The program includes largely senior high schools and a few junior high schools, and a "600" school, an experimental sheltered workshop in New York City. Pupils perform paid work in private industry as a supervised school course. In some instances stipends are used, when the school must find work assignments in schools or in other public agencies.

The program attempts to create a climate favorable to change of attitudes to make transition from school to work easier, and to attack the problem of juvenile delinquency. Teacher-coordinators work with both industries and parents and also serve as guidance counselors. The major concern in the job training is the development of proper work habits and attitudes.

Pupils are not isolated from the rest of the school. They spend at least a two-period block together in the morning and work in industry in the afternoon. They attend some classes with other pupils and participate in school activities.

These programs, as well as job upgrading programs in other cities, have selected the pupils who have poor records of achievement, indifferent or negative attitudes, delinquent behavior, and irresponsibility. One city selects dropouts after they have been out of school and unemployed long enough to see the futility of it and wish to return to school. Many schools do this in different programs, including those for overaged ninth and tenth graders.

One city has an after-school program for 14- to 17-year-old youth when training is given in low-order skills. Each shop produces a saleable item not being manufactured by industry. A number of programs may run short courses to make youth employable in the shortest period of time.

A second type of project in cooperation with the community is based on the community service concept. Service to one's fellow men has been the focal point of Peace Corps activities. Similar activities could be conducted in local communities. There is no dearth of service opportunities in hospitals, orphanages, and economically deprived areas. In a junior high school in an Eastern state, a group of pupils from culturally disadvantaged areas took on as a project the improvement of a local park, where they constructed a fireplace and play areas.

Programs for Talented Underachievers

Some schools have made attempts to devise programs for the top 15 to 30 per cent who are underachievers. A senior high school in a New England state developed a three-year project beginning with thirteen tenth-grade pupils who had reading ability and mental ability above the 85th percentile, a history of superior academic performance at some level, and recent unsatisfactory achievement. The pupils were assigned to guidance counselors who had interviews with the pupils and their parents. These counselors met with the teachers of the selected underachievers in a case-study type of conference. Early in the study, one of the chief improvements noted was that the faculty learned how to deal with the pupil who had talent but was not utilizing it effectively.

Evaluation and Results

Some of the schools coordinating these projects have employed a program evaluator. At least one city system has a full-time research assistant in each school taking part in the study. Almost all of these schools make some attempts to evaluate the program but few have developed research studies on the level of a six-year controlled experiment in a Midwestern city.

The findings that are reported in the evaluations include reduced dropouts, reduced non-promotion, improved attendance, improved achievement, better school morale and citizenship, decreased reading retardation, greater motivation of pupils. The evaluation of the Higher Horizons program revealed that pupils gained an average of thirteen I.Q. points in three years, that 40 per cent more pupils finished high school than in similar groups in these same schools before the program began, and that three and one-half times as many went into some form of post-secondary education.[6]

The results also show that teachers develop more perceptive insights. They listen more, develop a teaching style suitable to these pupils, and understand them better as individuals. One of the most important factors that makes a difference is the assignment of appropriate teachers who understand these pupils, their homes, and their learning difficulties. As significant, perhaps, is the different attitude that parents take, becoming more supportive of their children

[6] Daniel Schreiber, "Promising Practices Gleaned from a Year of Study," *Phi Delta Kappan*, 44:220, February, 1963.

and the school. More than one of these projects found that the most significant changes occurred in pupils, teachers, and parents when a single school staff was involved with its community in working on its local problems.

THE SLOW LEARNER

The slow learner is usually considered as a pupil who because of somatic, cultural, social, and psychological factors is unable to achieve school tasks as well as the average pupils for his age and grade. The intelligence test categorization merely cuts the pie another way. In this case, the end result (I.Q.) is emphasized, not the cause of the difficulty (underprivileged, culturally deprived). It is a more absolute definition than "underachievers" since it assumes that once and for all a pupil will be classed as dull-normal. "Underachievers" is relative and presages a hope for betterment in the future. Factors that cause slow learning may be abnormalities of the brain or illness, or they may be cultural or psychological in nature.

Curriculum adjustments in the classroom usually include brief assignments, practical applications, frequent review, the teaching of skills and concepts at a slower pace, a variety of activities, use of audio-visual aids, planned experiences in success even in simple tasks, and assistance with reading problems.

In an English communications course in a Southern city, a great deal of practice in these skills is given in class, pupils are encouraged to read voluntarily, a number of paperbacks of simpler language are used, and failure is not emphasized. Another experimental English program for slow learners is characterized by unorthodox scheduling, lay readers, increased reading and writing assignments, and individual instruction in reading. A program in vocational training for slow learners aged 15 to 21 has been developed in a Midwestern city, in which ten staff members work with fifty pupils in a separate small building. A cooperative work–study arrangement has been developed with business and industry. A large Eastern county school system has corrective reading teachers in each school. Pupils leave their regular class to work with this teacher for one-half to one hour, three to five days a week.

A junior high school in a Western state has coordinated an experimental program for the "lower 30 per cent." This group will take four years to complete the three years of junior high school in an ungraded group. A reading program, study skills, and guidance are special areas of concentration in the curriculum developed for this group. Some of the most capable teachers with special preparation are assigned to teach in this program.

THE MENTALLY, PHYSICALLY, AND EMOTIONALLY HANDICAPPED

This section concerns those pupils in secondary schools who, because of their handicap, need to be placed in special classes in public schools, or, in the more severe cases, in special schools. It does not deal with the slow learner for whom curriculum adaptations were discussed in the last section. The I.Q., in many cases, is by far the least important criterion for placing a child in a special class.

The children of school age who need special education are estimated as constituting 10 to 15 per cent of the entire school population of the nation, less in some communities, more in others. Approximately one-fourth of these children are enrolled in special classes or other special programs. About 15 per cent of the children enrolled in special education programs are in the secondary grades. At the secondary school level, in 1958–1959 about 83 per cent of all school districts offered special provisions for the so-called mentally retarded, 44 per cent for the speech impaired, 39 per cent for the crippled, and from 9 to 33 per cent for other types of disabilities.[7] The types of handicaps are discussed in Chapter 11.

Often the special classes are ungraded and may typically contain children of both upper elementary and secondary school age. The same kinds of services described for elementary school pupils are available for secondary school pupils. Programs at the secondary level have adaptations similar to those discussed for elementary schools.

As frequently pointed out, the differences found among children with handicaps are differences in degree, not kind. Some learn more slowly than others because of their handicaps. Some cannot learn many things which a typical child can. Learning "up to grade level" is even more of a myth for handicapped pupils than for the others. Some children have multiple disabilities, but frequently teachers misjudge the hard of hearing, partially seeing, or emotionally maladjusted as also having lower mental learning potentialities than normal children.

[7] Romaine P. Mackie, *et al.*, *Statistics for Exceptional Children and Youth*, 1957–1958, Biennial Survey of Education in the United States, 1956–1958, Chapter 5, U. S. Department of Health, Education, and Welfare, Office of Education, Washington, D. C.: Government Printing Office, 1963, p. 4.

Most of the special education programs for handicapped pupils are full-time or part-time special classes or special day schools. The programs discussed here deal especially with pupils in regular public schools who spend part of their time in special classes and part in the regular classes. Deaf or blind children are usually provided for in special day or residential schools but the trend even with these children is to include them with normal children's classes as much as possible. Speech impaired pupils are assisted by speech therapists, who generally work with them individually. Handicaps such as cerebral palsy, cardiac disorders, epilepsy, emotional disturbances that need psychiatric care, glandular disorders, and severe mental retardation present problems which most secondary schools are not equipped to cope with. Many of these cases may be homebound.

The secondary schools have generally made provision for classes for the mentally retarded in which specially prepared teachers work with smaller groups, much of the time in individualized instruction. The classes are usually scheduled for a half-day or longer block of time for their general education, while the rest of the time they may be with other children in physical activities, music, art, or other special areas. Placement in these classes is a flexible arrangement, whereby a pupil may move back to regular classes full-time if judged ready to do so.

Special classes are provided on a district-wide basis concentrated in one or more secondary schools. Small school systems may band together to provide special instruction and services.

The programs for mentally retarded stress civic and social skills; physical fitness; mental health; manipulative tasks; learning how to communicate, to follow directions, to be a member of a family, to live safely, to manage one's money, and to appreciate music; leisure time activities; and occupational education that deals with work habits and simpler routine tasks. Field trips, community service, and many kinds of visual teaching aids are part of the experiences provided.

ISSUES AND POINTS OF VIEW

Of the issues that relate to provision for individual differences in the school, most are concerned with the pupil at the upper level of ability. No one questions the need for individualization. The "how" becomes the issue. At the same time, while there is a clamor for special attention to the gifted and organization upon organization works for the interests of the handicapped, the persistent and annoying question keeps buzzing in the background: What of the middle or so-called average group?

1. *Should the schools concentrate on creative acts or on creative people?*

We can ask ourselves a good many questions about what we do as teachers that affects a tendency toward being original and inventive. What behavior, for example, do these middle-class values produce in children? Be popular and well-liked by peers. Be energetic and industrious. Be willing to accept the judgment of authorities. Be receptive to ideas of others. These are traits ranked high by teachers. Do they help to produce a creative individual, or a socially acceptable individual? These are disturbing questions, for no one wants wholly unpopular, lazy, defiant, prejudiced children in a society that takes pride in principles of cooperation and human relations. However, the extremes are not well tolerated by society. Some of the most highly creative people in the arts were extremely unhappy souls at odds with the world.

But these extremes may represent non-creative acts, not non-creative people. A pupil can be courteous, popular, and receptive of ideas without being a conformist in thought. He is likely, however, not to care too much whether he says what everyone else says or whether he adopts manners and slogans which in themselves may be the height of discourtesy. The youngster who throws beer cans on the side of the road, drinks, and smokes is a conformist rather than a non-conformist. He may be rebelling against someone in authority, but such actions do not make him either liked, respected, or different. He is one of the "herd."

There are related questions that should also be asked. Is a pupil underachieving from the standpoint of creativity, if he does not measure up to what his intelligence test scores would indicate? Does the emphasis on academic achievement tend to stifle creativity? Some would contend that it does. Greater pressure and anxiety are no more helpful for the gifted than for the average child. Threat of heightened competition for college can build up such a pressure that it bursts in the form of increased mental breakdowns for secondary school youth—an unwise condition which mitigates against what its perpetrators hope to promote: optimum development.

2. *Should the academically talented secondary school student be accelerated in his school program, or should he proceed through the school years at the same pace as other students?*

Acceleration through school by such means as taking fewer years to complete high school and advanced placement in college has been opposed on the grounds that it will seriously affect the student's emotional and social adjustment. He may not be able to adapt himself to an older, more socially and physically mature group that has different interests. Some fear that the younger adolescent placed with college freshmen may become a recluse or run into serious social maladjustment. The accelerated student will have fewer chances for leadership experiences. The pressures may deny the able student time needed for reflection and exploration. Serious gaps may be left in his educational achievement. Moreover, an adolescent may mature more rapidly in some areas; wholesale acceleration would assume that he matures equally in all areas. The proponents of this point of view quote a few studies of Advanced Placement programs which show that students sometimes feel the placement in college classes earlier is not worthwhile.

The proponents of acceleration have presented arguments more strongly supported by research. They indicate that bright students who complete secondary school at age 16 or 17 are more likely to go on to college, do better in college, and are more likely to graduate than those of the usual entering age. Investigations of senior high school youth who had completed junior high school in two years instead of three show that they did as well or better than the non-accelerated. The students who entered college at the end of their junior year under the Ford Foundation experiment not only did better than their older colleagues of matched abilities but were reported by their parents as gaining in maturity. The studies of Pressey and others definitely reveal that the accelerated pupil adapts himself well to those who are older. More cogent arguments, perhaps, deal with the fact that a person's most creative accomplishments are in early adult life, that the saving of a year enables the student to enter into graduate work and a career earlier, now that the professions require more preparation, and that he can sooner contribute to professional manpower needs. Young people who go into medicine and law, for example, will be at the threshold of middle age before getting started on their career.

Yet, acceleration and enrichment are not mutually exclusive. The third position, and the most promising one, is a flexibility of advancement through school in a genuine individual, continuous progress where one year builds upon the next. Non-graded schools are based on this principle. So is the de-emphasis of completion of school for youth who will enter into semiprofessional and skilled occupations, and the emphasis instead on continued schooling whether full- or part-time. Where the student is placed in school might be flexible, for it is not as important a factor as how much he can learn in an age where more learning is required and more knowledge is available to be learned.

3. *Should exceptional pupils of any kind be segregated in special classes for instruction, or should they be taught in regular classrooms?*

The argument has been heated at times, especially concerning the gifted, but the issue concerns the handicapped pupil as well.

Snobbery and undemocratic procedures are the labels often attached to special classes for the academically talented by those who oppose them. They claim that students in other sections are likely to feel "lower" or inferior to those in the special groups. The most valid argument against special classes is the tendency of administrators or teachers to accept the fact of having the special group per se as adjustment in the curriculum, and the likely result of considering all students in the special class alike. This is not, however, a necessary result. There is much need for developing appropriate instructional materials adapted to the bright or the dull, otherwise grouping serves no purpose. Evidence in some studies seems to indicate that segregation of the extreme upper 2 or 3 per cent of the student body does not necessarily mean improved experiences.

Proponents of special classes for exceptional children point out that equality of opportunity does not mean an equal program for all. Special classes make it possible for the physically or mentally handicapped or the gifted to have a program best suited for them. Failure to provide for each individual to develop his potential to the utmost is undemocratic. When the range of differences is narrowed, the teacher has a greater possibility of meeting individual differences. Teachers can be prepared specially to work with children with different types of exceptionality, and size of class, programs, and materials can be more readily adjusted to their needs. Bright students succeed better and go at a faster pace in homogeneous classes.

The issue is much like the ones on grouping and on the self-contained classroom discussed in Chapters 10 and 11.

14

IMPACT OF TECHNOLOGY
ON THE CURRICULUM

Some of the more significant curriculum developments that have been presented in the preceding chapters are characterized by the continual search for individualizing instruction. This quest for the ultimate in learning for each child is a rational hope. The rather phenomenal growth of electronic devices that can aid learning may portend that this ideal is not as visionary or as illusory as it has seemed.

The discussion in this chapter centers on the meaning for the curriculum of the technological changes that apply to the educational process, the potentialities and limitations of different newer instructional media for improving teaching, and the issues that arise. Developments in television, programmed instruction, and other media are placed within the larger focus of the technological revolution as it affects society and the schools. The how-to-do-it and the mechanical intricacies and problems of using devices have no place in this discussion. The question of schedule is a minor question, irritating but solvable.

APPLICATION OF TECHNOLOGY TO THE
EDUCATIONAL PROCESS

Technology applied to instruction is but one of the aspects of the impact made on the curriculum by technical advances. It is but one problem in a much larger and more significant complex of questions discussed in Chapter 4. The definition of technology is pertinent to consideration of any devices to promote learning: the sum total of all tools and techniques invented by man since the beginning of time in order to make work easier or to perform some task more effectively.

The need for speedup of learning in a more efficient manner is unquestionable in view of the increase of knowledge and demand for greater specialization. We have known through research how to teach better; we have not always been able to apply this knowledge in the classroom. The possibilities for individualization of instruction are enhanced by the newer devices, and there is a promise of more self-control of learning and less adult supervision if we learn how to use them well. The sequential order of learning made possible is a type of control of learning.

Schramm makes the provoking statement that programmed instruction is essentially a revolutionary device that "has the potential to help free man from some of his bondage—the waste of human resources where there are no teachers or where people cannot go to school; the waste of time and talent where all students are locked into the same pace, and all teachers into the same routine; the tyranny of tradition which permits the study of a certain topic to begin only at a certain age, and expects a student to accomplish only so much as a questionable test of his ability says he can do; the inadequacy of outmoded and inadequate curricula. . . ." [1] Is he right, or is this just sales talk?

Since machines have no purposes, they are of dubious value in the hands of teachers who also have no purposes or whose purposes are fuzzy, obsolete, or inimical to a democratic society. The motion picture, for example, has had a checkered career as to its intelligent use for educational purposes.

It is, therefore, important to distinguish between unimaginative and creative uses of television, tapes, programmed instruction, computers, or other electronic devices or audio-visual aids. There is a danger of hardening some pattern of the use of these instruments into a rigid technology. This may come about if we focus on the machine instead of the learning process, the machinery instead of the idea. A parallel can be drawn for any innovation that crystallizes into a pattern and loses the vitality of the idea, the experimentalism, and the flexibility which were its substance. In some places machines are a status symbol. The administrator can show off the hardware. He can say that "we have *it*," just as schools may say they have team teaching, in order to be in the swing of things. This chapter attempts

[1] Wilbur Schramm, *Programed Instruction: Today and Tomorrow*, New York: The Fund for the Advancement of Education, 1962, p. 38.

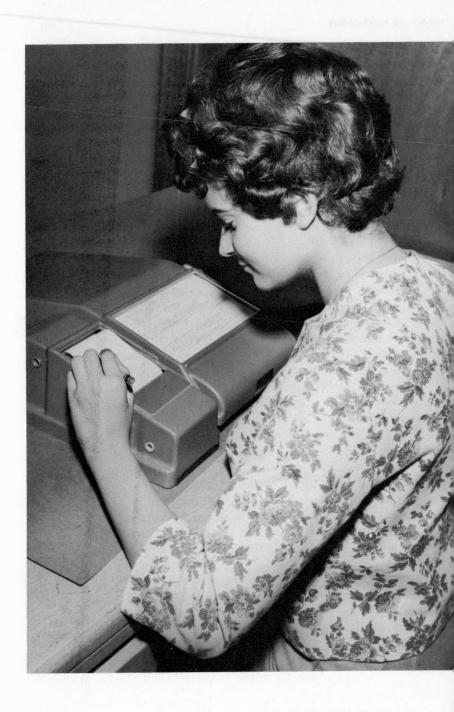

to focus on the potential imaginative and positive uses of the newer educational media, and the potential dangers of their undiscriminatory and unimaginative use.

The growth of instructional technology has been rapid since about 1935. World War II gave an impetus to its use in the post-war period. Earlier development included especially the projector, films, and slides. The application of television to instruction came about largely through Ford Foundation projects since 1955. The use of language laboratories and teaching machines has largely developed since 1960. Computers and instructional systems are of an even more recent origin.

Instructional technological developments in use at the time of this writing are listed below. This list will, in all probability, be augmented in a year or two.

1. Projection media: motion pictures (8 and 16 mm, sound and silent), photographic slides and handmade lantern slides, transparencies and overlays, pictures and objects for opaque projections, micro-projection, and the various projectors used with each of the above media.
2. Television and radio: closed circuit TV, airborne TV, stratavision and Telstar, videotape and kinescopes, including the portable videotape recorder.
3. Magnetic tape, making possible the use of the tape recorder, language laboratories, the computer; videotape.
4. Electronics teaching laboratories; language laboratories, mobile laboratories, classroom communication systems.
5. Duplicating devices, flexiwriter (automated typewriter), desk calculator, ditto, mimeograph, Xerox, and photocopy.
6. Self-instruction machines, and the programs for these devices.
7. Telephone recorders, teletest systems, and tele-lecture.
8. Recordings on conventional disc records, thermoplastic recordings.
9. Models, mockups, graphics, collections, and specimens.
10. Computers and data processing.
11. Simulators.
12. Instructional systems combining several types of media into an organized, logical system of instruction.

Discussed in this chapter are these more recent media: television, programmed instruction, computers and data processing, and the integrated systems approach.

TELEVISION

Growth of ETV

There is little doubt about the impact of television on the curriculum. In 1961, at least three million pupils in 7,500 elementary and secondary schools were receiving part of their instruction through courses on educational television stations. A study made by the University of Nebraska about the same time found 453 recorded television courses in existence, available for distribution throughout the country. The majority of these were for elementary and secondary schools, where the idea had taken hold faster than in colleges and universities.[2] By 1960–1961 there were 260 courses programmed live on closed circuit by schools and colleges and 569 courses given live by ETV stations.

The recent growth of television, and particularly educational television, can be visualized by the fact that in 1946 there were only six authorized, non-experimental television stations in the United States and only 6,500 receivers. Today's college student born in 1947 can immediately call to mind the present maze of television aerials even in the poorer districts of a city.

Educational television did not receive its impetus until 1952 when the Federal Communications Commission set aside 242 channels for educational purposes (since raised to a greater number). The first ETV station began operating in Houston, Texas, in 1953. By June, 1964, there were 88 such stations in operation, with about two new applications being filed each month. By 1966, there should be about 200 stations. Further growth was encouraged by the Educational TV Facilities Act in 1962, providing 32 million dollars to support TV as a teaching medium. The Ford Foundation has been interested in educational television and has helped to support its development in schools and colleges through grants for equipment and research.

An example of a state that has developed a program is Florida, where, in 1962, six ETV stations were coordinated by a Commission and sixteen channels were reserved for further expansion. It has a network of several stations, connecting by microwave relay the state-supported colleges and universities. There were in that year 286,000 students in Florida public schools and colleges receiving formal course instruction through television in nearly 900 educational institutions.

[2] Wesley Meierhenry and Jack McBride, "Exchange of Instructional Television: Report of the Nebraska Survey," in *Educational Television: The Next Ten Years*, Stanford: The Institute for Communication Research, 1962, pp. 266–85.

One-third of all ETV broadcasting time is required to be devoted to higher education in that state.

Two types of circuits for telecasting are available, the open and the closed circuits. The open circuits, used by all commercial stations, telecast by microwave on very high frequency (VHF) channels (a restricted number), or on ultra high frequency (UHF). Because of the availability of a larger number of channels on UHF, this is the type usually used by ETV. The closed circuit system is used by a greater number of educational institutions since it is more flexible, can carry several programs at once, and is more flexible for instructional programming. It uses the medium of a cable that is run to the various classrooms.

The rather recent replacement, by the videotape recorder, of kinescopes or filming of telecasts for future reproduction was a tremendous step forward since it provided through the use of magnetic tape a simpler process of high quality recording and storing of both the picture and the sound.

One of the more unique developments has been the Midwest Program on Airborne Television Instruction (MPATI). Covering parts of six Midwestern states, with headquarters at Purdue University, MPATI telecasts from a plane with a transmitter that can telecast five hours a day, Monday through Thursday, to an area requiring fourteen conventional transmitters. Financed by the Ford Foundation, it began in 1961 to offer such courses as modern algebra, new biology, general science, mathematics for the gifted, and foreign languages for the elementary grades. Courses are for elementary school, high school, and college levels. Plans were for more than seventy-five courses by 1965.

Research Findings

The general conclusion from many research studies both at the public school and the college level is that students learn about as much from a televised course as from a course using conventional classroom methods. In 1962, 425 studies of experimental instructional television with adequate research design were summarized. In 393 of these, TV teaching was compared with conventional methods. In these latter studies no significant differences were found in 65 per cent of the cases; significant differences in favor of television in 21 per cent of the cases; and significant differences showing that television instruction was inferior, in 14 per cent of the cases.[3]

[3] Wilbur Schramm, "Learning from Television Instruction," *Review of Educational Research*, 32:156–67, April, 1962.

Differences appear, however, among the subjects taught and grade levels. Subjects which gain from demonstrations, such as science, tend to be more successfully taught on television than language arts skills. The evidence indicates that television instruction is more effective in the elementary grades than in high school or college.

Studies of student attitudes toward instructional television indicate that elementary school pupils think they learn more from televised classes than do high school or college students. Home-bound pupils are also more favorable toward television.[4] As children grow older they become more used to television instruction. Perhaps the novelty "halo" wears off and young people become more sophisticated. However, attitudes seem to depend upon who teaches the course and reaction to the teacher, as well as what is taught.

Teacher attitudes vary with the fields but elementary school teachers tend to be the most favorable. College teachers are least favorable. The popular notion that educators are critical or fearful of television instruction is not borne out by these studies. In four large school systems in different parts of the nation, the proportion of teachers who believed students learned more from television classes was greater than those who believed pupils learned less.[5] It may be that those who have not participated in television instruction compose most of the skeptics.

Advantages, Problems, Disadvantages, and Unanswered Questions

The teacher and curriculum leader will find many advantages cited for television instruction. Most of them are the result of experience rather than research and need to be weighed carefully.

Television instruction makes it possible for outstanding teachers to reach more pupils.

When a teacher goes before a television camera, he must be better prepared. Both scholarship and teaching procedures are judged more rigorously. The dull, the ineffective, the poorly organized cannot survive.

More courses become available for small secondary and elementary schools. Small schools of fewer than 100 pupils in the Midwest Airborne Television area, for example, can offer subjects such as modern mathematics, advanced chemistry, art, music, or foreign languages, which would otherwise be impossible for most of them to offer since their faculty are not prepared in the particular field of specialty.

4 *Ibid.*, pp. 160–61.
5 *Ibid.*, pp. 162–64.

A more recent development of the portable videotape recorder for taping programs for repeated use on television, and for duplicate copies, makes it possible to bring TV programs to schools at much less cost than closed circuit television.

Television brings to pupils the resources of museums, art galleries, libraries, prominent artists and musicians, and industrial plants. Television brings to the classroom the actual national and world events live, as they occur.

More time is required for planning and the teacher is freed for planning and preparation time. Teams of studio and classroom teachers and members of the production staff work together.

Television capitalizes not only on competency but also on specialization. Undoubtedly, a number of teachers reading this book will have taken courses under Continental Classroom and other programs from outstanding specialists selected nation-wide.

Instruction by television is not without its problems, as many teachers and principals can verify. The scheduling problem bedevils the administrator. Buildings that were constructed for the teacher in a classroom of thirty pupils are not planned or equipped for this type of instruction. Perhaps the most serious handicap is the lack of feedback and discussion among students and teacher. This problem is being remedied so that there can be two-way communication, and in all probability will be advanced to allow even more interplay of minds in the next few years. The quality of the program is not always good, nor do all subjects lend themselves well to television instruction. But the same things can be said about the quality of teaching.

Substitution of large classes per se as a means of taking care of the teacher shortage is an actual hindrance to development of instructional television. It is a rather unimaginative use of the device, which can be used for other more promising purposes.

Many of the studies that make claims for improved results in teaching by television were not actually research studies under any rigid controls. Some of the proponents who have a missionary zeal for television have done studies that set out to prove something.

One can ask many kinds of questions about the use of television for formal instruction in the classroom. Why should there not be more research on the use of television as a complement to classroom procedures rather than comparisons with conventional means? Why do studies usually compare large-classroom TV instruction with smaller-sized conventional instruction? Does this not indicate a built-in concept that really does not free itself from traditional forms? Perhaps we have asked the wrong questions.

Is it possible that some mediocre teachers because they realize that television instruction enlarges the scope of the better teacher oppose the method? If pupils learn as much from television as from other classroom methods, should it be possible to devise other organizational schemes to use teachers effectively? The use of teams of teachers is one approach discussed elsewhere in this book.

Generally, one would expect less learning from television courses because of the lack of give-and-take. Some of the outcomes important in close-knit instructional groups are undoubtedly not measured in the experiments because of a lack of valid instruments. All of these kinds of learnings have not been taken into consideration in studies of the effectiveness of television courses: acquisition of facts, skills and habits, understandings, ideals and attitudes, social skills and habits, and growth that comes from group activities. Typically only the first one or two of these has been measured. The factor of greater time for preparation of TV classes has not generally been ruled out in research. What would happen if other teachers were given the same planning time as TV teachers? One of the significant findings for curriculum improvement in one large county school system was that it was soon discovered that a studio teacher could not carry the usual load of classes but that more planning time was required to do the job. No significant curriculum improvement can be done without time for preparation and planning!

Some of the pro and con arguments for television seem to forget that in cases where small secondary schools do not have teachers who are specialists in some field, the choice is not always between television instruction and conventional instruction. It may be between television instruction and no instruction. The teacher who has taught in an elementary or high school of 60 pupils in a rural area never would make that mistake.

Informal Adult Education

In most discussions of educational television, its greatest potential for education is overlooked. Generally, it seems to be assumed that education occurs only in classrooms in formalized situations. Yet, we know this is not true. As an instrument for adult education outside the classroom, television has few equals. Attitudes and cultural mores have been changed by television. Breakfast foods, cigarettes, or beer sales are stepped up by television advertising. Children learn many things—good or bad—from television.

But the great majority of commercial programs for adult viewing consist of westerns, reruns, soap-opera drama, artificial doctor shows, murder mysteries, quiz shows, and old movies—the "great wasteland" of television. There is perhaps no other instrument of communication that has such universal use for as great a length of time, reaching as many members in the family as television does, and such great potential for adult education.

Good programs are appreciated. In communities where such programs as courses in Shakespeare have been offered, the audience has been much greater than anticipated, if the formal course-credit idea is not considered. "Playhouse 90" was a live ninety-minute dramatic program with original and imaginative plays written especially for the medium, whose demise was regretted by many. Yet, the invalid rating scheme and consequent lack of sponsor caused its being taken off the air.

Perhaps some foundation with vision will put a substantial grant into testing whether over a period of time unsponsored programs of public affairs, good drama and music, parent education, language instruction, and the like will be accepted by the public and can be made worthwhile for commercial sponsors.

Educational TV includes both the cultural and information aspects for adult audiences as well as the televised lesson. Both can be significant for adult education. Ninety per cent of those who "register" for formal television courses do not take them for credit. The vast audience that is unknown makes up a considerable portion of the viewers of these courses. Television is a most powerful instrument for adult education.

PROGRAMMED INSTRUCTION

Early Development

In any discussion of programmed instruction, it must be recognized that this is a relatively new aspect of educational technology. Authorities date the development of programmed instruction devices to about the late 1950's and early 1960's, beginning with the work of B. F. Skinner, psychologist at Harvard University. Sidney L. Pressey, psychologist at Ohio State University, who in 1924 developed a testing machine, is generally credited with inventing the forerunner of the modern-day teaching machine.

Other terms often used in the literature as synonymous with programmed instruction are "automated teaching," "auto-instruction," "self-instructional devices," "programmed learning," and "teaching machines." Some of these terms refer to the mechanical or other device used and some to the total process. "Programmed materials" refers to any media on which programs are developed: books, tapes, or cards, etc., for use in machines. "Programmed instruction" is used in this book since it is the total teaching–learning process in which the teacher or curriculum worker is interested. It is a preferable term since it encompasses the idea and the process, as well as the device used.

Any number of self-instructional instruments are used for programming instruction, from the scrambled textbook to the complicated computer-based teaching machines. Texts using either a sliding panel or other device for covering up the answers, with pages "programmed" or "scrambled" so that they are not read by successive pages, were the most popular in 1964. The teaching machines were many and varied even at that early stage in the development of the technology. There were simulated teaching machines using punchboard devices, chemical answer sheets turning red or green, slides, card sorts, tab-pull devices, erasable silver overlays, all fairly much like the textbook type using printed media. The simpler type of actual machines used a paper-type written or constructed response. In addition, there were more complicated machines with a key response similar to a typewriter key, using printed media. Audio-visual machines of the projected media variety used magnetic tape, disc recorders, slides, or filmstrips, some having both the visual and audio aspects. Projected media types used constructed responses, audio responses, written responses, key responses. They varied from simpler machines to those using more complex keyboards. The computer controlled machine was the most complicated and highly developed of all.[6] Classroom communication systems using mass presentation with individual response by pressing keys, which made immediate group results available to the teacher, used combinations of the different technological media.

The visual portion of the program was on paper sheets, cards, discs, paper rolls, slides, filmstrips, motion pictures, computer tapes, punchcards, or in book form, depending upon the type of machine.

In a survey of programmed instruction in the United States in 1961–1962 the researchers found that 46 per cent of the schools responding had tried such programs on individual students and 80 per cent

[6] See James D. Finn and Donald G. Perrin, *Teaching Machines and Programed Learning: A Survey of the Industry, 1962,* U. S. Department of Health, Education, and Welfare, Office of Education, Washington, D. C.: Government Printing Office, 1962, pp. 35–49, for illustrations of types of machines.

on groups of students. About half of the schools using programmed materials were employing them for regular instruction. Other uses were for remedial instruction and for enrichment. Programs were used to a greater extent in secondary schools, the greatest number in the field of mathematics.[7] It was estimated that some 630 programs were available in 1962.

The data are given as a stage of development since in this field of technology as in others the changes are extremely rapid. Developments go on at an accelerating pace, outdistancing the research to test the concepts.

Theoretical Concepts and Research

Programmed learning has generally been based on two psychological principles: reinforcement and sequential steps. Learning itself is the stimulus and the reward. Since correct answers are made immediately available to the pupil, learning is reinforced by intrinsic rewards.

Some defining principles basic to programmed learning are:

1. Information is presented and frequent responses are required.
2. Immediate feedback is presented to the learner, informing him of the results.
3. The learner works individually, progressing at his own rate.
4. The material is sequential so that the learner proceeds to the next step only when he has learned the previous one.

In this communications system, the relation between the learner and the medium is a direct one. He learns from it without an intermediary in the process. The three basic elements of the system include the pupil, the program, and the device. For the teacher or curriculum worker, the program and the pupil are the essential elements, not the device. It is only a means to achieving learning by the pupil through the program. The program is based on the objectives of the school and the teacher.

Two main concepts of programming predominate at the time of

---

[7] Center for Programed Instruction, Inc., *The Use of Programed Instruction in U. S. Schools: Report of a Survey of the Use of Programed Instructional Materials in the Public Schools of the United States During the Year 1961–62*, U. S. Department of Health, Education, and Welfare, Office of Education, Washington, D. C.: Government Printing Office, 1963, pp. 10–11, 26.

this writing: linear or constructed response programs, identified with Skinner, and branching or intrinsic programming, identified with Dr. Norman Crowder. Considerable controversy exists as to which type is superior.

In linear programming, a pupil reads the questions or frames in the same sequence but proceeds in a straight-line fashion from the beginning to the end of the program. The pupil constructs a response from memory, assisted by cues in the beginning. Skinner holds that recalling an answer is superior in the learning process to recognizing one, as in choosing from several alternatives. The very act of recalling tends to cause learning. Another characteristic of linear programming is the short step, or small learning increments, by which it is made difficult for the learner to make a mistake. Essentially, then, this point of view regards programmed instruction as a teaching device that reinforces correct responses and minimizes incorrect ones. The Skinner program is based upon the reinforcement of a learned response.

In the branching type of program, the learner may branch off into more than one direction, since there may be more than one right answer. The learner is challenged by several alternative answers from which he must choose. Each alternative leads somewhere in a sequential learning pattern. Where wrong choices are obviously made, the learner is branched off and reviewed on materials missed and retested until he is able to return to the main program. The response is used mainly in guiding the learner through the program; wrong answers are not avoided. Errors are corrected before the learner proceeds. Teaching of concepts seems to be better suited to the branching style. Scrambled texts are of the branching program type.

Most important, of course, for the person interested in curriculum is the programming, no matter what the program type. Programmers need to be curriculum specialists, subject specialists, and specialists in learning and programming, working as a team. One suggestion for steps involved in a good program includes the following:

1. Specific and clear objectives for the program must be established at the outset.
2. The body of content involved in reaching the goal(s) must be identified.
3. Content must be broken down into small bits of learning (or increments) that are easily understood and mastered by the learner.
4. Increments must be arranged in learning sequence, together with the insertion of "cues" and "prompts" and review increments to assist in the assimilation process.
5. Each increment is arranged to be followed by a challenge in the

form of a question to be answered, a problem to be solved, or a function to be performed.

6. Provision is made to inform the learner of his success or to provide reinforcement after each challenge has been met.[8]

Programming experimentation involves using relatively short units, such as "Vocabulary Growth" and "Our Solar System."

The number of studies to test the hypotheses concerning programmed instruction are increasing rapidly. Most of those summarized here were conducted in the early 1960's. Two summaries of studies give more complete details of the findings and furnish the basis for these generalizations.[9]

The results have generally tended to favor programmed instruction when compared with conventional instruction. Although the differences are not great, it is generally concluded that programmed instruction is at least as good as conventional instruction when testing conventional outcomes of information and understanding, and perhaps more significant for the curriculum worker, that it takes less time, and that it is better than no instruction at all.

It is quite clear, however, from these studies that the machine is not what makes the difference. There was no significant difference between programs on teaching machines and programmed texts.

The findings do not always agree. Some of the studies found that as much can be learned in a given time by reading as by reading and responding. Some showed that students learn as much and require less time with covert responses (thinking the answers) as with overt responses. Pressey, who is a strong advocate for using programmed instruction as an adjunct to other modes of instruction, found that such adjunct instruction is superior to conventional classroom instruction alone. He also found that programmed materials were useful as an adjunct to planned independent study. In this use of programmed instruction to assist with independent study may be the important clue for curriculum workers.

The differences for fast and slow learners seem to offer interesting clues. Some linear programs become boring to bright pupils. Larger increments may be more suitable for the pupil who can move faster in his learning. The more promising results with slow learners

[8] Association for Supervision and Curriculum Development, *Using Current Curriculum Developments*, Washington, D. C.: National Education Association, 1963, p. 102.

[9] "Instructional Materials: Educational Media and Methodology," *Review of Educational Research*, 32:179–93, April, 1962.

"The Teacher and the Machine," *Journal of Educational Research*, 55:396-531, June–July, 1962.

should cause teachers and schools to examine their ways. In studies using mathematics content, for example, children who are labeled as "slow learners" have shown that this is what they actually are, not "non-learners" as often seems to be assumed. Slower-learning pupils learn the more difficult concepts—although more slowly—when they have the opportunity to take a step at a time. Usually, what happens in the classroom is that once the slow learner falls behind (in so-called "homogeneous" classes as well) he soon loses interest because he cannot keep up with the class. The pacing was not right for him as an individual.

This spread in the rate of learning argues for individualization of instruction. Research shows that in using programmed learning within a homogeneous group of pupils, some students will learn three times as fast as others. With college students as subjects, investigations report that students have completed individual courses in one-fourth of the usual time and that some students have completed a four-year undergraduate program in two calendar years. The speedup of learning in a time of explosion of knowledge is not an inconsequential matter. The best use is probably for different purposes and different kinds of learners.

The research throws no light on the question of whether linear programs or branching programs are superior. The results are rather contradictory. Some seem to indicate that for final results it makes no difference whether the learner gets the right answer 50 per cent of the time or 100 per cent of the time.

Undoubtedly, the greatest contribution of the reinforcement theory had been the upsurge of interest in learning studies, including the studies of how children learn different subjects. It may or may not be true that branching programs are more useful for learning concepts and choosing alternatives, and linear programs are best for learning rote materials. However, it is important to find out more about how children learn different behaviors, and what children learn best from what means. The most consequential outcome of these studies will probably be their contribution to learning theory. In that sense, programmed instruction represents a breakthrough in the unknowns of learning.

Potentialities for Curriculum Development

Programmed instruction is not manna from heaven. Nor is it the solution to all curriculum problems. The administrator who buys hardware in order to have an up-to-date school typifies the antithesis of a curriculum leader's or teacher's thoughtful, inquiring, more sensible approach. Although its greatest promise may be in the field of research on learning, programmed instruction offers a new way of looking at instructional problems. It offers some potentialities for curriculum development that bear examination. In that spirit, these potentialities are discussed here. Much still remains to be learned in determining how they may best be used.

1. **Individualization of instruction.** The thinking educator knows that we have nowhere come within sight of the goal of individualizing instruction in the public schools. The thousands of children added to the rolls every day in public schools; the extreme concentration of population in suburban areas, which has magnified the problem many times for school districts in those areas; and the shortage of qualified teachers have all contributed greatly to this failure. Another factor has been the lack of knowing how to do it. The critic who condemns the schools but who never works for bond issues and more funds for operating expenses makes the problem even harder.

The curriculum leader should be the first to see the potential that programmed instruction has for making individual instructional programs a reality. It offers, first of all, a way of talking about individual differences. The focus placed on the learning process and on how children learn under different conditions is promising. The fact that there is a differentiation in the time taken for children of different pacing abilities in learning takes the idea of individual progress out of the talking stage to the action stage. Yet, programmed instruction has by no means reached its potential. Giving bright, average, and dull children the same materials is not individualizing instruction.

We have grouped children in classrooms for learning and have given differentiated assignments to a certain extent. We have further subgrouped in ability groups or within classes to take care of individual differences. We have constructed tracks to follow. But we have only guessed at whether or not the children were following a track of their own, building learning upon learning, at a really individual place. Actually, all kinds of groups—large or small—may have kept us from building programs for individuals.

Probably the most provocative idea engendered by programmed instruction experimentation is that learning has no limits for the individual, at least no absolute limits that may ever be discovered. The pacing of learning so that material is learned in different lengths of time suggests this. The sound barriers of knowledge about learning may be broken through, but such an event will be only a step.

Schramm, Director of the Institute for Communications Research at Stanford University, makes this statement:

Just as the classical concepts of absolute time and space in Newtonian physics hindered for a long time the development of relativity theory, so did the classical concepts of absolute thresholds, absolute ability and intelligence, absolute readiness, and so forth, for a long time hinder the development of a true science of behavior, and in particular the application of such a science to education.[10]

2. Development of sequence in the curriculum. The promise held for developing sequence in terms of the individual pupil relates directly to individualizing the program for him. If he learns at his optimum rate, he has the possibility of having a sequence that can move him to higher levels of learning—that is, if curriculum workers know how to write programs that will accomplish this objective. The problem is discussed further in Chapter 6.

3. Development of objectives in behavioral terms. Curriculum and research leaders have long spoken out against broad, vague kinds of objectives that cannot be translated into behavior. The psychologist, working with the educator on programmed learning experiments, has insisted that these objectives be in terms of what the pupil does. This is essential to breaking learning activities up into small sequential steps. It is one of the important characteristics of making a program effective. The desired end product must be specified clearly.

4. Constant re-examination of subject matter. As discussed in Chapter 6, the greatly increased accumulation of the world's knowledge has created a problem for updating the curriculum as well as for selecting what is to be learned. Programming requires that content be examined as to how it is organized and how it can best be learned. Should programming find a way to keep knowledge fresh and stimulating, it will contribute to the curriculum workers' solution of this monumental problem. The reduction of teaching time is another means by which programmed instruction may contribute to the solution of this problem.

5. Introduction of new subjects. The process of adding new subjects to the curriculum in small schools where the number of teachers is limited has always been a problem. The shortage of competent teachers in a number of fields, and in rural areas, has intensified the problem. The programming of subjects offers the possibility of pu-

10 Wilbur Schramm, *Programed Instruction: Today and Tomorrow,* New York: The Fund for the Advancement of Education, 1962, p. 20.

pils' being introduced to fields for which no competent teacher is available.

Problems and Unanswered Questions

The unanswered questions in programmed instruction will be by far greater than the answered ones at any year in which this book may be read. For new discoveries about learning and programming for learning will open up many other avenues for inquiry.

One of the needs is to study the various uses, techniques, and conditions under which programmed instruction will be most effective. Few studies compare the adjunct use of programmed learning with conventional approaches used alone. Should programmed instruction be used for a whole unit or course? Is the best response to use the open-ended one or the structured (constructed) response? Could independent study alone accomplish as much? What should be the size of steps? How many cues should be provided? Is there something wrong with a process that does not result in more active learning than the constructed response?

Broader and more significant questions include the following: For what kind of teaching can it be most effectively used—remedial work, practice, enrichment? What subjects, skills, concepts, or levels of learning can best be taught through this means? For what kind of learner are its various forms most useful? What shall be programmed? State or city courses of study?

Can conventional standardized tests be used with programmed instruction to measure primarily how far an individual has gone in his learning? Should test-makers conceive of their objective as selecting the kinds of instructional methods best suited for different individuals?

Will learning accomplished through conditioning be synthesized by the pupil into a total pattern? Do human beings organize their learning in the linear fashion? What quality in programming produces effective learning? Will the success built into programs provide the necessary motivation for underachievers? Will it increase the numbers of classrooms where subjects can be taught at an earlier age?

Some of the problems facing schools are whether or not to use programmed learning, in what kinds of situations to use it, and what type to use in view of effectiveness and costs. Questions of a fundamental nature are determining the limits of what can be accomplished by this instructional process. Should it be used in connection with independent study alone or for a total program? One of the limitations is the insight into values that can be gained. Programmed instruction still is rather limited in learning skimming for main ideas, problem-solving, concept formation, synthesizing, making judgments, integrative behavior, although the proponents make claims for many of these types of learnings. Its use has largely overemphasized facts.

There has been somewhat of an unfortunate tendency for some commercial companies to sell the machines as the important aspect of programmed instruction. A lucrative market has been offered, although the product has been untested. The emphasis on the machine overshadowed that on the program. "The lay public and many school boards and school administrators had filed programmed instruction with water-coolers and air-conditioning, rather than with curricula and teaching method.[11]

The challenges to well-accepted practices are great enough to make us uncomfortable about classrooms with all pupils taught at the same pace, about the concept of what is teaching, and about the concept of testing. One of the challenges facing the teacher and programmers is to use the programs in exciting, new ways with perhaps variations of combinations of schedules, units, and types of programs. Programs could be built for pupils of different achievement levels. Pupils' attitudes and reactions need to be considered. Teacher educators need to prepare teachers in programming techniques and in the intelligent use of programmed instruction.

One thing seems unmistakably clear. Our notion of the teacher's role is being shaken up. The teaching machine or other means of programming instruction will do the presentation of facts better than a teacher can. This changing concept, long advocated in the professional literature, has been slow in coming. This does not mean replacement of the teacher, a weak argument often used by mediocre teachers to cover up their inadequacies, but a freeing of the teacher from some tasks in order to do others. There is left more room for creativity, sensitivity to pupils' needs, interaction of minds, evaluation activities, and individual work with pupils. The problem is that only creative teachers can use creatively the time freed from more routine tasks. The task-maker tends to love his chains. The 1962 survey of programmed instruction in the United States found that 60 per cent of the schools saw the role of the teacher as an active supplement to the program, and only 11 per cent saw the teacher's role as being limited to that of proctoring only.[12]

11 *Ibid.*, p. 16.
12 Center for Programed Instruction, Inc., *op. cit.*, p. 32.

COMPUTERS AND DATA PROCESSING

Less research and discussion have been devoted to the digital computer as a medium for instruction. Yet, here is a system of storage and retrieval that is a revolution in itself. Already librarians with foresight are seeing the value for them of computer science as a field. It has limitless possibilities for storing, recalling, selecting, and transmitting data. These are the basic elements of instruction.

Perhaps the reason is that computers have been used at first largely for recording and storing pupil data, test data, and teacher data, for registration, for scheduling, and for financial and payroll purposes. These are more of the bookkeeping type of chores done by school systems. As data were fed into computers for storage and future use, it became obvious that such information about pupils could be used for finding out more about the pupil population. Studies could be made comparing different pupil and teacher groups, marks, test scores, and the like.

The computer has come into its own as a significant research instrument. The fact that data can be processed at incredible speed has been a boon to researchers. In fact, no respectable university that hopes to do research can today afford to be without a large-scale computer. It marks the beginning of a new era of research with possibilities for the treatment of multiple variables in educational research.

This chapter is concerned with the broader aspects of instruction, not mere record-keeping and transmittal. The processing of educational data, the scheduling of students into classes, storing of test data, storing information on diagnostic interviews, supplying forecasts for school management decisions, automating library services, and conducting research are all important activities complementary to instruction. The fact that all data about pupils in a school system can be processed and studied and made available instantly to teachers through the use of the computer, is not an inconsequential matter. Serving up information about pupils on demand by the teacher provides a basis for individual attention. The possibilities for storage and immediate transmittal from library to library all over the world not only for research findings, but any written materials, staggers the imagination. An individualized high school schedule for each pupil enrolled, programming him into a section and a classroom, makes for efficiency and greater possibility for individualizing programs of studies.

Computers can also be used more directly for instruction. They can be used as an auto-instructional device for adapting instruction to individual differences and have potential for handling pupils of varied learning rates. Computer-based teaching machines are being used as research tools in universities and other institutions.[13]

The computer differs from other teaching machines in that it is the only instrument that can determine the item sequence and knowledge of results to be presented to the student as well as carry out the processing upon which this determination will be based. Computer-based teaching machines may use slides or films, for example, for presenting a visual display. The typewriter keyboard handles the input by the student. Evaluation information for the student as to his performance may be presented on the page printer of the typewriter used for input.

In 1963, a majority of the junior colleges in one state were offering to students some type of training in the use of automatic data processing, varying from simple machine skills training to programming of large-scale computers. By 1964, some sixteen subjects were taught by computer to high school pupils in one state.

In addition to processing data on teachers' retirement, certification, and accreditation, on facilities, and on pupils, state departments of education in some states program textbooks and are able to give information regarding what, for example, might be contained in textbooks used in the state.

The computer is a language system limited only by the extent to which people are capable of feeding it information. A large part of what has been called thinking can be done by computers, according to computer science experts. Such questions as what processes can be described by means of certain language and how one can translate one such language into another are being studied by computer scientists.

INTEGRATED EDUCATIONAL SYSTEMS

At the apex of instructional technology stands the potential integrated educational system, a total communications system. Proposals have been made for automated, computer-controlled electronics systems of total teaching, data storage and processing, and research.

[13] Don D. Bushnell, "Computer-Based Teaching Machines," *The Journal of Educational Research,* 55:528–31, June–July, 1962.

This type of system, which may seem like science fiction to the teacher, is already a reality in the minds of researchers and scientists. Research has just begun toward the use of such integrated systems that would combine with the computer many of the media now in use such as television, films, slides, and tape recorders. The future of most of the typical audio-visual aids is in all likelihood as parts of combinations of media. A systems approach would mean that objectives, learning process, content, methods of presentation, would be studied and combined into a system of instruction.

There already are prototypes of this type of system. The language laboratory exemplifies a system of instruction that utilizes both mass instruction and individual instruction. The laboratory in its better developed form permits the teacher to monitor all individual pupil stations, record and summarize their answers, and give individual instruction as necessary. The language laboratory, in some schools, has been used in a broader way, for independent study and for music instruction as well. Experimentation is taking place with visual devices as a part of the system and with the use of the laboratory as a complete, programmed, self-instruction course.

Another currently used system, in a simpler form, is the classroom communications system which uses mass presentation and individual response, already mentioned. Slides, tape, television, or filmstrips are used in combination as a part of the system.

The potential integrated system would simulate many of the functions of the teacher in a digital computer combined with other types of media. Such a system would contain means for unlimited storage of information for counseling and teaching. Not only that, but it would perform the teaching act in mass and individualized instruction form, and many of the counseling acts. Instructor-instruction characteristics data would be used for quality control. Fast access to data would be available for student classification, guidance, effectiveness of instruction, evaluative studies of other kinds, and programmed instruction. Revision of information for instruction could be handled by the computer, with day-by-day or week-by-week upgrading and revision of the programmed instruction.

Simultaneous individual instruction would be possible for up to over a thousand students. Long-distance data links with other communications centers would be possible (some are now in use). Continual re-evaluation of the student in light of his own personal data would be possible. So would student group interaction. Storage would be made of all instructional information required by the total education system. For individualized instruction, each pupil would follow his own schedule and his own rate with automatic generation of instructional sequences for individual pupil use.

The type of system envisioned would be capable of guiding the learning process on a scale never imagined previously. It would be sensitive to needs of learners of different types and their backgrounds and difficulties, with the possibility of arranging conditions suited to each. Each pupil would work at a pace suited to him. Any courses would be immediately available without the scheduling problems of airborne or other television programs. Since pupils would have access to immediate exchange of libraries all over the world, the pupil in one area would not be deprived of knowledge now available to those living in "favored" areas. Processing of all data for pupil transfer to other schools and colleges could take place with a moment's notice. The availability of and possibilities for use of data for research would be unlimited.

Is this a visionary picture? Some would say this is a daydream not likely to work out. Perhaps not; only time will tell. Every one of these processes now exists, in some cases in limited experimental form, but not in an integrated system. It certainly sounds like an educational Utopia. Perhaps a more important question is: What would we do with this "Utopia"? Would it be suppressed as have some inventions that might have ruined a flourishing industry? How do educators see it—as a boon to learning or as a threat? Do we have enough ingenuity and vision to discover how to use such a system effectively? That is a most crucial question we cannot afford to look at lightly. Whether or not it comes to pass, or will be in operation at some time during the useful life of this book is not a technical but a human question, with all the impact of any revolutionary industrial process. This discussion is not an argument for integrated systems; it is only an argument for an open-minded approach to the question.

ISSUES AND POINTS OF VIEW

In this chapter have been discussed the stimulus–response types of devices, such as programmed instruction, the computer, communications systems, and the stimulus device of television. Most of the devices such as the motion picture and slides, and the response devices, such as the desk calculator, which are not at present any great issue, have not been discussed at length. Their importance in instruction is recognized but they are, more and more, tending to become combined into more than one kind of device such as in the case of the tape recorder and the opaque projector. They are becoming, on the forefront of experimentation, integral parts of communication systems.

1. *To what extent will instructional technology replace the teacher, or to what extent will it enhance both the power and prestige of the teaching profession?*

This is not a simple question of will it or will it not replace the teacher. The alternatives may be replacement of the teacher by the machine or continuing in the same pattern of teaching that has existed for a long time. Either would be a futile outlook.

Some contend that automation of the teaching process is a real threat to the teacher. Such a picture of the potential of the future as drawn in the last section may uncommonly disturb us. These new instruments, and especially one that can simulate the functions of an ideal teacher, tend to place an emotional block in front of us, preventing any thoughtful or analytic approach. We may act like the staunch party member who, when someone from another political party discusses an opposite point of view, does not hear a thing. The things we stand for in education, such as the platform or policies adopted by the national professional organization to which we hold allegiance, the emotional arguments, the educational cliches—all may get in the way.

These new instruments can frighten us because they seem to be able to do more than man. So could the "new" invention of the automobile, the airplane, and gunpowder. But they proved useful or destructive instruments as man learned to use them. There are weaknesses and limitations of programmed instruction and television but most of these are limitations of the programmer, not the instrument. Even the camera cannot be blamed for the likeness its products reveal.

There is not likely to be any technological unemployment because of the use of newer media of instruction. But there is likely to be a modification of the traditional role of the teacher or the librarian. Much depends on how we define the act of teaching. If it is simply telling, then the machines of various types are likely to be able to do it as well or better. If it is a lively interaction and interplay of minds, ideas, and feelings, then we will use the machine as an adjunct to teaching better than we have ever taught before. If the machine requires that as teachers on any level we define teaching objectives in behavioral terms, what we want children or youth to learn to do, then it may indeed be a welcome device. It is well to keep in mind that the pupil learns from the program fed into the machine, not from the machine.

There is probably little doubt that instructional technology may or even should replace some ill-prepared teachers, who either cannot or will not keep up with content or technological developments and who function like machines, doing damage to the child's emotional development. Teacher education institutions for years ahead, according to the best estimates, will not be able to supply the needs for teachers fully certificated to teach. Some educators say that we have outgrown the myth of replacing the teacher but the question seems to crop up disturbingly every now and then in teachers' minds.

It would scarcely be possible, however, for any kind of highly complex machine to replace the teacher and the warm, human relationships between teacher and pupil, unless we saw learning as having a ceiling. If there is a known point to which man (or any pupil) can go in his learning and not possibly be able to go any further, then the replacement argument becomes a tenable one. But even programmed instruction itself, or the devil "teaching machine," points toward the view that there is no such limit, even for the mentally handicapped. Other research implies the same thing. A limited view of learning is not compatible with the development of instructional technology, which has a potential of helping the learner to learn more in less time than ever before.

2. *What will be the role of the teacher in a time when a communications system can perform as well or better some of the tasks that he now performs?*

Some advocates of auto-instruction say the teacher's being freed to do concept teaching and more creative teaching through use of instructional technology is a spurious argument. For, they say, programmed instruction can do more than routinized tasks and rote learning. It has potential for teaching concepts, problem-solving, critical thinking, generalization, appreciation, and the like. Any behavior that can be defined operationally can be programmed. If creativity has any significant meaning, it implies that the unknown barriers of knowledge can be broken through.

Others hold that the teacher will be freed to do more creative tasks if he knows how to be creative. He will need to be far more highly specialized because undoubtedly he will perform more specialized tasks. Among these will be the important task of programming the machine. Programming requires knowledge of objectives and content to a fine degree. The television teacher found that he had to be a better prepared teacher but also a *different* teacher from a straight lecturer. We will need teachers who will decide what machines should do and how to put together into systems what is to be learned. Freeing a teacher may mean freeing him to do individual counseling, helping, diagnosing learning difficulties, developing individual programs on the basis of background and capabilities, integrating educational experiences, interpreting implications, working with pupils on value-choice and interpreting and analyzing data, individual experiments, and—by all means—helping to extend learning into unexplored, complex fields. Such teaching should sound exciting to bright young people who may consider teaching as a possible profession.

The teacher's role will be modified. He will find more use for all resources of the school and the community. No longer will he see "teacher" as a person in front of the room dispensing questions. The teacher in the language laboratory is not such a figure, except one who was heard to use the apparatus for asking pupils to translate and read back to him, one at a time, their translations!

What if the future means that teacher contacts with pupils will be far more of the individual type than in a mass group? The classroom as a means of instruction is by no means the only effective organization.

3. *Will mechanization and automation of instruction lead to curriculum rigidity and stereotyped learning, or will it enhance the possibilities of a more individualized and creative type of learning?*

The real threat lies in the direction of stereotyping learning, making it a deadly, dull process. We should recognize that the potential is there. If educators are fascinated by the hardware, become manipulators of gadgets, and want to teach only facts, there is indeed this possibility. The superficial concept of technology could lead to overlooking the essential elements of learning, the human touches, the emotional side, the development of attitudes and appreciations, and contacts with interesting human beings with their consequent social gains.

Cited as arguments against the use of programmed learning, or caution in its use, are these:

1. The program by its nature tends to emphasize facts and neglect other important learning.
2. A poor reader is handicapped by any medium which demands the use of reading skills.
3. The programs are not well suited to the bright or the dull child.
4. A linear program is a relatively fixed and arbitrary sequence set up by an adult specialist.
5. Programmed textbooks make it possible for the pupil to cheat.

6. It does not make adequate provision for individual instruction since it emphasizes differences in rate of learning only, not needed differences in instructional materials that will appeal to youngsters who are different in interests, backgrounds, and needs.
7. There is no substitute for teacher–pupil interaction in the classroom.
8. Any other kind of teaching device is more expensive than books if one is to provide it in sufficient quantity.[14]

Is it appropriate provision for individualized instruction to have all children use the same programmed materials, only faster? Would that develop their capacities? Perhaps no more so than the same book material. But the question again hinges on how well teachers can learn how to use the machine (any auto-instructional or audio-visual device), which is neutral. It could serve evil ends or good ends. Teachers and society as a whole would still have to choose educational objectives. If unimaginative, stolid teachers programmed into tapes, computers, television, or other device materials that stultified thinking, taught wrong concepts, and made for rigidity of the mind, those are the results that would likely occur. The danger of focusing on passive reception in a formalized program is a real one.

On the other hand imaginative, human, interesting, and competent teachers can use educational technology creatively. There is little doubt that some audio-visual aids and other media will be able to utilize programs for more of the creative types of learning—although much remains to be done. They may cause us to look at the "fat" in the curriculum, and, even more important, to scrutinize objectives in relation to procedures and content more carefully.

The answer lies in the individual who programs and operates the machine. We should not minimize the dangers of increasing conformity of answers through applying technology to the educational process, teaching by television or by machine that allows for no feedback or interaction or by any stimulus–response process. Devices do not change educational goals. The question-and-answer, the discussion, the lecture, or any technique of presenting knowledge can and most certainly has been used for purposes of increasing conformity to the teacher's beliefs. Technology can devour creativity only if the goals and methods foster conformity and sameness.

[14] See Harl R. Douglass (ed.), *The High School Curriculum*, New York: The Ronald Press Co., 1964, pp. 157–59 and 204–5; and Harl R. Douglass, *Trends and Issues in Secondary Education*, Washington, D. C.: Center for Applied Research in Education, Inc., 1962, pp. 46–47.

4. *Is there an inherent danger in the development of instructional control of programs falling into the hands of powerful commercial interests or the national government, or will national origin of programs lead to a gradual breakdown of regionalism and of state lines without any adverse effects?*

There is, of course, the danger of any powerful instrument of communication being controlled by certain groups who do not always have the best interests of the public in mind. Witness the commercial television programs. But the controls over education exercised through state departments of education and local boards of education would seem to be an adequate safeguard. Some would feel that it would be well if we had a national curriculum with the control of evaluation as well resting in the federal government. Most Americans doubtless are averse to such a policy.

But educators need to be vigilant so that groups with the capital do not make the educational decisions as to what is to be programmed. The age of technology, which makes for centralization, argues even more strongly for local control over education.

State lines and regional or provincial attitudes have little meaning for education that is aiming toward developing more international understanding. Perhaps the national origin of programs will serve for greater unification of people. International programs, exchange of programs, and transmission of data may do the same on a worldwide scale. It has this potential.

SELECTED REFERENCES

Alberty, Harold B., and Elsie J. Alberty. *Reorganizing the High-School Curriculum.* 3rd ed. New York: The Macmillan Co., 1962, Section II. This section on determining the structure of the curriculum has numerous examples and discusses issues concerning general education, specialized education, and the scope and sequence of the modern secondary school curriculum.

American Association of School Administrators, and Research Division, National Educational Association. Circular No. 2. *School Programs for the Disadvantaged.* Washington, D. C.: National Education Association, 1963, 63 pp.
Presents summaries and descriptions of special projects or other efforts in behalf of the disadvantaged in forty-two local school districts.

Anderson, Vernon E., and William T. Gruhn. *Principles and Practices of Secondary Education.* 2nd ed. New York: The Ronald Press Co., 1962, chaps. 7–11, 20.
The present author and a colleague discuss at greater length trends, principles, and issues in the secondary school curriculum.

Association for Supervision and Curriculum Development. *Individualizing Instruction.* 1964 Yearbook. Washington, D. C.: National Education Association, 1964, chaps. 1, 4, and pp. 159–68.
Challenging and forward-looking statements on the relationships of teacher and individual learner as a basis for individualizing instruction.

Association for Supervision and Curriculum Development. *The Junior High School We Need.* Washington, D. C.: National Education Association, 1961, 37 pp.
Discusses the junior high school of today and the future, in the nature of a position statement.

Blough, Glenn O. *You and Your Child and Science.* Washington, D. C.: Department of Elementary School Principals and National Science Teachers Association, 1963, 28 pp.
An overview of elementary school science written for the layman by a specialist in the field.

Brickell, Henry M., et al. *Commissioners' 1961 Catalog of Educational Changes.* Albany, N. Y.: State Education Department, 1961, 200 pp.
Of value only for a quick overview of changes in secondary schools. Contains very brief statements of the changes and a few facts about them. A number describe secondary school practices.

Burton, William H., and Helen Heffernan. *The Step Beyond: Creativity.* Washington, D. C.: National Education Association, 1964. 30 pp.
Helps teachers look at creative activities of children.

Bushnell, Don D. (ed.). *The Automation of School Information Systems.* Monograph No. 1. Department of Audiovisual Instruction. Washington, D. C.: National Education Association, 1964, 134 pp.
School applications of electronic data processing, including chapters on retrieval of educational information and computer-based instructional systems.

Conant, James B. *Slums and Suburbs*. New York: McGraw-Hill Book Co., 1961, 147 pp.

A hard-hitting report on the conditions under which children live in city slums, and their schools as contrasted with those in wealthy suburbs; also, what the schools are and should be doing about the problems revealed.

Conant, James B. *The American High School Today*. New York: McGraw-Hill Book Co., 1959, 140 pp.

Contains recommendations for improving secondary education, some of which deal with curriculum organization problems. A significant, influential report based on visits to high schools.

Congreve, Willard J. "Learning Center—Catalyst for Change." *Educational Leadership*, 21:211–13, 247, January, 1964.

A picture of students working independently in a learning center in a high school laboratory school.

Copley, Frank O. *The American High School and the Talented Student*. Ann Arbor: University of Michigan Press, 1961, 92 pp.

Observations on acceleration, enrichment, the advanced placement program, early admission to college, and ability grouping. Written for parents and educators.

"Course Content Development in the Social Sciences." *Science Education News*. Washington, D. C.: American Association for the Advancement of Science, April, 1964, 8 pp.

Brief descriptions of ten major projects in the social sciences.

Dale, Edgar. "Technology Is More than Tools." *Educational Leadership*, 21:161–66, December, 1963.

An expert discusses issues and problems of educational technology.

Deans, Edwina. *Elementary School Mathematics: New Directions*. U. S. Department of Health, Education, and Welfare, Office of Education, Bulletin 1963, No. 13. Washington, D. C.: Government Printing Office, 1963, 116 pp.

Descriptions of programs devised to improve elementary school mathematics.

Douglass, Harl R. (ed.). *The High School Curriculum*. 3rd ed. New York: The Ronald Press Co., 1964, chaps. 8, 10, 13, 15, 17–25, 28–29.

One of the most up-to-date publications on the high school curriculum. Chapters written by specialists on trends in each of the subject areas.

Douglass, Harl R. *Trends and Issues in Secondary Education*. Washington, D. C.: Center for Applied Research in Education, 1962, chaps. 1–7, 10, 12.

A brief but comprehensive volume on such topics as curriculum offerings, content of subjects, team teaching and programmed learning, adapting instruction to the individual.

Educational Policies Commission. *Contemporary Issues in Elementary Education*. Washington, D. C.: National Education Association, 1960, 27 pp.

A brief examination of some of the issues current in 1960.

Educational Policies Commission. *Education and the Disadvantaged American*. Washington, D. C.: National Education Association, 1962, 39 pp.

A position statement on what the schools should do for children from culturally disadvantaged homes.

Educational Television: The Next Ten Years. Stanford: The Institute for Communication Research, 1962, 375 pp.

     A comprehensive compilation of information about television in education; articles written by various experts in the field.

Fleming, Robert S. (ed.). *Curriculum for Today's Boys and Girls.* Columbus, Ohio: Charles E. Merrill Books, Inc., 1963, chaps. 5–13.

     Directed to the teacher as a guide to the improvement of programs for elementary school children. These chapters deal with trends in the fields of elementary school curriculum.

Ford, Edmund A. *Rural Renaissance: Revitalizing Small High Schools.* U. S. Department of Health, Education, and Welfare, Office of Education, Bulletin 1961, No. 11. Washington, D. C.: Government Printing Office, 1961, 54 pp.

     Forward-looking experiments in small secondary schools in order to improve their programs and enrich their offerings.

Frazer, Dorothy M. *Deciding What to Teach.* Washington, D. C.: National Education Association, 1963, chaps. 3–6.

     The NEA's Project on Instruction reports on individualizing instruction, establishing balance in the curriculum, and teaching controversial issues, and makes a series of recommendations.

Frazier, Alexander (ed.). *Freeing Capacity to Learn.* Washington, D. C.: Association for Supervision and Curriculum Development, 1960, pp. 40–97.

     Discusses research studies on underachievement of able students and the mentally retarded.

Gallagher, James J. *Teaching the Gifted Child.* Boston: Allyn and Bacon, Inc., 1964, chaps. 8–9.

     Good all-around reference on the gifted child, with these chapters devoted to creativity, discovery, and inquiry.

Getzels, Jacob W., and Philip W. Jackson. *Creativity and Intelligence.* New York: John Wiley & Sons, Inc., 1962, chaps. 1–4.

     Explores relationships between creativity and intelligence and reports on studies made by the authors and others in exploration with gifted students.

Goodlad, John I. *Planning and Organizing for Teaching.* Washington, D. C.: National Education Association, 1963, 190 pp.

     One of the reports of the Project on Instruction. Discusses curriculum organization, school organization, classroom organization and use of time, space, and personnel. Contains a number of recommendations pertaining to both elementary and secondary schools.

Goodlad, John I. *School Curriculum Reform in the United States.* New York: The Fund for the Advancement of Education, 1964, 96 pp.

     A report on the major curriculum projects in the subject fields of mathematics, the sciences, the social sciences, English, and foreign languages. Also contains recommendations and an analysis of problems and issues.

Goodlad, John I., and Robert H. Anderson. *The Nongraded Elementary School.* Rev. ed. New York: Harcourt, Brace & World, Inc., 1963, 248 pp.

Reports research related to the non-graded school and describes organizations and practices in detail.

Haan, Aubrey. *Elementary School Curriculum: Theory and Research.* Boston: Allyn and Bacon, Inc., 1962, chaps. 8–10.

Presents frontiers in scope and sequence, experimental programs in science, mathematics, social studies, language arts, the arts, music, physical and health education in elementary schools. Stresses "the growing edge."

Haring, Norris G., and Lakin E. Phillips. *Educating Emotionally Disturbed Children.* New York: McGraw-Hill Book Co., 1962, chaps. 1 and 4.

Stresses the simplicity and practicality of a structured classroom for emotionally disturbed children. Emphasizes how teachers and parents can help the recovery of the emotionally disturbed child.

Hartsell, O. M. *Teaching Music in the Elementary School.* Washington, D. C.: Association for Supervision and Curriculum Development, 1963, 53 pp.

An overview of answers to teachers' questions about the music program, drawn from research and practice.

Havighurst, Robert J., *et al. Growing Up in River City.* New York: John Wiley & Sons, Inc., 1962, chap. 5.

The progress of youth through school and a study of the dropout problem in a high school of a Midwestern city.

Heath, Robert W. (ed.). *New Curricula.* New York: Harper & Row, Publishers, 1964, 292 pp.

Describes goals, history, and status of the significant curriculum projects in the subject fields.

Keesee, Elizabeth. *Modern Foreign Languages in the Elementary School: Teaching Techniques.* U. S. Department of Health, Education, and Welfare, Office of Education, Bulletin 1960, No. 29. Washington, D. C.: Government Printing Office, 1963, 65 pp.

Entire bulletin is devoted to effective procedures for teaching foreign languages in elementary schools.

Kough, Jack. *Practical Programs for the Gifted.* Chicago: Science Research Associates, Inc., 1960, Section III.

Identifies and describes some of the outstanding gifted child programs in the United States. Designed to be used as a reference work.

Lewis, Gertrude M. *Educating Children in Grades Four, Five, and Six.* U. S. Department of Health, Education, and Welfare, Office of Education, Bulletin 1958, No. 3. Washington, D. C.: Government Printing Office, 1960, Part II.

Emphasizes the responsibilities of the public elementary schools to children in a democratic society. Information on the curriculum in the middle grades.

Lounsbury, John H., and Jean V. Marani. *The Junior High School We Saw: One Day in an Eighth Grade.* Washington, D. C.: Association for Supervision and Curriculum Development, 1964, 78 pp.

A fascinating report of "shadow studies" in which skilled curriculum workers followed 102 eighth-grade youngsters throughout the school day, recording what they heard and saw. This study shows what the curriculum actually was like for these pupils in a junior high school.

Manpower Report of the President and a Report on Manpower Requirements, Resources, Utilization, and Training. U. S. Department of Labor. Washington, D. C.: Government Printing Office, 1963, 204 pp.

A resource reference on employment trends in the occupations, product demand, mobility of workers, and the future manpower needs and sources.

Money, John. *Reading Disability.* Baltimore: The Johns Hopkins Press, 1962, chap. 3.

Discusses in detail dyslexia as an educational phenomenon; its recognition and treatment. Summarizes the results of a corrective reading program and calls for the early identification of severe reading disabilities.

Moore, Bernice Milburn. *Juvenile Delinquency: Research, Theory, and Comment.* Washington, D. C.: Association for Supervision and Curriculum Development, 1958, 68 pp.

A useful brief summary of research on juvenile delinquency.

National Association of Secondary-School Principals. "A Look at Acceleration and Achievement." *Bulletin of the National Association of Secondary-School Principals,* 47:1–106, December, 1963.

Discusses latest trends and issues in specialized high schools, acceleration and enrichment, educating the academically talented and the gifted.

National Association of Secondary-School Principals. "Changing Secondary Schools." *Bulletin of the National Association of Secondary-School Principals,* 47:33–144, May, 1963.

Part II contains illustrations of changes in team teaching, flexible scheduling, the non-graded school, instructional technology, and curricular innovations. Descriptions of programs in specific schools.

National Association of Secondary-School Principals. *Locus of Change— Staff Utilization Studies.* Washington, D. C.: National Education Association, 1962, 321 pp.

The final report on the staff utilization studies dealing with use of team teaching, large and small classes, lay readers, and other innovations.

National Association of Secondary-School Principals. "Secondary-School Curricular Areas: Issues and Developments." *Bulletin of the National Association of Secondary-School Principals,* 47:1–168, November, 1963.

Contains recent information on trends in content and procedures in all of the secondary school subject fields.

National Association of Secondary-School Principals. "The Junior High School." *Bulletin of the National Association of Secondary-School Principals,* 47:1–86, October, 1963.

Position papers on junior high school issues and descriptions of curriculum changes in junior high school.

National Association of Secondary-School Principals. "What's Happening in English?" *Bulletin of the National Association of Secondary-School Principals,* 48:1–134, February, 1964.

Reports on experimental programs in secondary schools and developments under Project English.

National Education Association. *Schools for the Sixties.* Washington, D. C.: National Education Association, 1963, 146 pp.
A summary of recommendations made by the NEA's Project on Instruction. Contains thirty-three specific recommendations that would point the way to the future of secondary education, as well as elementary education.

National Education Association, Project on the Academically Talented Student. *Administration: Procedures and School Practices,* 1960, 223 pp. *Research on the Academically Talented Student,* 1961, 92 pp. Washington, D. C.: National Education Association.
These and several other bulletins published in 1959–1961 by the Project present research findings, practices in different subjects, practices in acceleration, grouping, and enrichment.

National Society for the Study of Education. *Individualizing Instruction.* Sixty-first Yearbook, Part I. Chicago: University of Chicago Press, 1962, chaps. 11–14.
This section deals with school practices for individualizing instruction, acceleration, ungraded school, grouping, presenting historical perspectives and current practices.

Parker, Don H. *Schooling for Individual Excellence.* New York: Thomas Nelson & Sons, 1963, 285 pp.
Based on the assumption that both traditional and progressive philosophies have failed in producing schooling for individual excellence, advocates pupils moving at their own rate in a "multilevel philosophy" with training (skills) and knowledge (using skills) considered separately in a structure of schooling. Raises good questions about the present organizational plans and procedures.

Programs for the Educationally Disadvantaged. U. S. Department of Health, Education, and Welfare, Office of Education, Bulletin 1963, No. 17. Washington, D. C.: Government Printing Office, 1963, 105 pp.
Contains papers presented at a conference in 1962 which described programs used, such as Higher Horizons and others in large cities.

Rosenbloom, Paul C. (ed.). *Modern Viewpoints in the Curriculum.* New York: McGraw-Hill Book Co., 1964, chaps. 5–16.
Reports of trends in secondary school curriculum fields written by scholars in these fields. For example, the new mathematics programs; the science programs in chemistry and biological sciences; and trends in art, music, and English are presented.

Russell, David H. *Children Learn to Read.* Boston: Ginn and Co., 1961, 612 pp.
A comprehensive and positive treatment of the total reading program.

Schramm, Wilbur. *Programed Instruction: Today and Tomorrow.* New York: Fund for the Advancement of Education, 1962, 74 pp.
A challenging, brief pamphlet on programmed instruction.

Schramm, Wilbur. *The Research on Programed Instruction: An Annotated Bibliography.* U. S. Department of Health, Education, and Welfare, Office of Education, Bulletin 1964, No. 35. Washington, D. C.: Government Printing Office, 1964, 114 pp.

Contains a well-annotated bibliography and a good introductory summary of the research to date.

Schramm, Wilbur, *et al. Four Cases of Programed Instruction.* New York: Fund for the Advancement of Education, 1964, 119 pp.
Contains a brief summary chapter on developments in programmed instruction and describes such programs in four different school systems.

Shane, Harold C., June Mulry, Mary Beddin, and Margaret Gillespie. *Improving Language Arts Instruction in the Elementary School.* Columbus, Ohio: Charles E. Merrill Books, Inc., 1962, chaps. 9, 15.
A comprehensive treatment of the language arts and their relation to child growth and development. Chapters 9 and 15 have suggestions for creative expression in the language arts. Contains an extensive bibliography on children's literature.

Shaplin, Judson T., and Henry F. Olds, Jr. (eds.). *Team Teaching.* New York: Harper & Row, Publishers, 1964, 430 pp.
The first textbook on team teaching. Contains a helpful appendix listing team teaching projects and available articles or pamphlets about them, plus a complete additional bibliography.

Strickland, Ruth. *The Contributions of Structural Linguistics to the Teaching of Reading, Writing, and Grammar in the Elementary School.* Bulletin, Vol. 38, No. 4. Bloomington, Indiana: Bureau of Educational Studies and Testing, School of Education, January, 1964, 44 pp.
Examines linguistics in relation to each of the above aspects of language arts.

Stoddard, George D. *The Dual Progress Plan.* New York: Harper & Row, Publishers, 1961, 225 pp.
Presents a plan for dividing subject matter into a core of basic studies in charge of the classroom teacher and the "cultural electives" in charge of special teachers. A controversial plan presenting a different approach as an alternative to the self-contained classroom.

Suchman, J. Richard. "Learning Through Inquiry." *NEA Journal,* 52: 31–32, March, 1963.
Discusses stages in inquiry training with children, focusing on children's questions to help them learn the skills of inquiring into a problem.

"Teaching Machines and Language Laboratories." *Theory into Practice,* 1:1–60, February, 1962.
Articles on usefulness, limitations, and probable future of these newer instructional media.

"The Teacher and the Machine." *Journal of Educational Research,* 55:405–531, June–July, 1962.
A special issue devoted to research studies in programmed learning. Reports on actual studies and is not a general summary.

Thompson, Elizabeth E., and Arthur E. Hamalainen. *Foreign Language Teaching in Elementary Schools.* Washington, D. C.: Association for Supervision and Curriculum Development, 1958, 46 pp.
Examines the issues and develops criteria for establishing programs.

Trump, J. Lloyd, and Dorsey Baynham. *Focus on Change: Guide to Better Schools.* Chicago: Rand McNally & Co., 1961, 147 pp.

This readable pamphlet is a report on the four years of experimental studies under the Commission on the Experimental Study of the Utilization of the Staff in the Secondary School, including team teaching, schedule modification, teacher assistants.

VanTil, William, Gordon F. Vars, and John H. Lounsbury. *Modern Education for the Junior High School Years.* New York: Bobbs-Merrill Co., Inc., 1961, chaps. 3, 5, 9–16, 22.

Much recent information on trends in the junior high school curriculum. Has an excellent section on the core curriculum.

Venn, Grant. *Man, Education and Work: Postsecondary Vocational and Technical Education.* Washington, D. C.: American Council on Education, 1964, 184 pp.

A report on the history, needs, and issues in vocational–technical education related to both secondary and postsecondary education.

Washington County. *Closed Circuit Television Report.* Hagerstown, Maryland: Washington County Public Schools, 1964, 80 pp.

The report on the Washington County Closed-Circuit Educational Television Project, giving the history of the project and the results of the five-year study.

Wiles, Kimball. *The Changing Curriculum of the American High School.* Englewood Cliffs, N. J.: Prentice-Hall, Inc., 1963, chaps. 4–7, 9, 14–15.

A dynamic approach to the high school curriculum. Interesting concept of the high school of the future.

Willis, Benjamin C., and Panel of Consultants. *Education for a Changing World of Work.* U. S. Department of Health, Education, and Welfare, Office of Education, Washington, D. C.: Government Printing Office, 1963, 292 pp.

The report of the panel of consultants on vocational education prepared at the request of the President of the United States. Contains historical background, the contemporary program and evaluation of that program, and needed redirection and improvement in vocational education.

V

CURRICULUM
DEVELOPMENT
IN THE CLASSROOM

15

CURRICULUM GUIDES
AND RESOURCES

One of the striking contrasts between the modern school and the school of a few decades ago is the great variety of resources—both material and human—that are now available to the teacher. He has curriculum guides prepared by the school system, the state, or in some experimental program; resource units prepared either locally or commercially; instructional materials of such abundance that his problem is one of selecting wisely what pupils should use for optimum learning. He finds for his choice not only textbooks but also workbooks, classroom library books, paperbacks, the school and the community library, periodicals, bulletins, films, slides, tapes, radio and television programs, curriculum laboratories, classroom laboratories (whose equipment contrasts with yesterday's as today's remote-controlled and mechanical toys do with the stationary toys of a generation ago), tele-lecture, computer-stored information, programmed courses, and all the vast resources of the community in which he lives.

True, every teacher does not have all this wealth of material at his fingertips. Nevertheless, all of it is available to any state or community, even the poorer districts, that values it enough to make an effort to obtain it. The National Defense Education Act has illustrated that additional equipment can be obtained for schools if the federal government sees its responsibility in obtaining it.

It is probably also true that there are more materials available to a teacher than he either secures or knows how to make use of. A homely example is what he finds in his surroundings: the people, farms, fields, and factories, or the tons of public relations materials produced and distributed free every day by industries, business, the government, and organizations—much of it propaganda materials. Each of these may be good or bad, depending upon how it is used.

What guides and materials then can the teacher use to make a classroom a laboratory for learning and how should he cull the useful from the useless?

THE COURSE OF STUDY

Each year some 2,000 curriculum bulletins in current use, published by school systems, state departments of education, and universities and colleges, are displayed at the annual conference of the Association for Supervision and Curriculum Development and listed in a publication entitled *Curriculum Materials*.[1] The list includes handbooks, manuals, bulletins on such topics as promotions policy and reporting to parents, audio-visual aids bulletins, television courses, counseling and testing bulletins, and programmed curriculum materials; but the great proportion of the bulletins are courses of study from kindergarten through adult education, for all subjects, for the handicapped as well as the gifted.

Kinds of Curriculum Guides

The early course of study was chiefly an outline of content to be covered. This type can be found in only a few school systems today. It usually contained some general objectives, a subject matter outline, and a few suggestions for "learning aids," such as terms to learn, persons to identify, places to locate, vocabulary to define, and events to remember (for a history course). Its purpose was to designate what was to be taught and the order in which it should be taught.

The modern course of study is usually known as a "curriculum guide" to designate that it is a flexible plan to be adapted by the teacher. Its purpose is to assist the teacher and give him suggestions from which to choose for his particular group of pupils. It indicates the broad framework of the scope and sequence within which each teacher has a great deal of latitude to work. Illustrative titles are *Guidelines for School Health Programs, K–12; Language Arts Cur-*

[1] Available from the Association for the current year, 1201 16th Street, N. W., Washington, D. C.

riculum Guide, 10–12; A Teacher's Guide to Appreciating Poetry, Elementary; Interpreting Modern Mathematics, K–6; and *A Guide for American History in the Junior High School, 7–9.*

A majority of the curriculum guides cover a span of a few grades, such as K–3, K–6, 7–9, 10–12, or only one grade or high school subject. The voluminous bulletins that contain courses for all of the grades are not particularly useful nor economical to publish. Teachers find helpful bulletins that deal with a certain age level of youngsters or the primary grades, for example. Each guide can contain the general framework of the total scope and sequence.

At the elementary and secondary school levels, a common practice is to publish guides dealing with curriculum problems that cut across subject fields or are of a more general nature. Examples of titles are *The First Day at School; Work Habits and Study Skills; Reporting Pupil Progress; Selection and Use of Standardized Tests; Behavioral Growth Patterns.* Some describe the services available to teachers in the school system or resources upon which to draw, such as *Curriculum Centers and Library Resources; Catalog of Teaching Aids; Instructional Materials Center; Library Materials for Remedial Reading; Research Services; Instructional Television; Guidelines for the Selection of Programmed Materials; Pupil Personnel Services; Community Resources; The Children's Museum.* Others are in the form of handbooks or policy statements: *Procedures for Textbook Adoption; Teachers' Guide for Homework Assignments; Handbook for Teachers; Teachers' Handbook on Marking and Reporting; Health Policies.*

One of the newer trends is the publication of bulletins for use by parents or to describe the school program to the community. Examples are *We're Off to Kindergarten; Parents' Handbook; Your Guide to the Schools; Know Your Schools; The Five-Year-Old in the School; What We Teach in First Grade; You Can Help Your Child Learn.* These types of bulletins and newsletters supplement the superintendent's annual report, which often was the only report previously made to the community.

Among the curriculum publications can be noted several other trends. Some publications report on projects or experiments: *The Teaching Team Project; Botanical Garden Project; Report of Gifted Child Study; Ungraded Primary Curriculum; Factors Associated with Underachievement.* Some treat a particular problem or phase of a subject: *Teaching about Communism; Africa: Its People and Problems; Indian Cultures in the Pacific Northwest; The Principles of American Freedom; Tropical Fish; Exploration of Outer Space; Think-*

ing *About Sets and Numbers; Creativity through Language Arts*. Some describe a technique or teaching method: *The Micro-Projector; Suggested Demonstrations in Agricultural Mechanics; Using Maps and Globes; A Guide for Laboratory Procedures; Note Reading Guide for Elementary School Music; Graphs and How To Make Them; Speech Improvement Through Puppets; The Language Laboratory; Glass Craft; Identification of the Gifted*. The use of more colorful titles is characteristic of a number of publications: *Turn to the Ocean; Now Is the Time; Infinite Riches* (creative writing); *It's All in the Game—About Children at Play; Our Children's Eyes; Do Adolescents Like Art? Yes, If; More Willingly to School; Each Child a Challenge; The World Belongs to Those Who Prepare for It*. Resource units are often made available: *A Resource Unit on Alaska; The Canning Industry; Science Resource Units; Developmental Reading Unit; The Roaring Twenties and Aftermath; Instructional Units in Conversational French; Life in Mexico*.

Contents of the Modern Curriculum Guide

Modern courses of study contain suggestions such as how to determine the needs of children and youth and how to plan with pupils in setting up objectives, in addition to the more common materials. More specifically these guides may include:

Suggested goals or directions for the curriculum, with illustrations of how to translate these general goals into behavioral terms. Such statements often include the point of view concerning the curriculum.

Suggestions on how to plan with pupils, indicating how each teacher can develop with pupils the problems on which the group will work. Techniques for using the problem-solving approach may be included.

The general framework for the scope and sequence of the curriculum. Usually this is presented in a chart form showing the areas of experiences, areas of content, social functions, or some other general category around which the curriculum is planned for the different grades and age levels.

Suggestions on how to study children, indicating specific kinds of techniques to use and the types of records to keep.

A statement of characteristics, needs, and developmental tasks of children and youth.

A list of types of experiences to assist children in their growth toward desired kinds of behavior changes, with suggestions for selecting, organizing, and developing these experiences with the children.

Identification of resources upon which to draw, such as the community, people, books, films, charts, maps. To be helpful, these resources should be annotated and some indication should be given as to the maturity level or the reading level to which the materials are best suited.

Suggested means of evaluation. Suggestions are included to assist teachers in evaluating growth toward various kinds of behavior outcomes.[2]

INSTRUCTIONAL MATERIALS AND RESOURCES

In this age of abundance of instructional materials, the problems facing the teacher are manifold. He faces the question of how to use the new kinds of materials and the new equipment. Perhaps he has never before ventured to use an opaque projector or an overhead projector. "Overlays" is a term unfamiliar to him. He has hesitated to ask pupils to build equipment for their classroom experimentation, for he has failed to learn the skills of using tools and the different media of industrial arts. Moreover, he has the problem of selecting from the many kinds of books, pamphlets, periodicals, leaflets, radio transcriptions, films, slides, recordings, tapes, television programs, and now even the computer-based programs or other programmed instruction to add to the enormity of the task. Consequently, he falls back on the use of the single textbook, which is a simple method. Even the use of many materials may sound like a buzz of confusion in the classroom.

It is extremely doubtful that any book can instruct the teacher in learning to use these new aids. He will need practice in their use. He will need courses in colleges and universities, many of them offered at his back door, or assistance from specialists or teachers in the building or school system. Supervisors and principals who themselves are competent are glad to help. The one who wants help can find it. The fearful, the insecure, and the incompetent will continue to use materials as limited in scope as their own horizons.

This section concentrates, therefore, on the problems and reasons for use of a variety of materials, the resource centers for materials, and the principles for selecting materials to serve instructional purposes.

[2] See Eleanor Merritt and Henry Harap, Trends in the Production of Curriculum Guides, Nashville, Tenn.: Division of Surveys and Field Services, George Peabody College for Teachers, 1955, 43 pp.

Problems of an Up-to-Date Curriculum

As knowledge increases by phenomenal strides, the question of timeliness of instructional materials becomes a serious one. Books may be out of date before they are published. The school that uses a science textbook published five years ago may be teaching misinformation and omitting much important new knowledge. In the school of today and tomorrow, the textbook will not be able to keep up with the changing world. That is the function of television, radio, other newer media, and more fugitive types of printed materials. There will be greater need for supplementary books, for reference books, newspapers, magazines, trade books, mimeographed and dittoed materials, arts and crafts materials, maps, globes, slides, films, tapes, and videotape. For this reason the cost will be considerably greater. A modern school cannot be run on a 1950 budget.

In spite of the abundance of books and pamphlets, there are some deficiencies. One of the real needs of which publishing companies are becoming cognizant is the type of book that is on a mature interest level, but on a *low reading level,* for use in the upper grades and the secondary school. Materials written at different reading levels are needed for the bright and the dull student. There is also a demand for more materials dealing with the local area, the state, or the community. In some cases school systems large enough to do so have published pamphlets, books, or films dealing with their own communities.

No doubt the teacher will meet obstacles in using sources of information. There will be budget problems to overcome, but the same amount of money that will buy forty copies of one book will also buy one copy of forty different books. There will probably be some regulations that handicap the conducting of field trips. Some teachers find the handicap largely in themselves; they are reluctant to take field trips because of the legal responsibilities involved. These are problems that will have to be worked out by the school system and the community as a whole. Many communities have found that citizens' study of school problems helps to solve them.

Use of a Variety of Materials

The use of varied materials is desirable from the standpoint of learning principles. If a pupil is to investigate, to find solutions to problems, to seek answers, he needs many resources to which he can go. What he studies and what he reads must have meaning for him.

He should not "read" words in books that are meaningless or too difficult for him, nor should he read books that present no challenge in learning new vocabulary, new ideas, and new concepts. The teacher needs different books on different levels and suited to different interests. In any one class in sixth grade, for example, there are pupils who are interested in stories about horses; those who are interested in the space age; those interested in romance or adventure; those interested in stories about nurses, aviators, or explorers; and those interested in inventions; and even those interested in anthropology, astronomy, physics, and Asian languages and cultures.

Undoubtedly having many books, pamphlets, and periodicals easily accessible to pupils in the classroom and in the school library encourages wider reading. A number of studies have shown that when pupils are exposed to many sources of reading materials dealing with varied interests, they will read more than if they are in classrooms barren of anything but the text itself.

Actually the problem is really one of how to keep a wide variety of materials *out* of the school, if one were so disposed. Industries, councils created by industries, insurance companies, transportation companies, unions, temperance organizations, medical societies, left-wing and right-wing organizations publish free materials available for use in schools. Many furnish accurate information. Others present only one side of an issue. Some are of a propaganda nature. Properly used, they can furnish pupils an opportunity to learn to select their reading materials with care and to judge information on the basis of its source. There can be little hope of pupils developing those skills unless they are allowed to read examples of propaganda and advertising types of pamphlets that are entirely slanted.

Teachers should be cautioned, however, against using only publications biased from one point of view. The fact that many attractive pamphlets are free may result in pupils' having very few contacts with the point of view expressed by organizations that do not have the resources for such a vast publications program. Teachers need to guide pupils in the study of biased publications, helping them to evaluate the sources and the purposes of published materials.

A variety of materials makes possible the use of a problems approach. Pupils investigate different phases of the problem. When committees are formed to work on a problem-solving basis, they will use available materials suited to their needs and their interests. They will search out new sources of information and new materials. In many cases, pupils have helped in developing the classroom as a laboratory through gathering the pamphlet type of materials. Some children will have magazines and pamphlets in their homes that they can contribute to the room.

If pupils are going to be helped to explore, to find out more about the world in which we live, to study their culture and their historical background, teachers will need to give them limitless opportunities to read on their own. Teachers will need to help them develop new interests so that they become widely read individuals rather than people who read textbooks in school and scarcely become acquainted with other kinds of books. After they leave school, youth may have no more desire to read, since they may have found their textbooks dull and uninteresting.

The Classroom as a Laboratory

Not long ago the classroom laboratories found in the typical secondary school were the science laboratory, the home economics laboratory, the commercial classroom, and the industrial arts shop. Some schools had art rooms, music rooms, and vocational agriculture rooms and shops. In all other classrooms, one room resembled the next. More recently, there have been added foreign language laboratories, electronics laboratories for business subjects, speech laboratories, social studies laboratories, and English laboratories.

In a well-equipped school, the classroom may now have television screens, tape recorders, an overhead projector, or multiple-screen telemation combining a number of audio-visual devices such as a tape recorder, a movie projector, an opaque projector, a transparency projector, and perhaps three translucent screens.

The classroom that offers optimum possibilities for learning and for independent research and study is a laboratory. Classrooms have their own collections of books, pamphlets, newspapers, periodicals, maps and globes, realia, models, and pictures. Self-contained classrooms in the elementary school also have centers for sciences, for arts and crafts, for mathematics, and for reading. Bulletin boards, displays, art objects, movable furniture, tables, sinks, and storage space are a part of the classroom laboratory.

The classroom library especially in the elementary school is a supplement to the central library, keeping materials where the children can easily work with them. Arrangements can be made whereby books can be borrowed from the central library for classroom use.

In secondary schools, the trend is toward scheduling more and shorter periods per day, providing opportunity for independent study. More use is being made of central libraries and resource centers by the secondary schools, and less of supervised study in the classroom.

The Central Library

The library is one of the most important instructional resources in the school, for both elementary schools and secondary schools. In a world of profusion of books and periodicals, there is little excuse for a community in the United States that does not equip its school buildings with modern libraries. States are neglecting their obligations where they allow such conditions to exist either because of local poverty or indifference.

Some communities use the bookmobile from the central library to supplement the collections of books in different schools. Some rural communities have found that the use of a bookmobile from a cooperative library for several schools is the best solution under their condition of limited finances. Other schools use a central library for each of different age groups rather than a single large unit. Elementary schools, particularly in larger school systems, have added central libraries and librarians to their staffs.

In one large school system the services of the elementary school library for children and teachers are described as follows:

1. To provide reference material for children and teachers. This includes books, magazines, pictures, and pamphlets.
2. To supply and circulate recreational reading materials.
3. To teach the use of books and materials within the library.
4. To arouse enthusiasm and interest in reading through sharing of book discussions, story hours, book reviews, related musical groups, library clubs, use of audio-visual aids, and exhibits of classroom projects.
5. To help children to become discriminating in their choice of reading.
6. To work with teachers in developing reading interests and hobbies with individual children.
7. To introduce children to the services of the libraries within the community.
8. To help develop in children *the life-long habit* of reading to have fun and reading to find out.
9. To provide parents and teachers with special book lists of good literature for children.[3]

The services of the library to the modern secondary school also are many. By means of its books, magazines, newspapers, clippings, pamphlets, and other resources, the library serves as a coordinating

[3] Hartford Public Schools, *The Library Program in the Hartford Elementary Schools*, Hartford, Conn.: The Public Schools.

center for the instructional program. In some schools it may also be the center for films, filmstrips, slides, recordings, and other audio-visual materials. It may contain a listing of the resources that are available for use in the community. It provides through its wide variety of up-to-date materials a place for investigation and research activities on the part of pupils. It is also the source of materials for creative activities in dramatics and art.

The library serves as a focal point in educating pupils in the use of library techniques and references. Classes are scheduled in libraries for periods that are used for browsing and for research for classroom committees and projects. In a junior high school in a Western city, teachers make weekly appointments for their classes to work in the library, and the librarian visits classrooms on invitation to give instruction and book reviews. It is not a function of the library to be used as the old-fashioned study hall where all pupils who do not have a class are placed. Such a practice does little to develop library skills or other good study habits.

A publication of the New England Development Council indicates a list of typical activities that take place in the library:

A committee of fourth-grade children, whose classmates have made a collection of sea shells, looking for reference materials to answer questions which the group has raised

A group of seventh graders seeking ideas for wild life programs which might be pertinent in their local community

Three fourth graders bringing in a mural which they ask to have hung in the library

A slow learner in the fifth grade receiving help from the librarian in choosing books on her level to aid in setting up her Indian exhibit

A first-grade teacher coming in to borrow recordings of nursery rhymes

A kindergarten class listening intently to a new story or looking at picture books together

A second grader looking for pictures of winter birds to illustrate a report he is preparing; his teacher borrows a film on the same subject

A twelfth-grade secretarial class receiving instruction in the use of reference books most often found in a business office

A group from a Current Problems class, in preparation for a panel discussion, using the newspapers and *Reader's Guide to Periodical Literature* for pertinent current materials

The commercial geography class working on a project on Canadian trade which requires research in pamphlets, books, encyclopedias, year-books and maps

A group of eighth graders, preparing to work out a puppet show, searching for books on puppetry and directions for ventriloquism

Members of the Library Club, preparing a book program for a radio broadcast, discussing some of the new books

A group of physical education students preparing bibliographies of fact and fiction on their favorite sports which will be used with exhibits at an all-school playday

A group of seniors preparing for job interviews by studying books which tell how to make a good impression on a prospective employer

An Industrial Arts student copying plans of a sailboat from a current magazine in preparation for building a boat

The Science Club displaying its photography in the library

Fans of television science programs attempting to learn more about "those reptiles" seen on the screen.[4]

The librarian needs to be a person skilled in human relationships, in working with teachers, in helping them with their class projects. In this sense, the librarian is a supervisor and consultant. The traditional librarian regarded the library as a place where books were to be carefully guarded. The modern librarian helps pupils and teachers in every way to facilitate the use of materials and books. In a medium-sized Midwestern school system, the librarian is responsible for correlating materials with the learning situations, which involves being familiar with the curriculum of each grade level. The librarian works with teachers by observing in classrooms, consulting with teachers, and participating with them in workshops. The librarian works with children and serves as a resource person in teaching the skill of library use. A librarian may serve more than one small elementary school in the district. On her days in the schools, the librarian in cooperation with room teachers advises and instructs children as a core of assistants, a plan that has been developed to allow children to share in the responsibility of managing library routine.

Audio-Visual Materials

Many large school systems and counties have an audio-visual center which services the schools. In some large high schools, a center has been developed in the individual school unit. The center is concerned with the distribution and use of films, filmstrips, exhibits, specimens, objects, still pictures, maps, globes, charts, recordings, tapes, programs, television, radio, posters, and cartoons. It houses and distributes equipment for the use of these aids, such as motion picture, slide, opaque, linked slide-tape, and overhead projectors; record players; and tape recorders. In the modern center, facilities are provided for the teachers to produce overhead transparencies, slides, study prints, over-

[4] New England School Development Council and New England School Library Association, *Every School Needs a Library*, Cambridge, Mass.: The Council, 1952.

lays, tapes, videotapes, charts, flash-cards, and other materials that will assist in instruction. The center provides instruction to teachers in the use of equipment and production of aids.

Because many of these materials are costly, they need to be kept in a central pool and distributed for use by the schools. In the case of some types such as pictures, objects, and specimens, the center supplements the materials kept regularly in the classroom and keeps a record of where such materials can be found in the school. It is a central coordinating agency.

Although a plan for distribution may be established on a county-wide basis, every school building ought to have someone who serves as a coordinator. In the smaller schools, the teacher with this responsibility may be given some free time for carrying on these activities. Schools of medium size as a rule have a part-time audio-visual director, and larger schools generally have full-time directors. The director serves as a consultant to the school, arranging sessions for previews and evaluation of instructional materials, ordering audio-visual materials requested, developing a system of distribution to schools, working with building coordinators, making recommendations to teachers for materials to use in specific units, conducting in-service sessions in the use of equipment and aids, helping teachers in the production of materials, and consulting with principals.

Since the main function of an audio-visual director is that of consultant, clerical service is provided for handling the details and mechanical service for repairing the equipment. Students are given valuable training in audio-visual centers and are utilized in distributing, taking care of, and repairing equipment, and serving as operators. This is another example of how the school community can serve as a source of learning experiences.

Curriculum Laboratory

The concept of a curriculum laboratory varies from that of a place or room with equipment and materials to that of a service in which leadership in the use of these materials, facilities, and equipment is also provided. Consultant service to teachers is an important part of the curriculum laboratory. Some school systems consider the whole curriculum division or bureau of curriculum service as the curriculum laboratory, in some instances known as a curriculum center.

The broader concept of the laboratory or center provides services to teachers and carries on major activities in curriculum revision and development, including the collecting and assembling of curriculum materials, advising and directing curriculum studies, assisting in experimentation and evaluation, producing and publishing curriculum bulletins, lending and distributing materials, sponsoring curriculum conferences, and arranging for in-service courses.

The curriculum laboratory is a place where teachers can find resources of the "fugitive" type to help them in their curriculum problems. Because of its collection of the latest pamphlet material, it is a rich source of ideas and challenges. Its collections of courses of study; bulletins from school systems and professional organizations; bulletins produced by the U. S. Office of Education; periodicals; reports of research; samples of handbooks, records, programs, and units from school systems; professional books, periodicals, and indexes; textbooks from publishing companies; and, in a few cases, trade books or children's literature provide a variety of sources for information and suggestions on any school problem. Teachers find here a wealth of materials from which they may choose. Committees use the laboratory for selecting books for adoption or purchase.

A study found that in seventy-three curriculum laboratories in colleges, city school systems, county school systems, and state departments of education, the following kinds of materials were contained in descending order of frequency: courses of study, pupil texts, general bulletins, professional books, workbooks, sample tests, reference materials, bibliographies, maps and charts, supplementary materials, audio-visual aids, trade books, manipulative materials.[5]

It is recognized that only the larger school systems can furnish all of these materials, but it is possible for the county, the state department of education, or the state university or college to provide them on a loan basis to schools of the state. Local schools can supply them on a small scale. Some schools have a section of the library devoted to professional materials. Other schools have found it to their advantage to set up such a professional library in the teachers' room.

The kinds of pamphlets that can be secured for the curriculum laboratory are illustrated by the major subject listings of pamphlets in a university curriculum laboratory which has a full-time consultant in the laboratory and which is utilized extensively by schools of the state.

[5] Eleanor Antan, *The Material Resources of Curriculum Laboratories*, Curriculum Bulletin No. 1, Storrs, Conn.: Curriculum Center, School of Education, University of Connecticut, 1951, p. 9 (mimeo.).

Administration
Adult Education
Agriculture
Art
Attacks on Schools
Audio-Visual Aids
Aviation
Business Education
Child and Adolescent Development
Civil Defense and Mobilization
Community
Comparative Education
Connecticut Bulletins
Conservation Education
Consumer Education
Core Curriculum
Curriculum
Distributive Education
Education for Minority Groups
Elementary Education and Curriculum
Evaluation and Reporting
Extraclass Activities
Foreign Language
General Curriculum Guides
Group Dynamics
Guidance
Handwriting, Spelling, Word Study
Health Education and Services
Higher Education
Home Economics
Industrial Arts

Instructional Materials
Junior College
Juvenile Delinquency
Kindergarten and Preschool
Language Arts
Library
Mathematics
Methods
Music
Physical Education
Programmed Learning and Teaching Machines
Reading
Religious Education
Research in Education
Resources for Curriculum Improvement
Rural Education
Safety and Driver Education
School Improvement
Science
Secondary Education and Curriculum
Social Studies
Special Education
Speech
Staff Utilization
State and Federal Reports
Teacher Education
The Teaching Profession
Team Teaching
Vocational Education
Youth [6]

Consultant services are essential to assist teachers and students in the utilization of the curriculum laboratory. Preferably, consultants should have a varied background of teaching experience. The system of filing the materials is somewhat mechanical and routine and can be readily learned, but the insight and understanding that are necessary for assisting teachers to find materials for curriculum study are far more important.

[6] Curriculum Center, University of Connecticut, Storrs, Conn.

An expanded concept of a curriculum laboratory includes other materials, such as manipulative materials prepared in the Instructional Devices Development Laboratory at the University of Connecticut. California State Department of Education's Curriculum Laboratory newsletter visualizes the laboratory as having the following resources of materials for assisting with action research:

1. Examples of different types of learning materials which may become models.
2. Diagnostic devices beyond those found in print.
3. Materials so familiar to the laboratory staff that they may be used for different purposes. For instance, they might suggest a health film for use not for health study but for analysis of stereotypes.
4. Within particular subject areas and topics, materials organized around different teaching styles—to provide for individual differences among teachers.
5. Some models for curriculum designs; for example, for a teacher of a class containing fourteen slow learners.
6. A file of materials developed in completed projects, or pictures of them if storage is a problem.
7. Models of planning, execution and evaluation of action research projects.[7]

Community Resources

The community offers many possibilities for enriching the curriculum and furnishing pupils with valuable learning experiences.

Some systematic kind of classification of resources needs to be made in order to secure maximum use by teachers. A constantly revised file of resources can be kept in the library of the school. In some schools the audio-visual director has a list of such resources and assists teachers with field trips. One medium-sized city school system has a special consultant with the title of school-community-coordinator, who works as a liaison person between the schools and the community, assisting the schools in various ways to utilize community resources. A number of school systems publish mimeographed bulletins on school trips that list suggested field trips by units, age levels, courses, or areas of interest. A committee of teachers worked with the coordinator of instructional materials to provide a community resources file in one system. Neighborhood schools, in turn, developed such files. Some schools make it a practice to keep lists of community resources on file cards in a central location to supplement the information placed in the hands of each teacher.

---

[7] *California Curriculum Newsletter*, Vol. 6, No. 3, December, 1962, Sacramento: Curriculum Laboratory, State Department of Education, p. 3.

In a workshop in a small school system, a group of elementary and secondary school teachers studied the problem of how they could utilize community resources such as the places of business, historic spots, and interesting persons. The teachers made a preliminary list after a survey of the places that eventually might serve for field trips. They visited all of these places and selected the ones that would provide good resources for learning experiences. These were organized into a booklet entitled *Field Trips and Resource Visitors.* For each resource, information was given concerning the units, grades, or classes for which it was recommended, the location, how reached, time to be allowed, person in charge to contact, recommendations for visiting hours, number of children who could be accommodated, special instructions to children in regard to behavior or safety, suggestions by persons in charge, and things to be pointed out to children. For the resource visitors, the name of the person, the subject or teaching levels for which the resource visitor might be used, and the background of the person were given.

A few schools have acquired special resources for learning experiences for the pupils. Some own a farm on which agriculture students develop various kinds of projects in connection with their class instruction. Others own a school forest in which reforestation work is done. Others have developed school museums. Several schools in Midwestern states are among those that own camps for their camping programs.

The Instructional Materials Center

The NEA Project on Instruction has recommended that "in each school system there should be one or more well-planned instructional materials and resources center, consisting of at least a library and an audio-visual center. In each school building, there should also be an instructional resources facility." [8] The Committee which produced this significant report envisions the school system of the sixties as having at least one of these centers to serve its schools. It also reflects the trend toward a comprehensive type of materials center.

Since the written word is not the exclusive source of stored information in the 1960's, a center which teachers may use as a resource should contain the variety of instructional media now available. Instead of having separate resource centers for audio-visual, curriculum library, and other types of materials and services, school systems are

[8] National Education Association, *Schools for the Sixties,* New York: McGraw-Hill Book Co., 1963, p. 98.

finding an advantage in a combined service that includes audio materials, visual aids, forms, community resource suggestions, exhibits, maps and globes, reference books, periodicals, curriculum guides, school realia, audio-visual equipment, museum collections, models, specimens. Textbooks are also distributed through the center.

A suburban school district has an educational services center in a separate building in which are housed also the administrative and supervisory personnel and the special services. It represents a centralization of services to the schools of the district. Teachers may browse and select library books, supplementary textbooks, films, filmstrips, records, study prints, and other instructional aids. They have the use of a library room, preview facilities, booths for listening and for study and selection of the materials. Mechanical devices facilitate the distribution of the materials to the individual buildings. Workshops, university courses, committee meetings, and other meetings are held in this busy instructional center. Consultants in different fields and in materials help teachers in the center and in the schools. A feature of the center is the constant evaluation done by teachers, who fill out evaluation forms for new materials examined. Coordinators of instructional materials in each building work with the central coordinator to insure the most effective use of the center.

SELECTION OF MATERIALS

Should textbooks be selected on a city-wide basis or by individual schools? What part should the teacher play in selecting books and other learning materials? Who should decide what materials are to be purchased? These kinds of decisions must be made in selecting materials and resources. Guiding principles are presented here to assist teachers and faculties in their choice of instructional aids.

Selection of instructional materials should follow a study of the program and its objectives. In order to secure the best kinds of learning materials for children and adolescents, teachers need to spend time in thinking about the purposes of the program and about the kinds of materials that will serve those purposes. Some curriculum committees consider their main problem to be the choice of texts and supplementary books. In the case of a language arts committee, it may start out with the question: What books shall we choose for reading, language, or English texts? Consideration should first be given to the nature of the program in reading, language, or English. To select books without really knowing their purpose is a blindfolded process. Perhaps the language arts program has not been carefully studied for years; yet, the committee mistakenly believes that it can choose books intelligently without any concern for the purposes and kinds of experiences desired in the total program.

To the greatest extent possible, the choice of materials and resources should be the responsibility of those who use them. In recent years larger school systems have been moving away from the centralization of selecting instructional materials. The purchase of such standard items as pencils, paper, and notebooks may be done more economically and efficiently through a central purchasing agency. But choosing textbooks and other supplementary materials is too closely related to local curriculum problems to be relegated to a central agency. Some schools have found that the person at the head of the purchasing becomes rather powerful in policy-making through selection of instructional materials.

The basic reason for the change, however, is the desire to choose materials that are best suited to the individual school and community. In terms of adapting materials to curriculum needs, there is a real advantage in allotting each school its own budget for the purchase of instructional materials, including textbooks. Actual purchasing can be done in the central office, but the selection should be the responsibility of the individual school. The principal and the teachers car work together in choosing the kinds of materials that will best suit their pupils' needs and the program and purposes. In any school system there is variation from school to school in the philosophy of the use of materials. No school that wants to use a variety of materials rather than a single text should be handcuffed by a school policy of purchasing only single textbooks.

The job of the administrator is to make the choice of materials by the teacher easy, informed, and in terms of an acceptable philosophy developed by the staff. Above all, his responsibility is to see that choices are made wisely, in terms of purposes for which the instructional materials are to be used. This is true for small as well as large school systems. When teachers were poorly trained, there was more reason for the superintendent choosing the textbooks.

A number of states have some form of textbook adoption by a state agency. In such states as Texas, Oregon, and California, textbook commissions have been installed by the state legislature for state-wide adoption of texts. Once desirable, this practice is now dangerous and undesirable. Both a multiple-choice system and a single textbook plan are used in state adoptions. In the former, the state department of education selects a list of approved books from which local school districts may choose. In the latter, the state department selects only a single text for each grade level subject or each class. Some school systems have also followed the practice of giving greater flexibility through adopting a list of books from which the individual school faculty may choose. The great majority of school systems are free to choose their own materials.

If this principle is seriously applied, the teacher in cooperation with his pupils will have an important part to play in the selection of materials. One of the powerful incentives to experimentation is the encouragement given to the teacher through freedom to select the media for such experimentation in the classroom. The teacher should have a role in the making of city-wide policy, in the making of policy and selection of materials for the individual school, and in the selection of materials for use in his own classroom.

The process of assisting in the selection of learning materials can be made into a valuable learning experience for pupils. Committees in a number of school systems have placed in the hands of teachers books that are being considered for selection. Teachers in turn have put these books in their rooms for use by the children. The reaction of the children is a significant factor in the selection of the books.

The choice of materials and resources should be based upon the purposes, maturity, and background of the group. In selecting instructional materials, the teacher needs to ask himself such questions as: Does the book promote the kinds of understandings of other peoples that are important? Does it make clear the need for distinguishing between propaganda and factual information? Is it suitable for use in developing the kinds of attitudes and appreciations that are important? The chief criterion for selection is the goal of instruction.

The maturity and background of the group need to be taken into consideration. Why does a teacher want one book instead of a variety of books? Who is served by the policy used, the teacher or the pupils? Would one book serve the purpose of all the pupils? A single social studies text in the elementary school cannot be equally well suited to children who range in reading ability from grades one through six. Likewise, no anthology of literature can include enough selections to fit all the interests of any group of high school students, to say nothing of their reading ability. The use of a single text without supplementary materials is not realistic in terms of the differences among individuals in any class. Sets of five or ten different books are often used to take care of these differences.

Children who have grown up on a farm cannot be expected to profit most from reading books that are based on life in the city. In recent years more attention has been given to this problem in the development of readers for the elementary schools. More needs to be done in producing books and materials that are based on the background of the children. Some cities have produced their own materials, more true to life for the children of their schools.

Both purposes and maturity need to be taken into consideration in selection from the profusion of free and inexpensive materials that multiplies as fast as "junk" mail. Commercial companies or organizations may attempt to use the school for their own interests by flooding the school with free pamphlets, workbooks, posters, units, packets, films, and other types of materials. The fact that material is free may make it attractive to those operating on restricted educational budgets. Educators are faced with decisions that require drawing a line between admitting all free materials without any restrictions and excluding them. The latter is contrary to the principle of guaranteeing access to materials that are essential to good learning. Learning to distinguish between slanted or biased materials and accurate information cannot be done without studying both.

Although some selected lists of these types of materials are made available by commercial companies, they in no sense can select for a school what serves its purposes.

Some schools develop criteria for the choice of these materials. The Joint Council on Economic Education in the Greater Hartford (Conn.) area, through one of its committees, developed the following criteria for selecting free and inexpensive materials dealing with basic economic issues:

1. The source and sponsorship of any piece of literature or teaching aid should be clear, so that students may make judgments as to its probable bias.
2. Resource materials should arouse interest in our economic life. They should give insight into problems inherent in our economic society, including those of human relationships.
3. In the over-all selection of materials, there should be a wholesome balance among the various points of view. However, the fact that an individual piece of literature has a one-sided point of view does not disqualify it as a useful aid to economic understanding.
4. Materials should be on the students' level of understanding and interest. It is recognized that in most high school classes there will be pupils with mature abilities and interests and others whose abilities and interests are immature. Attempts should be made to secure variety of materials in terms of maturity of presentation to meet the needs of a variety of students.

5. The above criteria should be considered in the use of various types of resource materials, including speakers, films, recordings, field trips, and interviews as well as pamphlets and other printed materials.[9]

The principle of choice based upon purpose, maturity, and background applies also to the use of resources. Many Eastern secondary schools follow the practice of having each senior class take a trip to Washington, D. C., in the spring. The trip means a great deal of preparation throughout the year in order to raise funds. Some schools undoubtedly make good instructional use of these trips in their classes, preparing for it ahead of time and following it up after the class has returned.

In the case of traditional, long field trips, teachers need to question seriously: What educational purpose does the trip serve? Would it be more valuable to schedule trips to other places of interest, where some social or economic problems could be studied, such as a coal mining area? A sixth grade in a small New England school system made a class project out of a visit to an underprivileged school in West Virginia. The class had a great deal of correspondence ahead of time with the West Virginian children, exchanging pictures, letters, and information about their respective schools and communities. The fund-raising activities for the trip were made an integral part of the instructional program.

Materials and equipment to take care of a variety of individual interests, development, and abilities should be selected for every classroom. Child development studies indicate that, if a rich environment is provided, learning will be facilitated. Young children tend to choose the more appropriate kinds of materials if given the opportunity through a process of self-selection. Modern elementary classrooms need to have reading centers, science centers, art centers, idea centers, equipment for construction work, laboratories for the study of social living.

The classroom laboratory should be like a department store with a range of goods to serve many pocketbooks, tastes, and interests. The pocketbooks of cultural background and previous experience determine with what degree of wealth a child can procure other experiences. The range of reading levels, of interests, and of topics in the average classroom can be served only by a rich source of materials from which to choose.

[9] Greater Hartford Council on Economic Education, *Aids in the Improvement of Education for Economic Understanding,* Bulletin No. 1, Hartford, Conn.: The Council, 1950, p. 2.

The same principle holds for equipment. Group discussion, committee work, and individual projects require flexible equipment. There ought to be equipment for experimentation, for use of audio-visual materials, and for drawing and construction work. Some of this equipment can be pooled in one room of a school building and borrowed for use in many classrooms. One of the valuable learning experiences is to teach pupils how to use equipment such as that in the audio-visual field.

The staff should establish or adopt criteria for selection of materials to be purchased for the school. When a committee has the responsibility for choosing materials based on the study of the program, it should determine the criteria for selection before it begins to study the books, maps, or globes themselves. The establishment of criteria means that the objectives will need to be examined to determine what kinds of experiences are desirable. Such matters as authenticity, vocabulary, organization, consistency, teaching and study aids, style, and format need to be considered.

In one city school system, the following standards were established for the selection of related materials for classroom libraries by a committee.

Some of the definite reading interests to remember are:
1. Biography
2. Personal adventure
3. Informational books
4. Stories of vocations, adventure, mystery, school and animals.

Books of biography should:
1. Be about heroes of action and achievement
2. Deal with outward events and struggles rather than with character analysis
3. Be presented sympathetically
4. Be idealistic without being didactic.

Books of personal adventure should be:
1. Vividly written but without undue exaggeration
2. Wholesome exploits worth reading about.

Informational books should have:
1. The same characteristics of accuracy, good organization, and presentation as in younger children's books
2. In addition, splendid indexes and bibliographies where the subject calls for them.

Fiction in general should have:
1. An authentic background

2. Characters which are not types
3. Genuine character development
4. A plausible plot
5. Wholesome and normal relationships
6. Problems of interest to adolescents, the solutions of which may be helpful in their own lives.

The committee also developed a rating sheet on which each teacher on the committee and others could make a rating of the books. The rating sheet included places for rating physical makeup (attractiveness and durability), content (range of interests and vocabulary and contribution to child growth and to purposes), and pupils' evaluation (the books were placed in classroom for use and evaluation by children).

The following excellent list of criteria for evaluating books, pamphlets, and periodicals for the secondary schools were established by a school system that uses a systematic means of arriving at selections.

CONTENT:

How well does the material cover the essentials in the field?

How suitable is the vocabulary for the grade level?

How adequate is the material in scope and interest appeal to meet teacher and student needs at the grade level for which it is being considered?

How factually correct is the material?

How up-to-date is the material?

How well does the material suggest and discuss applications to everyday life?

If an anthology, how genuinely representative of the thought and culture of the period and area to be studied are the selections?

How well do the problems of life presented stimulate students to meaningful consideration of right and wrong behavior?

How adequately presented is that aspect of American civilization with which the book deals?

How well does the author support his generalizations with reliable information and logical deductions?

In the study of democracy how well are both its accomplishments and problems considered?

How well does the material offer means and methods for arriving at solutions to the problems?

In dealing with the individual American's relationship to government, are his obligations stressed as well as his rights?

How adequately does the material help students to develop sound methods of propaganda analysis to be applied to all situations?

For judging basic texts: If controversial issues are considered, how adequately are representative points of view included and treated objectively?

For judging supplementary materials: How well does this material contribute to an appropriate balance of all representative points of view in your school or library?

For judging plays, newspapers, and other periodicals: How sound is the reputation and integrity of the editorial board?

How well does this text help students to understand and appreciate the historic traditions of the American system of government as expressed in the Constitution?

FORMAT:

How clear, readable, and attractive is the type?

How suitable is the paper for this type of textbook?

Is the binding attractive but still suitable for extended student use?

How appropriate is the size for the students of the grade for which the material is being considered?

How adequate for student reference work is the index?

INSTRUCTIONAL AIDS:

How well does the bibliography encourage and aid the students in carrying on research?

How effectively used are such reading aids as variations in type, center heads, side heads, italics?

How clear, well-designed, and meaningful are the illustrations?

How challenging and stimulating are study aids such as self-tests, summaries, reviews, and suggested activities (including instructional trips, films, dioramas, etc.)?

How adequate and practical are such instructional aids as suggested problems or projects, tests, bibliographies, appendices, glossaries, and maps?

AUTHORSHIP:

How well-qualified is the authorship in the field and grade level for which this material is being considered? [10]

Guidelines have also been established for the evaluation of newer kinds of learning media. A joint committee of the American Educational Research Association, the American Psychological Association, and the Department of Audio-Visual Instruction of the NEA developed these criteria for programmed materials:

The use of self-instructional programed learning materials in teaching machines and similar devices represents a potential contribution of great importance to American education. But this contribution can best be realized only if users have information with which to evaluate self-instructional materials. Accordingly, the following interim guidelines have been prepared.

1. Teaching machines do not, in themselves, teach. Rather, the teaching is done by a program of instructional materials presented by the teaching machine. Any evaluation of a teaching machine thus requires an assessment of the availability and quality of programs for each type of machine, as well as its mechanical dependability.

[10] Adapted from forms used by the Pasadena City Schools, Pasadena, Calif.

2. A variety of programed materials is becoming available, but not all programs will fit all machines. Thus only those programs compatible with a particular machine can be considered as available for use with it. A list of commercially available programs and devices can be obtained by sending a request to the Department of Audio-Visual Instruction, National Education Association.

3. In evaluating the specific content which a self-instructional program purports to teach, the program can be examined to determine what the student is required to do and whether the student's responses reflect the kind of competence which the educator wishes to achieve. Like other educational materials, programs labeled with the name of a particular subject matter vary widely with respect to content and instructional objectives.

4. Just any set of question and answer material does not constitute a self-instructional program. One major type of self-instructional material proceeds by small steps requiring frequent student responses. These steps can be examined to see if they embody a careful, logical progression of the subject matter. Items in such a program are designed so that the student will respond to the critical aspects of each item or will perform the important operation which that item was meant to teach. Furthermore such programs generally provide a wide range of examples illustrating each principle or concept.

5. Self-instructional materials are designed to adapt to individual differences by allowing each student to proceed at his own rate. Some types of self-instructional materials further adapt by "branching" to alternate materials. For this purpose, questions are designed to diagnose the student's needs, and to provide alternate material suited to those needs. The material is designed so that the choice of answer to a particular question determines which items will be presented next. Incorrect answers take the student to items containing information designed to correct the error before continuing through the sequence.

6. An important feature of almost all self-instructional materials is that a record of the student's responses provides a basis for revising the program. The prospective purchaser should ask about the extent to which revision has been based on student response and how the preliminary tryout was conducted.

7. The effectiveness of a self-instructional program can be assessed by finding out what students actually learn and remember from the program. The prospective purchaser should find out whether such data are available and for what kinds of students and under what conditions the data were obtained.

8. Active experimentation with self-instructional materials and devices in school systems is to be encouraged prior to large scale adoption.[11]

[11] *Programed Instruction,* Vol. 1, No. 1, New York: The Center for Programed Instruction, Inc., May, 1961, pp. 4, 7.

A revised, more lengthy statement on criteria for assessing programmed instructional materials is found in the February, 1963, issue of *Audio-Visual Instruction* and in the Spring, 1963, issue of *The Journal of Programed Instruction.*

Teachers should never lose sight of all important objectives in selecting materials for programmed instruction, as well as materials of any other type. If they do, they may select materials which contribute little to some types of objectives, such as ideals, interests, attitudes, social skills, and habits.

In selecting instructional materials, schools should guard against being influenced by outside pressures, direct or indirect, that would limit the freedom to teach and learn. Statements concerning "loyalty" and "non-subversion" which appear in connection with selection of materials show that schools are cognizant of critics in the community and of the tendency of some groups to level charges against instructional materials as containing "subversive" materials or statements, often taken out of context. The danger is that these pressures will unduly influence school people in their responsibility to help pupils examine and criticize ideas.

There is no doubt that the atmosphere of regarding liberal ideas with suspicion has influenced the selection of textbooks and other instructional materials. One unfortunate result appears to have been a tendency in some schools toward greater centralization of the process of selection. The safeguards can become so formalized that it becomes difficult, or at least discouraging, for a teacher to secure the necessary current materials on up-to-date problems and issues.

One way to avoid being influenced by such pressures to the extent that learning is adversely affected is to work with regularly established citizen groups in developing policy for the selection of materials, as is done in a growing number of communities. (See Chapter 3.)

In making the choice, all resources should be considered. The human elements in the learning situation are one of the most important resources. The teacher himself is generally recognized as a resource of utmost importance. Not so generally accepted or understood is the valuable resource of the pupils. In any class of twenty-five children, youth, or adults, some of the most helpful assets can be found in the group. There will be children who have moved from other sections of the United States, who have traveled to various parts of the country, or who have lived in other countries; there will be children from middle-class homes, lower-class homes, and upper-class homes; there will be children from different races and religions; there will be children who have had experiences in other schools.

There are the resources in the school community, such as the lunchroom, the halls, the school grounds, the books to be taken care of, the traffic to be regulated, supplies to be inventoried and stored. There is the community, with its rich resources in governmental institutions, welfare institutions, business places, industries, homes, farms. There are people in the community, people who have interesting backgrounds, people who have interesting hobbies, people who have ideas that may differ from others' ideas, people engaged in various occupations. In the community there are the trees, the woods, the soil, the rock formations, illustrations of erosion and conservation practices, wild life, game animals, tame animals—all of these are rich and wonderful resources at hand for every school.

ISSUES AND POINTS OF VIEW

The issues develop largely in the use of materials and represent differing philosophies of education.

1. *Is the textbook an essential aid to learning, or is it a crutch that fosters the use of a subject-centered approach?*

There is nothing wrong with textbooks or workbooks in and of themselves. Textbooks in this country have been highly developed with attractive formats, illustrations, questions, suggested learning activities, and other learning aids. They are good sources of information. The issue lies almost entirely in their use.

The workbook is misused when it is placed in the hands of every child and all do the same exercises, whether or not they need practice in a particular skill. It is misused when it becomes a lazy man's way of teaching and children learn to fill in exercises rather than to think clearly about problems and to read with understanding.

In like manner, the textbook has been considerably misused. When it is followed slavishly and pupils are assigned a chapter to study day by day, learning suffers. In such instances, one can observe children peeking into the book to find the right answers as the teacher is asking the questions. Little thinking occurs. The child learns to repeat what the book says.

Instead, the textbook should be used as a source like any other book. It is referred to for information, for suggested learning activities, and for further references. If a teacher is interested in helping pupils to learn how to seek information from different sources and how to get different points of view, as well as in adjusting the difficulty of the materials to the ability of the pupil, it makes good sense to use a number of different texts rather than a single one. Yet, one persistent problem that remains is that very few appropriate textbooks have been published for the bright or for the dull pupil.

The textbook can serve as a common base for the investigation of problems. The class might read sections of the text and then together develop problems for investigation, questions that they would like to know more about, problems that have aroused their curiosity.

In the study of instructional practices, sponsored by the NEA Project on Instruction, the principals rated the textbook as the resource most useful for a teaching program, when compared with locally prepared materials, state courses of study, and materials prepared by professional associations, educational foundations, and national studies.[12]

2. *Should the course of study be used as a guide to the curriculum, or as the curriculum to be followed?*

This question is still argued. Many hold that, in order to facilitate transfer of children from school to school and district to district, a common course of study should be used. They tend to see courses of study as a nationally prepared and used document.

Others argue that courses of study should be flexible in order to suit the teacher, the class, and the community. They believe that no amount of coercion to get teachers to follow a state course of study would achieve the slightest uniformity, except superficially, since children vary so greatly in backgrounds, learning rate, and achievements.

3. *Should the selection of instructional materials be done locally or by the state?*

The movement to have state adopted textbooks has gained some headway. One of the reasons for the more recent upsurge of interest is the desire of some groups to protect children from the immoral, the subversive, and the un-American. Other more rational arguments have been the economy of state selection and the fact that education is a state obligation.

Opponents of this point of view point out that investigation of textbooks occurs often when people are frightened during periods of crisis. They ponder that, although schools should not put into children's hands the obviously shoddy and pornographic literature, there is a problem of where censorship ends. Selection of materials for instructional purposes and the use of materials intelligently, they argue, protects children far more effectively from inroads of undesirable ideas, moral or political, than outright censorship. State selection of textbooks moves dangerously close to censorship.

Interestingly enough, this question does not often arise concerning the obviously unfit materials or obviously outright propaganda but

---

[12] National Education Association, *The Principals Look at the Schools*, Washington, D. C., 1962, pp. 23–24.

concerning passages taken from some respectable book. *The Merchant of Venice,* for example, has been attacked for its portrayal of an ethnic group.

It is probably only a matter of time before censorship groups move into the area of newer instructional materials. Motion picture censorship has long been a point of controversy. The real issue is what promotes democratic ideals and freedom of thought.

16

THE UNIT ORGANIZATION
OF CLASSROOM EXPERIENCES

The major task of curriculum development is organizing a plan of instruction for the classroom. The teacher, no matter what his point of view about the curriculum, has to plan the work in the classroom for his particular group of pupils. In the end, the kinds of experiences that children have in his room are his responsibility.

The planning of classroom experiences is carried on within the framework of the curriculum established by the school district. In some cases, especially in smaller schools, the teacher's only course of study may be his textbook. In other cases, he has virtual freedom to plan within the general guidelines of purposes and suggestions for content, experiences, and materials. In a few instances, he may be told what and how to teach. The likelihood is, however, that the teacher will have more freedom than he can use.

School tasks should have a unity for the child. He must see the different parts of the school program as having unity in relation to himself and the problems that he faces. How such unity can be achieved through the planning and organizing of classroom experiences is the concern of this chapter. The problem is not a simple one. But steps can be taken to move away from the limited view of what the teacher demands to one in which the pupil shares with the teacher the long-range design for the class. For many teachers, moving from daily to weekly assignments would be a major step.

THE UNIT ORGANIZATION

Meaning of a Unit

The unit of work is a well-accepted concept in education; yet it has many meanings. Textbook publishers use the term to refer to a particular chapter or block of subject matter. Many teachers use it in the same way with reference to sections within their own subject. Other teachers use it to signify a series of related activities in which children engage. As used here, a *unit* is an organization of experiences and content around some problem or goal to aid the pupil in integrating his learning.

The important distinctions to be made are these: For whom does the experience or information have unity? Around whose problems or goals are the experiences organized? The source of unity is the significant factor. It may lie in the subject matter or in the learner. If it rests in the subject matter, there may be no unity for the learner. There is a vast difference between a unit taught for the purpose of learning a certain block of subject matter and one that is taught to achieve some purpose of the learner and to satisfy his needs.

The basic difference between units as taught in the classroom is the extent to which the experience-centered [1] or the subject-centered approach is used. The differences between these approaches to the development of the unit lie in the purposes for which the subject matter is used, how it is used, the degree of emphasis on change of behavior as the goal, the consideration given to quality of experiences and to pupil purposes and needs, and the extent to which the learner participates in planning his goals and experiences. The unit in which the subject-centered approach is paramount centers in the past and has a "backward look," while in the experience-centered unit the teacher and pupils look toward the future for taking some action on a problem.

The experience-centered unit is a planned group of experiences around a problem or purpose of the pupils, using any subject matter needed to solve the problem or achieve the purpose. It results in the achievement of change of behavior of pupils, some of the goals being inherent in the process of planning and executing the unit. Titles of experience-centered units do not distinguish them from subject-cen-

---

[1] Throughout this discussion, the term "experience-centered" will be used. If the reader prefers the term "problem-solving," or if it has more meaning for him, it is suggested that he substitute it for "experience-centered."

tered ones. They are more likely to be in the nature of problems, such as "How Can We Improve the Unsafe Conditions in the Streets of Our Community?" Both the subject matter and the process used in the unit are means of helping the learner to achieve his goal in the experience-centered unit.

The maturity of the learner, the extent to which he is a beginner in the study, and the degree of general education or specialization represented by the content will determine how remote the goals are, the amount of use that can be made of vicarious experiences, and the extent to which the experience-centered approach can be used. As the learner matures and as he studies more specialized areas of knowledge, he works toward goals that are not immediate. As a pupil advances in understanding and in specialization, he can profitably make greater use of vicarious experiences.

A *resource unit*, or as it is sometimes called, the source unit, is an organized plan of suggestions centered around some problem, which serves as a source of ideas for objectives, learning activities, evaluation, and materials to assist the teacher in planning the teaching of a unit. The resource unit contains more suggestions than can actually be used. It is planned for an appropriate age or grade level.

A *teaching unit* is a unit as actually carried out with the children or is used to refer to the teacher's unit plans for a specific group of children.

A resource unit can be used for preplanning the teaching of either a subject-centered unit or an experience-centered unit. Only in teaching the unit can the differences be clearly distinguished. If all of the subject matter is carefully preplanned and the teaching unit is outlined ahead of time in great detail, the teacher is using more of a subject-centered approach. If, on the other hand, the preplanning consists of determining the objectives that he wants to stress, the kinds of experiences that he hopes to use, and the kinds of materials that he will have in the classroom, he will be using more of the experience-centered approach. It is important to understand that the subject-centered approach and the experience-centered approach represent a continuum. The teacher applies more or less of the concepts of either approach in any type of unit that he teaches.

Advantages of the Unit Organization

The unit has an advantage over daily assignments only if it achieves some unity of experiences for the pupil. There is no inherent magic in the unit organization that will achieve unity in learning. It is not immune to the deadly formalism that can transform any teaching method into a ritual.

The very procedure of developing a unit closely approximates the steps in the process of learning. The pupils are motivated toward a goal; they are then confronted by a problem-solving situation which must be overcome if the goal is to be reached. The next step is carrying on various kinds of activities in order to solve the problem situation. They discover or learn successful ways of reaching the goal. As further units are studied, there is a repetition of similar problem-solving until behavior is changed.

If the experience-centered approach is used in the teaching of the unit, it will be more in accord with learning principles. Pupils solve problems that are vital to them. There is motivation in the problem-solving process. Change of behavior—developing new attitudes, understandings, skills, and appreciations—is emphasized rather than learning subject matter for its own sake. The subject matter is drawn from various subject areas as needed in order to solve a problem, rather than being divided into artificial subject lines, each to be learned by itself. Where children work on various phases of the problem, attention to all types of growth can be given since the teacher works among pupils. The pupil has an opportunity to participate through planning, carrying out, and evaluating his experiences throughout the unit. A variety of activities can be planned in order to suit the varied abilities in the class.

The teaching of a unit centered around a problem gives an opportunity to practice democratic procedures in the process itself. Pupils have the opportunity to make choices, to plan together in groups, to decide upon what is to be done, to share ideas, to select committees, to select leaders in the various groups, to take responsibility, to investigate and get the facts, to draw conclusions. These behaviors represent the heart of the democratic process. The teaching of an experience-centered unit is a cooperative, interactive process.

Applicability of the Experience-Centered Unit

The extent to which the experience-centered approach to unit organization can be applied varies considerably with the maturity of pupils, the degree of specialization of the content, and the teacher's understanding of the theory behind the approach and how to apply that theory.

The more mature in mental development and background the pupil is, the greater is his skill for relating new experiences and ideas within his own framework of previous experiences. He is able to handle more abstract concepts and materials and to do more independent study. His social goals are more remote. Consequently, a more systematic organization of subject matter is appropriate.

The experience-centered approach can be applied more effectively to the area of general education, such as social studies, than to the area of specialized education, such as advanced mathematics. When specialized education begins, the field is more circumscribed, or confined mainly to skills as in the case of typewriting or machine shop. In such a situation, it is obviously not so feasible for pupils and teachers to center planning around problems that meet the pupils' social and personal needs and interests. The problems are special and the field becomes a narrower one. Since subject matter cannot be drawn from various areas to solve the problem, there cannot be as much freedom in planning.

In order to carry out the experience-centered unit effectively, teachers need to understand the theory behind the approach, believe in it, and know how to carry it out. These conditions do not exist in the majority of the schools today. Many teachers do not feel secure enough in a situation where there is a great deal of latitude for planning the curriculum with pupils. In order to achieve competency and security in this approach, teachers need to do cooperative planning among themselves, led by someone skilled in the process.

However, these limitations do not mean that the experience-centered approach applies only to elementary schools. There are general education programs in both secondary schools and colleges that stress unity of learning. There is no logical reason why the teacher in the field of general education should utilize the same procedures that are used in training a specialist. The purpose of general education is to develop an intelligent citizen who can think for himself and solve problems in the world today, one who has an integrated personality and who knows how to live and work with people. These goals determine the kinds of behavior changes that the teacher is working toward in developing such a person. The goals for specialized education are different and are intended to educate a person for a vocation or for a special kind of interest.

Even in courses with more specialized purposes, a number of important aspects of the experience-centered approach can be applied to unit organization. Emphasis can be placed upon change of behavior as a goal, working toward achieving the kinds of behavior that a specialist in the area exhibits. The quality of experiences can be stressed. Students can participate to a certain extent in planning goals and experiences even though the limits are circumscribed.

College faculty involved in professional teacher education should be able through the professional courses to give future teachers practice in cooperative planning and in organizing of objectives and activities. Even though there is a body of accumulated knowledge that the instructor may want students to become familiar with, they can develop problems cooperatively part of the time. This is especially true of in-service teachers or administrators who have problems of curriculum development in their own classes or in the school system. Teachers cannot be expected to learn how to use the experience-centered approach by listening to someone talk about it. They learn through experience in their courses.

Selection of a Unit

There is a significant difference between organizing a unit in advance and selecting the problem for the unit in advance. This distinction is not always clearly made. Units that are organized in advance are subject-centered rather than experience-centered, for they inescapably limit the amount of planning and participation with the pupils in determining their own goals and in meeting their needs. Problems selected in advance do not necessarily have such limitations.

Certain criteria can be suggested for assisting the teacher in the selection of a unit or problem. They furnish the basis for thoughtful decisions as to problems selected. These are guides to assist in that decision:

Is the unit related to the interests and needs of the pupils?
Is it appropriate to the maturity level of the group?
Does it have good potentialities for developing patterns of desired behavior?
Is it based on a purpose or problem that is real to the majority of the pupils rather than a problem that is the teacher's only?
Does it build upon and grow out of the past experiences of the pupils and lead to further significant experiences?
Is the problem socially significant?
Will it offer opportunity for cooperative teacher–pupil planning in selecting, executing, and evaluating?
Will it make possible the use of life experiences of the pupils in school and community?
Are there sufficient resources available for the study of the unit?
Will it offer possibilities for utilizing materials from various fields?

Is there sufficient time to study a problem of such scope?
Will it furnish opportunity for a good balance and variety of activities, individual and group?
Will it give each child a chance to succeed in what he undertakes and use talents and interests in contributing to the group?
Am I sufficiently prepared to guide the work with confidence?

The source of units may be the courses of study, which may list required units or suggest units to the teachers; cooperative planning with other teachers or teams of teachers of the same grade or subject; collections of units in the instructional materials center; leads that come from units studied so that one unit leads to another and the work has continuity; or teachers working with pupils. The teacher's own imagination in examining the framework for the curriculum and the subject content should be one of the best sources.

PREPARATION AND USE OF RESOURCE UNITS

Considerable variation exists in the format of units. A school system may have its own familiar pattern that it prefers to use. A study of some 400 resource units in social studies revealed a number of rather common basic ingredients: introduction or overview, objectives, content, activities, evaluation, and materials.[2] No matter what pattern of outline may be used, these may be considered the essentials of a unit.

The resource unit has been employed to a great extent in assisting teachers in the planning of their work. Teachers in curriculum workshops and courses have prepared resource units that they and other teachers could use in their classes. Many school systems have a file of resource units to supplement the general course of study. Curriculum libraries ordinarily contain a large number of resource units prepared by school systems, professional organizations, and individual teachers. Resource units have generally proved effective in planning by committees or teams of teachers working together. Their main value is to the person who constructs them.

The resource unit is a way of planning for teaching of units of work. As noted before, it is not something to be followed slavishly and taught in its entirety. Resource units are used as a guide, a reference, and a service from which the teacher can draw ideas and information. The

---

[2] Wilhelmina Hill, "Designs for Social Studies Resource Units," Section Two in *Planning for Instruction*, Thirty-Second Yearbook, National Council for Social Studies, Washington, D. C.: National Education Association, 1962, p. 263.

planning of the resource unit is the process of seeing the totality of the unit, from the setting up of objectives to evaluation of outcomes.

The Introduction or Overview

The overview is a brief statement of the purpose and scope of the unit. It gives some idea of the unit's content and its possible uses. It should indicate the social significance of the unit and its relation to pupil needs. In addition, the reader should gain from the overview an idea as to grade or age level for which it was planned. A series of leads to the problems, theories, or topics to be considered may also be included.

The Objectives

The statement of objectives in the unit represents the kinds of outcomes planned for by the teacher. They form a resource list from which to draw.

It is important that the objectives be stated in specific terms. In many courses of study or units, objectives have been stated in such broad terms as "to adjust oneself to society," "to secure more accurate and adequate information about Central America," "to learn how to live democratically." It is little wonder that such objectives seem to bear limited relationship to the suggested activities and the materials. In other cases, objectives have been stated as facts to be studied. These are nothing more than lists of content to be covered.

The primary criterion for stating objectives is that they should be put in behavioral terms. It is helpful to state them in terms of what the *pupil* does so that the focus is always on the pupil and the behavior that he is expected to develop as a result of his learning experiences. A good test of statements of objectives, to see whether they are specific enough, is to determine whether they are capable of being evaluated. If it is impossible to ascertain whether the change of behavior has occurred, the statement is too general.

Objectives in a resource unit represent ideals that the teacher has in his mind as his goals of teaching. He does not expect that all pupils will approach these ideals. He also understands that a single statement of objectives cannot indicate different levels of achievement, but he expects different pupils to make varying degrees of progress toward achieving these objectives. He also understands that pupils have objectives of their own.

Although types of behaviors are not learned separately, they are listed in the resource unit under a number of categories in order to be sure that the teacher will be aware of all types of outcomes. The purpose is not to indicate that those behaviors are learned in an atomistic manner but to show how objectives are related to experience and evaluation. Understandings, appreciations, attitudes, and skills as controls of behavior cannot be attained without unity, for without unity knowledge exists in a vacuum. It is the configuration of all of these learnings into a behavior pattern that is important.

There is considerable advantage in stating specific objectives as what the pupil does, says, values, enjoys, or understands. The pronoun "he" conveys the idea that the pupil behaves in a certain way. If one uses the infinitive "to," the emphasis may be on what the teacher does to the pupil, for example, "to help the child realize . . . ," and it is easier to slip into the error of stating objectives as experiences that the teacher provides, i.e., "to provide for individual differences." If a person has a particular attitude, appreciation, skill, or understanding, he acts in certain ways different from the way he would act if he did not have them, or if he had learned different controls of his behavior. Interests, habits, and ideals are subsumed under these four classifications.

1. **Attitudes.** An attitude is a mind set or a readiness to react to situations in a certain way. An attitude can be expressed only in terms of how the person behaves if he has this particular attitude. Examples of statements of desired attitudes are:

He welcomes differences of opinions.
He withholds judgments until he has all of the facts.
He accepts the consequences of his own actions.
He respects authorized leadership and regulations.
He treats others with the same respect that he demands for himself.
He attempts to see the other person's point of view.
He wants to help other people.
He asks many questions.

2. **Appreciations.** An appreciation represents feeling or awareness about the value or significance of something. It is largely emotional in character. The liking or disliking of an experience causes a person either to want to repeat or to avoid the experience because of his interest in or aversion to it. Examples of statements of desired appreciations are as follows:

He enjoys the quaintness and charm of colonial heirlooms.
He chooses to attend good concerts.

He enjoys listening to music of all types.
He enjoys beauty and color in his own surroundings.
He likes to read books in his spare time.

3. Understandings. Understandings are concepts, principles, ideals, or generalizations of experiences which are used to guide future experiences. They result from the ability to organize, interpret, and relate experiences. If, for example, pupils learn to understand that when people make their own regulations they are more likely to abide by them, this understanding will govern future actions.

Understandings are not stated as understanding something "about" a certain phase of life, such as, "He understands about minority rights." In fact, the use of the prepositions "about," "how," and "of" cannot be used in stating understandings specifically. Instead, one understands *something* about minority rights; that "something" is significant: "He understands that minority rights must be protected within majority rule."

Understandings are built on experience; they are not learned by the student through memorizing them. The teacher has certain understandings in mind, actually as sample generalizations that might be drawn upon. He knows that many other kinds of understandings will grow out of the pupils' experiences. However, if he wants them to gain an understanding, for example, that group discussion can be improved by attention to group process, he will plan certain kinds of experiences that will give them an opportunity to evaluate their group procedures.

The following are examples of understandings:

He understands that citizenship in a democracy demands a responsible, actively participating people.
He understands that the individual who places the interests of his racial, cultural, religious, or social group above the good of society as a whole endangers his own freedom.
He understands that man's environment affects his way of living, his food, his clothing, and his behavior.
He realizes that the countries of Central America have been the melting pot of various races.
He understands that problems must be defined specifically in the use of the scientific method.
He understands that the modern computer has accelerated the possibilities for discovering new knowledge.

4. Skills or abilities. A skill is something a person has learned to do with ease and precision either mentally, socially, or physically. It is a type of behavior that varies from one that can be carried on rather automatically to various degrees of difficulty and complexity. A complex of skills is often called an ability. The following are examples of statements of skills:

> He knows how to use the index of a book.
> He knows how to skim in reading.
> He can use the library for research.
> He speaks clearly and distinctly.
> He interprets road maps.
> He writes with legibility.
> He writes with complete sentences.
> He can make a useful bibliography.
> He is able to draw up a hypothesis for testing.
> He can make a mortise-and-tenon joint.
> He can report interestingly upon his findings.
> He can introduce a friend properly.
> He knows how to dance.

It should be re-emphasized that skills, attitudes, appreciations, ideals, interests, habits, and understandings are *interwoven* in learning.

The Developmental Sequence

The developmental sequence lists various means by which the teacher can approach the unit, methods of planning with pupils the goals and experiences, and the probable learning experiences that can be used in order to achieve the outcomes desired. This section of a resource unit is intended to suggest the steps in planning a unit with the pupils and to provide a fund of resources to which the teacher can turn in the constant planning with the group.

1. **Approaches.** An approach or an orientation to a unit is a carefully planned means of stimulating the interest of pupils in some problem or topic or of using the ongoing environment as an opportunity for beginning a new unit. The first questions in the teaching of a unit are: How shall I get started? How will I get the pupils interested in something worthwhile? If required units are specified for the entire program, the teacher's task becomes more difficult, for he must attempt to find different approaches that will stimulate pupils in wanting to study what has been predetermined. If the situation is one in which there are many suggested units in the course of study, only a few of which may be required, the job is simpler since the teacher can utilize the environment of the pupils and their interests and purposes as a means for an approach to a unit.

Probably the best type of approach is one that comes out of the continuing work of the class. Some approaches of this nature are: (1) one of the committee reports or individual reports may stimulate pupils to carry on further study and investigation in this area; (2) the discussion, questions, arguments, readings, and other activities of pupils will indicate interests that are aroused; (3) field trips as a part of the unit often will stimulate an interest that is related to the previous topic; (4) speakers that are brought to class may have opened some new avenue of interest among the pupils; (5) questions arise from class groups; (6) the preceding unit suggests an additional one. With a more mature group of pupils, it is possible to discuss frankly the problems growing out of the previous study and to work on the basis of a problem census.

The second type of approach is one in which opportunities present themselves through daily events and occurrences not necessarily a part of the class work: (1) materials brought by the children from home, such as pets, hobby materials, and souvenirs collected; (2) trips that children have taken; (3) visitors to the school from a foreign country, from other states or localities, or from the community; (4) any event related by the pupil from his experiences and background; (5) some magazine article, book, or news item that a pupil has read and tells about in class; (6) some need for improvement in the school that has grown out of the deliberation of the student council; (7) any current event that draws the attention of the pupils; (8) the lunch program. An alert teacher capitalizes on events in the environment outside of school.

The third type of approach, which does not come spontaneously from the environment but must be arranged for deliberately by the teacher, is illustrated by the following: (1) the arrangement of an exhibit on a table or the bulletin board; (2) news items of interest called to the attention of pupils by the teacher; (3) stories that the teacher tells from his own reading; (4) arrangement of a field trip to stimulate interest; (5) the use of audio-visual aids in order to present some topic and to open up possibilities for problems.

If one approach is unsuccessful, another one should be tried. If several have been tried but failed to stimulate the interest of pupils, it would be wise to give up the unit at least for the time being and await some more opportune moment. If interest cannot be aroused, the chances are that pupils see no purpose in the problem, and that the quality of experience and learning would be inferior. In that case, the teacher would be better off to drop the unit.

After a problem has been suggested, time needs to be spent by the class on the analysis of the problem, discussing its meanings for them. The class can look at the issues and questions involved. Questions such as these ought to be considered: What is the importance of the problem for us? What could we do about the solution of a problem of this nature? If we did study it, what would be some of the issues involved? What are the kinds of things we visualize doing in getting information on the problem?

The following illustration of suggested approaches is taken from a resource unit on the cultural heritage.

1. After the class has become acquainted, the teacher begins a discussion of careers. Pupils discuss careers in which they are interested, and gradually certain members of the class tell what kind of work they would like to do when they finish school. The teacher further encourages the class to discuss the advantages and disadvantages of certain types of work. Questions arise, and from those questions certain problems are formulated. It is decided to seek answers to some of these problems. Soon, someone is asking about the kind of men who have been successful in business, or law, or labor-organizing.

2. The teacher designs a simple test utilizing popular advertisements from magazines and periodicals that stress some "cultural" slant. The actual cut-out advertisements should be used, and the children should be asked to explain the mythical illustration, name, or allusion. This test should be designed to interest the pupil by arousing his curiosity. It should offer a good stimulating introduction to the unit by posing as many general and varied questions as possible related to the scope of the unit.

3. The teacher exhibits certain personal family heirlooms to the class and discusses them. The following day, each pupil is to bring some "cherished possession" to class and give a short talk on it. This is a direct method of introducing our "cultural heritage" to the contemporary life of the student, and it opens more specific approaches and problems within the scope of the unit.

4. The teacher asks the class: "What do you think is meant by an 'individual's philosophy'?" The class discusses the question. Different aspects of a "code of living" for high school pupils are considered. Someone asks, "How do people determine their philosophies or 'living codes'?" The teacher is alert, and develops any seemingly "common interest" of the class that will lead into the work of the unit.[3]

2. Planning period. In this section of the resource unit, suggestions are given as to how to plan with the class. What steps can be taken?

[3] The examples in this chapter are taken from units developed by the Portland, Oregon, Public Schools.

What are some kinds of questions that I should ask the pupils? How can I elicit questions from them? Most helpful as a part of the pre-planning is an indication of how the planning will be done, how the pupils' questions may be listed and discussed, how the class in turn makes a selection or organizes all of the questions that have been asked into categories around which the work in the unit can be centered. The main purpose of this section is to focus on the importance of planning at the beginning and throughout the unit and to assist the teacher in the steps in planning.

The approach or introduction to the unit blends imperceptibly into the planning period. It is not possible to distinguish between when the introduction ends and the planning begins. In fact, in an experience-centered unit, pupils will be participating in the discussion from the beginning.

Following the decision of the class to study a problem, the group needs to go into a rather extensive period of planning its goals and determining its ways of working. Although planning occurs throughout the unit, this concentrated period at the beginning is the time when the teacher and the pupils work together on developing the framework and over-all plans. At this time classes of older pupils analyze further the issues and questions within the scope of the total problem to determine which ones are to be studied. The teacher defines the problem with the pupils, raising questions with them, having them indicate what they are interested in knowing, what questions they want answered, and what specific interests they have in the problem.

The class, through its questions, indicates the objectives that it has for the study of the unit. These can be listed on the board. They ought to be written in the pupils' words, not the teacher's, with any clarification of meanings being done together with the class. The teacher should avoid interpreting the pupils' statements according to the meaning he would like to read into them. After all the goals have been indicated, the group can work on organizing the items listed, either as an entire class or through a small committee. This phase of the class activity is in answer to the question: What do we want to know?

The next questions to consider are these: What do we need to do in order to find answers to our questions? Where can we find the information needed? This is the time when the teacher and the class determine their ways of working together and the materials needed. Many possibilities should be suggested and investigated by the pupils and teacher cooperatively. Ordinarily the questions will be so many that it will be obvious that the class cannot as a group study all of them. The class will usually need to be divided into committees to gather information or to perform the various jobs that need to be done in the study of the unit.

The teacher has a very important responsibility here. He has the obligation to help the pupils see the alternative ways of attacking the problems. He needs to discuss with the group what it would mean in terms of kinds of work to be done, the kinds of materials needed, the time required, and the like, in order to carry out the various suggestions that have been made. In other words, the teacher's role is to assist the pupils in arriving at more mature judgments based on an understanding of the alternative plans or proposals. Although the teacher does not come into the classroom with a cut-and-dried armful of subject matter that must be learned by the pupils, he does come with ideas, a background of experience, and a knowledge of the subject and the pupils and their interests.

The teacher needs to be patient at this stage, to realize that it takes time for pupils to think carefully about their goals. Planning should not be hurried. Some teachers feel that the planning stage is not "teaching" and that, unless the group is actually busy working to find answers, they are not "studying." Learning is going on in such planning.

The following illustration of planning activities is taken from a resource unit on Oregon:

The class will begin with a present day area of experience, such as the growth of Portland as a city, that will lead into the areas of the past. Several days will be spent in class discussion in order to develop and determine the pupils' objectives. Then selections of individual or group fields of interest will evolve. Since all activities are continuous and since all activities merge, the planning for each work period will contain suggestions from the group as to questions directed toward necessary readings; demonstrations; experiments; and creating, summarizing, and evaluating activities.

The class will usually work in committees of five to ten pupils. The chairman of each committee will be responsible for the assembling of the material and the active participation of each member of his group under teacher guidance. At the beginning or end of each work period, the class will evaluate the accomplishments of its respective committee or individuals and make plans for further execution of their area of experience before the reassembling of the committee.

The class as a whole will determine what type of plan they wish to use for a culminating activity; furthermore, suggestions will be offered for the continuation of this area of experience, which will lead to higher levels of achievement.

3. Probable learning experiences and content. In the resource unit, the next section makes suggestions for content and learning experiences that follow and blend into the planning with the class. In this discussion, the manner in which these resource activities can be listed in the unit is presented first. Then the ways in which the teacher can put the resource unit into operation in the classroom are suggested.

The list of probable learning experiences anticipates some of the problems that might come up in connection with the unit and suggests various kinds of activities and procedures that the teacher can use in working with the pupils in order to accomplish the objectives. These are all suggestions that will assist pupils in the solution of the problems. Such lists help teachers in their thinking about how they will work with pupils in committees, carry on group and individual activities, and secure the kinds of resources they will need to tap. The list should provide for individual differences, for talented, creative, dull-normal, or unusually industrious pupils.

These activities should be related to the objectives. For example, if pupils are expected to learn judgments on the basis of consideration of different points of view, the activities and the materials should indicate means by which different sides of a question can be explored.

One form used is stating the problems, the activities, and the materials in three parallel columns. The "problems" point out questions or possible subproblems. The "activities" indicate the types of experiences, such as reading, speaking, writing, listening, taking field trips, planning, constructing, drawing, interviewing, conducting a discussion, presenting reports, organizing, dramatizing, figuring, conducting surveys. The "materials" suggest the kinds of construction materials, films, maps, charts, recordings, exhibits, books, and other reference materials that the pupils can use in the study of the problem.

In an illustration from a unit on physical and mental health (see page 446) note that the activities and materials show a direct relationship to the possible problems that may arise. A similar listing can be made showing the relationship of objectives to activities. A long list of activities without any organization is not of as much value. The problems represent the samplings of content to be used for the unit. Some teachers prefer to delineate the content further.

1. *Attacking the problem.* This stage in the development of the unit is often called the "working period" since it is the time when pupils work at the plans they have developed. It is the period for

Problems	Activities	Bibliography
Phobias, fears, anxieties: a. How can we organize our social and personal lives to minimize the fear factor? b. What are the social origins of fear? c. How do fears affect our mental lives? d. How do fears affect our physical lives?	Make a list of the irrational fears that you have experienced and see if you can explain them. Do the same for anxieties. If your fears and anxieties arise from some social situation, can you suggest some way of changing the situation? Make a list of people you know whose lives have been marred by fears. Talk to one of them to discover possible causes and effects.	*Our Changing Social Order* (Gavian, Gray, Groves) *Be Glad You're Neurotic* (Bisch) *Why Men Fail* (Fishbein and White)
Alcoholism: What are the social origins of this problem? How does it affect family life? How does it affect individual health and efficiency?	Visit alcoholic clinic in Portland area. Visit "drunk tank" at city jail. Attend lectures being given by specialists.	*Man Against Himself* (Menninger) *Social Adjustment* (Dexter) *American Government* (Magruder)
Inheritance: Are our physical illnesses inherited?	Make a sociological chart of your family or some other family showing all the pertinent facts you are able to assemble.	*Social Adjustment* (Dexter) *Heredity and Disease* (Mohr)
The family: How does the well adjusted family promote personal morale and mental health? How does a broken or unhappy family affect mental health? How to account for antagonisms between parents and children? Between siblings?	Compare yourself and your parents with respect to: a. family life (brothers, sisters, etc.) b. education c. cultural facilities d. economic opportunities e. relationship between parents and children.	*Current Social Problems* (Gillette) *Recent Social Trends* *Our Changing Social Order* (Gavian, Gray, Groves)

study, for collecting information, for pooling information, and for individual and group activities in the solution of the problem.

After the committees have been formed, instruction needs to be given as to how committees operate; how leaders are selected; the kinds of leadership roles required, such as leader, recorder, and observer. The teacher works with the pupils, guiding them in how to tackle and analyze a problem. This is a most difficult stage even for adult committees of teachers, who usually need similar help. Up to this point, the problem has been defined by the class. Each committee will need to define its job further and break down the responsibilities of the group.

This time is rich in opportunities for the teacher to guide the group in becoming more proficient in its ways of working together in the solutions of problems. It is a laboratory for learning group processes. Most important of all is the quality of thinking that goes on in the group: where there is a give and take of ideas; where facts need to be searched for; where group opinions of different people are weighed; where there is opportunity for reading from many sources; where children learn how to interview people; where they meet people in the community; where they make contacts with community organizations, industries, labor unions, government; where they consider the social functions carried on in the school.

Among younger children, this period will be devoted to individual work and group work, with the teacher leading the total group as well as smaller groups. They will need more teacher direction than more mature pupils.

The working time for the unit should give opportunity for the class as a whole, as groups, or as individuals to work on skills for which the need is evident—skills in writing, spelling, interviewing, reading, speaking, and presenting reports.

Another problem in the working period is the presentation of progress reports. In some way the whole class should be informed from time to time as to what the different groups are doing. Reporting provides an opportunity for teaching the skills of oral communication and organization of information. The progress report gives other pupils a chance to make suggestions to the group and to ask questions of the committees. This phase of the working period is often neglected. It is a mistake for committees to work without any communication among the groups. If they do, pupils may fail to grasp how the problem studied by their committee relates to the whole problem.

It should be obvious that class time must be used for committee and individual investigation. However, some teachers still have the holdover concept from the days of lesson-hearing, namely that class time is for some kind of reciting, reporting, discussing, testing, or "teaching" activity and that study and preparation by the pupils should be done outside the class. Many consecutive days may be needed for pupils to work on committee or individual investigations, with the teacher assisting the different groups and at times calling the groups together to help them on some mutual problem. Unless sufficient time is given for investigation and research, little use is likely to be made of the community, audio-visual materials, individuals outside the school, and resources other than reading materials. Provision is made for individual activities and responsibilities, some for the talented and gifted, others for the slow, others for those with special interests. Not all of the class time is spent in small-group work. At times class members work as individuals, depending upon purposes and abilities. There is planning to be done by the individual pupil and the teacher, according to how much assistance the pupil needs. The goal is to guide the pupil to assume responsibility for his own actions and to gain independence in study.

Cooperative evalution of the progress toward the goals is done periodically. When a class makes decisions, it needs to look frequently at the consequences of those decisions. How far have we progressed toward our goals? What are we failing to do well? What have we accomplished to date? Evaluation of process is an integral part of ongoing work. Throughout the work, the teacher is constantly observing and evaluating in many ways.

2. *Culmination: Summarizing or action-taking stage.* At the end of the unit the teacher should plan with pupils some way of bringing the study to a satisfactory close, so that they will feel a sense of satisfaction and achievement with the work that they have done. This is the time for generalizations, conclusions, and action based on the decisions growing out of the problem studied. Although evaluation has been a part of the entire unit, at this stage the class looks at its goals, its progress, its ways of working, evaluating cooperatively what it has done.

If a genuine problem-solving approach has been used, the study will come to a natural conclusion with the teacher guiding the pupils in deciding when they will present their findings to the class. The class can set some deadline when the committees should have their findings or recommendations ready.

One of the perplexing questions faced by teachers is the matter of achieving variety in reports, in order to avoid their becoming boring to the pupils. Various reporting devices can be used: tape recordings, role-playing situations, panel discussions, a report by some member or members of the committee followed by general discussion, the presentation of findings on slides made by the group, the use of charts and graphs to highlight the report, written reports, and dramatization. Again the teacher needs to work with pupils to assist them in devising interesting ways of presenting the information to the class that in themselves are valuable learning experiences.

Another perplexing question is how to tie the reports together so that they are not separate entities. At this point teachers need to remind the class that there was a common problem, so large that many groups were needed for its solution. All reporting should help toward the solution of that problem.

If the problem has been a real one that concerns the pupils' own environment, they will do more than listen to reports. As a group, they will need to come to some conclusions with regard to the reports through a discussion of the findings. In some cases, group conclusions may mean a revision of the recommendations made by committees. Any final recommendations for action represent the thinking of the class as a whole.

Only in the case of this kind of a problem can social action be taken as a result of the study. Teachers should be on the alert to see what kinds of action pupils can take. For example, in a number of schools, classes have studied safety and have drawn up safety rules for bicycle traffic that have been presented to the city council and have been adopted. In some problems of democracy or civics classes, as a result of the study, the pupils wrote to their Congressman to request certain changes. In a high school social studies class, the pupils studied the reasons why industry was moving out of some New England communities. A group of citizens in the city had organized a committee to buy the woolen mill that was to be vacated. The class decided to raise money and contribute to the committee. Their contributions amounted to about $200.00. Thus, the pupils were taking action to make a real contribution to the community.

Not all units need to "culminate" in the stereotyped sense of the word. Summarizing activities and cooperative evaluation of what has been done are important. But far better than to end all units with a program is to strive to develop units of study around problems of children, where the study will lead to some action on their part. They will then be learning one of the most significant skills for living in a democratic society.

Evaluation

The section on evaluation in a resource unit suggests to the teacher how to evaluate progress toward the objectives. Evaluation is a constant process throughout the unit. The listing of the means at this point in the resource unit does not signify that evaluation is left to the end of the unit. Many of the suggestions designate how teacher and pupils can evaluate together and how pupils can evaluate their own progress.

In considering the means of evaluation, the teacher should look at specific behavior changes to which, as indicated in the objectives, the unit would make definite contributions. The desired outcomes should have been stated in terms of understandings, attitudes, appreciations, and skills as possible controls of behavior that would emerge from the study of the unit. Evaluation, then, must be concerned with the extent to which these controls of behavior have emerged. How can we find out whether the pupil is growing in the directions signified by these changes of behavior?

The discussion of objectives indicated that they should be stated specifically enough to be evaluated. The statement concerning evaluation should indicate how each of the specific objectives or groups of specific objectives can be evaluated. For example, if the objective were, "He uses the facilities of the library efficiently" then the resource unit might indicate the following evaluation: "The teacher should observe the pupil when he works: (a) Does he use the card catalog? (b) Does he use the *Reader's Guide?* (c) Does he follow the index numbers of the books on the shelf? (d) Does he show increasing knowledge of the library's arrangement, as to the location of magazines, biographies, and other reference aids?"

Further examples from a resource unit on "Our Cultural Heritage" are given here.

Understandings

Outcome	Means of Evaluation
Students will realize that clear sound thinking precedes good writing and good speech.	Students will be asked to give examples from their experience in class as evidence of this in a test. Teacher will note in log individual and class indications (through remarks in class and in written papers) of their realization that sound thinking must precede good expression. Application of this realization will be noted by individual improvement in writing and speaking.

Students will understand that such factors of our "democratic heritage" as free speech, free press, the right to vote and to hold office, equality before the law, etc., represent much struggle and sacrifice on the part of those that went before us.

Teacher will note in log such understanding when manifested in discussion and written papers. Teacher can also check through different tests given the class.

Attitudes and Appreciations

Students will have an appreciation of good stories.

Teacher will note enthusiasm and interest of student in regard to his individual reading. The amount and quality of each student's reading will be indicative of this appreciation. Independent reading for pleasure should especially be noted. The teacher will talk to individual students about their reading in order to evaluate and develop this appreciation.

Students will appreciate the school.

Teacher will note interest and attitude toward school particularly in regard to type and degree of student participation in school affairs. At this level, the teacher must pay particular attention to the *wish* to participate, for the students are mainly adjusting to their new school environment. Most direct participatory activity will be confined to the class.

Students will have respect for the other fellow, for his rights, his opinions, and his welfare.

Teacher will observe manner in which each individual cooperates with the class and what his attitude is in regard to contributions of others. The students can evaluate themselves and each other in an impersonal way. Reaction of other teachers to same students in their respective classes can be checked in regard to these attitudes.

Skills

Students will be able to work a problem through to a satisfying conclusion.

Teacher can note indications of this in arguments of individual students during class discussion. Teacher will check in log for number of problems solved by each student. Reasons for non-solution of problems must be considered by teacher before making final evaluation.

Students will be able to utilize the dictionary, source materials, and the library facilities efficiently.

This ability will be indicated to great extent by individual's quality of work produced. The librarian can observe work of committees in library. The class can be given an objective test covering this material.

Students will be able to write clearly and punctuate logically.

Through constant individual attention, teacher will note improvement in student's papers as to style. Teacher will go over each paper with student carefully drawing attention to errors and suggesting improvements.

Bibliography

For many teachers who are well acquainted with planning with pupils and utilizing a variety of activities, the bibliography is perhaps one of the more valuable features of the resource unit. It should contain a rather extensive but well-selected list of references that can be used by pupils in the classroom. In the materials section under "probable learning experiences," brief mention has been made of the materials. The bibliography should contain complete bibliographical data concerning the reference, including the author, title, name of publisher, place of publication, date, and pages. It is important that these items in the bibliography be complete in order that they may be found or purchased by someone not familiar with them.

In addition to the pupils' references, a section of the bibliography contains teachers' references: selected books, professional periodical articles, courses of study, curriculum bulletins, and other publications to which the teacher can refer in order to get further information on the unit. These references will contain books that discuss the content of the unit and those that deal with teaching procedures.

Other types of instructional aids, such as films, slides, recordings, videotapes, that are especially pertinent to the unit should also be listed.

ISSUES AND POINTS OF VIEW

Most of the issues that arise concerning organization and planning of classroom experiences concern the part that the pupil plays in curriculum development.

1. *Do pupils participate most effectively in curriculum development by serving as members of school curriculum councils and committees, or by helping to plan the curriculum with the teacher in the
classroom?*

This issue is a somewhat academic one. Yet, it does get at the
question of just how do pupils participate in curriculum improvement.
If one takes a limited view of what constitutes curriculum activities,
the obvious way for pupils to participate would be to serve on curriculum councils.

From an expanded perspective of curriculum development, pupils
participate in many ways. They participate in curriculum experimentation, as members of demonstration classes in workshops, as subjects of study groups; fill out checklists and rating forms; assist in
school and community surveys; help in evaluating the school program; plan their out-of-class activities; serve on student councils;
conduct interviews with citizens; and do other activities that are
a part of the total curriculum improvement process. Some would say
this is enough, or too much.

But it is in the day-by-day and week-by-week planning of goals
and activities in the classroom where pupils are at all odds the most
effective curriculum makers. This is the time and place where pupils
sharing in the process can have the most influence. This chapter
and the one that follows are, in a sense, a description of how the
pupil participates in this way.

2. *Should the teacher do all of the organizing of content and activities of a unit, or should the pupils participate in the process, and
to what extent?*

Some would exclude the pupil from classroom or any other curriculum-making activities. Children, youth, or even young adults
are not mature enough, they say, nor do they know enough about
the subject to help plan the curriculum. This is the experts' and the
teachers' job, who know what younger pupils or older students should
learn and can best make these decisions. Unstructured planning will
result in leaving out many important phases of the curriculum.

Those who believe in teacher–pupil planning of a unit contend that
the classroom participation by the pupil is the means by which he
enters into the processes of purposing, questioning, sharing, planning,
and evaluating. These are fundamental skills in themselves, necessary to a democratic society. They are learned through guided practice under skillful supervision. Besides, the curriculum can be adjusted to a pupil's needs, interests, and background if he is a part of
the process. After all, the teacher is still the responsible leader of the

class who can see that important learnings are not omitted. The unit does need to be entirely unstructured to permit planning by pupils.

3. *Does the unit plan of organization promote unity in learning, or does it become a ritualistic, stilted form that confines more than it frees teachers to be creative?*

This kind of question ought to be asked about every form of organization used in education. For it is the user that is imaginative, not the pattern. Any pedestrian, dull teacher can cause a plan to be routine and lifeless. It is easy to go through the motions. All one has to do is learn the formula or the steps. It is difficult to put life into a plan or an idea.

Whether or not a unit promotes unity depends on whether or not the teacher sees its potentialities for unity, the maturity of the pupils, and the nature of the subject matter. Perhaps some children ought to have a maximum of independent study, a minimum of group activity. For others it should be the other way around.

The greatest value of the unit organization of experiences may be in the fact that the teacher, in his planning, must relate objectives to content and experiences and to evaluation. This is a fundamental concept in curriculum development.

17

CLASSROOM PLANNING
FROM GOALS TO APPRAISAL

How does the teacher develop the curriculum in the classroom? What should be the teacher's and the pupil's roles in the day-by-day decisions that have to be made concerning the experiences that pupils will have in school? What the teacher does and what the pupils do in working together in the classroom to evolve goals and activities and to evaluate learning are the gist of this chapter. Principles and criteria for planning and putting plans into operation are presented. This is fundamentally curriculum development. The classroom is the focal spot for all national, state, system-wide, and local school curriculum improvement. It is the place where improvement becomes visible.

COOPERATIVE TEACHER–PUPIL PLANNING

The topic of teacher–pupil planning has been the butt of considerable ridicule, especially from those who would be insecure in the use of such a procedure. Some teachers are guilty of having helped to perpetuate mistaken ideas about planning with children. Some of the misconceptions are that teacher–pupil planning involves pupil planning alone, that it is without direction and purpose, that it requires no planning ahead of time, that planning caters only to the immediate interests and whims of pupils, that planning is done to get children to accept the teacher's ideas, that it is an easy way of teaching, that individuals may lose their individuality in the group, that children fail to select what they need or what is important, and that time will be wasted in planning. These misconceptions are discussed in interpreting the meaning of cooperative planning.

Principles and Meanings

These principles clarify the meaning of teacher–pupil planning. However, actual experience in planning with pupils is the only way to understand thoroughly the meaning of the concept.

Teacher–pupil planning means cooperative planning on the part of pupils and teacher. It is a matter of teamwork. Cooperative planning means teacher *and* pupil planning. It implies that the teacher is a member of the group, working with pupils in developing goals and experiences, finding materials, and evaluating progress. The teacher guides and assists the group. The extent to which the teacher needs to guide the planning depends upon the pupils' maturity, age, and previous experience in planning. By virtue of his greater experience, education, and maturity, he helps pupils to set up significant and attainable goals and to achieve those goals. Some people have the idea that the teacher comes into the room and asks the pupils what they want to do, and the group takes off in that direction. Anyone who has done planning with a group to identify its problems knows well that it takes time to decide upon problems for group study. If the process is a hurried one, the problems will probably be those that the teacher wants to study. Planning is deliberative, cooperative decision-making, not catering to the immediate interests and whims of pupils.

It means working together on common purposes or goals. Since classroom teaching usually involves group teaching, cooperative planning is the means of arriving at common purposes that will be accepted and understood clearly by the group as a whole.

Work that has been carefully planned by the teacher and the pupils is very likely to have a very definite purpose in the minds of both. When the teacher makes all the decisions, the purpose is in the mind of the teacher alone. Careful planning establishes directions for the group, usually of a long-term nature for a week, six weeks, or a semester. In fact, teacher–pupil planning has a more clearly defined purpose for all concerned than does the traditional procedure. It has more specific direction because it requires the teacher and pupils to think through for some time in advance where they are heading. In the daily assignment type of procedure, where the teacher does all the planning in making the assignments, the visibility of direction is zero.

It means sharing and making decisions and thoughtful judgments. The children assist the teacher in making these decisions. For them, it is a learning experience in acquiring new skills. As children become more proficient in making thoughtful judgments, they are given a greater share in participation.

It does not mean getting children to accept the teacher's ideas and making them believe that these ideas are their own. This is an authoritarian concept of planning as a way to fool the children into doing what the teacher wants to do. Such a notion does not consider the teacher and the pupils as a group working together. It belittles the children's ideas. Nor is it sharing.

There are limitless possibilities for utilizing children's and adults' ideas within required units or subject matter. Mature young adults should be able to do planning, becoming more independent in their thinking, in self-direction of their activities, and in clarifying their goals.

It means constant appraisal of progress toward goals. The teacher considers evaluation a joint venture with pupils throughout the learning experience. He realizes that children's perceptions of themselves and their progress is important. This is consistent with the principle of learning, that pupils should be aware of progress toward their goals. It is quite different from the pupil's being aware of his progress only when he sees marks posted on a bulletin board.

It means pointing up pupil needs. Cooperative planning is a way of finding out the needs of pupils. As pupils indicate their interests, their problems, and their questions, they reveal their needs. In fact, a group planning with the teacher is more likely to select content that is better suited to its own level of ability. They indicate what is important to them.

A common fear expressed by teachers who are hesitant to do any cooperative planning with children is that children may not select what they need or what is important. The experiences of teachers who have planned with children and older pupils should dispel such fears. Pupils do not suggest just their own whims, inconsequential problems, insincere questions, or work that is easy. Indeed, teachers have found that in many cases they must guide the pupils to avoid selecting problems that are entirely too difficult for them to accomplish.

It means innumerable hours of preparation. Successful teacher–pupil planning is not haphazard. It requires an inventory of the resources within the group, an inventory of information and assistance that can be secured outside the class, a diagnosis of what the pupils are like, an analysis of the kinds of experiences that will be helpful in developing desired behaviors. A sure way to fail in successfully carrying out cooperative planning is to avoid any planning before the class meets.

One of the drawbacks to wider use of teacher–pupil planning is that it requires a great deal of hard work on the part of the teacher. This procedure actually requires a broader background in the subject than the lecture or question-and-answer method of teaching. The latter is a relatively simple procedure in which the various factors can be easily controlled. Teacher–pupil planning is more difficult because the teacher cannot foresee all of the possible avenues to which the planning might lead. Intellectual curiosity on the part of the pupils will probably lead them into areas that the teacher had never imagined they could deal with intelligently.

It means accepting pupils' ideas as of value. A teacher who would be successful in planning with pupils needs first of all to believe that pupils' ideas and opinions have value. He will accept all ideas as important and help the group to sift them in order to determine which are the most important. Criteria will be developed with the class by which to judge suggested goals or activities.

One of the principles of group process is that everyone's ideas are accepted as being worthwhile for discussion. Instead of submerging the individual, this process actually strengthens the importance of individual thinking within the group. Teacher–pupil planning by the group strengthens rather than eliminates individual study and creative work. The individual does not reach his ultimate in isolation. The group enlarges the field in which he may function in order to arrive at his potential.

It means having courage and faith in oneself. Planning with pupils means having faith in one's ability to carry out plans that evolve from the situation, faith in children, and courage for going into a situation that may be different from the usual. Teachers with such courage and faith who have taught for many years using more direct procedures develop some of the best skills in planning with pupils. Teachers with a feeling of insecurity are unlikely to be successful in planning with children. They need the security of a single textbook, a lecture, detailed notes, or some other crutch on which they can lean. They should not even attempt it.

It means giving children, youth, and adults a chance to learn democratic skills. The crux of planning is to give pupils experiences in learning how to live with others. Planning skills are democratic skills. Teachers may think of cooperative planning as a waste of time. The "saving of time" by reliance upon an authoritarian approach is a delusion. Similar criticism is made of democratic government. However, in the long run, it is actually the most efficient method. Since it involves people in thinking and planning, they accept the conclusions as their own and are more likely to carry them out with greater enthusiasm, purpose, and efficiency.

It means planning when needed as the group is faced with a problem. If planning is done only at set times, it may become so formalized that it defeats its own purpose. It should be done when the group is faced with a problem, whether that be at the beginning of a unit in deciding goals and procedures, or as the work of the class proceeds. Whenever he sees the need for planning, the teacher should take time to do it with the class.

Planning by the Neophyte

The teacher who has never planned with pupils before needs to begin gradually. He cannot expect immediate success if he suddenly begins to work with pupils in a way unfamiliar to both him and the pupils. The gradual development of pupils' attitudes and skills is a learning process.

Begin in small ways. Perhaps the sale of stamps, the Christmas party, an assembly, or an excursion will offer an opportunity for planning with pupils. In these instances, the pupils are already motivated and will have ideas as to what to do. Pupils may assist in developing the rules of conduct in the classroom. Or the teacher can develop suggestions with the class as to how a certain activity can be improved. The class might make suggestions concerning the environment of the classroom. Pupils can be asked to answer such questions as whether they have pursued a topic far enough to clarify it for them, and whether they are ready to go on to the next topic. From these small beginnings the teacher can stem out into more extensive types of planning.

Plan for concrete tasks. The arrangement of the room, the selection of leaders to carry on discussions, choosing people to take part in a dramatization, and getting ready for a visit from the parents are more concrete subjects for planning than what the group wants to accomplish over a longer period of time. These are specific tasks that can easily be envisioned and can, consequently, be planned more readily. Pupils can be given experiences in this kind of planning before they begin working together on long-range goals for the classroom work.

Plan for short periods of time. Setting up a plan for a particular day in a self-contained elementary school classroom, planning for some of the activities for the next few days in a secondary school classroom, or discussing the work for the next meeting or two in a college classroom involves relatively easy planning. Beginning in this way, the teacher has an opportunity to correct his mistakes and to gain greater confidence for long-range planning.

Plan first in a school activity. Teachers who lack confidence in being able to plan in the classroom may be able to begin in a pupil activity. In such activities, pupil participation is the accepted practice. The teacher will find himself more secure in cooperative planning, serving in the role of adviser to pupils in an extraclass activity, than he would in the classroom where tradition has tended to put him in the role of a person who makes all the decisions.

Work with another teacher or two. It is always helpful for two or three people who are trying something new to get together for mutual support. By the very process of planning together, talking over what they hope to do, their successes and failures, they will learn more of the skills of planning with children in the classroom. Moreover, they will reinforce each other in their attempts, finding out that their mistakes are not unique.

Begin planning wherever we are. Of course, there is no other place to begin. However, the whole point is that the teacher should not attempt at once to do all the possible kinds of planning that he finds suggested in professional articles and textbooks.

Relation to Teacher–Teacher Planning

The question arises: How can we plan goals and activities with pupils in the classroom and still have planning among teachers? Will not the latter result in decisions that will limit the teacher in planning with pupils? If the cooperative teacher planning is concerned with organizing the lessons that are to be presented in the classroom, naturally it will restrict the possibilities for teacher–pupil planning. However, teacher–teacher planning can be concerned with getting some agreement among the teachers as to the goals, experiences, and ways of evaluating the achievement of the goals. Planning may also deal with the opportunities in the school and in the community for learning experiences and with the cooperative use of materials. By sharing ideas, all of the teachers will be enriched, not restricted in what they can do in the classroom.

Most important of all, joint planning by teachers should be continuous. Teachers should have an opportunity to talk over experiences in their classes and to exchange ideas. It can lead to some cooperative work among the pupils of different classes.

There is still another value to be considered in teacher–teacher planning. Working with one's fellow teachers in planning gives the teacher experience and confidence in being able to do planning with his pupils.

PLANNING OF GOALS

The Teacher's Goals

The teacher's goals are the directions by which he operates. They are his guidelines for selecting content and activities and for evaluating what he is doing. There can be no intelligent judgment or appraisal without objectives.

The previous chapter indicated how goals are stated objectively and specifically in a resource unit. Formal or informal, written or unwritten, the teacher's goals need to be visualized in terms of pupils' behavior. A goal that has meaning is one that communicates to others the person's intent and excludes the greatest number of possible alternatives. This degree of objectivity is as necessary in stating goals for teaching as it is for research.

As the teacher gains skill in formulating objectives, he does not necessarily write them out, but he has them definitely in mind. He sees them as parts of a behavior pattern, in which attitudes, appreciations, skills, and understandings are unified and interrelated.

Planning with children does not mean that the teacher is without purposes of his own. It does mean that his concept of goals differs from the traditional ones, which may consist of a book to be read, a certain library selection to be studied, or a specific problem to be assigned. Why should these particular problems, this particular book, or this selection be studied; why not some other book, or some other selection, or some other problem?

If the teacher has in mind certain understandings as desirable outcomes of instruction, will he predetermine all generalizations that pupils make and, consequently, minimize the thinking process? Generalizations cannot all be preplanned. The pupil must have freedom to arrive at his own conclusions. This is a goal in itself, of utmost importance. The teacher can list only the *kinds* of generalizations which may develop from a problem-solving situation. Certain types of understandings are necessary to a well-educated person; for example, the concept that freedom involves responsibility as well as privileges, or the understanding that hypotheses need to be formulated and tested in order to arrive at valid conclusions. Generalizations cannot be taught merely by having the teacher state them. They are outcomes of experiences (and more than one experience, by the very nature of a generalization).

The Pupils' Goals

For some it is difficult to understand how the teacher can have goals for instruction and still plan with pupils their goals in the classroom. The two are not antithetical. In fact, they are complementary. There is no conflict between the teacher's and the pupils' goals *unless* the teacher's goals are confined to the subject matter to be learned. The teacher uses the pupils' stated goals to develop the behavior patterns he has in mind.

The teacher is the status leader who assists and guides the pupils in learning how to select and define the problems on which they work. This is a part of the process of teaching pupils how to carry on their activities independently. It is also teaching pupils how to work as a group in defining goals. It should be remembered that this is a learning process. The younger child naturally needs more guidance in planning his work.

Pupils state their goals in terms of what they want to know or what they want to learn to do. They do not deliberately set out to change their own attitudes. A group of eight-year-old children studying a problem of how to attract birds to the schoolground listed, among other things, what they wanted to find out:

> What birds visit our school?
> What birds stay here all winter?
> How are birds alike?
> How are birds different?
> What foods do birds eat?
> How do birds help us?
> How can we help birds?
> How do birds protect us?
> How do birds build their nests?

These were some of the goals set up by a laboratory class at the junior high school level in a summer workshop:

> How to stand up before a group to talk
> How to choose class officers

How to vote properly
How to listen while others are speaking
How to carry on conversations and discussions
How to work together so that the class can accomplish what it wants
    to do.

In a fifth-grade unit on "How Our Town Has Changed to What It Is Today," the pupils first gave reasons why they should study their town: "Because we are going to grow up and live here," "Because we go to school here," "Because people will ask us about our town, but I don't know about it," and others. They listed such questions as these for their study:

1. Has Seymour always been the town name?
2. How did Center School replace the high school?
3. How is our town government organized?
4. What is our relationship with neighboring towns?

In these illustrations, it is apparent that the children's goals would not conflict with the teacher's. In some cases, they may well have extended those the teacher had in mind. With older pupils and adults, the goals of the teacher and the students become very much the same.

SELECTING EXPERIENCES

Experiences are planned to bring about the desired behavior changes indicated by the goals. The teacher deliberately creates situations in which particular skills will be used and in which there will be opportunity to develop desirable types of attitudes and understandings. For example, if he wants pupils to like to read and to select materials of their own for leisure-time reading purposes, he will need to establish conditions in which they can browse and select books of their own liking.

Criteria for Selection of Experiences

In addition to the main criterion of furnishing a medium for developing the desired goals, certain other tests may be applied to determine desirability.

Are the experiences appropriate to the maturity of the group and do they build upon previous experiences? One of the teacher's most important tasks is to find out about the pupils' past experiences.

Only if he knows these somewhat in detail can he judge the pupils' maturity and readiness for new experiences. He should not expect pupils to be able to make a study of the community through interviewing citizens in the community unless someone has assisted them in building up skills for interviewing and in acquiring some knowledge of community problems. Children are taught the concepts of motion and change by using familiar objects in their environment, with which they have had experience.

Do they give each pupil a chance to succeed and to use his own talents and interests in contributing to the group? The teacher's responsibility is to use and develop pupils' talents and interests. He should help pupils plan group experiences in which everyone will have a share in the solution of the total problem. He should know pupils well enough to utilize their potentialities and special abilities. Who can draw well? Who is artistic? Who has ability to talk to people easily? Who is mechanically inclined? Who knows how to work with people easily? Who is interested in collecting insects?

Are they varied enough to provide for a balanced development of the pupil? In planning experiences with pupils, a variety should be provided, both to take care of individual differences and to foster development of the child physically, mentally, socially, and emotionally. A range of activities includes research and investigation, presentation of materials, creative types of activities, drill, experimentation, organization and evaluation, writing reports, listening to conversations or talks, carrying on group discussions, giving reports, observing others, using audio-visual materials, analyzing relationships, drawing graphs, using maps or charts, constructing models, playing games.

Are they recognized by pupils as means of achieving their purposes? Unless pupils perceive activities as ways of achieving their own purposes, it is doubtful whether they will be particularly helpful in bringing about desired behavior changes. When the teacher assigns questions for study, he disregards whether or not the pupils see any purpose to studying the questions. What reasons do they have for answering them? To please the teacher? To get a good mark? These are not intrinsic purposes but artificial means by which teachers believe they get pupils to "learn." As the curiosity of pupils is aroused to learn more about atomic energy, repairing a radio, China's relation to the United States, or the growth of white mice under different diets, the experiences related to these purposes have meaning for them.

Do they broaden and expand the pupils' interests and concerns?

Trivia are not worthwhile learning experiences. Pupils need guidance to improve their judgment as to which school experiences are significant. For example, looking at a motion picture because it is available in the school may be an activity that is readily suggested by the pupil, but if it is done just for the sake of "seeing a movie," it has doubtful value. Teachers also need to be mindful of guiding pupils toward developing their concerns for other human beings and broadening their interests into new fields.

Are they challenging and do they lead to further worthwhile activities? Planned experiences should arouse the curiosity of the pupils. Reading lessons over and over so that they can be repeated to the teacher is perhaps one of the most boring kinds of experience that could be provided for pupils. Retaining a pupil in a grade and reteaching the same content will leave him still unchallenged. Furthermore, are the experiences of a terminal nature or will they lead into other worthwhile kinds of activities? Will they promote interest along new lines, new avenues, so that the class can pursue these activities either as a group or as individuals?

Are the materials, resources, and equipment needed available, or can they be discovered or constructed by the pupils? Teachers should not encourage pupils to carry on activities for which the resources are unavailable. However, pupils can assist in discovering such resources, bringing materials from home, or constructing those needed. Science teachers often have pupils construct equipment for experiments. If little children are interested in bringing their pets to the classroom, they can help to find the materials needed to construct housing. A valuable learning experience is the collection of specimens, illustrations, or pamphlet materials related to some particular goal.

Do they make it possible to use the community and the child's own community as laboratories for learning? Learning that is confined only to books does not have the most favorable setting for promoting changes in behavior. Situations in which a child uses his school and his community are far more useful than is apparent in many schools. What are the opportunities in the lunchroom, in hall traffic, in regulating safety in the schools, in school government, and in studying the community?

Do they furnish an opportunity for the teacher to study the pupil as an individual and as a member of a group? When the teacher stands at the front of the room directing the class or asking questions, he loses all opportunity for close contact with pupils. He needs to work among the pupils so that he can see them in their re-

lationship with others, study them as they work individually, find
out what their habits are in attacking problems. In a discussion, he
can have pupils act as leaders so he can observe how pupils behave
in the situation. As they work in small groups, he can move among
them and observe them more closely. Only if it is possible to get
to know pupils, can teachers plan effectively for suitable learning
experiences that will meet pupils' needs.

*Does the experience provide continuity for this individual child to
increase his knowledge?* In order to provide for individual differences, experiences are planned for individuals as well as for groups.
The principle of continuity of learning means an increasing difficulty,
complexity, and range of experience for any one child. What does
the child already know upon which I can build? Diagnosis is an
important factor.

Selection of Subject Matter

The teacher is concerned with the kind of subject matter utilized
to bring about the desired behavior changes. How can he select
subject matter that is important and that will do the job of achieving
the goals? How does he select from the many books available, from
the various resources, from all of the content in the field? Suggestions in answer to these questions have been made throughout the
book up to this point. For example, in the discussion of learning,
social values, child and adolescent development, and knowledge,
consideration has been given to principles that apply to selection of
content. This section serves as a summary and more direct focus for
some of the things that have been said about content.

Subject matter is defined as the principles, techniques, facts, values,
processes, and modes of response that man has learned about the
world in which he lives, himself, and his relationships to his environment. Since it encompasses more than is found in a particular book
on a specific subject, the selection of subject matter involves more
than the selection of books. The selection involves more than accepting the organization of subject matter. Subjects were organized
in a logical fashion to preserve the culture, not to teach it. Organized bodies of subject matter are resources for learning, not something
to be learned verbatim. They represent the organization of material
that has already been learned.[1]

Principles are suggested for selection of subject matter that will

[1] See William H. Burton, *The Guidance of Learning Activities,* New York:
Appleton-Century-Crofts, 1962, pp. 337–40.

help provide experiences of high quality. They apply to any level of teaching. The subject matter used is chosen by teacher and pupils in the class within the framework of school policy and agreements arrived at by the staff as a whole. The principle of flexibility gives the teacher and pupils the needed latitude for developing their significant problems and purposes.

The pupil's total environment is accepted as a source of content. This is a much broader concept than considering content as what is found in the course of study or in the textbook. It includes the opportunities for providing experiences that are found in the school, in the classroom, and in the community. It includes relationships with other pupils in classrooms and other school functions. The arguments that arise on the playground, the adjustments required to be made to a new school, the difficulties caused by pupil cliques, the bond issue for a new school, the issues in the local election—all are subject matter provided by the environment. The immediate environment furnishes an opportunity for gaining an understanding of the principles, values, processes, and modes of response which man has learned.

Subject matter is selected to suit the purposes of society and the school and to bring about the behavior changes that are consistent with these purposes. Subject matter should be chosen to suit the purposes, the times, and the problems at hand. One kind of content will be best suited to develop the purposes of a totalitarian society; another kind, the purposes of a democratic society.

Subject matter dealing with India, China, Burma, Pakistan, the United Arab Republic, Israel, Ghana is necessary to developing an understanding of the problems involved in the United States' relations with these rapidly developing countries. Change of attitudes toward Asiatic and African peoples can come about through as many contacts as possible with the background and thinking of these people.

It contributes to the understanding and improvement of society. Through the subject matter which is a part of the school experience the child learns to understand his society, the world about him, the scientific discoveries and principles, the development of man, different kinds of people, the earth and its geography, the products of man's mind, the techniques and skills that man has developed.

Nothing is more important in the school of the last half of the twentieth century than promoting skills and techniques for good human relations and developing an understanding of social forces, social change, and persistent social problems. Without such understanding that will lead to intelligent behavior in the closely inter-

woven world of today, scientific developments may well prove to be
the monster that man could not control because of his backwardness
in social insights. Content from such areas as these is not for the
concern of social studies alone: culture of American and other societies, social change, geographical understandings, democratic values,
moral and spiritual values, totalitarian societies and methods, why
people think as they do, the moral fiber of today, efforts to obtain
world peace, the question of disarmament and world organization for
peace, space exploration. Instead, understandings from such areas are
basic to the school program whether the subject studied is called
science, English, or social studies. The teaching of intelligent reading
and the selection of what appears on newsstands should deal with
such live social issues. The implications of scientific developments
and the scientific method are significant content of science.

*It is relevant to the pupils' life problems, everyday living experi-
ences, and purposes.* In selecting subject matter, the teacher should
have in mind the experiences that pupils have in their environment,
the problems that they face, the purposes that they have in their own
lives.

Content ought to reflect the right of the pupil to examine critically the experiences and the institutions that are a part of the history of his world. City planning, the housing problem, the problem
of water supply, community recreation needs, the growing juvenile
delinquency, the relations of labor and management in local strikes
or in industries without such difficulties, industry moving out of the
city, a local citizen committee's efforts to clean up a political scandal,
all are proper content from the pupil's environment that lead to an
understanding of his society and an improvement of that society.

In a growing number of schools, especially junior high schools,
teachers are using content from pupils' personal and social life problems: one's beliefs and values, sex education, managing personal
affairs, selecting a vocation, and one's appearance. Psychology courses
for senior high schools deal with mental health problems that young
people face. Psychological problems may be studied through literature, such as physical deformities' effect on behavior, family influences on behavior, emotional conflicts, and social pressures.

It is related to the development and maturity of the pupil. The
matter of giving a pupil something suitable to read used to be a
simple procedure of giving him a book written for his particular
grade. The content of the material that is used needs to be suited
to the child's development and to his maturity. Problems that are

planned with pupils and interests that are observed lead to the study of subject matter that is suited to the maturity of the pupil.

It is related to the pupils' interests and needs. The study of developments in physical sciences may be of interest to an eighth-grade boy, but not to a twelfth-grade girl. A study of twelfth-grade English attempted to discover the needs and interests of pupils by means of a questionnaire to high school seniors, recent high school graduates, and teachers of English. The respondents were asked to check on a long list the things they thought should be included in the twelfth-grade English course. The excerpt on page 470 from a table in the report of the study compares the selection of topics and activities for the three groups. The items are listed in the rank order of the selections of the high school students. These include the first ranked twenty-five of forty-seven items.

Subject matter is timely and accurate. Both are fundamental characteristics of content used in the schools. The teacher will need to be a student of society and of his particular field in the secondary school, if he expects to keep up with the growing knowledge in any field. The materials that he uses should include at least an access to references that reflect current discoveries and events. Deliberately slanted or biased information to suit regional prejudices has no place in school textbooks. Teachers can find enough of such biased information to teach the skills of distinguishing propaganda from fact.

EVALUATING PROGRESS TOWARD GOALS

Another integral part of developing the curriculum in the classroom is the evaluation of progress toward goals. Evaluation is a continuous process operating as a part of setting the goals, planning experiences, and determining to what extent the goals have been achieved. The procedures for evaluation under the experience-centered approach to curriculum development are markedly different from those under the subject-centered approach. Those who cannot accept these rather radical departures from traditional practices will find that they will be unable to use the experience-centered approach effectively. Evaluation as an integral part of the learning process is contrasted here with the concepts of measurement, testing, and marking.

No other factor in the teaching situation will govern the way curriculum experiences are planned and carried out so much as the manner in which evaluation of outcomes is done. How a person evaluates the results of his instruction reveals a great deal about how

Item Number	Topics and Activities	Per Cent of Respondents Recommending Inclusions of Items		
		Students	Recent Graduates	Teachers of English
1	Tours out of school	84	83	48
2	Developing personality	82	81	62
3	Club activities	80	79	°
4	Speaking in public	78	84	°
5	Solving teen-age problems	73	51	40
6	Informal "get-togethers"	73	78	°
7	Becoming socially acceptable	72	77	54
8	Friendship (problems of)	72	71	°
9	Understanding meaning and choice of words	71	80	54
10	Wise spending	66	60	°
11	Marriage	66	60	°
12	Interviewing (conduct, attire, etc.)	64	74	43
13	Writing original stuff	63	63	°
14	Family life	63	71	18
15	Improving spelling, punctuation, etc.	63	75	°
16	Leading or participating in discussion	62	84	64
17	Making grammar helpful	61	74	72
18	Making conversation	59	82	48
19	Courtship	58	29	°
20	Discrimination (problems of)	57	41	°
21	Intolerance (problems of)	55	°	°
22	Speaking before a group	55	88	100
23	Taking part in a meeting according to parliamentary procedure	55	65	62
24	Introducing a speaker	55	75	64
25	Round-table discussion	54	72	29

° No response because of differences in questionnaires.

SOURCE: Central New York School Study Council, Committee on English 12, *A Guide for the Teaching of English*, Syracuse, N. Y.: The Council, 1949, p. 14.

he teaches. Whether they realize it or not, for a good many teachers evaluation is the tail that wags the dog.

Evaluation is a much broader concept than measurement. Since measurement commonly refers mainly to testing with objective or standardized instruments for quantitative data, it is just one aspect of evaluation. Evaluation, on the other hand, is the making of appraisals or value judgments based on all types of data, qualitative as well as quantitative. Moreover, evaluation looks at the total situation rather than just at its respective parts. It is concerned with feelings, emotions, meanings, values, attitudes, interests, and purposes—factors that measurement specialists call the "intangibles" because they are more difficult to measure objectively and quantitatively with valid and reliable instruments.

In a nutshell, the modern concept of evaluation is the continuous examination of the growth of the child as a total personality. Evaluation is concerned with interests, critical thinking, social sensitivity, needs, values, personal and social adjustments, beliefs, human relations, concepts, tastes, physical development—all phases of a pattern of behavior. In order to evaluate, teachers must be alert to what is happening in the class, in activities, on the playground, in halls, and even outside of school. They also need to create situations in which evaluation of behavior can occur, individually and cooperatively: writing ideas, experiencing feelings, reacting to films, action on field trips, remarks during discussions, undisturbed conferences. In these situations, the teacher gets to see and hear what is taking place in the child's development.

Principles of Evaluating Pupil Progress

The principles of evaluation of curriculum improvement discussed in Chapter 9 apply to pupil progress as well. The concepts that should govern evaluation in the classroom are stated here briefly in terms of a teacher working with pupils.

The teacher's evaluation is in terms of specific behavior changes as the goals of instruction. The changes of behavior that are the goals of instruction furnish the basis for evaluation. Evaluation done without reference to goals is without direction.

Evaluation occurs continuously as learning activities are carried on in the classroom. Teacher and pupils from time to time stop to consider together what progress has been made. As pupils plan together, they consider ways in which they will check up on themselves to see whether or not they are proceeding satisfactorily with their plan. The teacher can help them think about how well they are achieving their purposes, both as individuals and as a group.

In a junior high school class, the log written by the pupils records how the group stopped to evaluate why it was not achieving its purposes. They discussed "why our committee didn't accomplish very much," and listed these reasons:

1. Too much fooling
2. We didn't settle down

3. Wasted too much time talking about other things
4. Everyone talked at once
5. Were not well organized
6. Others interrupting our group
7. People wandered around too much
8. Not enough interest in the meeting
9. Not enough time
10. Arguing
11. Leaving group to go to another group.

Thus, evaluation in the classroom is concerned both with the constant evaluation by the teacher and pupils of individual progress and of the group's progress toward its objectives.

Evaluation follows, rather than precedes, the establishment of objectives. First of all, pupils and teacher determine the objectives for their work; then, using those objectives as a base, they decide how they are going to evaluate progress. This process is the exact opposite of studying for the purpose of passing a final examination. In the latter case the examination comes first and is the governing factor. The experiences are provided in order to help pupils pass the examination.

Pupils and parents participate in evaluating pupil progress. Evaluation is a cooperative job among teachers, pupils, and parents. Pupils have conferences with their teachers to discuss their progress; they keep records and charts of the work that they do; they do self-evaluation through checklists. Parents through conferences with teachers should be aware of the goals of the school. They need to talk frequently with the teacher about the kinds of behavior the child exhibits at home and at school.

Evaluation considers the pupils' environment, individuality, background, abilities, present learning status, and total growth. Evaluation is by no means merely a rating of a child against the abilities of the rest of the group or those of children of the same age throughout the country. It is an appraisal of a child's individual growth and his personal equipment, such as his background, his emotional problems, his record in school, his previous achievement, his abilities. It looks at him in his setting.

Growth is evaluated by using the pupil's previous growth as a reference point. Evaluation needs to be of a longitudinal nature, through recording the pupil's growth over a period of time, including growth that can be seen in anecdotal records, as well as tests and other means of appraisal.

Evaluation should be a valuable learning experience in itself. If examinations are an integral part of the teaching–learning process, they can be valuable learning experiences. In such cases the teacher and the pupils will follow through on the basis of the test to discover what has been learned and what pupils have failed to learn. Other kinds of evaluative procedures discussed in this section, such as evaluation of products and growth in attitudes, are in and of themselves an integral part of the teaching–learning situation.

In evaluation, actions are cooperatively examined in terms of consequences. Once pupils have achieved a goal which demands doing as well as knowing, they need to examine the consequences and results of their action. What effect did it have on us? On others? How well did we do what we set out to do? When a field trip is taken, a valuable part of the learning experience is evaluating the trip, what was accomplished, mistakes made, insights gained, opportunities missed. As committees give reports, evaluation of the significance and the interest aroused should be made. The most valuable learning in giving an assembly program probably occurs in the cooperative evaluation led by the teacher after the program has been given.

Means of Evaluating Instructional Goals

The procedures are discussed and illustrated briefly to indicate the varied means that can be utilized in evaluating progress toward goals.

Teachers' records of pupils' behavior. There are many ways by which teachers can make a record of children's behavior. Some are more systematized than others.

1. *Log and diaries.*

The teacher keeps a log or an account of the work carried on in the class and a diary of happenings during the day.

2. *Rating scales.*

The teacher indicates on some scale of values the rating of the child on different aspects of his growth. The scale is used to record the judgment of the observer, such as a handwriting rating scale. On some numerical scale or descriptive rating scale the teacher may rate personality, study habits, work habits, work experience, leadership, or in fact most of the school objectives.

3. *Checklists.*

These lists may ask questions, such as: Does the pupil look for necessary data by himself? Does he work for the best interest of all? Checklists of evidence of responsibility, cooperation, getting along with others, hobbies, attitudes shown in games, work habits, steps in a production job, and other activities and characteristics generally give subitems in detail to be checked.

4. *Inventories.*

The teacher through some kind of an inventory form (similar to checklists) keeps a record of accomplishments and work done in class.

5. *Sociometric techniques.*

In constructing a sociogram, the teacher asks questions in order to obtain a picture of friendship structures and other group relations in the class. The sociogram reveals natural groupings and indicates who are the accepted and rejected children. The questions are usually given in connection with some ongoing activity such as seating, or choosing committees. The teacher makes a graphic picture through which relationships become more apparent concerning leaders, isolates, cliques, and individual children's social relations. Sociograms are often combined with interviews after the sociogram has been given.

Other sociometric techniques that discover social relations among children are a social acceptance scale or a social distance scale in which pupils reveal whether they accept or reject other pupils and the "guess who" technique in which short descriptions of people are given and the pupils indicate which classmate the paragraphs describe. Pupils may be asked to give reasons for acceptance or rejection in the use of any sociometric technique.

6. *Projective techniques.*

In projective techniques, the individual projects his feelings and unique personality characteristics into new situations. He responds to an unfamiliar task, meaningless in itself, to which he gives his own interpretation. For example, ink blots, pictures, drawings, paintings, word association, films, cartoons are all used as materials for the test. These techniques have been used largely in connection with evaluating personality adjustments. Most teachers are not trained in their use, although increasing numbers of guidance counselors are.

7. *Records of voluntary activities.*

Records are kept of the nature of activities or services that individual children volunteer to do.

8. *Recordings.*

The teacher makes tape recordings of some phase of the class work that can be used later for evaluation purposes.

9. *Library readings.*

These readings may be recorded by librarians or by teachers for each individual child.

10. *Contributions of individuals.*

The teacher keeps a record of the various kinds of contributions that pupils make: services to the room, leadership, contacting speakers, bringing information, greeting visitors.

11. *Observation and anecdotal records.*

One of the most fruitful means of evaluation of pupil growth is the observation of behavior. Only through such observation can a teacher determine whether or not a pupil is growing in the development of attitudes and appreciations, feelings, values, and interests. In addition to the ways listed above, the anecdotal record affords a means of studying changes in behavior. The teacher records what the pupil says and does in different situations, not his interpretation of that behavior, selecting the more important incidents to record. Samples of behavior over a period of time reveal behavior patterns and growth. This kind of evaluation requires creating opportunities in which to observe pupils. Summarizations and analyses are made from these cumulative records.

Pupils' records of their activities. One of the ways in which children participate in evaluation is through keeping a record of their activities in class. These may vary from the more detailed log which is kept day by day by a class recorder to simple records of the books read.

1. *Diaries of activities.*

Such records furnish concrete evidence not only of the things that children do but of their feelings as well. Pupil diaries may be kept of class activities or activities outside of school.

2. *Lists of voluntary reading.*

These readings are listed by the children either on library cards or cards they prepare. The class may have a library committee that takes charge of these records.

3. *Records of trips.*

These may be class trips, committee trips, or travel done by individual pupils during their holidays.

4. *Time charts of week's activities.*

Pupils keep a chart or record of the time spent in study, in play, in work activities, or in doing nothing. Such time charts kept even for part of the school day are revealing to pupils as to the amount of time they spend on concentrated work as opposed to meandering, talking to other pupils, and fooling around.

5. *Checklists of activities connected with a unit.*

These checklists can be constructed to include such items as: had an interview; read newspapers; worked on a committee.

6. *Logs.*

These are usually kept by the class, which appoints a recorder from day to day to keep the log. It is a record of what the curriculum is like. Class secretaries who keep a day-by-day log are of invaluable assistance to the class and to the teacher for evaluating or giving an overview of the work of the class.

7. *Questionnaires and inventories.*

Questionnaires filled in by students concerning their home background, their past schooling, their hobbies, their likes and dislikes are useful in the total evaluation picture. Vocational interest inventories are used by secondary school and college guidance counselors. Teachers construct interest inventories to find out about pupils' interests in school, leisure reading, movies, radio and television programs.

Pupils' reactions and self-appraisal. Children's records of their activities may be used either by the pupil or by the teacher as a means of evaluation. Through these procedures, the pupil appraises himself against some standard or looks critically at his own growth over a period of time.

1. *Profile charts of growth in specific areas.*

Through drawing a line profile, the pupil may keep a chart of his progressive scores on tests of reading speed or comprehension. He may keep scores on arithmetic tests to check up on his computation skills.

2. *Progress charts.*

The pupil keeps an actual comparative record of scores over a period of time rather than making a profile in the form of a graph.

3. *Written evaluation of accomplishments or experiences.*

The teacher may ask the pupils to write at intervals what each one feels he has accomplished in the class or course, having in mind goals that he has developed in conference with the teacher. During and at the conclusion of an experience, pupils write evaluations of their experience.

4. *Rating scales.*

On scales constructed by the teacher or by the class, pupils rate themselves as to the quality of work that they have done, according to a particular kind of scale, varying from excellent quality to poor quality. Usually such scales have three to five points, each described by a specific kind of behavior. Self-rating scales of work habits, cooperation, character traits, effectiveness in group discussion are examples.

5. *Conferences or interviews.*

Through conferences with the teacher, the pupils react to the work that they have done, evaluate their own progress, and appraise their own contributions. These conferences are an extremely important part of the total evaluation. They give the teacher a means for finding out more about feelings and values, gathering information about the child's home, gaining insight into his needs, helping him to gain a better picture of himself.

6. *Group appraisal.*

The kinds of group evaluation procedures discussed in Chapter 2 for studying the group structure and evaluating group process are applicable to the elementary and secondary school classroom.

7. *Role-playing.*

In playing roles of some other individual or replaying a situation in which the child acts as himself, new insights can be gained by pupils. Role-playing affords an opportunity for more objective analysis or evaluation of some situations in school that, at the time the event occurred, were too highly charged with emotion to be discussed objectively.

Performances and creative products. One of the means widely used for evaluation of growth is the actual performance or production of the pupils. It may be a demonstration or may consist of articles made by pupils. It is usually a creative product of the child's: a drawing, a model, a poem, a story, a dramatization, a pantomime, an idea for improving the classroom, a birdhouse, or metal jewelry. The judgment of the teacher is used in appraising the performance as related to his past performances and to his individual abilities and maturity.

1. *Oral and written reports.*

Teachers with the assistance of pupils appraise constantly ongoing activities in a classroom: reporting on individual research, giving committee reports, giving talks, writing reports of a study, writing requests to people, and writing reports of field trips. Samples of written work from different spot checks throughout the year, kept in the pupil's folder, are used as a means of evaluating his growth in skills and understandings. Written papers, such as autobiographies, are used by teachers to find out backgrounds as well as values that pupils hold.

2. *Scrapbooks and notebooks.*

Pupils keep scrapbooks and notebooks for projects in the classroom. These products furnish evidence of what is accomplished.

3. *Creative work.*

The actual products of the pupil's work in art, in industrial arts, in home-making, or in whatever area he exhibits creativity are tangible means for evaluation. The actual product, not a test on the product, is the best evaluation of the pupil's ability to act in certain ways.

4. *Exhibits.*

Pupils exhibit their work, often as a part of a culminating activity where the parents have an opportunity to evaluate what the child has done.

5. *Dramatizations.*

Dramatization is a type of performance activity which can be judged on various points of merit, on the basis of a number of performances.

6. *Pictures, movies, and tape recordings.*

Still pictures, motion pictures, and recordings made of activities in which pupils engage form a means of record and appraisal. Pupils may keep as part of their log a picture record of their activities in a unit.

7. *Demonstrations.*

Pupils can be asked to demonstrate techniques that they have learned, such as tumbling, playing a game, operating a mimeograph machine, or finishing a product in the shop.

8. *Experiments.*

A teacher can observe the process by which a pupil performs an experiment.

Parents' reactions to children's growth. The parents' evaluation of a child can help to give the teacher a total picture of the child's growth in and out of school.

1. *Conferences.*

The conference has replaced or supplemented some of the traditional methods of reporting to parents. If the conference is well-planned, the teacher can gather valuable information about the child, and plans can be made by teacher and parents in order mutually to help the child in his progress.

2. *Questionnaires.*

Questionnaires are often sent home to parents to gather data about their children's interests, hobbies, out-of-school activities, and information about the work of the parents.

3. *Visits to homes.*

This type of a conference has a special purpose. Only through visitation in the homes can the teacher become well informed about the environment in which pupils live and the home background that influences the child. Evaluation lacks accuracy and completeness unless it is considered in the light of all of the factors that influence the pupil.

4. *Letters.*

Frequently, teachers write to parents comments on report cards, and in turn comments are made by parents. Even better are the occasional letters that teachers may write, not only about the failing pupil or the pupil who is in trouble but also about the pupil who is doing well.

Tests. Tests are valuable as *one* source in gathering information about the growth of the pupil. They have been used rather exclusively by many teachers to judge growth, whereas at their present state of development they can be used to judge only a segment of such growth. Standardized tests of achievement are useful for evaluating growth of the class as a whole and growth of individuals over a period of time.

Many new developments in standardized tests and evaluating instruments are promising for appraising beliefs, understandings, skills in critical thinking, and interests. Problem situation tests are of value in testing for aspects of critical thinking such as logical reasoning, interpretation of data, applying generalizations to new situations. The pupil is presented with a problem or a case study and asked to respond to what he would do in the situation, or he may choose from a number of situations and give reasons for his choice. The essay examination, even though it cannot be scored as accurately, is better suited to finding out to what extent the pupil is able to analyze problems, to think them through, to attack a question intelligently, to arrive at conclusions, to organize information, and to see relationships.

The chief purpose of tests is to evaluate pupil growth. Standardized tests are necessary instruments for testing hypotheses and carrying on research in the classroom. However, in this total list of means of evaluating instruction, they are only one means.

Case studies. The case study combines many of the different means of evaluation discussed. It is an intensive study of a pupil, made through gathering data about him from as many sources as possible, such as anecdotal records, previous school work, conferences with the child and the parents. Case studies cannot be done for all pupils on a regular basis, but they are means used by teachers in making a study of pupils who need special kinds of help. Case studies can be done profitably on superior students or others who do not seem to have any particular problem. Through the very process of doing such a case study, the teacher will gain insights into how better guidance can be given to the superior student.

ISSUES AND POINTS OF VIEW

The issues that deal with planning, developing, and evaluating classroom experiences are deeply embedded in one's philosophy of teaching and learning.

1. *Is teacher–pupil planning a significant means of learning, or is it a waste of time that should be spent on teaching?*

Those who believe in cooperative planning of the teacher and pupils contend that the skills of planning are significant behaviors to be learned by the pupil. They represent the resourcefulness and proficiency needed for self-discipline and for independent action. The statements in this chapter give the arguments for pupil participation in planning. This issue crops up not only in unit planning but in all kinds of planning in the teaching process.

The conflicting point of view sees no value whatsoever in the pupils' doing the planning. Often, for the sake of argument, they liken it to deciding what one wants to do today. It is disorganization, not organization. It leads to inconsequential byways, to trivia, to minutiae of daily life, and to innocuous life adjustment. Instruction in schools should deal with the intellectual, the facts, information, the fundamentals, and subjects to be learned.

Fundamentally, the issue rests on the interpretation of the art of teaching. One sees it to be imparting information or skills by verbal means. When a teacher is planning with pupils, he is not teaching. The other sees it as guiding pupils through experiences in which they are active participants. One sees evaluation as doing something to the individual; the other, as something done by the individual, with the assistance of others.

2. *Is subject matter what is to be learned by pupils, or is it a means to learning specified behaviors?*

This section of the book has attempted to indicate that planning the curriculum for the classroom is a process of determining specific goals, planning subject matter and activities to help pupils learn those goals, and evaluating to see whether the behavior has been learned.

This process has been presented as an integral one, with no sharp lines among the three facets of curriculum development.

Those who hold that subject matter is what is learned may believe that since achievements in subject matter or in fundamental skills are the only outcomes that can be measured, they are the ones upon which teaching should concentrate, or that learning is a process of memorizing, being able to repeat, verbalize, read, write, and compute. Learning these intellectual tasks represents conditioning or training of the mind. Many teachers have no stated philosophy of the curriculum process in the classroom. Nevertheless, they function as though they saw no connection among goals, experiences, and evaluation. Learning of subject matter is measured by what one knows about the subject. This is logical, makes sense.

3. *Are marks or "grades" given for the purpose of evaluating the pupil and largely for motivation, or are they a means of communicating information?*

The dilemma of marking has been the inability of the system to prevent the mark from becoming an end in itself. The symbol is confused with the outcome. When marks in and of themselves become the important objectives, significant learning suffers. One of the main topics of conversation on college campuses and in high school corridors is marks received in courses. The first thing pupils look at when a paper is returned is the mark rather than any comments or suggestions for improvement.

Practices of teachers have set these conditions. We have measured time by "marking periods"; we have jotted down marks in record books for each contribution a pupil makes in class; we have used marks as incentives in many ways, subtle or otherwise. We may have used the practice of threatening failure if a pupil does not carry out the assignments we have made.

Evaluation for marking is only a small segment of total evaluation. A review of the means of evaluating outcomes discussed in this chapter will indicate that many of those listed do not possibly lend themselves to recording a mark.

Marks are given for one valid purpose only: to give information to pupils, to parents, to other schools, to other teachers, and to colleges. They are a shorthand means of reporting on the quality of work that the pupil has done. Reporting, of course, serves the same purpose.

Thus marks serve to report on the evaluation that we have placed on the pupils' accomplishments. However, the difficulty is that in our marking system we have generally come to accept the practice of using a single symbol to represent a great many kinds of accomplishments.

In other words, we have narrowed down the whole gamut of growth into a single mark. Schools have recognized the fallacy of this practice and have listed various kinds of growth on the report card under attitudes, habits, and the school subjects, showing the progress of a child by means of a symbol or a check mark.

Sequential progress in the curriculum, as it is conceived of in this book, involves an expanding and deepening process, not something that can be contained in any single symbol, book, unit, or course of study.

SELECTED REFERENCES

Alcorn, Marvin D., and James M. Linley (eds.). *Issues in Curriculum Development*. New York: Harcourt, Brace & World, Inc., 1959, chap. 6.
Discusses issues with regard to textbooks, audio-visual materials, free and inexpensive materials, and curriculum resource centers.

Association for Supervision and Curriculum Development. *Curriculum Materials—1964*. Washington, D. C.: National Education Association, 1964, 38 pp.
A comprehensive list of curriculum bulletins and guides published by school systems, state departments of education, and colleges which produce materials for public schools, published largely since 1960. Supplements the publication by Merritt and Harap, below. Published annually by ASCD since 1954.

Association for Supervision and Curriculum Development. *Individualizing Instruction*. 1964 Yearbook. Washington, D. C.: National Education Association, 1964, chaps. 4–5.
Suggests guidelines for teachers working with individual learners and presents ideas concerning the use of human and material resources.

Bloom, Benjamin S., *et al. The Taxonomy of Educational Objectives. Handbook I: Cognitive Domain*. New York: David McKay Co., Inc., 1956, 196 pp.
Analysis of objectives with a classification of types. Presents idea of specific objectives that can be evaluated.

Burton, William H. *The Guidance of Learning Activities*. 3rd ed. New York: Appleton-Century-Crofts, 1962, chaps. 12–17.
Excellent discussion of the planning and developing of units. Contains illustrative parts of units. Suggestions for utilization of teaching aids and materials.

DeBernardis, Amo. *The Use of Instructional Materials*. New York: Appleton-Century-Crofts, 1960, 250 pp.
Presents principles of using a wide variety of materials and resources for instruction.

Douglass, Harl R. (ed.). *The High School Curriculum*. 3rd ed. New York: The Ronald Press Co., 1964, chaps. 10–12, 14.
The types and selection of instructional materials, the planning and preparing of a unit of work, and the construction of courses of study as applied particularly to the secondary school.

Elkins, Deborah. *Reading Improvement in the Junior High School*. New York: Bureau of Publications, Teachers College, Columbia University, 1963, 76 pp.
This pamphlet is far more than a discourse on teaching reading; it discusses language arts experiences in relation to other classroom work in an integrated approach. Has excellent suggestions on planning.

Ellsworth, Ralph E., and Hobart D. Wagener. *The School Library: Facilities for Independent Study in the Secondary School*. New York: Educational Facilities Laboratories, Inc., 1963, 143 pp.
A new concept of the secondary school library as a place to facilitate independent study, adapted to the newer educational media.

Fleck, Henrietta. *How to Evaluate Students.* Bloomington, Ill.: McKnight
& McKnight Publishing Co., 1953, 85 pp.
   A helpful, brief bulletin, especially for evaluating the more intangible
   objectives.
Fleming, Robert S. (ed.). *Curriculum for Today's Boys and Girls.* Co-
lumbus, Ohio: Charles E. Merrill Books, Inc., 1963, chaps. 8–10, 15.
   These chapters deal specifically with intellectual experiences in prob-
   lem-solving and clarifying values and evaluating learning. Well illus-
   trated.
Gwynn, J. Minor. *Curriculum Principles and Social Trends.* 3rd ed. New
York: The Macmillan Co., 1960, chaps. 8, 10–11, 15, and 18–19.
   The influence of the textbook on education, trends in organizing and
   evaluating experiences in elementary and secondary schools, curricu-
   lum materials centers, and propaganda analysis in teaching.
Hill, Wilhelmina. *Unit Planning for Teaching in Elementary Social
Studies.* U. S. Department of Health, Education, and Welfare, Office
of Education, Bulletin 1963, No. 23. Washington, D. C.: Government
Printing Office, 1963, 82 pp.
   A bulletin of wider application for elementary schools, as well as sec-
   ondary schools, dealing with selection, preparation, and use of units.
   Derived from a study of over 500 social studies units.
Hock, Louise E. *Using Committees in the Classroom.* New York: Holt,
Rinehart and Winston, Inc., 1958, 55 pp.
   The use and purpose of pupil committees in instruction and the role
   of the teacher in committee work.
Krathwohl, David R., *et al. Taxonomy of Educational Objectives. Hand-
book II: Affective Domain.* New York: David McKay Co., Inc., 1964,
196 pp.
   A companion volume to Handbook I in the cognitive domain. The
   classification of objectives relating to values, attitudes, appreciations,
   feelings.
Leese, Joseph, Kenneth Frasure, and Mauritz Johnson, Jr. *The Teacher in
Curriculum Making.* New York: Harper & Row, Publishers, 1961, chaps.
7–10.
   Four chapters under a section entitled "Individual Action for Better
   Experience" which deal with planning and organizing learning activities, use of courses of study, unit plans, the production and use of resource units (with illustrations), and the selection and use of instructional materials.
Lounsbury, John, and Jean V. Marani. *The Junior High School We Saw:
One Day in the Eighth Grade.* Washington, D. C.: Association for Supervision and Curriculum Development, 1964, 78 pp.
   One of those rare publications that actually describe what the curriculum is like as experienced by the pupil. Records what happened to
   102 eighth-grade pupils in 98 schools shadowed for a day by an observer. The day's record of five samplings and some principles and
   suggestions drawn from the study are significant.
Mahar, Mary Helen. *The School Library as a Materials Center.* U. S. Department of Health, Education, and Welfare, Office of Education, Circular No. 708. Washington, D. C.: Government Printing Office, 1963,
84 pp.

Changing concepts of the library as a materials center as related to preparation of librarians and preparation of teachers in the selection and use of instructional materials.

Merritt, Eleanor, and Henry Harap. *Trends in the Production of Curriculum Guides.* Nashville, Tenn.: Division of Surveys and Field Services, George Peabody College for Teachers, 1955, 43 pp.
A comprehensive survey of courses of study published from 1951 through 1953.

National Education Association and Magazine Publishers Association. *Magazines in the Classroom.* Washington, D. C.: National Education Association, 1960, 32 pp.
Practical suggestions and obstacles to using magazines in instruction.

Parker, J. Cecil, *et al. Curriculum in America.* New York: Thomas Y. Crowell Co., 1962, chap. 3.
An analysis of problem-solving activities as choice-making by pupils in the classroom.

Parrish, Louise, and Yvonne Parrish. *Teacher-Pupil Planning for Better Classroom Learning.* New York: Harper & Row, Publishers, 1958, 160 pp.
A helpful reference on understanding what teacher–pupil planning means and how it works.

Shuster, Albert, and Milton E. Ploghoft. *The Emerging Elementary School Curriculum.* Columbus, Ohio: Charles E. Merrill Books, Inc., 1963, chaps. 4–5, 14.
Information on unit teaching, the elementary school library, use of materials and resources, and evaluation of pupil progress.

Smith, B. Othanel, William O. Stanley, and J. Harlan Shores. *Fundamentals of Curriculum Development.* Rev. ed. New York: Harcourt, Brace & World, Inc., 1957, chaps. 5–7.
Principles of selection of objectives and content.

Snyder, Edith Roach (ed.). *The Self-Contained Classroom.* Washington, D. C.: Association for Supervision and Curriculum Development, 1960, 88 pp.
Valuable for showing what planning of experiences can be done in the self-contained classroom, including teacher–pupil planning and units, but not as an argument for this classroom organization as compared to other types.

Taba, Hilda. *Curriculum Development: Theory and Practice.* New York: Harcourt, Brace & World, Inc., 1962, chaps. 14, 16–20.
More at the idea and principles level; discussion of behavioral objectives for teaching. The selection of experiences, organizing learning experiences, evaluating outcomes, and an especially helpful chapter on developing a unit.

Thornton, James W., Jr., and John R. Wright. *Secondary School Curriculum.* Columbus, Ohio: Charles E. Merrill Books, Inc., 1963, chaps. 2–4.
The teacher's development of the curriculum in the classroom.

Wood, Hugh B. *Foundations of Curriculum Planning and Development.* Seattle: Cascade-Pacific Books, 1960, chaps. 8–13.
The principles of selecting, organizing, and evaluating learning experiences and of selecting materials.

INDEX OF NAMES

[All page numbers in italics indicate listings in the "Selected References" sections. Roman type indicates text discussion or footnote citations.]

GENERAL INDEX

Academic learning, issues in, 137
Academic organizations and scholars
  influence on curriculum, 75, 78–79
  leadership in curriculum, 156
Academically talented; *see* Gifted children
Acceleration in school, 290–92, 334–36, 357–59
Accrediting agencies, 71–72
Action research
  characteristics of, 233–35
  collecting data, 238–39
  communicating findings, 241
  defining problems, 237
  definition of, 231–32
  developing hypotheses, 238
  drawing conclusions, 241
  evaluating curriculum improvement through, 235–36
  gathering evidence, 240–41
  issues regarding, 242–44
  as means of curriculum study, 231
  means of gathering data in, 239–40
  participants in, 236–37
  steps in, 237–41
Administration related to curriculum development, 56, 68–69; *see also* Leadership
Adoption of new ideas, 54–55
Advanced courses, 327
Advanced Placement Programs, 335, 358
Advisory councils, lay, 208–9
Aesthetic subjects, 295–97
Appreciations, statements of, 438–39
Art, 296–97
Attacks on schools, 62–66; *see also* Community attitudes, Cultural values, Freedom to teach
Attitudes, statements of, 438
Audio-visual materials, 410–11
Auto-instruction; *see* Programmed instruction

Basic skills (elementary schools), 258–59
Behavior, study of human, 344–45; *see also* Learning
Bibliography, in a unit, 452
Board of education
  as a curriculum maker, 68–69
  policies regarding freedom to teach, 66–69
  relation to citizen participation, 201–2
Book censorship, 66–68
Buildings, adapted to newer curriculum trends, 325–27

California, legislation on curriculum, 70
Case studies, 479–80
Censorship, 66–68
Central office staff, 174–75
Change; *see also* Curriculum change, Curriculum improvement
  acceleration of, 92–93, 361
  concept of equilibrium in, 21–22
  diversity of values, 103–9
  preparation to cope with, 94–96
Child development; *see* Growth and development
Child study, 138–39
Citizen participation in curriculum study
  advisory councils for, 208–9
  on citizens' committees, 208–9
  on curriculum committees, 200–1, 207
  on curriculum councils, 207
  issues regarding, 214–17
  leadership in, 200
  parent organizations, 211–12
  principles of, 198–204
  as resource people, 214
  role of the citizen, 202–6
  on school surveys, 211
  in study of the community, 210–11
  in working directly with teachers, 212–13
  in workshops, 209–10
Citizens' roles in curriculum study, 202–6
Class size, 323–24, 367–68
Class structure; *see* Social class
College courses, for curriculum study, 180
College entrance requirements, 72
Colleges; *see* Universities
Commission on Evaluation, ASCD, 220–21
Commission on the Experimental Study of the Utilization of the Staff in the Secondary School, 321, 324
Committees, curriculum; *see also* Advisory councils, lay
  issues regarding, 196–97
  lay participation in, 200–1, 207
  in organization for curriculum study, 176–78
  selection of, 177
  size, 177
Communication, channels of school–community, 199, 206–14
Communications skills, 260–61, 315